CANONICAL THEOLOGY

CANONICAL THEOLOGY

The Biblical Canon, *Sola Scriptura*,
and Theological Method

John C. Peckham

WILLIAM B. EERDMANS PUBLISHING COMPANY
GRAND RAPIDS, MICHIGAN

Wm. B. Eerdmans Publishing Co.
2140 Oak Industrial Drive N.E., Grand Rapids, Michigan 49505
www.eerdmans.com

22 21 20 19 18 17   2 3 4 5 6

ISBN 978-0-8028-7330-9

Library of Congress Cataloging-in-Publication Data

Names: Peckham, John, 1981- author.
Title: Canonical theology : the biblical canon, sola scriptura, and theological method /
    John C. Peckham.
Description: Grand Rapids : Eerdmans Publishing Co., 2016. | Includes bibliographical references
    and index.
Identifiers: LCCN 2016027077 | ISBN 9780802873309 (pbk. : alk. paper)
Subjects: LCSH: Bible—Criticism, interpretation, etc. | Theology. | Bible—Canon.
Classification: LCC BS511.3 .P43 2016 | DDC 220.1/2—dc23
    LC record available at https://lccn.loc.gov/2016027077

Abbreviations in this volume follow *The SBL Handbook of Style* (2nd ed.).

To my students

Contents

Foreword

Every age presents its particular theological challenges. Luther rightly argued in his context that justification is the article by which the church stands or falls. In our day Alister McGrath has left us all in his debt with his magisterial *Iustitia Dei: A History of the Doctrine of Justification*, which is now in its third edition. The new perspective on Paul has indeed led to a lively debate about justification, but I doubt that this important doctrine could or should be seen as just as critical as it was in Luther's day.

Indeed, the debate about justification rests on a pre-understanding of Scripture as the canonical literature of the Christian church and it is here that we find one of the most serious issues facing Christian faith today. Already in 1975 David Dungan predicted that major challenges to traditional understandings of the canon were on the horizon,[1] and he has proved to be correct as the "Canon Debate" has moved front and center.[2]

When I was at Oxford I had the privilege of getting to know Roger Beckwith and he kindly gave me mimeographed copies of what became his seminal *The Old Testament Canon of the New Testament Church and Its Background in Early Judaism*.[3] James Barr and John Barton were also at Oxford during this time and they articulated liberal views of canonicity often highly critical

1. D. L. Dungan, "The New Testament Canon in Recent Study," *Int* 29 (1975): 339-51.
2. Cf. Lee Martin McDonald and James A. Sanders, eds., *The Canon Debate* (Peabody, MA: Hendrickson, 2009). A strength of Brevard Childs's work is his familiarity with German debates around canon. See his and the other essays in Craig G. Bartholomew et al., eds., *Canon and Biblical Interpretation*, Scripture and Hermeneutics Series 7 (Milton Keynes: Paternoster; Grand Rapids: Zondervan, 2006).
3. Eugene, OR: Wipf and Stock, 1985, 2008.

of Beckwith. During these years, under the influence of Karl Barth, Brevard Childs's canonical hermeneutic emerged as he courageously sought to redirect biblical studies along lines which took the Bible seriously as canon while retaining the insights of historical criticism. Several of Childs's students, notably Christopher Seitz and Stephen Chapman, as well as many others, have continued to develop Childs's canonical approach.[4] In recent decades Stephen Dempster has done important work on canonical biblical interpretation within the evangelical tradition and Michael Kruger has addressed the issue of canon in his works *Canon Revisited: Establishing the Origins and Authority of the New Testament Books*[5] and *The Question of Canon: Challenging the Status Quo in the New Testament Debate.*[6]

The issues involved in the canon debate are complex and multiple.[7] At their heart, however, as John shows in this book, they come down to where we locate final authority, whether in Scripture or some version of "the community." The issue of authority is central to the current challenges facing modernity, and this is as true of Western societies as it is of the church. Thus, where we land on canonicity really matters! There is hardly a major issue dividing Christians today that does not come down finally to the question of the intrinsic authority of Scripture, i.e., canonicity. In our day it takes courage and wisdom to grasp the nettle of canonicity and John Peckham manifests both in this important new book.

The role of the theologian is to reflect on Scripture and the tradition and to articulate the contours of Christian faith for a particular age. In this book John does just that. He takes hold of what I argue is one of the most pressing issues facing the church today, and does so clearly, with a refreshing and astonishingly wide range of engagement, pushing towards the conclusion that Scripture is intrinsically authoritative as the Word of God.

Much of the above work referred to relates to biblical studies rather than theology. In my view, contrary to the history of religions approach, theology is indispensable to the canon debate, *and* canonicity is vital for healthy theology. Part of the importance of this book lies in the fact that as a theologian John moves beyond the canon debate to develop a theological method built on the

---

4. See most recently Stephen Chapman, *1 Samuel as Christian Scripture: A Theological Commentary* (Grand Rapids: Eerdmans, 2016); Christopher R. Seitz, *Joel*, International Theological Commentary (London: Bloomsbury, 2016).

5. Wheaton, IL: Crossway, 2012.

6. Downers Grove, IL: InterVarsity, 2013.

7. See Craig G. Bartholomew, *Introducing Biblical Hermeneutics: A Comprehensive Framework for Hearing God in Scripture* (Grand Rapids: Baker Academic, 2015) 251-78.

intrinsic authority of Scripture and then devotes several chapters to testing his model in relation to themes such as the doctrine of the Trinity and the doctrine of the love of God, about which he has already published two important books.

In my view this is precisely the sort of work we need our best and brightest theologians to do today. Doubtless readers will disagree with John at points. I myself look forward to discussing and debating aspects of the book with him! But wherever we land on these issues, it is to John's credit that he has put the issues so clearly, firmly, winsomely, and integrally on the table for discussion, and for this I am profoundly grateful.

CRAIG G. BARTHOLOMEW
Hamilton, Ontario
March 2016

Acknowledgments

This book is the culmination of a number of years of reflection on the nature of the biblical canon relative to the doing of systematic theology. Over the course of these years I have benefitted greatly from learning from a number of individuals. I am especially grateful to Fernando Canale, who first sparked my interest in investigating the biblical canon during my graduate studies and first introduced me to theological method and the importance of attending to operative presuppositions. I likewise owe profound thanks to Richard M. Davidson who was instrumental in shaping my conception of biblical hermeneutics, particularly when I began to explore in earnest the intersection of philosophical and biblical hermeneutics some years ago.

I am deeply thankful to my colleagues in the Theology and Christian Philosophy Department of the Theological Seminary of Andrews University, especially for the many conversations we've shared individually and collectively regarding the issues dealt with in this book and many others. It is a privilege and joy to work with each of you. Thanks are also due to the numerous individuals who read part or all of this work and provided feedback and encouragement. I am also especially thankful for the interest and encouragement of my students.

I would also like to thank a number of people for their support and help as I wrote this volume. I would like to especially thank the entire Eerdmans team. In particular, I am indebted to Michael Thomson, acquisitions editor, for his interest in publishing this work and all of his help in making it a reality. I am likewise thankful to Andrew Knapp, project editor, for his careful work on this manuscript. I am also very grateful to Craig Bartholomew for his willingness to write the foreword to this book.

This book grows out of a number of previous research projects and special thanks are due the editors at *Trinity Journal, Themelios, Didaskalia*, the *Mid-America Journal of Theology*, and *Perspectives in Religious Studies* for granting me permission to reuse material from the following articles, significant portions of which I have revised and expanded upon in this book:

1. "The Canon and Biblical Authority: A Critical Comparison of Two Models of Canonicity." *Trinity Journal* 28/2 (2007): 229-49.
2. "Epistemological Authority in the Polemic of Irenaeus." *Didaskalia* 19 (2008): 51-70.
3. "Intrinsic Canonicity and the Inadequacy of the Community Approach to Canon Determination." *Themelios* 36/2 (2011): 203-15.
4. "The Analogy of Scripture Revisited: A Final Form Canonical Approach to Systematic Theology." *Mid-America Journal of Theology* 22 (2011): 41-53.
5. "*Sola Scriptura: Reductio ad absurdum*?" *Trinity Journal* 35/2 (2014): 195-223.
6. "Theopathic or Anthropopathic: A Suggested Approach to Imagery of Divine Emotion in the Hebrew Bible." *Perspectives in Religious Studies* 342/5 (2015): 341-55.

Finally, I am most thankful to my family. My parents, Ernest and Karen, have been a source of great encouragement and support. Most of all, I would like to thank my amazing wife, Brenda, and our beloved son, Joel. Spending time with you both is the best part of every day.

CHAPTER 1

Canon vs. Community?

Recent generations have seen a proliferation of Christian denominations, sparked by numerous doctrinal divides. Many believe that this fragmentation of Christianity stems, at least in part, from very different answers to some complex and crucial questions: What is the role of canon and community respectively when it comes to the understanding and articulation of doctrine? Should the church be the doctrinal arbiter in the twenty-first century?

With regard to both the issue of canon specifically and the wider issue of the relationship between canon and doctrine there exists a divide regarding the role of the community. Perspectives on the biblical canon are split between those who favor an intrinsic canon perspective (wherein God is the determiner of the scope of the canon) and the community canon approach (wherein a community determines the scope of the canon). In a similar and related fashion, debate continues over the role of the canon and community in establishing doctrine. Some advocate the exclusive authority of the canon for all matters of faith and practice (canonical approaches) while others consider the community to be the arbiter of doctrine and/or the final interpreter of Scripture (communitarian approaches), with a wide spectrum of opinions in between. This divide has been the subject of considerable discussion among evangelicals in the past few decades, with an abundance of recent scholarship offering communitarian alternatives to, and/or interpretations of, the Protestant Scripture principle.[1]

This chapter introduces the ongoing controversy regarding the nature of the biblical canon and the proper relationship between Scripture, community,

---

1. See chapter 4.

1

and Christian theology by briefly summarizing the contemporary landscape regarding these issues, particularly the canon debate between two competing models of canonicity and the long-standing debate over *sola Scriptura*. The chapters that follow will take up these issues and the relationship between them, addressing the question of canonicity, the *sola Scriptura* principle, and the tension between canonical and communitarian theological methodologies.[2]

THE CANON DEBATE

There has been more than a little debate over the definition, nature, and function of the biblical canon, that is, the collection of biblical books that Christians view as authoritative scripture. Why some ancient books are viewed by Christians as "canonical" has received considerable attention, with various divergent views operating within the academy and in popular literature. Although Scripture is nearly universally cherished throughout Christianity, various communities differ over the nature and contents of the biblical canon. Accordingly, the questions of which books are canonical, and why, hold considerable implications for Christianity generally and for theology specifically. The prime question of the canon debate, for our purposes, is: Who determines the canon?

At the heart of this debate is the vital philosophical division between those who believe that the canon is a community-determined construction (the community canon model) and those who believe that the canon is divinely appointed and thus recognized, but not determined, by any given community (the intrinsic canon model). The intrinsic canon and community canon models posit different definitions of the canon, see the nature of the canon differently, and consequently identify different functions for the canon.[3]

2. Focusing on the debate between canonical and communitarian approaches, both of which are oriented toward theological practice after modernity, this work addresses the modernistically-oriented divide between liberalism and conservatism only as it relates to the canonical/communitarian conversation.

3. These models are representative of contemporary divergent views regarding canonicity, with considerable diversity within the models themselves, focusing primarily on contemporary perspectives regarding the *nature* of canonicity.

The Community Canon Model

The community canon model defines the canon as a set of writings that are determined by the community as a standard. Accordingly canonicity is viewed as imposed upon writings by the community.[4] Thus, the authority resides in the community to select the writings that are in the canon and thus used for theology.[5] But this model is not monolithic. The diversity among those who believe the canon is determined by the community might be illuminated by consideration of two quite different examples.[6]

The Roman Catholic Church is representative of the view that canonicity is determined by the authority of the Church and its tradition, accepting as canonical those books which have been declared so by the institution (the ecclesial fixed canon view).[7] Therefore the canon was determined by the approval of the church as demonstrated in the lists of the church fathers and councils,

4. Some hold this view as an extension of Walter Bauer's influential hypothesis that there was no single orthodoxy in early Christianity but a diversity of competing Christianities. Here, the canon is a later imposition by the "orthodoxy" that emerged from the struggle among various forms. See Walter Bauer, *Orthodoxy and Heresy in Earliest Christianity*, trans. Paul J. Achtemeier (Philadelphia: Fortress, 1971); cf. Harry Y. Gamble, *The New Testament Canon* (Philadelphia: Fortress, 1985), 11-13. For an excellent critique of the Bauer hypothesis, see Andreas J. Köstenberger and Michael J. Kruger, *The Heresy of Orthodoxy* (Wheaton, IL: Crossway, 2010).

5. Here, canon "denotes a fixed standard or collection of writings that defines the faith and identity of a particular religious community"; see Lee Martin McDonald, *The Formation of the Christian Biblical Canon* (Peabody, MA: Hendrickson, 1995), 13; cf. Lee Martin McDonald, *The Biblical Canon: Its Origin, Transmission, and Authority* (Peabody, MA: Hendrickson, 2007), 54.

6. There are significant differences between representatives of these models, regarding their overall view of Scripture, its inspiration, function, and interpretation, and other matters of doctrine and belief. Their commonality consists of their view of canonicity as determined by some community or communities. No comparison beyond this is intended.

7. For example, Peter Kreeft, *Fundamentals of the Faith: Essays in Christian Apologetics* (San Francisco: Ignatius, 1988), 275, depicts the "church as writer, canonizer, and interpreter of scripture." Compare the view of the Orthodox church in this regard, wherein the "later Church Fathers . . . viewed the entire corpus of Scripture . . . as directly inspired by God," yet the "official evidence for the authority and primacy of scripture is its canonisation as a sacred corpus in the Church's tradition over the first four centuries of church life"; see Theodore G. Stylianopoulos, "Scripture and Tradition in the Church," in *The Cambridge Companion to Orthodox Christian Theology*, ed. Mary Cunningham and Elizabeth Theokritoff (Cambridge: Cambridge University Press, 2008), 22. Some Protestants make a similar communitarian argument regarding the church's role in canon formation; see Craig D. Allert, *A High View of Scripture? The Authority of the Bible and the Formation of the New Testament Canon* (Grand Rapids: Baker Academic, 2007).

notably the Council of Carthage (AD 397) and the later, perhaps more official, affirmation at the Council of Trent (1546).[8]

A significantly different approach within the community canon model views the canon as flexible to a given community (the adaptable canon view). In this approach, the community determines which books are considered canonical for that specific community such that the canon is relative to the community's standard in a constantly shifting context.[9] Accordingly, the canon is flexible to whatever the contemporary needs of a specific community may be. Over time, this adaptability may allow for a change in the writings that the community accepts as canonical. Here, the authority to determine the canon does not reside in a particular institution but belongs to the contemporary consensus of *any* given community.

Many who define the canon as a collection of books determined by the acceptance of a community focus primarily on the dates of such acceptance and/or the usage of such canonical books throughout history as determinative of canonicity itself. Proponents often appeal to Gerald Sheppard's influential definitions of canon 1 and canon 2, where the former refers to books used *functionally* as authoritative and the latter refers to a fixed or permanent collection of writings.[10] Sheppard explains, "one can say that Christian scripture had a canonical status (canon 1) long before the church decisions of the fourth

---

8. However, Roman Catholicism includes differing understandings of the community's authority relative to canonicity. On one hand, papal legate to the Council of Trent Stanislaus Hosius claimed: "The Scriptures have only as much force as the fables of Aesop, if destitute of the authority of the Church" (Confutatio Prolegomenon Brentii, *Opera*, 1.530, quoted in Michael J. Kruger, *Canon Revisited* [Wheaton, IL: Crossway, 2012], 40). Conversely, Joseph T. Lienhard, *The Bible, the Church, and Authority: The Canon of the Christian Bible in History and Theology* (Collegeville, MN: Liturgical, 1995), 71-72, contends: "No Catholic would want to say that the authority of the Bible derives simply from the decree of a council. Trent recognized the Bible; it did not create it. The Bible is in the Church but not from the Church."

9. Here, the canon is "basically a community's paradigm for how to continue the dialogue in ever changing socio-political contexts"; see James A. Sanders, "The Issue of Closure in the Canonical Process," in *The Canon Debate*, ed. Lee Martin McDonald and James A. Sanders (Peabody, MA: Hendrickson, 2002), 262; see also James A. Sanders, *Torah and Canon* (Philadelphia: Fortress, 1972); *Canon and Community: A Guide to Canonical Criticism* (Philadelphia: Fortress, 1984).

10. See Gerald T. Sheppard, "Canon," in *The Encyclopedia of Religion*, ed. Mircea Eliade (New York: Macmillan, 1987). Andrew E. Steinmann, *The Oracles of God* (Saint Louis: Concordia, 1999), 17, however, criticizes this as "purposely confus[ing] two different meanings of canon" for "ideological reasons," that is, "in order to argue that the canon was not closed until a relatively late date."

century delimited a fixed list of books (canon 2)."[11] Accordingly, some apply this distinction of canon 1 to the history of the canon to emphasize the fluidity of the "canon" in early times, sometimes arguing that the concept was foreign to early Christians, while canon 2 applies only to a closed and fixed list of authoritative books (no earlier than the fourth century).[12] On this basis the books are considered authoritative not when they were written but later when the books were purportedly determined to be canonical by the community.

The Intrinsic Canon Model

In the intrinsic canon model, the books of Scripture are not canonical based on the determination of the community, but in virtue of the intrinsic nature of the books as divinely commissioned. In this view, divinely appointed books are intrinsically canonical independent of extrinsic recognition. That is, the books of the Bible are inherently canonical even if they are not recognized as such, similar to the way in which Jesus is truly the Messiah even though many do not recognize him.[13]

The recognition of canonical books bears on the function of the canonical

---

11. Sheppard, "Canon," 65. See also McDonald's claim that "canon" in the sense of canon 2 became widely used from the fourth century AD onward (*Formation*, 15). McDonald makes considerable use of this distinction and Albert Sundberg's similar distinction between Scripture and canon, saying "Scripture has to do with the divine status of a written document that is authoritative in the life of a community of faith." Canon "denotes a fixed standard or collection of writings that defines the faith and identity of a particular religious community" (*Formation*, 13). Cf. Albert C. Sundberg, *The Old Testament of the Early Church* (New York: Kraus, 1969).

12. In conjunction with this, the lateness of the use of the term "canon" has been argued as evidence of a lack of the concept in early Christianity. Eugene Ulrich, "The Notion and Definition of Canon," in *The Canon Debate*, ed. Lee McDonald and James A. Sanders (Peabody, MA: Hendrickson, 2002), 23, states that if canon were so important, "one would expect that authors would discuss or at least mention it."

13. In this view, canonical "Scripture is something given by God" such "that only he can determine what it is. The role of the church, therefore, is essentially receptive, to recognize what he has given"; Charles E. Hill, "The New Testament Canon: Deconstructio ad Absurdum?" *JETS* 52/1 (2009): 119. Thus, in virtue of what they are, books are "'recognized' as canonical"; Gerhard F. Hasel, "Divine Inspiration and the Canon of the Bible," *Journal of the Adventist Theological Society* 5/1 (1994): 69. Cf. Michael J. Kruger's view, *The Question of Canon: Challenging the Status Quo in the New Testament Debate* (Downers Grove, IL: IVP Academic, 2013), 39, that "the canonical books are what they are by virtue of the divine purpose for which they were given, and not by virtue of their use or acceptance by the community of faith." However, Kruger uses the phrase "intrinsic canon model" in a different manner than I do; see chapter 2.

books, but not on the intrinsic canonicity of those books. Whereas books must be recognized as canonical in order to be *functionally* authoritative within a given community, canonical books are *intrinsically* authoritative as the rule and norm of theology due to their divine origin/commission. Thus, intrinsic canonicity is independent of community recognition and, accordingly, the particular dating of canon recognition (whether earlier or later) is not crucial or determinative regarding the question of canonicity itself. Rather, on this definition, divinely commissioned books are intrinsically canonical as soon as they are written.[14] Nevertheless, the community plays a crucial role in (among other things) correctly recognizing those books as canonical that were divinely commissioned as such.[15]

The intrinsic canon model's distinction between determination of canonicity and recognition of canonicity constitutes the essential departure from the community canon model, locating the determining factor regarding canonicity in divine commission rather than community determination.[16] This presupposes the providential interaction of God in relationship to humanity. If the possibility of such divine guidance is denied *a priori*, the intrinsic canon model is, consequently, precluded.

Impasse with Theological Implications

There is thus a significant impasse regarding the very nature, definition, and function of the biblical canon, with abundant implications for Christianity in general and Christian theology specifically. Whereas an intrinsic canon approach naturally undergirds an approach to canon as the rule or standard for theology, the community canon approach is used by some to undergird the purported theological authority of the community (as normative interpretive arbiter or otherwise; see below). For example, Craig Allert uses a community

---

14. The "canon developed at the very point when the biblical books were written under inspiration" (Hasel, "Divine Inspiration," 73).

15. According to the view that canonical books are intrinsically so in virtue of divine commission, such books possess traits on the basis of which they might be recognized as canonical (i.e., criteria of canon recognition). See the discussion in chapter 2.

16. Anthony C. Thiselton, "Canon, Community, and Theological Construction," in *Canon and Biblical Interpretation*, ed. Craig G. Bartholomew et al. (Grand Rapids: Zondervan, 2006), 13, thus contends that "the church did not 'make' the canon, but through its life and identity recognized the formative impact of divine revelation through the call of the 'prophets and apostles as a whole.'"

canon perspective to undergird a determinative role for the community in, among other things, the interpretation of Scripture.[17] Conversely, Michael Kruger cautions against "viewing the canon as a purely community-dependent entity" and against the tendency of some to "artificially inflate the role of official church declarations about the canon — as if those declarations somehow 'created' or 'established' the authority of these books."[18]

In my view, at issue is not just whether and to what extent the role of official church declarations has been inflated in some discussions of canon but also the need for careful evaluation of the validity of the common view that books *become* canon in virtue of the authoritative action of the church (which can be held even on a more organic functional view of canonicity). These two models will be taken up further beginning in the following chapter but, first, we turn to another impasse that further contributes to the divide between the authority of the community and that of the canon, the debate over *sola Scriptura*.

THE DEBATE OVER *SOLA SCRIPTURA*

Traditions 0, I, and II

Although many Protestants in recent decades have afforded an increasing role to the community as doctrinal (and/or interpretive) arbiter, the debate over *sola Scriptura* is often depicted as a long-standing disagreement between those who posit "extra-biblical oral tradition" (ecclesial tradition) as an additional source of revelation (Tradition II or "two-source" theory) and those who hold that "Scripture has final authority" while embracing "a traditional way of interpreting scripture within the community of faith" (Tradition I or "single-source" theory).[19] According to this latter view, influentially framed by Heiko Oberman, the "Reformation was not a protest against tradition as such" but

---

17. See Allert, *High View*, 67.

18. Kruger, *Question*, 38, 36. He particularly finds misleading Allert's statement that the "Bible was not always 'there' in early Christianity" but "the church still continued to function in its absence" (Allert, *High View*, 12).

19. Craig D. Allert, "What Are We Trying to Conserve? Evangelicalism and *Sola Scriptura*," *EvQ* 76/4 (2004): 333. Heiko A. Oberman, *The Dawn of the Reformation* (Edinburgh: T&T Clark, 1986), 280-96, here 294, suggests that "Tradition II developed . . . out of Tradition I when the theologians and canon lawyers discovered that all the truths actually held by the Church could not be found explicitly or implicitly in Holy Scripture."

"simply a call to return from Tradition II to Tradition I."[20] Building on this framework, Keith Mathison contends that Tradition I was "the concept that the Church universally held for the first three centuries," "the majority of the Church held for the bulk of the Middle Ages," and the magisterial reformers "re-emphasized under the banner of *sola scriptura*."[21] According to this view, Scripture is "the sole source of revelation" and "the only infallible, final and authoritative norm of doctrine and practice," but it must be "interpreted in and by the church" and "according to the *regula fidei*."[22] For Mathison, this is the "only historical concept of scriptural authority that does not reduce to either autonomy or absurdity."[23]

Anthony Lane, however, differentiates the view of the magisterial reformers from both what he calls the "supplementary view" (Tradition II) and the pre-Augustinian "coincidence view" (Tradition I). He claims, contra Oberman, that the magisterial reformers did not promote a return to the coincidence view, wherein "the teachings of the church, Scripture and tradition coincide"; instead they advocated a merely ancillary role for tradition (the "ancillary view").[24] Because the magisterial reformers believed the contemporary tradition of the church had been corrupted such that contemporary church teaching contradicted Scripture, "the teaching authority of the church had to be soundly rejected."[25] Whereas the "patristic writers were concerned to show the identity of ecclesiastical with apostolic teaching," the magisterial "Reformers sought to do the opposite."[26] Nevertheless, the magisterial reformers "did

20. Allert, "What Are We Trying to Conserve?" 336. Cf. 332. Thus, Oberman contends that Luther's "*sola scriptura* principle . . . does not necessarily imply a rejection of the so-called coinherence of Church and Scripture" (*Dawn*, 283); cf. Anthony N. S. Lane, "Scripture, Tradition and Church: An Historical Survey," *VE* 9 (1975): 42. D. H. Williams, "The Search for *Sola Scriptura* in the Early Church," *Int* 52/4 (1998): 356, 357, likewise refers to "a blind spot common to Evangelicals that wrongly construes the Protestant conflict with Catholicism as one of scripture versus tradition" when the conflict was "rather a clash over what the traditions had become, or between divergent concepts of tradition."

21. Keith A. Mathison, *The Shape of Sola Scriptura* (Moscow, ID: Canon, 2001), 281.

22. Mathison, *Shape*, 299.

23. Mathison, *Shape*, 281.

24. Lane, "Scripture," 39-43. Cf. Allert, "What Are We Trying to Conserve?" 332, 336. Mathison, conversely, prefers Oberman's categorization and claims that Lane's view is incorrect, contending that "the early Church's view contained elements of the 'ancillary' view, and the Reformers' position contained elements of the 'coincidence' view" (*Shape*, 86).

25. Allert, "What Are We Trying to Conserve?" 338. Williams adds, "scripture alone was the bulwark affording the grounds to reject the Roman claim as the sole interpreter of the church's Tradition" ("Search," 357). Cf. Lane, "Scripture," 44.

26. Lane, "Scripture," 43.

allow for an interpretative tradition not adding to Scripture but did not see either this tradition or ecclesiastical teaching as infallible."[27] Tradition, then, was not seen "as a normative interpretation of Scripture" or "as a necessary supplement to it but rather as a tool to be used to help the church to understand it."[28] Accordingly, whereas the church fathers "accepted the inherited faith because it was [considered to be] apostolic tradition," the magisterial "Reformers accepted the (traditional) creeds only because they believed them to be scriptural."[29]

Alister McGrath added the category Tradition 0 to describe the radical reformers' "understanding of theology which allocates no role whatsoever to Tradition."[30] This view is often pejoratively referred to as "solo *Scriptura*," which numerous advocates of *sola Scriptura* sharply differentiate from their own view, criticizing it as a self-defeating and unworkable extreme (among other things).[31] Brad Gregory, however, considers such a distinction between magisterial and radical reformers in this regard "untenable" because neither deferred to tradition "relative to their respective readings of scripture" but "rejected" the "traditional authorities . . . at each point of disagreement. In principle and as a corollary of *sola scriptura*, tradition thus retained for them *no independent* authority."[32] McGrath contends, however, that "it is totally

27. Lane, "Scripture," 43. Allert comments that Luther "rejects contemporary church authority," but "this does not imply a rejection of tradition," contra what Allert considers the widespread mischaracterization of Luther's view ("What Are We Trying to Conserve?" 338, 342). As D. H. Williams, *Evangelicals and Tradition: The Formative Influence of the Early Church* (Grand Rapids: Baker Academic, 2005), 97, puts it, "Magisterial Reformers such as Luther and Calvin did not think of *sola scriptura* as something that could be properly understood apart from the church or the foundational tradition of the church, even while they were opposing some of the institutions of the church. The principle of *sola scriptura* was not intended to be *nuda scriptura!*"

28. Lane, "Scripture," 43.

29. Lane, "Scripture," 43.

30. Alister E. McGrath, *Reformation Thought: An Introduction*, 3rd ed. (Malden, MA: Blackwell, 2001), 154. While McGrath lays out these three different categories, the specific definitions of Traditions 0, I, and II are conspicuously absent from the 2012 edition; see Alister E. McGrath, *Reformation Thought: An Introduction*, 4th ed. (Malden, MA: Wiley-Blackwell, 2012), 100.

31. Williams, for example, laments that the "scripture-only principle" exemplified by the "Radical Reformation" has created "greater problems which have plagued Christianity ever since" ("Search," 356, 358); cf. Christian Smith, *The Bible Made Impossible: Why Biblicism Is Not a Truly Evangelical Reading of Scripture* (Grand Rapids: Brazos, 2011), 4-5.

32. Brad S. Gregory, *The Unintended Reformation: How a Religious Revolution Secularized Society* (Cambridge, MA: Belknap, 2012), 95 (emphasis his). Gregory claims the difference

wrong to suggest that the magisterial reformers elevated private judgment above the corporate judgment of the church or that they degenerated into some form of individualism."[33] The magisterial reformers did not abandon the "concept of traditional interpretation," though they did view the authority of any church or tradition as subordinate to that of Scripture.[34]

Accordingly, Mathison claims that, in large part due to the prevalence of a "more anabaptistic notion of solo *scriptura*," the "predominant Evangelical theory of authority is an incoherent mass of theological self-contradictions" while "Evangelical practice is an incoherent mass of denominational self-contradictions."[35] D. H. Williams similarly laments that the "longstanding and prevalent [evangelical] conception" is that "*sola scriptura* is compromised by any acceptance of extracanonical authority."[36] This line of criticism against Tradition 0 is often furthered by reference to extreme examples of heretical views held by some radical reformers, leaving little room (if any) for a nuanced position that might depart from both the coincident and ancillary views.[37]

It is questionable, however, whether any of the above categorizations adequately represent the various nuances and complexities of the historical or contemporary Christian landscape. Neither the magisterial nor the radical

---

between magisterial and radical reformers was in their biblical interpretations, "not that the former accepted some patristic writers, conciliar decrees, and ecclesiastical tradition as authoritative and the latter none. Rather, they *all* rejected *every* putative 'authority' whenever the latter diverged from what each regarded as God's truth, based on scripture as they respectively and contrarily understood it" (*Unintended Reformation*, 96, emphasis his).

33. McGrath, *Reformation Thought* (4th ed.), 102.

34. McGrath, *Reformation Thought* (4th ed.), 102. Williams adds in a similar vein, "In no way did Luther or Calvin reject the authority of Tradition, although it had to be regulated by scripture" ("Search," 357).

35. Mathison, *Shape*, 296, 307. Mathison roundly criticizes "solo *scriptura*" as turning to "self as the ultimate authority by which all things (including Scripture) are to be interpreted," which he views as "inconsistent" with the "Reformation," "logic," and "Christianity" itself (*Shape*, 311).

36. D. H. Williams, *Retrieving the Tradition and Renewing Evangelicalism: A Primer for Suspicious Protestants* (Grand Rapids: Eerdmans, 1999), 19. This dovetails with his concern that, among evangelicals, tradition is often viewed as "antithetical to the absolute authority of the Bible" (*Retrieving*, 18).

37. Sebastian Franck, Faustus Socinus, Thomas Müntzer, Caspar Schwenkfeld, and others are mentioned in this regard. See Mathison, *Shape*, 124-28; Allert, "What Are We Trying to Conserve?" 341. While both Mathison and Allert distinguish between more and less radical reformers, "extreme" examples are used to illustrate "just how far" sola *scriptura* "may be taken when the right of private judgment is retained at the expense of tradition as a tool to help understand scripture" (Allert, "What Are We Trying to Conserve?" 340).

reformers were a monolithic group[38] and the Eastern Orthodox view does not fit well within any of these oft-used categories.[39] Moreover, contemporary Protestant proponents of Tradition I offer historical and contemporary understandings that differ considerably from one another, as do some Roman Catholic scholars.[40] The historical theology regarding this issue is thus heavily debated, with competing past and present categorizations offered by adherents and opponents.[41]

Finally, it seems to me that some use Tradition I in a way that blurs the important distinction between those who advocate for an extracanonical, normative, interpretive arbiter alongside *sola Scriptura* and those who do not and/ or who seek to dismiss the latter perspective by associating it with Tradition 0. However, there is in fact a large and critical gap between total dismissal and ignorance of tradition (the purported Tradition 0) and adoption of a normative extracanonical interpretive arbiter. For these (and other) reasons, this book categorizes Protestant perspectives on *sola Scriptura* under reductionist *sola Scriptura*, canonical *sola Scriptura*, and communitarian *sola Scriptura*.[42]

Canonical vs. Communitarian *Sola Scriptura*

At the juncture of these perspectives stands the question: What or who (if anything or anyone) stands as the "rule" of theology and theological interpre-

---

38. As Alister McGrath, *The Intellectual Origins of the European Reformation*, 2nd ed. (Malden, MA: Blackwell, 2004), 182, himself notes, "the Reformation is best conceived as a series of initially essentially independent reforming movements with quite distinct agendas and understandings of both how theology was to be done, and what its role might be within the life of the church."

39. For a recent Orthodox treatment of the issues involved, see Edith Humphrey, *Scripture and Tradition: What the Bible Really Says* (Grand Rapids: Baker, 2013). For a defense of the *sola Scriptura* principle in dialogue with Eastern Orthodox criticism, see Torsten Löfstedt, "In Defence of the Scripture Principle: An Evangelical Reply to A. S. Khomiakov," *EvQ* 83/1 (2011): 51. See also the brief discussion in chapter 4.

40. For example, consider the differences (above) between Mathison and Oberman on the one hand and Allert and Lane on the other, regarding whether the magisterial reformers held the coincidence view. With regard to the Roman Catholic view there is ongoing discussion as to whether there are two sources of revelation or one. See the further discussion in chapter 4.

41. This leaves it to anyone who would use the historical categorizations the task of first deciding who is accurately interpreting the history and tradition.

42. Note, however, that some of the Protestant communitarian approaches reject or avoid the phrase *sola Scriptura* altogether.

tation?[43] A reductionist *sola Scriptura* approach would take Scripture alone to be the "rule," but with the view that Scripture requires no interpretation alongside an isolationist (and perhaps anti-intellectualist) standpoint that purports to interpret Scripture apart from the influence of any tradition. Such a view, however, enables superficial (*prima facie*) reading of Scripture wherein interpreters of Scripture are unaware of the contributions of their own conceptual frameworks to their readings of Scripture, and ignorant of what might be learned from the readings of others. Such a reductionist approach tends to yield impoverished, solipsistic theology that is thus blindly beholden to the idiosyncrasies of private interpretation. However, while some Christians appear to (wittingly or unwittingly) practice such an approach, I am not aware of any serious academic exemplar of this approach. Its isolationism leaves little context for fruitful engagement and, as such, does not appear to warrant extended engagement. While the remainder of this book indirectly provides ample reasons as to why such a reductionist approach is not deemed to be viable, this work focuses its engagement on the potential viability of the canonical and communitarian *sola Scriptura* approaches.

Canonical *sola Scriptura* contends that the canon *qua* canon is the rule and standard of Christian theology, while recognizing that the canon requires interpretation (cf. Luke 10:26) and rejecting isolationism and the private interpretation of Scripture. The canonical approach to theology further suggests *tota* and *analogia* Scriptura as safeguards, especially in recognition of the various horizons of interpretation, resulting in an intentionally continuous spiral between reader and the text as canon (as explained in later chapters).

Conversely, a communitarian *sola Scriptura* approach proposes a community-determined, extracanonical rule as interpretive arbiter. Such approaches typically include past tradition (or some part thereof) and/or the present spirit-directed community as interpretive arbiter (i.e., rule or hermeneutical key).[44] As such, communitarian *sola Scriptura* contends that an authoritative extracanonical interpretive arbiter of Scripture is necessary for the

---

43. This question will be taken up at length in chapter 5.

44. With regard to the latter, John R. Franke, "Scripture, Tradition, and Authority: Reconstructing the Evangelical Conception of *Sola Scriptura*," in *Evangelicals & Scripture: Tradition, Authority, and Hermeneutics*, ed. Vincent Bacote, Laura C. Miguélez, and Dennis L. Okholm (Downers Grove, IL: InterVarsity, 2004), 210, believes that "Scripture and tradition must function together, each in its proper fashion, as coinherent aspects of the ongoing ministry of the Spirit. Viewed in this fashion, the Christian tradition provides a crucial, indispensable and authoritative hermeneutical context and trajectory for the life and witness of the church." See the discussion of this and other views beginning in chapter 4.

production and maintenance of sound Christian theology and the mitigation of the deleterious results of individualism and rampant hermeneutical diversity.[45]

In this regard, a number of prominent criticisms of *sola Scriptura* undergird either the rejection of the phrase *sola Scriptura* altogether or a definition of *sola Scriptura* along communitarian lines. The most prominent of such criticisms include the charge that the *sola Scriptura* principle (1) is self-defeating — as itself unbiblical or the product of circular reasoning; (2) isolates Scripture to the exclusion of any other revelation, the proper use of reason and scholarship, and/or interpretive communities past and present; and (3) leads to subjectivism and/or hyper-pluralism.

I argue in this book, however, that such criticisms do not defeat canonical *sola Scriptura*. That is, this approach is appropriately derived from Scripture itself and thus is not self-defeating and, over and against isolationism and private interpretation, it advocates the proper use of reason and scholarship alongside engagement with interpretive communities past and present, all of which are subordinate to the data of Scripture itself. Finally, canonical *sola Scriptura* posits the canon itself as rule without suggesting that the canon requires no interpretation or asserting that the canon as rule will eliminate or assuage hermeneutical diversity. Rather, this canonical approach does not believe that *any* extracanonical rule or normative interpreter would actually eliminate hermeneutical diversity. On this view, then, the canon is adequate to function as the rule for theology as the standard against which all theological proposals are brought, with the recognition that hermeneutical diversity will remain.[46]

In this and other ways, it will be argued that the unique sufficiency and epistemological primacy of Scripture as canon (with regard to theological doctrine) is logically consistent and practicable toward a canonical theological method that is preferable to communitarian approaches and, perhaps, preferable even on communitarian grounds.

---

45. Whether one takes a coincidence or ancillary view of the Scripture-tradition relationship (or something else), insofar as an extracanonical normative interpreter is adopted the position falls under the broad label "communitarian," as defined herein.

46. This approach recognizes the *ministerial* intra-communal doctrinal authority of communal bodies to draft, and expect members to abide by, descriptive doctrinal statements (insofar as they remain members of that community), but it does not suggest that any community (or other extracanonical arbiter) possesses the authority to determine (or be the normative interpretive of) theological doctrine prescriptively.

Toward a Canonical Theological Method:
Canon-Ruled Theology

The outcomes of these canon and *sola Scriptura* debates hinge upon the relative authority of the canon and community and, accordingly, hold significant implications for theological method. Perhaps most obvious is the fact that one's view of the canon will itself set parameters of how the canon could legitimately function theologically, particularly in relationship to the Christian community. If the canon is merely a human construct, then it follows that the canon could not offer divine theological authority. If the canon's authority is community-imposed, then it follows that the community *might* possess authority to impose theological interpretations as normative. If the canon is determined by God and merely recognized by humans, then it follows that the canon holds a divinely commissioned authority independent of human recognition and the intra-community functionality of the canon. The sharp divide regarding the nature of the canon thus holds significant implications regarding the canon's theological role.

In a similar fashion, *sola Scriptura* proponents debate whether (and to what extent) an extracanonical interpretive arbiter should be adopted as a rule for Christian theology. Whereas adoption of the community canon model does not require adoption of communitarian *sola Scriptura* or vice versa, it seems natural that one who adopts a community canon model would be open to the adoption of a community-determined extracanonical interpretive arbiter (and, thus, communitarian *sola Scriptura*). Given the view that the community possesses the authority to determine the canon, the community might likewise possess the authority to determine normative interpretation of that community-determined canon.[47]

Conversely, if the canon possesses divinely commissioned authority (intrinsic canon model), then it follows that the canon might be appropriately recognized as (under God) *the* standard or rule (*canon*) of Christian theology along the lines of canonical *sola Scriptura*. That is, if the canon is divinely determined to function in a theological authoritative role, it follows that one's theological method should allow the biblical canon to function canonically (i.e., as "rule").[48]

---

47. Cf. the Roman Catholic depiction of the "Church as writer, canonizer, and interpreter of scripture" (Kreeft, *Fundamentals*, 274-75).

48. See the discussion of the minimal definition of canon as "rule" or "standard" in chapter 2.

In my view, an intrinsic canon model undergirds (without requiring) canonical *sola Scriptura*, both of which support a robust canonical theological method. However, someone who rejects the intrinsic canon model and/or *sola Scriptura* (canonical or otherwise) could nevertheless appropriate much of the canonical approach to theological method offered in this work, at least minimally. No individual component (canonical model, canonical view of *sola Scriptura*, and canonical method/hermeneutics) requires the others out of logical necessity, but the components together are greater than the sum of the disparate parts. Together they set forth an internally coherent, theologically robust, and practically preferable approach to the nature of the canon and its theological function within Christian community.

Conclusion

This chapter has outlined the crucial divide among Christians regarding the relative authority of the canon and community for theology, with particular attention to the divide regarding the origin and attendant function of the canon *qua* canon and the ongoing debate relative to *sola Scriptura* about whether (and to what extent) an extracanonical interpretive arbiter should be adopted as a "rule" for Christian theology.

Toward addressing this divide and advancing the conversation, the chapters that follow take up the questions of the nature and function of the biblical canon (chapters 2 and 3), communitarian approaches to theology and the identification and application of the rule of faith (chapters 4 and 5), a working approach to *sola Scriptura* as preferable to communitarian approaches (chapters 6 and 7), and an explication of canonical theological method, concluding with a step-by-step explication of its implementation in practice (chapters 8-10).

CHAPTER 2

Defining the Intrinsic Canon

There is considerable ongoing debate and confusion regarding just how "canon" should be defined and understood, what the nature of the canon is and what it includes, and whether and to what extent the biblical canon is (or should be) authoritative. This chapter outlines a theological approach to the issue of canon by way of an explication of the intrinsic canon model, focusing on two primary issues: (1) competing definitions and understandings regarding the nature of the canon, particularly what or who makes the biblical canon "canonical" and determines its scope; and (2) the nature and scope of the biblical canon according to an intrinsic canon perspective.

DEFINING THE CANON OF SCRIPTURE

The canon debate hinges on the way that the term "canon" is defined and requires attention to what *kind* of definition is in view, whether regarding the canon's nature (what *is* the canon?) or its historical function (when did the canon function as such?). Perspectives on the nature of the canon are split between those who define the canon as a corpus of divinely determined books (the intrinsic canon) and those who view the canon as a collection of community-determined books (the community canon). Perspectives on the historical function of the canon are further divided regarding *when* the canon functions as canon and when the term "canon" ought to be applied.[1] The predominant framework of the canon debate in recent times has been

1. See the discussion in chapter 3.

relative to this latter *kind* of definition, which some take as bearing on, or even determinative of, the former. For our purposes, however, we turn first to the canon's nature.

What Is the Nature of the Canon?

In my view, the crucial theological question that cuts across the canon debate is: what makes the canon "canonical"? One might approach the canon as the result of historical phenomena, apart from weighing in regarding whether and to what extent God played a role in the canon's history. Framed this way, the question is whether one considers the biblical canon "an extrinsic phenomenon" wherein "a later ecclesiastical development [was] imposed on books originally written for another purpose," on the one hand, or as a notion that "developed early and naturally out of the Christian religion."[2]

Whereas I view the canon as a historical phenomenon, I am most interested in the particularly theological form of this question: Is the canon determined by humans or by God?[3] The intrinsic canon model and community canon model sharply diverge regarding precisely this question, with significant theological implications.

In the community canon model, the community determines the canon. This tends toward reducing the definition of canon to a collection of books deemed authoritative (and thus made canonical) by a given community.[4] As such, the canon might be viewed as an extension of community authority.

2. Michael J. Kruger, *The Question of Canon: Challenging the Status Quo in the New Testament Debate* (Downers Grove, IL: IVP Academic, 2013), 7, 22. Kruger makes a strong case for the latter, that canon was a natural development in early Christianity. Cf. Michael J. Kruger, *Canon Revisited: Establishing the Origins and Authority of the New Testament Books* (Wheaton, IL: Crossway, 2012).

3. I posit here a distinctively theological treatment of canon, which makes no pretense of neutrality. Every investigation requires starting points and mine is the supposition that God has revealed himself to humans (most fully in Christ) in a way that is recognizable. This is a minimal belief of Christianity which does not require the *a priori* supposition of an overarching theological system and itself appears to be a fundamental supposition of the NT (thus, it methodologically and theologically coheres with the canonical theological method laid out in later chapters). Accordingly, I devote considerable attention here to the internal testimony of the Bible regarding the nature of its contents.

4. See n. 5 in chapter 1 above. See also Kruger's delineation of three types of community-determined canon models (historical-critical, Roman Catholic, and canonical-critical model); see his *Canon Revisited*, 30-57.

The community canon model is itself split in this regard between those who believe the canon was fixed by the church at some time in the past (the ecclesial fixed canon view) and those who favor a more fluid definition of the canon as shaped by contemporary community consensus (the adaptable canon view).

Within the community canon model's broad scope, then, some suggest that "canon" is an anachronistic imposition on selected writings by external community forces.[5] Others reduce the notion of canon to the decisions of a Christian community such that "biblical canons depend for content and order on the denomination or communion in view."[6] Here, canon is "something officially or authoritatively imposed upon certain literature." As such, it is "basically a community's paradigm for how to continue the dialogue in ever changing socio-political contexts."[7]

Others attribute less fluidity to the canon yet retain the centrality of the community in canon-determination. Paul McGlasson states, "*Canon* by definition refers to a sacred text treasured in an ongoing community of faith."[8] Charles Scalise similarly points out, "Including a text in the canon means that it has theological importance for the communities who read it as Scripture."[9]

---

5. Such community forces external to the canon might be Christian (ecclesial) forces or, in some theories, primarily political forces. See, for example, David L. Dungan, *Constantine's Bible: Politics and the Making of the New Testament* (Minneapolis: Fortress, 2007). Cf. Robert W. Funk, "The Once and Future New Testament," in *The Canon Debate*, ed. Lee Martin McDonald and James A. Sanders (Peabody, MA: Hendrickson, 2002); Harry Y. Gamble, *The New Testament Canon: Its Making and Meaning* (Philadelphia: Fortress, 1985), 11-13, 57-67. See, further, the discussion of various supposed forces including political, ecclesiastical, heretical, and (Greek) philosophical, among others in Kruger, *Question*, 17-20.

6. James A. Sanders, *Canon and Community: A Guide to Canonical Criticism* (Philadelphia: Fortress, 1984), 15. Sanders delineates this in the context of scholarly "devalu[ation]" of "the meaning of the word canon in order to apply to the Bible the developing tools of historical investigation" (*Canon and Community*, 1).

7. James A. Sanders, "The Issue of Closure in the Canonical Process," in *Canon Debate*, 252, 262.

8. Paul McGlasson, *Invitation to Dogmatic Theology: A Canonical Approach* (Grand Rapids: Brazos, 2006), 54. Cf. John R. Franke's view, "Scripture, Tradition, and Authority: Reconstructing the Evangelical Conception of *Sola Scriptura*," in *Evangelicals & Scripture: Tradition, Authority, and Hermeneutics*, ed. Vincent Bacote, Laura C. Miguélez, and Dennis L. Okholm (Downers Grove, IL: InterVarsity, 2004), 200, that "canonical Scripture is, on the one hand, constitutive of the church, providing the primary narratives around which the life and faith of the Christian community is shaped and formed and, on the other hand, is itself derived from that community and its authority." Thus, "Scripture and tradition" are "inseparably bound together through the work of the Spirit."

9. Charles J. Scalise, *From Scripture to Theology: A Canonical Journey into Hermeneutics* (Downers Grove, IL: InterVarsity, 1996), 45.

Despite variations regarding fluidity and authority, then, the common denominator of community approaches is the location of canon-determination in the community such that the canon is defined as those books that some community makes authoritative (and thus "canonical").

Conversely, according to the intrinsic canon model, divine action is the determining factor regarding the nature and scope of the canon. God determines the canon, which the community *merely* recognizes.[10] Writings, then, are "canonical" insofar as God divinely commissioned them as the rule or standard of faith and practice. Whereas the community's recognition of the canon holds crucial implications regarding its function within that community, community-recognition does not bear on canonicity *qua* canonicity. The divide, then, is not over *whether* the community plays a role with regard to the canon but precisely *what* that role is, particularly regarding what makes the canon "canonical" and by whose authority the canon is the "rule" or "standard."

Intrinsic Canonicity

I define the intrinsic canon as the corpus of writings commissioned by God to be the "rule" or "standard" of Christian faith and practice.[11] Thus, the intrinsic canon refers to those writings that are *intrinsically* canonical by virtue of what the canon *is* as the result of divine action (i.e., via divine commission).[12] This

10. Anthony C. Thiselton, "Canon, Community, and Theological Construction," in *Canon and Biblical Interpretation,* ed. Craig G. Bartholomew et al. (Grand Rapids: Zondervan, 2006), 13, comments, "the church did not 'make' the canon, but through its life and identity recognized the formative impact of divine revelation through the call of the 'prophets and apostles as a whole.'" For Milton Fisher, "The Canon of the New Testament," in *The Origin of the Bible,* ed. Philip Wesley Comfort (Wheaton, IL: Tyndale, 1992), 77, further, "what is really meant by canonization — [is] recognition of the divinely authenticated word." Cf. Brevard S. Childs, *Biblical Theology in Crisis* (Philadelphia: Westminster, 1970), 105; F. F. Bruce, *The Books and the Parchments* (Glasgow: HarperCollins, 1991), 86–104; Kruger, *Question,* 39.

11. Therefore, as Gerhard F. Hasel, "Divine Inspiration and the Canon of the Bible," *Journal of the Adventist Theological Society* 5/1 (1994), 73, contends, the "canon developed at the very point when the biblical books were written under inspiration."

12. Kruger adopts a "historical approach to the canon," leading him to an "ontological" definition, which "focuses on what the canon is in and of itself" (*Question,* 40). Here, "the canonical books are what they are by virtue of the divine purpose for which they were given, and not by virtue of their use or acceptance by the community of faith" (*Question,* 39). Kruger uses the phrase "intrinsic canon," however, to refer to something else and contrasts his use of this phrase with my own by framing his as not in reference to "the authority of the canon but" to "the *historical development* of the canon" (*Question,* 22 n. 27, emphasis his). See

does not mean that the canonical writings result from exclusively divine action but that their intrinsically canonical nature is derived from the uniquely divine activity that, combined with human activity, resulted in the product of Scripture (cf. 2 Tim 3:16; 2 Pet 1:20-21).[13] Hereafter, I will use "divine commission" as an umbrella term for the various divine activities in the production of the canonical writings.[14]

This intrinsic canon view rests on a minimal definition of the word "canon" (κανών) in the sense of "rule" or "standard."[15] Paul appears to use the term κανών in this minimal sense (though not of the biblical canon) when he states, "as many as walk according to this rule [κανόνι], peace and mercy be upon them" (Gal 6:16).[16] With this minimal definition of "canon," the intrinsic canon of Scripture is those writings commissioned (in the broad sense) by God to be the "rule" or "standard" (κανών) of faith and practice.

Given that God is the ruler of the universe, whatever God commissions

---

John C. Peckham, "The Canon and Biblical Authority: A Critical Comparison of Two Models of Canonicity," *TJ* 28/2 (2007): 229-49. By intrinsic canon, however, I do not refer *merely* to the authority of the canon but to what the canon *is intrinsically*. Canonical writings are intrinsically authoritative *as* intrinsically canonical and they are intrinsically canonical in virtue of what they are due to divine action.

Whereas by "intrinsic" I mean intrinsic *to the canon itself* in virtue of what it is, it seems that by "intrinsic" Kruger means intrinsic *to Christianity* in the sense of flowing "organically from within the early Christian religion itself" (Kruger, *Question*, 21), as opposed to extrinsically imposed upon Christianity "from the outside." If this differentiation is correct, someone might adopt Kruger's intrinsic canon and yet fall under what I refer to as the community canon model (though Kruger himself would not, given his ontological definition; see *Question*, 44, 46). Whereas Kruger's primary concern in *The Question of Canon* appears to be whether the concept of canon is a late development imposed upon Christianity (arguing that it is not), my concern focuses on whether canonicity is imposed upon books by humans (whether from inside or outside Christianity) or intrinsic to the canonical writings in virtue of divine action.

13. 2 Timothy 3:16 likely refers specifically to OT Scriptures, but the theological import of the verse may apply to later writings insofar as those writings are also genuinely "Scripture" in this sense (cf. 2 Pet 3:15-16).

14. The phrase "divine commission," then, does not require commitment to a particular model of revelation-inspiration. For my view, in this regard, see chapter 8.

15. On κανών, see Bruce M. Metzger, *The Canon of the New Testament: Its Origin, Development, and Significance* (Oxford: Clarendon, 1987), 289-93; Eugene Ulrich, "The Notion and Definition of Canon," in *Canon Debate*, 21-35; and Hermann Beyer, "κανών," *TDNT* 3:596-602.

16. Such use in the sense of "rule" or "standard" also appears in early Christian writings of a *canon* of faith or *canon* of truth (Irenaeus, *Against Heresies* 1.9.4; Clement of Alexandria, *Miscellanies* 6.15; cf. Eusebius, *Ecclesiastical History* 6.25.3; see chapter 5). The term also appears elsewhere in the NT and LXX with a broader range of meaning beyond "rule" or "standard." See 2 Cor 10:13, 15, 16; cf. LXX Judith 13:6; 4 Macc 7:21; Micah 7:4.

as the rule or standard is thereby canonical. According to the words of Christ in Luke 11:49, God commissioned, or sent (ἀποστέλλω), "prophets and apostles" as his authoritative spokespersons and witnesses. Further, Eph 2:19-20 describes the "household" of God as "built on the foundation of the apostles and prophets, Christ Jesus Himself being the corner *stone*" (cf. Eph 3:5; 4:11; 1 Cor 12:28-29; 2 Pet 3:2; Rev 18:20; translation following NASB).

Such divine commission of prophets and apostles closely relates to the covenantal context of Scripture. A strong case can be made that the canon is a covenant document, depicting and regulating the relationship between God and his people. In this context, many biblical writers describe their prophetic and/or apostolic activity as responsive to divine command such that they disseminate not merely their own thoughts but divine revelation written down under the guidance of inspiration. The nature and authority of such writings derives from divine commission.[17]

Indeed, biblical writers repeatedly describe their teachings and/or those of others as theologically authoritative in virtue of their divine origin. For example, Paul contends: "All Scripture is inspired [θεόπνευστος] by God and profitable for teaching, for reproof, for correction, for training in righteousness" (2 Tim 3:16). Further, 2 Pet 1:20-21 emphasizes the divine origin of Scripture, explaining "that no prophecy of Scripture is a matter of one's own interpretation, for no prophecy was ever made by an act of human will, but men moved by the Holy Spirit spoke from God." In these instances and others, the term "Scripture" is used in reference to writings originated through divine action and theologically authoritative in virtue of divine action (i.e., commission). As such, any writings that are properly "Scripture," in this sense, are thereby "canonical" in the minimal sense defined above.[18]

17. Cf. the redemptive-historical approach wherein Scripture is a "product of God's revelatory activity in the history of redemption"; Herman N. Ridderbos, *Redemptive History and the New Testament Scriptures,* 2nd rev. ed. (Phillipsburg, NJ: Presbyterian and Reformed, 1988), ix. Here, "the apostles' [Christ-commissioned] role in the history of redemption was unique and unrepeatable. . . . Christ established a formal authority structure" as "source and standard" (*Redemptive History,* 13). Christ thus bestowed authority on the canon, which is finally closed based "on the once-for-all significance of the New Testament history of redemption itself," which required "a *written form*" to "exist permanently" beyond the apostles (*Redemptive History,* 25). The NT canonical writings are thus inherently authoritative due to their location in redemption history.

18. Contra Sundberg's influential but artificial distinction between "Scripture" and "canon" (see chapter 3). As Iain Provan, "Canons to the Left of Him: Brevard Childs, His Critics, and the Future of Old Testament Theology," *SJT* 50/1 (1997): 10, notes, the very "idea of scripture" itself implies "the idea of limitation, of canon, even if it is not yet conceived that the limits

Note, at this juncture, that the above texts are not being used to bear on *which* extant writings are "canonical" but as evidence of the claim that canonical writers believed that divine commission (broadly) invested their teachings (oral and written) with divine authority (cf. 1 Thess 2:13). If such claims are true, any such written (inscripturated) teachings would be properly "canonical" in the minimal sense defined above and would be so before and apart from community recognition (and, indeed, often set directly against community consensus; see chapter 3). Thus, whereas those who believe the canon is the product of external imposition often contend that biblical writers did not "conceive of themselves as producing authoritative texts," biblical writers "do provide substantial indications that they understood their message as authoritative, and often do so quite plainly" (see the further evidence below).[19]

Recognizing the Intrinsic Canon

With the intrinsic canon model, then, God is the one who makes the canon canonical and, accordingly, determines (via divine commission) the contents of the canon. Among the community's duties, then, is to properly recognize the divinely commissioned canon. Accordingly, the intrinsic canon approach looks for evidence of divine commission. The biblical data itself provides key evidence via internal claims to such divine commission, indicating some criteria that might aid in recognizing which writings were divinely commissioned as covenantally authoritative (i.e., canonical).

The Canon as Christocentric Covenant Document

The contents of the intrinsic canon arise from within the context of God's covenant relationship with his people wherein there is a "tight connection between the giving of covenants and the production of canonical texts."[20] Fol-

---

have been reached." As such, "the necessity of a strict demarcation between Scripture and canon largely disappears" (Kruger, *Question*, 20; cf. Kruger, *Canon Revisited*, 35-38). Here, the crucial matter is not the term(s) used but the way biblical writers describe the nature and authority of biblical writings.

19. Kruger, *Question*, 24.

20. Kruger, *Question*, 61. See the compelling case in this regard in Andreas J. Köstenberger and Michael J. Kruger, *The Heresy of Orthodoxy* (Wheaton, IL: Crossway, 2010), 109-15. They conclude that "canon is inherent to and derives its function from the concept of covenant" such

lowing the Exodus, the Torah depicts Moses as divinely commissioned to write down divinely authoritative teachings, prescribed as a covenantal rule or standard, to be preserved without alteration (Deut 4:2) and passed down to future generations (cf. Deut 6; 29:29; 31:10-13). As many scholars have recognized, Deuteronomy appears to share a similar structure with other ancient Near Eastern treaties, including (most significantly for our purposes) a "deposit of the written text of the covenant."[21] Further, the Ten Commandments themselves are proclaimed in the context of God's redemptive activity: "I am the LORD your God, who brought you out of the land of Egypt, out of the house of slavery" (Exod 20:2). Here and elsewhere, the "Old Testament pattern" is "that canonical documents are distinctively the result of God's redemptive activity on behalf of his people and function to proclaim that redemptive activity to his people (and to the nations)."[22]

Even as the OT canonical writings might thus be seen as depositing the written text of the covenantal relationship between God and his people, one might similarly view the NT as containing the Christ-commissioned canonical documentation of the new covenant, patterned after and building on the OT as covenant document. Indeed, "the concept of a written canon of Scripture is woven into the very covenantal fabric of both the Old Testament and the New Testament."[23] The OT's "archetypal redemptive event," the Exodus, is followed by the giving of the Law in the context of the wider covenant and written documentation thereof, the command to preserve and proclaim such "canonical" teachings, and the post-Mosaic generations of prophets as divinely commissioned proclaimers thereof (e.g., 2 Kgs 17:13; see below).[24]

A similar NT pattern emerges in that the Christ event, the redemptive event *par excellence*, is framed by Christ within the new covenant (Luke 22:20; cf. 1 Cor 11:25; 2 Cor 3:6) that he mediates (Heb 9:15; 12:24; cf. 8:8,

---

that canon is "the *inevitable result of covenant*" (*Heresy*, 112; emphasis theirs). For Kruger, then, "*the canon is a treaty document*" (*Question*, 61, emphasis his). Compare Meredith G. Kline's view, *The Structure of Biblical Authority* (Grand Rapids: Eerdmans, 1972), 45-75, here 75, that "canon is inherent in covenant of the biblical type" and thus "canonicity is inherent in the very form and identity of Scripture as the Old Testament and the New Testament."

21. Köstenberger and Kruger, *Heresy*, 111.

22. Köstenberger and Kruger, *Heresy*, 113. Cf. Richard M. Davidson, "The Divine Covenant Lawsuit Motif in Biblical Perspective," *Journal of the Adventist Theological Society* 21/1-2 (2010): 45-84.

23. Köstenberger and Kruger, *Heresy*, 113. Cf. Kevin Vanhoozer's view, *The Drama of Doctrine: A Canonical-Linguistic Approach to Christian Theology* (Louisville: Westminster John Knox, 2005), 134, cf. 137-39, of the "canon" as "a divinely initiated covenant document."

24. Köstenberger and Kruger, *Heresy*, 113.

13; Jer 31:31) alongside proclamation of the corresponding law of love upon which the "whole Law and the Prophets" depend (Matt 22:36-40).[25] Further, Christ commissions the apostles to preserve, proclaim, and disseminate his acts, teachings, and commands, and make disciples of all nations (cf. Matt 28:19-20). Accordingly, the Christ-commissioned apostolic generation preserved in writing for future generations their unique witness to the unrepeatable Christ event, depositing a permanent Christ-commissioned (and thus "canonical") testament.[26]

At the epicenter of covenant and canon, then, stands Christ. Many have recognized Christ as the center of the canon theologically; the OT points toward the Christ event and is fulfilled (without being nullified) therein (cf. Matt 5:17-18; Heb 1:1-2). However, Christ is also the center of the canon in that (broadly speaking) he appears to ratify the OT and commission the NT.

Christ repeatedly refers to the "Law and the Prophets" as authoritative (e.g., Matt 5:17; 7:12; 11:13; 22:40; Luke 16:16; cf. 16:29; Matt 11:13) and, in one particularly notable instance, states that "all things which are written about Me in the Law of Moses and the Prophets and the Psalms must be fulfilled" (Luke 24:44; cf. 24:27).[27] Some have suggested this may refer to the Law, Prophets,

---

25. Cf. Kline's view that the NT reflects the OT's covenantal structure (*Structure*, 68-75). Cf. also the typology of Christ as second Moses.

26. Regarding the claim that Christ did not explicitly commission the NT *writing*, see below. Compare Adolf von Harnack's comment, *The Origin of the New Testament and the Most Important Consequences of the New Creation* (New York: Macmillan, 1925), 13, that the "conception of the 'New Covenant' necessarily suggested the need of something of *the nature of a document*; for what is a covenant without its document?" (emphasis his).

27. While the precise books to which Jesus refers are unidentified, as Craig A. Evans, "The Scriptures of Jesus and His Earliest Followers," in *Canon Debate*, 195, notes, Luke 24:44 manifests "awareness of additional authoritative writings" although "the contours of a third division of Scripture remain undefined"; cf. also Christopher Seitz, *The Goodly Fellowship of the Prophets: The Achievement of Association in Canon Formation* (Grand Rapids: Baker Academic, 2009), 97-100. Consider further Christ's reference to "Daniel the prophet" in Matt 24:15. Note also that 2 Macc 15:9 records Maccabeus encouraging his men "from the law and the prophets." Cf. 4QMMT[c] 10; b. Baba Batra 13b; Sir 39:1; Philo, *Contempl. Life*, 25. Additionally, Josephus, *Against Apion* 1.8, delineates (without naming each book) a three-part corpus as five books of Moses, thirteen of the Prophets (from the death of Moses to the time of Artaxerxes), and four containing "hymns to God and precepts for the conduct of human life" (translation following Josephus, *The Life; Against Apion*, translated by H. St. J. Thackeray, Loeb Classical Library 186 [Cambridge, MA: Harvard University Press, 1926], 179). Kruger concludes, in this regard, "although it is disputed by some scholars, there are good reasons to think the threefold canonical structure of the Old Testament would have been established by the time of Jesus" (*Question*, 49). Cf. Roger T. Beckwith, *The Old Testament Canon of the New Testament Church*

and Writings sections of the Hebrew Bible, with "Psalms" perhaps designating the entire Writings section, of which it is the first book. Further, some point to Jesus's statement in Luke 11:51, "from the blood of Abel to the blood of Zechariah, who was killed between the altar and the house *of God*" as probably referring to the first and last martyrs in the Hebrew OT, thus encapsulating the Hebrew Bible from beginning to the end.[28] While inconclusive by themselves, these passages, coupled with other evidence such as the extensive use of the OT by Jesus and the apostles[29] and other evidence regarding recognition of a functional OT canon by the first century (see chapter 3), suggest that Jesus and his apostles held an OT canon of Scripture (at least in the minimal sense of a corpus that they recognized as a divinely commissioned "rule" or "standard"), the boundaries of which they knew and expected their audience to know.[30]

(Grand Rapids: Eerdmans, 1986), 110-80; Stephen B. Chapman, "The Old Testament Canon and Its Authority for the Christian Church," *ExAud* 19 (2003): 125-48.

28. This refers to Zechariah, the son of Jehoiada, as specified by the description of Zechariah's death (2 Chr 24:20-21). The parallel reference in Matt 23:35 introduces some confusion, also referring to this manner of death but identifying him as "the son of Berechiah." This patronymic is that of the prophet Zechariah (Zech 1:1), not the same figure whose death is recounted in Chronicles; it is likely a mistaken gloss (cf. Targum Lamentations 2.20). Evans takes this reference as "probably meant to sum up Israel's history, not Israel's sacred scripture" ("Scriptures," 190). However, given that Israel's history continued long after the death of Zechariah, as did the martyrdom of God's messengers (e.g., John the Baptist), this seems to me unlikely.

29. "According to the Synoptic Gospels, Jesus quotes or alludes to twenty-three of the thirty-nine books of the Hebrew Bible." He "alludes to or quotes all five books of Moses, the three major prophets (Isaiah, Jeremiah, and Ezekiel), eight of the twelve minor prophets, and five of the Writings" (Evans, "Scriptures," 185). Cf. R. T. France, *Jesus and the Old Testament* (Grand Rapids: Baker, 1982), 259-63. While the presence or absence of a quote or allusion may not itself indicate how a source was viewed (numerous sources are alluded to without connoting authority or inspiration; cf. Acts 17:28; Tit 1:12), it is notable that each section of the Hebrew Bible is very well represented by quotes and allusions throughout the NT (frequently quoted as authoritative Scripture). On Roger Nicole's count, "New Testament Use of the Old Testament," in *Revelation and the Bible*, ed. Carl F. H. Henry (Grand Rapids: Baker, 1958), 138, of "specific quotations and direct allusions," "278 different Old Testament verses are cited in the New Testament: 94 from the Pentateuch, 99 from the Prophets, and 85 from the Writings. Out of the 22 books in the Hebrew reckoning of the Canon only six (Judges-Ruth, Song of Solomon, Ecclesiastes, Esther, Ezra-Nehemiah, Chronicles) are not explicitly referred to" while there are "passages reminiscent of all Old Testament books without exception." Craig Blomberg, *Can We Still Believe the Bible?* (Grand Rapids: Brazos, 2014), 49, finds it "particularly telling" that the NT "explicitly quotes from a broad-section of Old Testament documents but never quotes from the OT Apocrypha," though "one may speculate about numerous possible references to both apocryphal and pseudepigraphic texts." For a list of possible references to the OT Apocrypha see McDonald, *Biblical Canon*, 452-64.

30. Thus, Childs believes, "From the evidence of the New Testament it seems clear that

Beyond the examples noted earlier (e.g., Luke 24:27, 44-45; 2 Tim 3:16; 2 Pet 1:20-21), Matthew writes, "all this has taken place to fulfill the Scriptures of the prophets" (Matt 26:56; cf. 1:22; 2:15-17, 23; Luke 1:70; 24:27, 44-45; Acts 1:16; 3:18). Similarly, Paul refers to what God had "promised beforehand through His prophets in the holy Scriptures" (Rom 1:2) and also speaks of God establishing believers both "according to my gospel and the preaching of Jesus Christ" and "by the Scriptures of the prophets, according to the commandment of the eternal God" (Rom 16:25-26; cf. 3:2; 15:4). Accordingly, Paul contends that he serves "the God of our fathers, believing everything that is in accordance with the Law and that is written in the Prophets" (Acts 24:14; cf. 23:5; John 1:45; 2 Cor 4:2). Elsewhere, Paul "for three Sabbaths reasoned with them from the Scriptures" (Acts 17:2) and "demonstrate[d] by the Scriptures that Jesus was the Christ" (Acts 18:28; cf. 1 Cor 15:3). This and other NT evidence suggests the "canonical" authority of some recognized corpus of OT Scripture.

Whereas the OT Scriptures appear to be ratified by Jesus and recognized by the apostles as, among other things, testifying of Christ (cf. John 1:45; 5:39; Acts 10:43; 1 Pet 1:10-12), Christ also commissions an enduring apostolic testimony and thus commissions (at least indirectly) the NT writings insofar as they are genuinely apostolic. Jesus himself "appointed twelve" to "be with Him" and to "send them out to preach and to have authority" (Mark 3:14-15). When sending them, Christ told them, you will bear "testimony" to "governors and kings" and "to the Gentiles" but "it is not you who speak, but it is the Spirit of your Father who speaks in you," so that those who do not "receive you, nor heed your words" will face judgment (Matt 10:18, 20; cf. Matt 10:14-15). Elsewhere, in John 20:21, Jesus declares to the apostles, "as the Father has sent Me, I also send you" (cf. John 17:8, 18). In this regard, Christ had previously promised: "the Holy Spirit, whom the Father will send in My name, He will teach you all things, and bring to your remembrance all that I said to you" (John 14:26) and

---

Jesus and the early Christians identified with the scriptures of Pharisaic Judaism" (*Biblical Theology*, 26). Cf. Peter Balla, "Evidence for an Early Christian Canon (Second and Third Century)," in *Canon Debate*, 372-85; Beckwith, *Old Testament Canon*, 165-66; F. F. Bruce, *The Canon of Scripture* (Downers Grove, IL: InterVarsity, 1988), 255. Whereas McDonald raises questions about this view, he does recognize that "many OT citations and allusions in the Gospels attest to the authoritative status of the OT in the life and ministry of the early Christian communities" (*Formation*, 9). Cf. McDonald, *Biblical Canon*, 31-32, 426. Consider, for instance, the way that Christ referred to and used OT Scripture as authoritative (e.g., Matt 4:4-10; 5:17-19; 11:13-14; 12:3-6, 39-42; 15:4-6; 19:4-9; 21:42-44; 22:29-32, 37-40, 43-45; 24:9-21; 26:31-32, 54-56; Mark 1:44; 7:6; 10:3; 12:26; Luke 8:21; 11:28; 16:16-17; 24:27, 44-45; John 2:22; 5:39; 10:34-35; 17:12, 17). See also the way the rest of the NT testifies to OT writings as authoritative Scripture (e.g., Acts 17:2; 18:28; Rom 1:2; 4:3; 9:17; 10:11; 11:2; 1 Cor 15:3, 4; Gal 3:8; 2 Tim 3:16; 2 Pet 1:20-21).

"will guide you into all the truth" (16:13). Accordingly, Christ told them, "the one who listens to you listens to me, and the one who rejects you rejects me," suggesting their commission as Christ's authoritative ambassadors (Luke 10:16).

Nevertheless, James Barr comments that "Jesus in his teaching is nowhere portrayed as commanding or even sanctioning the production of a written Gospel, still less a written New Testament. He never even casually told his disciples to write anything down."[31] However, that the NT does not portray Jesus as commanding things to be written down does not (and could not) demonstrate that he did not do so (cf. Acts 1:2). Further, even if Christ did not do so, it does not follow that the NT writings were not thereby commissioned, at least indirectly.[32]

Here, Peter's depiction of the apostles as "witnesses" (μάρτυς) of the resurrected Christ is of considerable significance (Acts 10:41). Peter and other apostles "who ate and drank with Him [Christ] after He arose from the dead" were "chosen beforehand by God" and "ordered" by Christ "to preach to the people, and solemnly to testify [διαμαρτύρομαι] that this is the One who has been appointed by God as Judge of the living and the dead" (Acts 10:41-42; cf. 2 Pet 3:2).[33]

If "apostles" were (at minimum) eyewitnesses to the risen Christ and thereby appointed as his witnesses (cf. Acts 1:2-4; 9:3-15; 26:12-18), then genuinely apostolic testimony would be restricted to that of this chosen group, whose testimony would possess intrinsically "canonical" authority in virtue of their unique relationship with, and commission by, the risen Christ.[34] If this

31. James Barr, *Holy Scripture: Canon, Authority and Criticism* (Philadelphia: Westminster, 1983), 12. McDonald similarly notes that Jesus did not write or command anything to be written except in "Revelation, where Jesus commands the angels of the churches to put his message in written form (Rev 2:1–3:14)" (*Formation*, 7; cf. McDonald, *Biblical Canon*, 426; Gamble, *New Testament Canon*, 57).

32. Mark Alan Powell, *Introducing the New Testament: A Historical, Literary, and Theological Survey* (Grand Rapids: Baker Academic, 2009), 50, goes further, claiming that the "authors of our New Testament did not know that they were writing scripture." However, one wonders just how Powell knows what NT authors knew and did not know. Further, McDonald claims that Paul "apparently was unaware of the divinely inspired status of his own advice ([1 Cor] 7:12, 25)" (*Biblical Canon*, 32). But in the very same chapter Paul explicitly claims to have the Spirit of God (1 Cor 7:40; cf. Rom 15:15; see the further discussion below) and many believe Paul's statement in verse 12 is simply a way of indicating that he is not quoting Jesus. Kruger, moreover, notes NT writers "expressly understood their writings to be apostolic in nature" and, as such, "functionally" the same as "Scripture" (*Question*, 153). Cf. N. T. Wright, *Scripture and the Authority of God* (San Francisco: HarperCollins, 2011), 51.

33. Notably, verse 43 adds, "Of Him all the prophets bear witness."

34. "Given the authoritative role of the apostles in early Christianity, and the manner in

is correct, fulfilling Christ's commissions regarding the worldwide spread of the gospel (not to mention the covenantal context and presumable impetus thereof) would seem to require that provision be made for the reliable and accurate transmission of this apostolic testimony after the apostles' deaths (cf. Acts 20:29-32; 2 Pet 1:13-15). The writing down of this apostolic testimony (by apostles themselves or their close contemporary associates) appears to have been the chosen way to permanently record their unique and unrepeatable apostolic witness beyond the limits of their personal presence (cf. Rev 1:11).[35] As such, the Great Commission by itself (Matt 28:19-20) would appear to require, and thus indirectly commission, something like the NT canon.[36]

Canon as Divinely Commissioned

Considerable evidence suggests that biblical authors viewed themselves as divinely commissioned and thus authoritative teachers. Whereas a claim to divine commission is, of course, not sufficient to conclude that one actually is divinely commissioned, such claims of biblical authors do indicate that a minimal intrinsic canon approach is not an external imposition.

Internal NT Evidence

Beyond the explicit NT claims regarding Christ's commission to disseminate his teachings widely (see above), further NT evidence suggests the apostles viewed themselves and others as divinely commissioned, often explicitly in

---

which they were commissioned to speak for Christ, an apostolic writing would bear the highest possible authority. Indeed, it would bear Christ's authority" (Kruger, *Question*, 153).

35. In Kruger's view, "the mission of the apostles" made "the resulting collection of authoritative books — a virtual inevitability" (*Question*, 76). Kruger includes in his study an extensive, compelling case that "written records and oral/eyewitness testimony were not in opposition to one another; on the contrary, written accounts were simply a way to make oral/eyewitness testimony permanently accessible" (*Question*, 72).

36. As George Lindbeck, *The Nature of Doctrine: Religion and Theology in a Postliberal Age*, 1st ed. (Philadelphia: Westminster, 1984), 116, notes, "purely customary religions and cultures readily dissolve under the pressure of historical, social and linguistic change," such that "canonical texts are a condition, not only for the survival of a religion but for the very possibility of normative theological description." Likewise, Kruger notes that the "need to textualize the oral tradition of founding members (or eyewitnesses) is a pattern that has also been recognized by scholars who study social and cultural memory theory" and "typically occurs within forty years of the community's founding" (*Question*, 72, 73).

virtue of their apostolic connection to the risen Christ. Jesus evidently considered his words to be an authoritative rule or standard, to be heeded and transmitted (Matt 7:24-29; 28:20; John 15:4; 17:8). Indeed, the words of Jesus, in virtue of who he was, are intrinsically authoritative and are treated thus by NT writers (1 Cor 7:10, 17; 1 Thess 4:15; Matt 28:18) and other early Christians (see chapter 3). The gospel is thus repeatedly described as the "word of God," which the apostles are depicted as preaching and spreading (Acts 8:14; 11:1; 12:24; 13:46; 17:13; 18:11; 19:20; John 17:14; Eph 1:13) and which was recorded by eyewitnesses and contemporaries and faithfully passed down (i.e., Luke 1:1-3; cf. 24:48; John 20:31).

The author of John self-identifies as "the disciple who is testifying [μαρτυρέω] to these things and wrote these things" (John 21:24; cf. 20:31), perhaps alluding to Christ's earlier statement that the "Spirit" would be sent to the disciples and would "testify [μαρτυρέω] about Me, and you *will* testify [μαρτυρέω] also, because you have been with Me from the beginning" (John 15:26-27; cf. Luke 24:48; 1 John 1:1-2).[37] Similarly, 1 John is presented as eyewitness testimony in writing (1:1-4) and 1 John 1:5 explicitly states: "This is the message we have heard from Him [Christ] and announce to you" (cf. Luke 1:1-3).

Further, Paul proclaims his divine commission as "an apostle" who was "not sent from men nor through the agency of man, but through Jesus Christ and God the Father" (Gal 1:1), claims to have the Spirit of God (1 Cor 7:40; cf. Rom 15:15), and emphasizes that the gospel he preaches was not "received" from "man" but received "through a revelation of Jesus Christ" (Gal 1:12; cf. 1 Cor 2:13; Eph 3:3-5; 1 Thess 2:13). Here, Paul explicitly notes that this apostolic status and message was not community-derived but divinely commissioned and revealed. As Acts 26:16 records, Christ "appoint[ed]" Paul "a minister and a witness [μάρτυς]" (cf. Acts 9:1-9; 22:6-15).

The gospel preached by the apostles, itself received from the Lord, is held up as the rule and standard from which no believer is to depart (Gal 1:8-12; cf. 2 Cor 11:2-4). Accordingly, Paul exhorts his audience to "retain the standards of sound words which you have heard from me" (2 Tim 1:13; cf. 2 Thess 2:15; 3:14; 2 John 9-10; Jude 3) and hold "fast the faithful word which is in accordance with the teaching" to "exhort in sound doctrine and to refute those who contradict" (Tit 1:9). Paul further commands the brethren "in the name of

---

37. Here and elsewhere the apostolic testimony is framed as "witness" (μάρτυς). See Luke 24:48-49; Acts 1:8, 21-22; 2:32; 3:15; 5:32; 10:39-41; 13:31; 22:15; 23:11; 26:16; 1 Pet 5:1; cf. Luke 1:2; John 15:26-27; 19:35; 20:30; 21:24; Acts 4:20; 1 Cor 15:15; Heb 12:1; 2 Pet 1:16; 1 John 1:1-4.

our Lord Jesus Christ" to "keep away" from those who live "not according to the tradition which you received from us" and "not associate" with "anyone" who "does not obey our instruction in this letter (2 Thess 3:6, 14; cf. Gal 1:8; 2 John 10).

The Bereans recognized "the word of God" that was "proclaimed by Paul" by "examining the Scriptures daily *to see* whether these things were so" (Acts 17:11, 13).[38] Accordingly, Paul describes the apostolic teaching of himself and others as not merely "the word of men" but "the word of God" (1 Thess 2:13). That the authority of Paul's teachings was not limited to oral proclamation is explicit in that Paul commands "by the Lord" that his letters be read to others (1 Thess 5:27; cf. Col 4:16; Rev 1:3), exhorts to "stand firm and hold to the traditions[39] which you were taught, whether by word *of mouth* or by letter from us" (2 Thess 2:15; cf. 3:14), and calls his readers to "recognize that the things which I write to you are the Lord's commandment" (1 Cor 14:37; cf. 38). 1 Corinthians 14:37 is representative of numerous examples where NT writers communicate their teachings as by the authority of Jesus himself (cf. 1 Thess 4:2-3, 8; 5:27).

Further, John is explicitly commissioned to "write in a book what" he sees "and send *it* to the seven churches" (Rev 1:11). He depicts the content of his writing as the "revelation of Jesus Christ, which God gave Him to show to His bond-servants" (Rev 1:1), wherein he "testified to the word of God and to the testimony of Jesus Christ" (Rev 1:2). Revelation thus testifies of itself as direct revelation from God and further evinces its "canonical" authority by concluding with an inscriptional curse against anyone who "adds to" or "takes away from" the "words of the book of this prophecy" (Rev 22:18-19; cf. Deut 4:2).

Finally, NT writers appear to treat other NT writings as "Scripture" in two noteworthy instances: 1 Tim 5:18 quotes as "Scripture" the same words that appear in Luke 10:7 (ἄξιος ... ὁ ἐργάτης τοῦ μισθοῦ αὐτοῦ), alongside a quotation from Deut 25:4.[40] Further, 2 Pet 3:15-16 declares the writings of Paul to be "Scripture" alongside "the rest of the Scriptures," thus identifying a group

---

38. Regarding the "word of God," see also Luke 3:2; 5:1; 8:11, 21; 11:28; Acts 4:31; 6:2, 7; 8:14; 11:1; 13:5, 7, 46; 17:13; 18:11; 1 Cor 14:36; 2 Cor 2:17; Eph 6:17; Phil 1:14; Col 1:25; 1 Thess 2:13; 1 Tim 4:5; 2 Tim 2:9; Heb 13:7; Rev 1:2. Notice also the instances where "word of God" explicitly refers to "Scripture" (Matt 15:6; Mark 7:13; Rom 9:6; Heb 4:12).

39. See the discussion of tradition, apostolic and otherwise, in chapters 5-6.

40. Whether this is a quote from Luke's gospel is a matter of much dispute. In this regard, Köstenberger and Kruger see Luke 10:7 as the "clear and obvious source for this citation." Given that this phrase occurs "*only* in these two texts," why "insist upon hypothetical and conjectural sources" (such as "Q or an apocryphal gospel)?" (*Heresy*, 130). See the discussion of scholarly opinions in Kruger, *Question*, 201-2.

of Pauline letters, with which he appears to suppose his audience is familiar, as (minimally) "canonical."[41]

In a similar vein, the early Christians are depicted as "continually devoting themselves to the apostles' teaching" (Acts 2:42) and there is strong evidence that the early post-apostolic Christians regarded genuinely apostolic writings as holding "canonical" authority in virtue of their apostolicity (see chapter 3). In all this, the NT records an abundance of self-testimony regarding its divine commission and attendant authority (i.e., its minimal "canonicity"), which points toward Kruger's conclusion that "the New Testament writings, generally speaking, were intended to be documents with an authority equivalent to that of Scripture."[42]

Internal OT Evidence

Beyond the evidence noted above that the NT writers viewed some corpus of (OT) Scripture as "canonical" (in the minimal sense, cf. 2 Tim 3:16; 2 Pet 1:20-21),[43] the OT yields considerable information about its status as divinely commissioned Scripture. Throughout the OT, writers are divinely commissioned to write down laws and/or teachings with continuing covenantal authority (Exod 17:14; Deut 6:4-8; 31:9, 12; Josh 1:8; 23:6; 1 Kgs 2:3; Neh 8:8-18; 9:3; Jer 30:2; cf. Deut 4:2).[44] Thus, God commanded Moses that his covenantal revelation be written, preserved, and passed on (Exod 17:14; 24:4; 31:18; 34:27; Deut 10:5; 29:29; 31:9-12, 25-26). Moses not only proclaimed the "words of the LORD" to the people but also "wrote all the words of the LORD" (Exod 24:3-4). After Moses, other divinely commissioned and inspired prophets carried on the writing of divine revelation (e.g., Josh 24:26; 1 Sam 10:25; Isa 30:8). For example, Jeremiah is commanded: "Thus says the LORD, the God of Israel, 'Write all the words which I have spoken to you in a book'" (30:2). Similarly, the LORD commanded Habakkuk to "record the vision and inscribe it on tablets" for future readers (2:2-3).

41. This evidence, however, is sometimes dismissed by dating 2 Peter as late as AD 180 (see McDonald, *Formation*, 9). However, if 2 Peter is genuinely Petrine, as I believe it is, this is strong evidence indeed. See the brief discussion of the dating of NT writings further below.

42. Kruger, *Question*, 154.

43. Further, the NT repeatedly appeals to OT writings as authoritative (Rom 4:3), including appeals to "Scripture" and "it is written" recurrent in the words of Jesus (Matt 4:4-10; 11:10; 26:24; Mark 12:10; Luke 4:21; 10:26; John 7:42; 10:35, et al.).

44. Of Nehemiah 8, McDonald comments, "the notion of scripture was clearly present in Judaism" (*Biblical Canon*, 30).

Later OT writers recognized and referred to earlier Scriptures as authoritative (Josh 23:6; 1 Kgs 2:3; 2 Kgs 23:1-3; Ezra 3:2; Neh 8–9; Jer 26:18; Ezek 14:14,
20; Dan 9:2; Mic 4:1-3; 2 Chr 35:6, etc.). The prophets continually called the
people to "hear the word of the Lord," which was to function as their covenantal rule of faith and practice (Deut 11:22; Josh 22:5; Amos 3:1; Jer 2:4; Ezek
6:3; Hos 4:1; cf. Zech 7:12; Neh 9:30). Finally, OT writers frequently use phrases
that explicitly denote their divine commission of Scripture as prophetic. These
include "by the hand of," "the Word of the Lord," "declares the Lord," and "thus
says the Lord."[45] According to Gerhard Hasel, such phrases are "the OT's way
of saying that it is God-derived and 'God-breathed'" and, as such, intrinsically "canonical."[46] With this abundant testimony of biblical writers regarding
divine commission and authority in mind, how might we go about further
discerning *which books* show evidence of this divine commission?

Criteria in the Recognition of the Canon of Scripture

Intrinsically canonical books, in virtue of their divinely commissioned nature, possess some traits that assist in recognizing them as "canonical." In
particular, we might identify three criteria of canon recognition: books must
be (1) divinely commissioned as prophetic and/or apostolic, (2) consistent
with past "canonical" revelation, and (3) self-authenticating. Here, "criteria"
is used to mean characterizing marks or traits, the recognition of which does
not impose canonicity on books or suggest that any recognizer possesses authority to judge the canon. The criteria merely manifest which books should
be properly accepted as "canonical" in virtue of being divinely commissioned.
These criteria of recognition are grounded in the canonical data (see below)
and there is evidence that at least minimal forms of them were used (at times)
in the history of canon recognition.[47]

---

45. See the instances regarding "the hand of the Lord" in Ezek 1:3; 3:22; 37:1; 40:1, and "the
word of the Lord came" or something similar in Jer 1:11, 13; Hos 1:1; Joel 1:1; Jonah 1:1; Mic 1:1,
et al. Note also "hear the word of the Lord" or something similar in Amos 3:1; Jer 2:4; Ezek
6:3; Hos 4:1; cf. Jer 1:9; Ezek 3:4. "Thus says the Lord" appears in many instances (e.g., Amos
1:3; Obad 1; Hag 1:7; Zech 12:1; Isa 7:7).

46. Hasel, "Divine Inspiration," 78.

47. Here, a canonical "trait" is something intrinsic to the nature of "canonical" writing.
A divinely commissioned prophetic and/or apostolic book will, by nature, be consistent with
past revelation and self-authenticating.

Propheticity and Apostolicity

If books are "canonical" in virtue of divine commission, it follows that those seeking to recognize "canonical" books should look for evidence of divine commission. As seen above, the canon identifies prophets and apostles as divinely commissioned and thus "canonically" authoritative messengers of divine revelation. God sent "prophets and apostles" (Luke 11:49; cf. Rom 16:25-26) and the very "household of God" is "built on the foundation of the apostles and prophets, Christ Jesus Himself being the *corner* stone" (Eph 2:19-20; cf. 3:3-5; Rev 22:6). Accordingly, Christians are exhorted to "remember the words spoken beforehand by the holy prophets and the commandment of the Lord and Savior *spoken* by your apostles" (2 Pet 3:2; cf. 2 Kgs 17:13; 2 Chr 24:19; Jer 7:25; 25:4; Zech 7:12; Luke 1:70; Acts 3:18, 21; Rom 1:2; Heb 1:1-2).[48]

As such, a genuinely "canonical" book must be the written record of covenantal prophetic and/or apostolic testimony, written either by a prophet/apostle or a close contemporary associate thereof.[49] Regarding the OT, a prophet is, by definition, one divinely authorized to speak for God (i.e., God's commissioned spokesperson, Jer 15:19; Luke 1:70; Acts 3:18, 21; cf. Deut 18:20). Accordingly, "prophecy of Scripture" is not "made by an act of human will, but men moved by the Holy Spirit spoke from God" (2 Pet 1:20-21; cf. 2 Tim 3:16). As seen earlier, the NT writers treat the "Scriptures of the prophets" (cf. Matt 26:56; Rom 1:2; 16:26) as a "rule" or "standard" (i.e., "canonical"); Jesus

---

48. Numerous similar references to the "prophets" and "apostles" appear elsewhere in early Christian literature. See Denis Farkasfalvy, "'Prophets and Apostles': The Conjunction of the Two Terms before Irenaeus," in *Texts and Testaments*, ed. Eugene March (San Antonio: Trinity University Press, 1980), 109-34.

49. The Gospels of Mark and Luke, for instance, are traditionally attributed to their namesakes and early Christian evidence suggests that both had close apostolic associations. Luke utilized the (apostolic) testimony of firsthand ministers and witnesses (Luke 1:1-5; cf. 24:44, 48; Acts 6:4; 26:16) and is identified as a close associate of Paul (Col 4:14; 2 Tim 4:11; Phlm 24; cf. Acts). Further, according to considerable patristic evidence, Mark recorded Peter's account (e.g., Papias cited in Eusebius, *Ecclesiastical History* 3.39.14-15; Justin, *Dialogue with Trypho* 106; Irenaeus, *Against Heresies*, 3.10.5; Tertullian, *Against Marcion*, 4.5; Eusebius, *Ecclesiastical History* 2.15.1-2; 6.14.6 [attributed to Clement of Alexandria]). The NT manifests Mark's apostolic associations (1 Pet 5:13; Acts 12:12-17, 25; 15:37, 39; 2 Tim 4:11) and the contents of Mark point to Peter as primary witness (cf. Acts 10:34-43); Richard Bauckham, *Jesus and the Eyewitnesses: The Gospels as Eyewitness Testimony* (Grand Rapids: Eerdmans, 2006), 125-27, 205-10. Indeed, some suggest he was the young man who fled in Mark 14:51-52. If the traditional view and/or the internal testimony of these gospels is accurate (see page 42), then both are genuinely apostolic.

himself frequently appeals to the Law and the Prophets as authoritative (see Matt 5:17; cf. 23:37; Luke 13:34).

Properly recognizing genuine covenantal prophets is, then, crucial.[50] Accordingly, Christians are exhorted to "test the spirits to see whether they are from God, because many false prophets have gone out into the world" (1 John 4:1; cf. Matt 7:15; Deut 18:20; Jer 7:25; 14:14; Ezek 13:6). Not only does this criterion appear to be in use (at least minimally) in the NT, the first-century Jewish historian Josephus also appears to employ something like it. In *Against Apion* 1.7, 8, he references a three-part corpus of "our books, those which are justly accredited" as of "the prophets" who wrote through "inspiration." Josephus numbers them "but two and twenty" and specifies that the authoritative writings were "until Artaxerxes," saying, "From Artaxerxes to our own time the complete history has been written, but has not been deemed worthy of equal credit with the earlier records, because of the failure of the exact succession of the prophets."[51]

Some have taken Josephus to mean that prophecy (at least of the covenantal kind deemed Scripture) had ceased such that "canonical" books would be limited to those written by the mid-5th century BC.[52] This would complement the view that appears to be reflected in many Jewish texts from the Second Temple and rabbinic periods that Israelite prophecy ceased around the beginning of the Second Temple period.[53] For instance, 1 Macc 9:27 refers to a time of "great distress in Israel, such as had not been since the time that prophets ceased to appear among them."[54] Whether or not Josephus believed proph-

---

50. Not merely any prophecy is "canonical" but only that which is covenantal witness to God's redemptive events/revelation (requiring genuine prophets in the covenantal history of Israel for the OT and apostolic witness to the new covenant for the NT).

51. *Against Apion* 1.7, 8 (LCL 186:179, 181). Josephus refers to twenty-two books, which many scholars believe are the same as the twenty-four books of the Hebrew Bible today but numbered twenty-two to correspond to the Hebrew alphabet. Cf. Beckwith, *Old Testament Canon*, 235-73.

52. L. Stephen Cook, *On the Question of the "Cessation of Prophecy" in Ancient Judaism* (Tübingen: Mohr Siebeck, 2011), 136, cf. 131-32, concludes that, whereas Josephus notes some prophetic phenomena in later ages and nowhere excludes the possibility that true prophets could reappear, he "does not seem to believe that true προφῆται (prophets) and προφητεία (prophecy) continued beyond the Persian period." He views Josephus as "assuming some beliefs — probably common among Jews of his day — about the relationship of the ancient prophets to the collection of Jewish Scriptures, and about a fundamental change in the prophetic tradition around the time of Artaxerxes" (133).

53. As Cook puts it, "Second Temple Jews did, on the whole, tend to believe that prophecy had ceased in the Persian period" (*On the Question*, 192, cf. 47-177). This is among the reasons Protestants cite for excluding the OT Apocrypha from the canon (see below).

54. Cf. 1 Macc. 4:46; 14:41.

ecy had ceased, he ascribes special authority to prophetic writings in the line from Moses to the time of Artaxerxes (ca. 465-424 BC), corresponding to the internal biblical testimony regarding the historical context of the last books of the Hebrew Bible and to the time that 2 Macc 2:13 has Nehemiah collecting "the books about the kings and prophets."

Similarly, the NT writings must consist of the testimony of apostles — those eyewitnesses to the risen Christ appointed as his witnesses (cf. Acts 1:2-4; 9:3-15; 10:41-43; 26:12-18). Accordingly, "the New Testament is filled with references to the apostles as Christ's foundational witnesses" (Luke 24:48; Acts 1:8, 22; 3:15; 5:32; 10:39-41; 26:16; cf. Eph 2:20).[55]

Genuinely *apostolic* testimony consists of direct witness to Christ and, therefore, must be written during the time of the apostles.[56] If F. F. Bruce is correct that the "four Gospels belong to the decades between 60 and 100, and it is to these decades too that all (or nearly all) the other New Testament writings are to be assigned," the NT writings possess the proper antiquity.[57]

---

55. See the earlier discussion of "witness" in the NT.

56. See the discussion of apostolicity further below.

57. F. F. Bruce, "The Bible," in *Origin of the Bible*, 9. However, McDonald questions the contemporary use of the criteria of apostolicity and antiquity because of the questions of authorship and dating of some NT books according to the historical-critical method (*Formation*, 230). Of course, the extant data regarding authorship may be interpreted against prophetic/apostolic authorship (and close contemporary association), and often has been. However, other interpretations of the *extant* data support faith in the propheticity and apostolicity of the biblical books. The scope of this work does not allow a satisfactory examination of the technical issues involved in such discussions. However, I do believe that (given minimal Christian beliefs) the weight of the *extant* evidence supports the view that the thirty-nine OT books and twenty-seven NT books are genuinely prophetic and apostolic. In my view, the purported counterevidence is inconclusive at best and rests heavily on speculative reconstructions that have little or no basis in extant historical data and often rely on presuppositions that contradict (a priori) the internal data of the writings under investigation. Because so many theoretical reconstructions are possible, I prefer to rely on the extant evidence and thus give little weight to speculative reconstructions. Compare C. Stephen Evans's incisive explanation, "Canonicity, Apostolicity, and Biblical Authority: Some Kierkegaardian Reflections," in *Canon and Biblical Interpretation*, 159, cf. 159-64, of why he is "skeptical about some of the skepticism" observed "among biblical scholars about the historical authorship of many New Testament books." See also the brief discussion in chapter 8. Given that one could claim that *any* book is not genuinely apostolic (without any extant evidence), it seems reasonable to suppose that a plausibly ancient book's claim of apostolicity (for instance) counts as evidence in favor of apostolicity unless there is sufficient *extant* counterevidence. Many NT books make an explicit (or implicit) claim to apostolicity and many of these are bolstered by the extant evidence from the earliest post-apostolic Christians (which should not be dismissed lightly, given their historical proximity). Regarding this sometimes murky yet quite helpful evidence, see chapter 3.

One might ask, however, why accept the apostolic claims of the NT books but not others?

Conversely, the Muratorian Fragment rejects *The Shepherd of Hermas* because it was written "after their [the apostles'] time."[58]

Here and elsewhere in the history of canon recognition, the importance of the writer's close connection to Jesus, either firsthand or by direct association with Christ's apostles, is apparent (see chapter 3).[59] Within the NT itself, Paul repeatedly emphasizes his handwriting to mark letters as truly from him, demonstrating the significance of apostolic origin (1 Cor 16:21; Gal 6:11; Col 4:18; 2 Thess 3:17; Phlm 19). Such a "temporary criterion" suggests both wariness of potentially pseudonymous writings and that the original recipients knew Paul.[60] Likewise, whereas many NT writings are anonymous, it is likely that their original recipients knew the authors and thus could vouch for their authentic apostolicity. This seems even more likely when one notes the NT insistence on properly recognizing divinely commissioned messengers over and against "many false prophets" (1 John 4:1; cf. Jer 14:14; see chapter 3).

Beyond what I take to be the self-authenticating witness of such books (see the third criterion), in my view (and that of the vast majority of Christians past and present) there is sufficient extant evidence to discount the claims to apostolicity made by some extracanonical books but there is insufficient extant evidence against the apostolicity of any of the twenty-seven NT books (not to mention the ways in which extracanonical books fail the other two criteria). For a case in favor of NT apostolicity, see D. A. Carson and Douglas J. Moo, *An Introduction to the New Testament*, 2nd ed. (Grand Rapids: Zondervan, 2005). Regarding OT propheticity, see Gleason Archer, *A Survey of Old Testament Introduction*, 3rd ed. (Chicago: Moody, 1998); Andrew E. Hill and John H. Walton, *A Survey of the Old Testament*, 3rd ed. (Grand Rapids: Zondervan, 2009). Cf. the discussion of NT apostolicity in Kruger, *Canon Revisited*, 174-94.

58. The Muratorian Fragment claims that *Shepherd* was written "very recently, in our times" during the time of Pius, bishop of Rome (ca. 140-154). It thus "cannot be read publicly to the people in church either among the prophets, whose number is complete, or among the apostles, for it is after their time" (lines 74, 78-80, in Metzger, *The Canon*, 307).

59. For example, *1 Clement* (ca. 96) comments, "Christ therefore was sent forth by God, and the apostles by Christ" and refers to the apostles as "the greatest and most righteous pillars [of the Church]" (42, 5; ANF 1:16, 6). Cf. Ignatius, *To the Magnesians* 7; Polycarp, *To the Philippians* 6; Irenaeus, *Against Heresies*, 3.1.1. *1 Clement*, Ignatius, Justin Martyr, and Polycarp also clearly distinguish their authority from the apostles (*1 Clement* 5; Ignatius, *To the Romans* 4; Justin Martyr, *First Apology* 39; Polycarp, *To the Philippians* 3).

60. Bruce, *Canon*, 256-58. Moreover, the arguments over authorship in the 2nd and 3rd centuries show "how important some degree of apostolic authorization seemed to be for the books which the church accepted as uniquely authoritative" (*Canon*, 258). Thus, "if a writing was believed to have been produced by an apostle, it was eventually accepted as sacred Scripture and included in the New Testament canon"; Lee Martin McDonald, "Identifying Scripture and Canon in the Early Church: The Criteria Question," in *Canon Debate*, 424. Cf. Kruger, *Question*, 77.

Given that historical certitude is beyond our reach, however, caution should be exercised in the application of the prophetic/apostolic criterion. While important historical referents may greatly assist in the recognition of canonical books, the historical data regarding propheticity/apostolicity is variously interpreted and should not be expected to settle the matter of canonicity. In this regard, it is helpful to consider two further criteria that themselves impinge upon whether a given book should be confidently recognized as prophetic and/or apostolic.

Consistency with Past Revelation

The second crucial trait of canonical writings is consistency with past revelation.[61] From early in Israel's history, the Law (of Moses) was set forth as the divinely revealed rule of faith and practice and subsequent revelation was to be tested thereby (cf. Deut 13:1-5). As such, any genuine new revelation would not contradict any genuine previous revelation.[62] In this regard, Isaiah 8:20 exhorts: "To the law and to the testimony! If they do not speak according to this word, it is because they have no dawn" (cf. v. 16). That is, new light from God will not contradict old light (Num 23:19; 1 Sam 15:29; Deut 4:1-2; Mal 3:6; Matt 5:17-18; 24:35; Tit 1:2-3; Heb 6:17-18; 13:7-9).

Application of this criterion of recognition in post-apostolic times would be analogous to the way those living while the canon was in process should have "test[ed] the spirits to see whether they are from God" (1 John 4:1). Israel was expected to do this in OT times (Jer 14:14; cf. Luke 6:26) and Christ and the apostles called on their contemporaries to do so in NT times (Matt 7:15; 24:44; Mark 13:22-23; 2 Pet 2:1). Implementation of such testing is exemplified by the Bereans, who "received the word with great eagerness, examining the Scriptures daily *to see* whether these things were so" (Acts 17:11), and in Paul's statement that he believes "everything that is in accordance with the Law and that is written in the Prophets" (Acts 24:14). Christians were further exhorted to "hold fast the faithful word which is in accordance with the teaching" and to refute "those who contradict" (Tit 1:9; cf. Gal 1:8-12; 2 Cor 11:2-4; 2 Tim 1:13; 2 Thess 2:15; 3:6, 14; 2 John 9-10; Jude 3).

61. This is similar to what some have called the test of orthodoxy but, here, the criterion is not conformity to tradition generally or the community's belief system but agreement with past revelation such that canonical writings might reform and change tradition (see chapter 3).

62. The prophets after Moses could be tested by the standard of the Law. The NT, then, could be tested and recognized in light of the OT as the fulfillment thereof.

It follows from this and the requisite of divine commission generally that only writings that are consistent with one another could be properly "canonical."[63] This criterion of consistency alone rules out many writings that have been put forth as prophetic or apostolic. Since evaluation regarding whether different texts are consistent depends upon how such texts are interpreted, it appears to be impossible to *prove* conclusively that the "canon" is internally consistent. The criterion of consistency, however, may nevertheless exclude some writings that are put forth as claimants, insofar as they demonstrably contradict previous revelation (e.g., the so-called *Gospel of Thomas*).[64]

Self-Authentication of Divine Commission

Although we can recognize characteristics of books that give us confidence in canon recognition, canonical books are finally self-authenticating (cf. John 7:17; 10:27; 1 Cor 2:10-14). The intrinsic canonicity of writings derives from divine action. Thus, whereas information regarding the human authorship of books provides important historical indicators, far more important is the divine authorship of "canonical" books.

Revelation and inspiration are, therefore, prerequisites of canonical writings.[65] However, not every inspired writing is thereby canonical. In numerous instances, the Bible refers to prophetic and apostolic writings that are not part of the canon.[66] Other books, such as *Shepherd of Hermas*, were considered by

63. In the NT a prophet was judged by a confession of Jesus Christ (1 John 4:2; 1 Cor 12:3, 10). The *Didache* 11, 16 instructs its audience to test the prophets. Consider also the case of Serapion at Rhossus, who originally allowed usage of the so-called *Gospel of Peter* but later rejected it altogether because it implied Docetism (Eusebius, *Ecclesiastical History* 6.12.1-6).

64. While a skeptic might "find" contradiction in nearly anything and, likewise, a dogmatist might "find" congruency in anything (via special pleading), one might approach texts via a charitable, ethical reading (see chapter 9) in an attempt to avoid doing either and letting texts speak for themselves as much as possible while recognizing there may be unity without uniformity (cf. the distinction between *ipse* and *idem* identity in chapter 8). On this approach, many extracanonical writings demonstrably exclude themselves. For instance, "Simon Peter said to them: 'Let Mary [Magdalene] leave us, for women are not worthy of life.' Jesus said, 'I myself shall lead her in order to make her male, so that she too may become a living spirit resembling you males. For every woman who will make herself male will enter the kingdom" (*Gospel of Thomas*, 114).

65. "All of the ancient church fathers believed that their canon of scriptures was inspired" (McDonald, *Formation*, 239). For an extensive case for the self-authentication of the biblical canon see Kruger, *Canon Revisited*, 88-122, 125-59.

66. Some examples of explicitly prophetic books are the book of statutes (1 Sam 10:25),

some to be inspired but were not recognized as canonical because they did not meet other criteria, such as apostolicity.[67] Inspiration is, then, a necessary but not sufficient characteristic of canonicity.[68]

There are important external and internal signs in canonical books, which have guided their recognition as canon and are still useful to us in our own acceptance of what God has done. That such books were at least recognized as worthy of preservation is evidenced in their extremely unusual level of preservation by the community.[69] Yet, *intrinsic* canonicity ultimately stems from the activity of God, not humans. As such, recognition of the intrinsic canon requires numerous faith decisions, though not blind ones, supported via faith-based interpretation of the available data (as is any other belief). Illumination by the Holy Spirit regarding such decisions is paramount (1 Cor 2:14).

A Notable Corollary

Some view community usage of writings as an important criterion of canonicity. It is of prime significance to the community canon model, particularly the version that stresses the adaptability of the canon to the community.[70] Community consensus is commonly offered as a criterion or attribute of canonicity on the view that the Holy Spirit directed the Christian community's recognition of the authentic canon.[71]

---

the book of Nathan the Prophet and of Gad the Seer (1 Chr 29:29), and the book of Shemaiah the prophet and of Iddo the Seer (2 Chr 12:15), among many others. Such prophetic books, and apparently some apostolic writings (1 Cor 5:9; 2 Cor 2:4; cf. Col 4:16), were not preserved through the ages for the present community.

67. See the earlier discussion, see page 36, note 58.

68. Accordingly, no post-apostolic inspired prophet would be "canonical"; see below.

69. For an introduction to the reliability of the OT and NT see Wayne Grudem, C. John Collins, and Thomas R. Schreiner, eds., *Understanding Scripture: An Overview of the Bible's Origin, Reliability, and Meaning* (Wheaton, IL: Crossway, 2012).

70. McDonald sees usage as "probably the primary key to understanding the preservation and canonization of the books that make up our current NT" (*Formation*, 249). Sanders, further, emphasizes adaptability and survivability: "Relevance or adaptability has always been the primary trait of a canon, early and late. When one speaks of a canon, in fact, one has to ask which canon of which community is meant, whether in antiquity or today" ("Issue of Closure," 259).

71. Indeed, even some who do not endorse a community-determined canon set forth community reception as an attribute of canonicity. See Kruger, *Canon Revisited*, 103-8, 120-21. For Kruger, community consensus does not make the canon canonical but is itself directed by God's activity.

While I do believe that God guided Christians in recognizing the canon,[72] it is self-evident that God did not guide each self-identifying Christian community to identify the same canon.[73] Thus, the application of usage or consensus as a criterion would first require deciding which community God (sufficiently) guided in canon recognition or what degree of consensus regarding canonicity is sufficient and during what time period. Yet, adoption of a *particular* community as standard raises a host of questions (see chapter 3).

If one does not propose a *particular* community as adequate in this regard, questions arise regarding the requisite extent of consensus. Is a simple majority sufficient? Even if something like an overwhelming majority is posited, the consensus view appears to require something like an adaptable canon (even if unintentionally) given that community consensus is malleable. One might argue that at certain junctures of past Christian history, differing scopes of the canon would be held by the broadest consensus of Christians (e.g., the Council of Trent). Even if it could be shown that this is not the case historically, it appears that nothing would guarantee that such consensus could not change in the future (as some scholars advocate).

While such a criterion is consistent with community canon approaches, it contradicts the intrinsic canon model, which holds that the canon just *is* those books that God deems canonical. Whereas one would expect canonical books to be preserved such that usage might be a product of canonicity, usage does not itself bear on whether a book is intrinsically canonical. As such, community recognition cannot be a proper trait of canonicity (where trait is something intrinsic to the nature of "canonical" writing) because canonicity does not depend upon community recognition.[74] Jesus was and is the Son of God whether or not his community recognizes him to be so. Similarly, the intrinsic canon is the canon whether or not any particular community recognizes it to be so (cf. Rom 3:3-4).

Nevertheless, while I do not view community usage/consensus as a proper trait of canonicity, I do believe that the data regarding historical usage provides extremely valuable (but not determinative) evidence relative to canon recognition. For instance, the NT books were so widely used that nearly the entire

72. As Bruce states, "it is easy to conclude that in reaching a conclusion on the limits of the canon they [Christians] were directed by a wisdom higher than their own" (*Canon*, 282).

73. Why God did not guide each self-identifying Christian to recognize the same canon is a question for a different study, relating as it does to models of God's providence, etc.

74. Whereas any genuinely canonical book would be covenantally prophetic and/or apostolic, consistent with past revelation, and self-authenticating, a writing could (theoretically) be canonical without being recognized as such by the community.

NT could be reconstructed from the writings of 2nd- to 4th-century church fathers.[75] In this and other respects, the community's witness throughout the ages provides powerful supportive evidence that coheres with other available evidence regarding canonicity. Although there is diversity regarding the scope of the canon, I do not believe it is a coincidence that there is a common canonical core of sixty-six books that is accepted by nearly all self-identifying Christians. Whereas some view more than sixty-six books as canonical, very few accept fewer than the thirty-nine books of the OT and the twenty-seven books of the NT.

CONFIDENT RECOGNITION OF CLOSED CANON?

Which books then are properly recognized as canonical?[76] Questions regarding the nature and scope of the canon are exceedingly complex and hinge upon many decisions and interpretations regarding various questions and points of data, the complexity of which cannot be done justice to in this brief treatment.[77]

Given our individual and collective epistemic limitations, fallible judgment, and the often murky nature of historical data, the intrinsic canon approach does not expect or require anything like absolutely certain or indubitable conclusions regarding canonicity. What is sought is *confident* recognition of divinely commissioned covenantal writings; seeking the best explanation of the available evidence given the minimal Christian belief that God has revealed himself to humans, most fully in Christ, in a way that is recognizable.[78] Based on my own investigation, I believe that the thirty-nine books of the OT and the twenty-seven books of the NT do in fact meet the criteria of recognition (i.e., they possess intrinsically canonical traits) and thus make up the divinely commissioned canon, authoritative for all faith and practice.

75. For a full tabulation see Norman L. Geisler and William E. Nix, *A General Introduction to the Bible: Revised and Expanded* (Chicago: Moody, 1986), 419-33.

76. Recall the crucial distinction between the intrinsic canon itself and what is believed to be the content thereof. The validity of the former does not hinge upon the latter and, thus, one might disagree with my conclusions regarding canon recognition but still adopt the intrinsic canon model of canonicity.

77. For a more detailed treatment, see Kruger's extensive case for the NT canon in *Canon Revisited*.

78. This minimal Christian belief is itself ruled by the canonical data; see page 17, note 3. Here, confident recognition refers to that which is discernible, demonstrable, and defensible but need not be persuasive to all nor assuage every doubt (see chapter 9).

It is, of course, beyond the scope of this work to explain sufficiently the application of the criteria to each individual book. I am convinced that the sixty-six books of the canon possess all three traits of canonicity, but it may be helpful to address briefly the first criterion. First, note that the recognition of the canonical books does not hinge upon identification of the authors in every case; it is sufficient to have reason to believe the books are prophetic or apostolic. While disputes abound regarding the authorship and dating of many biblical books, many books yield internal evidence regarding their prophetic or apostolic nature that merit due consideration (such is given priority on the intrinsic canon approach while speculative reconstructions are given little weight, see page 35, note 57).

With this in mind, there is strong evidence (particularly with, but not limited to, the internal evidence of the books) supporting the propheticity and apostolicity of the sixty-six books of the Protestant canon, reinforced (but not determined) by both Judaism's and Christianity's overwhelming recognition of at least these same books. With regard to the NT, insofar as the so-called Pauline epistles are, in fact, Pauline, they are thereby apostolic. These epistles make explicit claims to Pauline authorship (Rom 1:1; 1 Cor 1:1; 2 Cor 1:1; Gal 1:1; Eph 1:1; Phil 1:1; Col 1:1; 1 Thess 1:1; 2 Thess 1:1; 1 Tim 1:1; 2 Tim 1:1; Tit 1:1; Phlm 1), usually alongside claims to Paul's apostolicity (except Philippians, 1 and 2 Thessalonians, and Philemon). Hebrews, traditionally viewed as Pauline, is anonymous and its authorship is heavily disputed. Yet, whatever one concludes regarding authorship, Hebrews itself appears to claim apostolicity (Heb 2:3-4; 13:23).[79]

The gospels are also anonymous, but they too offer internal reasons for recognizing them as apostolic. Even apart from the tradition of authorship by apostles (Matthew, John) and close associates thereof (Mark, Luke, see page 33, note 49), the gospels lay claim to eyewitness (apostolic) testimony or write as personal (apostolic) witnesses (cf. Luke 1:1-3; John 15:26-27; 20:30-31; 21:24). The very term "gospel" itself was likely "a reference to the authoritative message of the apostolic preaching."[80]

This leaves the so-called general epistles and Revelation. Both 1 and 2 Peter explicitly claim to be written by the apostle Peter (1 Pet 1:1; 2 Pet 1:1, 16; cf. 2 Pet 3:2). 1 John puts itself forth as eyewitness testimony (thus appearing to claim

---

79. Cf. Kruger, *Question*, 147-48.

80. Kruger, *Question*, 131. For sustained argument that the gospels are substantially eyewitness testimony about Jesus, and that the eyewitnesses themselves would have remained through their lifetimes as accessible sources, see Bauckham, *Jesus and the Eyewitnesses*.

apostolicity, 1 John 1:1-5),[81] which would extend to 2 and 3 John if they are indeed written by the same author. James and Jude are thought to be written by brothers of Jesus, thus directly connected to Christ himself — Jude's author presents himself as the brother of James (Jude 1) and James presents himself simply as "a servant [δοῦλος] of God and of the Lord Jesus Christ" (1:1). Finally, Revelation explicitly claims to be the revelation of Jesus Christ and thus divinely commissioned as prophetic testimony (Rev 1:1-11).

The OT is even more complex than the NT and I thus make no attempt to survey each of the books. Here, consider the abundance of self-testimony regarding the propheticity of the OT contents (see the brief survey earlier). Note also the considerable testimony of Jesus and the apostles (including usage and the manner of such usage, see page 25, note 29), which I take to sufficiently ratify most (if not all) of the thirty-nine books of the OT Scripture in a way that appears to cohere with the evidence regarding Judaism's recognition of the Hebrew Bible.

Of course, no amount of internal or external evidence could place the propheticity or apostolicity of writings beyond any doubt. In my view, however, an ancient book's internal claim to propheticity or apostolicity counts as evidence unless there is sufficient counterevidence to defeat (or strongly question) such a claim and I believe that while there is sufficient evidence against all other known books, there is insufficient extant evidence against the propheticity or apostolicity of the sixty-six books of the canon, which show considerable evidence of their divine commission (relative to all three criteria).[82]

Conversely, all other books of which I am aware fail to meet the criteria of recognition. Indeed, I am aware of no claimants beyond the sixty-six aforementioned books that are genuinely (covenantally) prophetic or apostolic. Further, some prospective claimants in this regard demonstrably fail to meet the second criterion, consistency with past revelation.[83] Finally, and in an overarching sense, I believe that the sixty-six books evince a unique quality that self-authenticates them, which I do not find in any other claimants.

81. Cf. Kruger, *Question*, 151.

82. In this brief treatment I cannot detail all of my reasons for these convictions or enter into the complex debates regarding the authorship and dating of particular books (e.g., claims that some books such as 2 Peter are pseudepigraphal) but I would recommend, in this regard, the careful and excellent work of Carson and Moo, *Introduction to the New Testament*. Cf. Kruger, *Canon Revisited*, 174-94.

83. For instance, the aforementioned *Gospel of Thomas* (see page 38, note 64), which also appears to have been written too late to be genuinely apostolic. See Nicholas Perrin, "Thomas: The Fifth Gospel?" *JETS* 49/1 (2006): 67-80.

As noted above, (at least) these same sixty-six books have been recognized by the majority of Christians throughout the ages. Judaism and Christianity nearly unanimously agree that the thirty-nine OT books (or twenty-four as they are enumerated in the Hebrew Bible) are canonical. Further, the twenty-seven books of the NT are nearly unanimously accepted as canonical throughout Christianity. Among most Christians, then, the debate concerns not whether the thirty-nine OT books and twenty-seven NT books are genuinely canonical but whether there are other books that should be viewed as canonical, particularly the OT Apocrypha.

The reasons that Protestants give for excluding the OT Apocrypha from the biblical canon include: (1) the evidence appears to fall considerably against the propheticity of the Apocrypha given that, among other things, Jesus and the apostles do not appear to treat any OT Apocryphal books as Scripture whereas there is considerable evidence regarding their treatment of nearly all of the twenty-four books of the Hebrew Bible as "Scripture" (cf. the first-century writings of Philo, who quotes extensively from the OT but never from the NT); (2) the apparent belief of Second Temple Judaism and beyond that (at least Scriptural) prophecy had ceased in the Persian period (cf. 1 Macc 9:26-27), which Josephus suggests is the reason the Jews did not view such books as authoritative.[84] As Blomberg notes, "the earliest complete or nearly complete New Testament manuscripts still in existence (from the fourth and fifth centuries) have the LXX attached to them" and include the Apocrypha. Some suggest this is evidence that "Hellenistic or Diaspora Judaism thus must have had an expanded canon." However, the "actual discussions of the contents of Scripture in ancient Judaism show no trace of an expanded canon that included the Apocrypha."[85] He concludes that "no *Jews* ever seriously supported the canonization of any of the Apocrypha."[86] Further, many Protestants contend that the books fail the test of consistency with past revelation (e.g., 2 Macc 12:43-45) and self-authentication.

On the intrinsic canon approach, taken as a cumulative case, I believe that the available evidence suggests that only the sixty-six books of Scripture can be confidently recognized as canonical; that is, no other extant books possess the traits of canonicity.[87] However, what if a lost letter of Paul suddenly sur-

---

84. Josephus, *Against Apion* 1.8.

85. Blomberg, *Can We Still Believe*, 49.

86. Blomberg, *Can We Still Believe*, 51 (emphasis his). Cf. Bruce, *Canon*, 44-50.

87. Cf. Fisher's claim that "the method of determination is not one of selection from a number of possible candidates (there *are no* other candidates, in actuality) but one of reception of authentic material and its consequent recognition by an ever-widening circle as the facts of its origin become known" ("Canon," 75).

faced? Would not a genuinely Pauline letter meet the three criteria and, if so, would this not mean that other books beyond the sixty-six books might yet be canonical? This hypothetical scenario is difficult to judge in the abstract because the contents of any purportedly Pauline writing that might surface would impinge upon whether the second or third criteria might be met. Further, such a scenario would face the practically insoluble problem of lacking the historical evidence needed for confident recognition.

Recognition of genuine apostolicity in the twenty-first century necessarily depends upon historical evidence, including but not limited to the various ancient manuscripts that have been passed down and extant writings of other ancient writers regarding such writings. At best, it seems to me, one might remain agnostic about whether such a book was genuinely Pauline. Whereas all of the sixty-six canonical books might be recognized on the basis of not only the contents of their writing but also other extant historical evidence regarding their provenance, usage, and recognition, and the crucial preservation of numerous manuscripts that evince accurate transmission,[88] any purportedly Pauline book would lack such a historical record and thus the basis for confident recognition.[89] Without implying any authority of communities regarding canonicity, this should remind us of the crucial role of the community in the recognition of the canon, particularly in passing down and thus making available to future generations the means by which confident recognition might take place.[90]

88. Note, however, that this approach to canon specifically and canonical theology broadly does not require adoption of a particular text form of Scripture but leaves that open to the best results of ongoing examination via textual criticism (see also chapter 8). "It is the book, and not the textual form of the book, that is canonical" (Ulrich, "Notion," 30). In this regard, as noted by Evans, "evidence suggests that Jesus was not wedded to a particular text, but appealed to words, phrases and sometimes whole passages" in "an ad hoc, experiential fashion" ("Scriptures," 195). What about, however, potentially authentic Jesus traditions and sayings sources? According to this view, authentic Jesus sayings may appear in extracanonical writings and this is not problematic. However, it is extremely difficult to identify with confidence (let alone conclusively) extracanonical Jesus sayings (other than those very close in content to those within the canon already). Consider the wide array of mutually exclusive perspectives in historical Jesus studies and in source and form criticism regarding extracanonical and canonical Gospels. While such studies can be of great interest and I think the best results of textual criticism should be taken very seriously, I do take the results of higher criticism to be generally unreliable as speculative and constantly shifting. In any case, the results of such studies are not determinative regarding this model of canonicity.

89. Whereas a canonical book need not be recognized in order to be canonical, it is plausible to believe that all canonical books have finally been recognized by most Christians.

90. Conversely, if doctrinal or interpretive authority is believed to be infused via such roles,

One might ask further, however, why one should adopt or recognize a "closed" canon? As noted earlier, some within the community canon model favor an adaptable canon such that the contents of the canon are continually subject to change via community determination. On an intrinsic canon approach, however, if the OT and NT contain sufficient covenant revelation of God's activity in the history of salvation, the canon would be fittingly closed by the NT writings.[91] On the view that Jesus himself provided the ultimate revelation of God to humanity, and given that the apostles were commissioned as the uniquely elect witnesses to this revelation, the canon would be closed by the last written apostolic testimony and thus by the time of the death of the last living apostles. Alongside the OT Scriptures of the prophets, then, insofar as the NT includes the authentic divinely commissioned apostolic writings and thus sufficient witness to the teachings, life, death, and resurrection of Christ, no revelation thereafter could be the rule or standard (i.e., canonical) because the ruler himself had come, fulfilling (but not nullifying) the OT, himself being the ultimate canonical revelation, and commissioning the NT witness thereof via his apostles.

In this regard, Jesus promised that the Holy Spirit would guide the apostles into "all truth" (John 16:13), suggesting the sufficiency of the apostolic witness (cf. John 20:31; 21:25). Further, the NT depicts Christ as fulfilling, without nullifying, the OT as himself the full revelation of God (cf. Matt 5:17-18; John 14:9). In this regard, if the NT apostolic testimony to the Christ event is properly understood as the written document of the new covenant, it is possible that the inscriptional curse that nothing should be added or taken away at the end of Revelation (22:18-19) applies not only to that book alone, but to the NT covenantal witness itself (effectively signaling the close of the canon).

Whether or not the inscriptional curse of Revelation is taken to effectively close the canon, the authentic apostolic witness to the Christ event, inspired by the Holy Spirit, is sufficient to effectively close the canon. In this regard, Christ promised the apostles that the Holy Spirit would "teach" them "all things, and bring to" their "remembrance all that" Christ said to them (John 14:26). The prophetic voice of the OT and NT continues to the eschaton and there is no need for further covenant revelation. This does not mean that the Holy Spirit no longer bestows the prophetic gift, but that no post-apostolic prophet will

then on what basis would one exclude allowing interpretive authority to the extracanonical documents of the Qumran community, for instance?

91. "The closed nature of the canon thus rests ultimately on the once-for-all significance of the New Testament history of redemption itself, as that history is presented by the apostolic witness" (Ridderbos, *Redemptive History*, 25).

be canonical and must rather be tested by the canon, which includes the full revelation of God that culminated in the God-man Jesus Christ. In this way the Spirit continues to speak, but always in accord with God's previous revelation in the canon of Scripture (1 John 4:1; Isa 8:20).

CONCLUSION

In this chapter I explored the definition and scope of the biblical canon from a theological perspective. Whereas in the community canon model the community determines canonicity, in the intrinsic canon model writings are canonical in virtue of their divine commission (broadly construed) such that divine action makes the canon "canonical." Against this background, I proceeded to offer a positive explication of the intrinsic canon model, including a survey of the considerable internal data of the canon suggestive of its nature and status as a divinely commissioned covenant document. Having seen that intrinsic canonicity is not an external imposition on the biblical writings but congruent with its internal testimony, I turned to the recognition of which writings were indeed canonical. Toward this end, three mutually reinforcing traits intrinsic to canonical books were identified as criteria of recognition: divine commission as prophetic or apostolic, consistency with past revelation, and self-authentication by divine purpose. The application of these three traits appears to confirm the common canonical core of thirty-nine OT books and twenty-seven NT books.

Now that the intrinsic canon model has been explained, we are in a better position to take up the issue of whether the intrinsic canon approach is preferable to the community canon approach, with an eye toward implications for the divide between the canonical and communitarian theological methods.

CHAPTER 3

Intrinsic Canonicity and the Inadequacy of the Community Approach

The divide between the intrinsic canon and community canon models hinges upon how "canon" is defined, with crucial divergences over the nature and function of canon. As seen in the previous chapter regarding the nature of "canon," the community canon model views the biblical canon as determined by the community and thus an extension of community authority while the intrinsic canon model defines canon as a corpus divinely commissioned to be the covenantal rule of faith and practice.

This chapter turns to the significant conflict between these models regarding the *function* of the canon, raising the crucial question of the community canon model: which community (at which time) is adequate to determine the canon? If the canon is defined relative to its function within a given community, how does the concept of a community-determined canon cohere with the prominence of revolutionary community-opposed voices that are preserved in the received canon of Scripture? That is, what about radical propheticity? Toward addressing this and other questions relative to the adequacy of these competing models, we turn first to the widespread debate over just *when* the canon functions as canon.

WHEN DOES THE CANON FUNCTION AS CANON?

In recent decades the canon debate has predominantly focused on when the word "canon" ought to be applied to biblical books, with competing positions hinging upon what qualifies as "canonical" function. Can writings function as genuinely "canonical" without or prior to a once-for-all community-delimited and -fixed canon list?

Those who answer no to this question tend to adopt the sharp distinction between "Scripture" and "canon," advanced by Albert Sundberg roughly a half century ago, wherein "Scripture" is a fluid categorization of divine writings and "canon" is reserved for a fixed authoritative list of writings.[1] Others adopt Gerald T. Sheppard's influential distinction between canon 1 as a loose category of sacred writings that function as a rule or standard and canon 2 in reference to a fixed, definitive, authoritative list.[2]

Advancing the discussion, Michael Kruger distinguishes between the exclusive definition of canon as "a fixed, final and closed list of books" and the functional definition of canon as "a collection of books" that "functions as a religious norm, regardless of whether that collection is open or closed."[3] On the exclusive definition, books begin to function "canonically" for a community only as part of an authoritatively closed and fixed list. On the functional definition, conversely, books function "canonically" whenever and wherever a com-

---

1. Albert Sundberg, "Towards a Revised History of the New Testament Canon," *SE* 4 (1968): 452-61. Cf. David H. Kelsey, *The Uses of Scripture in Recent Theology* (Philadelphia: Fortress, 1975), 104-5; Geoffrey M. Hahneman, *The Muratorian Fragment and the Development of the Canon* (Oxford: Clarendon, 1992), 129-30; Harry Y. Gamble, Jr., "Christianity: Scripture and Canon," in *The Holy Book in Comparative Perspective,* ed. Frederick M. Denny and Rodney L. Taylor (Columbia: University of South Carolina Press, 1985), 46-47; Craig D. Allert, *A High View of Scripture? The Authority of the Bible and the Formation of the New Testament Canon* (Grand Rapids: Baker Academic, 2007), 44-47, 51. See also the discussion in Lee Martin McDonald, *The Biblical Canon: Its Origin, Transmission, and Authority* (Peabody, MA: Hendrickson, 2007), 49-50, 53-55.

2. Gerald T. Sheppard, "Canon," in *The Encyclopedia of Religion,* ed. Mircea Eliade (New York: Macmillan, 1987), 65. McDonald leans heavily on this distinction (*Biblical Canon,* 55-58). Cf. James Sanders's view that "canon as *function* antedates canon *as shape*" ("Canon: Hebrew Bible," in *ABD* 1:847. Andrew E. Steinmann, *The Oracles of God* (Saint Louis: Concordia, 1999), 17, conversely, criticizes this distinction as "purposely confus[ing] two different meanings of canon . . . in order to argue that the canon was not closed until a relatively late date."

3. Michael J. Kruger, *The Question of Canon: Challenging the Status Quo in the New Testament Debate* (Downers Grove, IL: InterVarsity, 2013), 29, 34. Cf. similar distinctions in Stephen B. Chapman, "The Canon Debate: What It Is and Why It Matters," *Journal of Theological Interpretation* 4.2 (2010): 277-79. Both of Kruger's definitions concern the community's reception of canon as opposed to what the canon is intrinsically or by nature, that is, what Kruger calls the ontological definition of canon (*Question,* 40; see chapter 2). Kruger posits all three definitions (exclusive, functional, ontological) as together capturing "the entire flow of canonical history: (1) the canonical books are written with divine authority; (2) the books are recognized and used as Scripture by early Christians; (3) the church reaches a consensus around these books" (*Question,* 43). Cf. Michael J. Kruger, *Canon Revisited: Establishing the Origins and Authority of the New Testament Books* (Wheaton, IL: Crossway, 2012), 57-59, 118-21.

munity treats them as such.[4] Because two different perspectives of canonical function are at work, the exclusive view contends that no canon exists until the fourth century AD (at the earliest) while the functional view posits canon(s) long before purportedly fixed canon lists appear in the historical record.[5]

How one defines the nature of "canon" governs how the canon might be identified and greatly affects one's understanding of, and approach to, such debates over the date of the "closing" of the canon. Whereas the community canon view is compatible with either an exclusive or functional definition, the exclusive definition presupposes a community canon view in that it restricts canonicity to a community-determined canon list.[6] Conversely, the intrinsic canon model does not define canonicity relative to its function within the community and is thus open (in principle) to earlier or later dating regarding *when* the canon functioned authoritatively within given communities, depending on the historical data.

Given an intrinsic canon view, that is, recognition of the canon bears on its *function* for the individual or community but does not bear on canonicity itself; the divinely commissioned canon is already intrinsically "canonical" apart from community usage or recognition.[7] Conversely, whether on an exclusive or a functional definition, the community canon model dates the canon at the time the books functioned "canonically" as determined by the community.[8]

---

4. See Brevard S. Childs, *The New Testament as Canon: An Introduction* (London: SCM, 1984), 25-26. Cf. Stephen B. Chapman, *The Law and the Prophets: A Study in Old Testament Canon Formation* (Tübingen: Mohr Siebeck, 2009), 107-10; Chapman, "How the Biblical Canon Began: Working Models and Open Questions," in *Homer, the Bible and Beyond: Literary and Religious Canons in the Ancient World*, ed. Margalit Finkelberg and Guy Stroumsa (Leiden: Brill, 2003), 37-40; Iain Provan, "Canons to the Left of Him: Brevard Childs, His Critics, and the Future of Old Testament Theology," *SJT* 50/1 (1997): 10-11.

5. Geoffrey Hahneman contends: "Once a distinction is made between scripture and canon, the idea of a New Testament canon does not appear applicable until the fourth century," while earlier "a 'core New Testament collection' might be spoken of, which, while remaining open, contained a number of works which were regularly appealed to for religious authority as Scripture" (*Muratorian Fragment*, 129-30; cf. Allert, *High View*, 51; McDonald, *Biblical Canon*, 57). Thus, as Chapman notes, "the dating dimension of the debate is largely secondary and derivative, arising from a prior semantic disagreement" ("Canon Debate," 273).

6. The "community" might be strictly ecclesial or, more broadly, political.

7. As Bruce M. Metzger, *The Canon of the New Testament: Its Origin, Development, and Significance* (Oxford: Clarendon, 1987), 287, puts it: "The canon is complete when the books which by principle belong to it have been written." Similarly, see Gerhard Hasel, "Divine Inspiration and the Canon of the Bible," *Journal of the Adventist Theological Society* 5/1 (1994): 73; Kruger, *Question*, 40.

8. Here there is considerable disagreement regarding not only the definition of canon and canonical function but also the relative weight that should be given to lists, quotations, allusions, etc., with the exclusive definition tending to focus on lists.

Even when the focus is limited to the dating of the functional closing of the canon, there remain a number of competing proposals that elude consensus. Some have hypothesized that the OT canon developed in three stages corresponding to the three sections of the Hebrew Bible, with the Law and Prophets appearing to have functioned at least as Scripture (or canon 1) by 400 BC and 200 BC, respectively,[9] but with ambiguity regarding the Writings.[10] However, some (focusing primarily on canon lists) contend that whether or not this is so, there is no adequate extant canon list until the late fourth century AD (if then), prior to which there was variance in collections and (apparently) no official church recognition of the OT or NT canon.[11] Conversely, others argue for a far earlier date for the recognition of a "closed" OT.[12]

Similar disagreements ensue regarding the dating of a "closed" NT canon. Many view the historical data regarding quotations and usage of the canonical books in early Christian writings as evidence of a "canon of faith" (i.e., Scripture or canon 1). But the finally authoritative function of these books as *closed* "canon" (or canon 2), purportedly identified on the basis of extant lists and records of councils, is often placed in the fourth or fifth century AD (or even later).[13] While the Council of Carthage (AD 397) is sometimes heralded

9. Lee Martin McDonald, *The Formation of the Christian Biblical Canon* (Peabody, MA: Hendrickson, 1995), 29, 32. See F. F. Bruce, *The Canon of Scripture* (Downers Grove, IL: Inter-Varsity, 1988), 36-37. This dating of the Law and Prophets is often based on Nehemiah 8–9 and 2 Macc 15:9, respectively, with earlier dates for both possible.

10. While many once believed the Writings were closed at the so-called council of Jamnia ca. AD 90, there seems to have been no definitive "council" but merely a discussion (which continued after) regarding whether Ecclesiastes and the Song of Songs defile the hands as sacred (cf. *Mishnah Yadaim* 3:5). The theory was originally proposed by Heinrich Graetz in 1871 and "a consensus had formed by repetition of what was at first a tentative suggestion"; Jack P. Lewis, "Jamnia Revisited," in *The Canon Debate*, ed. Lee Martin McDonald and James A. Sanders (Peabody, MA: Hendrickson, 2002), 151. Bruce states that the three-stage development (of the dating of canon recognition) "is completely hypothetical: there is no evidence for it, either in the OT itself or elsewhere" (*Canon of the New Testament*, 36).

11. See McDonald, *Biblical Canon*, 56-58; James A. Sanders, "The Issue of Closure," in *Canon Debate*, 253-54.

12. Some believe the OT canon was "closed" in the days of Ezra and Nehemiah. Others date the closing to ca. 164 BC via a collection by Judas Maccabeus (cf. 2 Macc 2:13-14). See Roger T. Beckwith, *The Old Testament Canon of the New Testament Church* (Grand Rapids: Eerdmans, 1986), 110-80, esp. 165; Sid Z. Leiman, *The Canonization of Hebrew Scripture: The Talmudic and Midrashic Evidence* (Hamden, CT: Archon Books, 1976); and David Noel Freedman, "Canon of the Old Testament," in *Interpreter's Dictionary of the Bible Supplemental Volume* (Nashville: Abingdon, 1976), 134. See the discussion regarding ambiguity in this regard in Bruce, *Canon of the New Testament*, 36-42.

13. McDonald, *Formation*, 195. The putative absence of authoritative canon lists from before

as providing the first official canon list, some scholars have argued that the council was a local gathering and thus not sufficiently ecumenical or "universal" to determine the contents of the canon.[14] This, however, raises the crucial question: Which community is (or was) adequate and authoritative to identify (or determine) the canon?

It appears that the debate over dating the closing of the canon itself rests on ambiguity regarding just what qualifies as the closing of the canon. If "canon" requires a fixed list of books *universally* agreed upon and accepted by self-identifying Christians, then there still is no canon because there remain differences between self-identifying Christians regarding which books should be deemed canonical.[15]

Short of universality, if biblical books are not "canonical" prior to being identified in an authoritatively delimited and fixed list, the crucial question becomes: What qualifies as such a list?[16] If books are identified as "canonical" only as part of a corpus that has been "closed" by community determination, one must either decide which particular community was and is adequate to close the canon or there still remains no canon.[17] It appears, then, that an exclusive definition either results in the absence of a canon or requires the positing of some community or communities as authoritative and adequate to determine the canon.[18] Even if one abandons the standard of a fixed list in

---

the fourth century is heralded as evidence of the late "closing" of the canon. Conversely, for arguments in favor of early recognition of the canon, see Peter Balla, "Evidence for an Early Christian Canon (Second and Third Century)," in *Canon Debate*, 372-85.

14. See Gamble, "Christianity: Scripture and Canon," 44.

15. Roman Catholicism, Eastern Orthodoxy, and Protestantism differ regarding whether the OT Apocryphal books are canonical and, if so, which ones. Yet, importantly, all accept at least the sixty-six books of the OT and NT (the common canonical core). A small minority of Christians does depart from this canonical core, however. For example, the Syrian Orthodox church follows a lectionary that uses only the twenty-two books of the Peshitta.

16. If "the closing of the canon refers to a formal, official act of the early church, then we are hard pressed to find such an act before the Council of Trent in the sixteenth century" (Kruger, *Question*, 31-32; cf. Chapman, "Canon Debate," 283; Gamble, "Christianity: Scripture and Canon," 44).

17. See Chapman, "Canon Debate," 281.

18. Indeed, "there was never a time when the boundaries of the New Testament were closed in the way the exclusive definition would require" (Kruger, *Question*, 32). As such, Chapman asks, "Why should scholars adopt as the correct usage of the term canon a meaning that does not correspond fully to any historical reality?" ("Canon Debate, 281; cf. Chapman, *Law and the Prophets*, 108). Kruger further asks: "Why should we be obligated to use the term *canon* in a way that prohibits the very approach to the canon that Christians have held for two millennia?" (*Question*, 41). Stephen G. Dempster contends that "reserving the terminology 'canon' for only

favor of the functional definition, insofar as canon is determined by communitarian function, this same question arises with force.[19]

Within the community canon model, some indeed contend that a past community authoritatively delimited the canon (e.g., Roman Catholicism), while others reject the notion of a fixed canon altogether and contend that, since the canon is a community construct, it is fluid and open to determination by contemporary communities (e.g., the adaptable canon view). Yet, this only further highlights the question, which community or communities?

This question, along with closely related ones regarding the coherence of a community canon given radical propheticity, might be helpfully illumined by engaging some intra-canonical cases of persecuted prophets wherein a purportedly authoritative community rejects a messenger that is later accepted as a truly prophetic, canonical voice.

Persecuted Prophets

If "canon" is what a particular community determines to be normative, what should be made of instances where a purportedly authoritative community rejects a genuinely prophetic voice? For example, despite later being recognized as one of the greatest prophets in Israel's history, Elijah faced severe persecution by his own community. Ahab and Jezebel sought to kill Elijah for his unfavorable messages (1 Kgs 18:7-10; 19:2). In the remarkable Mt. Carmel narrative, however, God's acceptance of Elijah's offering by fire, contrasted with the lack of response to the call of the hundreds of false prophets, manifests Elijah's true propheticity (1 Kgs 18:25-40). Whereas God's action finally distinguishes the true prophet from the overwhelming majority of false prophets, the community had failed to respond to Elijah's prophetic call (1 Kgs 18:21) and apostasy continues in the community thereafter.

In another instance, when Ahab (king of Israel) seeks the help of Jehoshaphat (king of Judah) against Ramoth-gilead, Jehoshaphat calls for prophetic guidance, specifically for the "word of the Lord" (1 Kgs 22:5). Roughly four hundred "prophets" of Israel counsel to attack Ramoth-gilead; Jehoshaphat seeks a prophet of Yhwh, yet Ahab is reticent to call Micaiah, a

---

the final collection of books obscures the continuity that exists at earlier times"; "Canons on the Right and Canons on the Left: Finding a Resolution in the Canon Debate," *JETS* 52 (2009): 51.

19. One might, alternatively, adopt a functional perspective regarding canon recognition without viewing the canon as community-determined.

prophet of YHWH, because his prophecies are unfavorable (1 Kgs 22:7-8). In the midst of further prophecies in support of Ahab's desire to attack Ramoth-gilead, Micaiah stands alone (despite counsel to provide an agreeable message and initially providing such) in revealing the devastation that will follow such a course of action, yet his prophecy goes unheeded (1 Kgs 22:9-29).

The difficult prophetic career of Jeremiah provides yet another example. Jeremiah's message of divine judgment against Judah was violently rejected by his own community (Jer 18:18; 37–39). Not only did the community dismiss Jeremiah's message, they beat and jailed him for an extended period (Jer 37:15-16) and afterward imprisoned him in a miry pit (Jer 38:6-9). Although Judaism and Christianity now recognize Jeremiah's writings as canonical, his immediate community rejected his unpopular prophetic message of judgment.

Authentic NT prophets likewise faced opposition and persecution within their own communities. John the Baptist was beheaded for his prophetic messages (Mark 6:21-29). Later, Stephen became the first Christian martyr, stoned for preaching before the Sanhedrin (Acts 7:1-60). Then there is Paul, first himself a persecutor and later himself repeatedly persecuted, beaten and imprisoned (Acts 14:19-20; 16:19-34; Acts 22; 2 Tim 4:6-8), and finally martyred.[20] In this manner, throughout history many of God's prophets were egregiously rejected (cf. Luke 11:49-51).

Yet, from a Christian perspective, such rejections pale in comparison to the rejection and crucifixion of Jesus himself. Jesus was persecuted by his own community, his opponents repeatedly sought to kill him for his prophetic messages (John 5:18; 7:1), and finally they succeeded in crucifying him as a blasphemer (John 19:30). Even the majority of his nearest followers, the twelve, temporarily forsook him. Afterward, prior to the resurrection, they remained in confusion and despair. Not merely a prophet, but the Son of God, the center of the biblical canon, Jesus himself was rejected and crucified by the putatively authoritative community of his day.

THE INADEQUACY OF THE COMMUNITY CANON APPROACH

What about Radical Propheticity?

In light of such examples of community rejection of authentic prophecy, even that of Jesus himself, we return to the question: What impact might a commu-

---

20. Of course, the martyrdom of Paul is not included in the canonical accounts.

nity approach to canonicity have upon the potential for a radically prophetic function for that canon? The examples above illustrate a key weakness in the community canon approach: communities, for obvious reasons, tend to reject critical messages and calls to reform, preferring favorable, pleasing words. Given that humans tend to avoid radical criticism (cf. Isa 30:10; 2 Tim 4:3), communities may reject prophetic messages that run counter to their own perceived interests, thus jeopardizing the prophetic function to call for reform and change. If a particular community is the final arbiter of canonicity, divinely commissioned revolutionary voices opposed to the value system of that community could be *legitimately* precluded in favor of community-sponsored pseudo-prophets.[21]

This is not to suggest that it is impossible for a community to accept prophetic critique or that a community could not preserve messages that are revolutionary or community-opposed. On the contrary, it is evident that some communities, both contemporary to the prophets and in the following generations, did accept prophetic voices. Nevertheless, under a community canon approach wherein the community holds primacy in determining the canon, such messages could be legitimately silenced. In other words, absent external standards or qualifications, whatever community is considered authoritative would be thus authorized to reject even divinely commissioned messengers.[22]

Which Community?

Which community, then, was or is legitimate and adequate to determine the validity or invalidity of purportedly prophetic messages? If the community is authoritative to determine canonicity, would not many of those whom the Bible calls "false prophets" actually have been genuine prophets by virtue of their community's support? After all, if the community is truly the arbiter of canonicity, whoever the community accepts is thereby an authoritative voice.

The biblical concept of a true prophet, however, refers to one divinely au-

21. By "legitimately" here I mean legitimate given the internal logic of the community canon approach.

22. As Kevin Vanhoozer, "The Voice and the Actor: A Dramatic Proposal about the Ministry and Minstrelsy of Theology," in *Evangelical Futures: A Conversation on Theological Method*, ed. John G. Stackhouse, Jr. (Grand Rapids: Baker, 2000), 80, puts it, "even believing communities, as we know from the Old Testament narratives, often get it badly wrong, and to locate authority in the community itself is to forgo the possibility of prophetic critique."

thorized to speak for God (Jer 15:19; Acts 3:18, 21).[23] There is then, by definition, a divinely appointed authority belonging to true prophets that is inconsistent with community determination. True prophets are commissioned by God regardless of whether any particular community accepts them.

One might reply that the community that rejected Elijah was apostate and thus disqualified from having a voice in canon determination. Yet, how does one know which communities are legitimate and which are apostate? If the community itself is judged as apostate or not by appeal to canonical revelation (or some other test of orthodoxy), then the community cannot at the same time be the authoritative arbiter.[24] Appeal to an external rule or standard actually supports the primary thesis of the intrinsic canon model, that communities are not authoritative to *determine* canonicity but that the community must apply external criteria to *recognize* canonicity.

The community canon advocate might, however, point out that in many (if not all) of the cases above, there was a minority that did recognize and receive the prophetic message. Further, many later communities accepted and preserved those genuinely prophetic voices. Yet these facts seem to highlight further the inadequacy of the community canon approach.

For example, the early Christian community accepted Paul's prophetic/apostolic authority, albeit after some reticence (Acts 9:10-30). Yet there were other communities, such as the Jewish leadership, who rejected Paul's message (Acts 23:1-15). This conflict between contemporary communities points back to the larger question: Which community? Indeed, what qualifies as a legitimate community? May any two or more constitute a community and thus legiti-

---

23. Thus, a prophet may be referred to as God's spokesperson, literally, his "mouth" (Jer 15:19; cf. Exod 7:1-2). In Acts, God is said to have spoken "by the mouth of his prophets" (Acts 3:18, 21; cf. Matt 1:22; 2:15, 17, 23). In Num 11:26, 29, true prophets are those upon whom God has put his Spirit. On the other hand, false prophets are those whom God has not commanded or sent (Deut 18:20; Jer 14:14; 23:21, 32; 28:15; Ezek 13:6), those willing to say what people desire to hear (Isa 30:10; Mic 2:11), and those with inconsistency between their words and those of previously recognized prophets (Isa 8:20; Deut 13:2-3). Peter proclaims that "no prophecy was ever made by an act of human will, but men moved by the Holy Spirit spoke from God" (2 Pet 1:21). Similarly, 1 John 4:1 exhorts, "test the spirits to see whether they are from God, because many false prophets have gone out into the world" (cf. Matt 7:15). These indicators of true or false prophets point toward divine commission, not human recognition, as the requisite of true propheticity. Thus, "a prophet is an authorized spokesperson for God with a message that originated with God"; Walter Kaiser, Jr., "Prophet, Prophetess, Prophecy," *Evangelical Dictionary of Biblical Theology*, ed. Walter A. Elwell (Grand Rapids: Baker, 1996), 642.

24. If one appeals to a "rule of faith" as the standard of orthodoxy, the question becomes: which rule? See chapter 5.

mately function as arbiters of their own canon? Why does the Damascus or Jerusalem Christian community possess authority to accept Paul in contrast to his former community?[25] Further still, by what authority is the NT added to the so-called OT?[26] Indeed, by what authority do Christians accept Christ in distinction from other communities that reject him? Community fiat will not suffice for the universal claims of Christianity.

If each community is authoritative to determine its own canon, then since mutually exclusive canons of sacred writings are posited by various communities, the "Christian canon" is not authoritative over and against the "canon" of any other community but is authoritative only within the community or communities that determine or recognize it. This amounts to a canonical relativism that is mutually exclusive to a universally authoritative biblical canon, appearing to contradict the canon's own claims to universal authority (cf. Matt 24:14; 28:19-20; Acts 17:30; 1 Thess 2:13; 2 Tim 3:16) and, indeed, to undercut the concept of "canon" itself as rule or standard.[27]

---

25. John Franke's postconservatism, "Scripture, Tradition, and Authority: Reconstructing the Evangelical Conception of *Sola Scriptura*," in *Evangelicals & Scripture: Tradition, Authority, and Hermeneutics*, ed. Vincent Bacote, Laura C. Miguélez, and Dennis L. Okholm (Downers Grove, IL: InterVarsity, 2004), 203, posits a "broader concept of inspiration," which "also incorporates the work of the triune God in the midst of the Hebrew and early Christian communities" (see chapter 4). Yet Christ's apostles were driven from communion with the very community that had gathered around the writings of the Hebrew canonical prophets, which testified of Christ (cf. John 5:39). Given that parts of these communities themselves became at odds over the recognition of Christ, how could an appeal to God's leading adjudicate between communities that claim to be led by God? As Franke himself recognizes, "Scripture contains sharp critique and condemnation of some of the attitudes and actions of the ancient faith communities" ("Scripture," 200). However, those communities that rejected prophets in the OT were also led by God but, apparently, being led by God (corporately) did not prevent them from rejecting divinely commissioned prophets. The internal canonical history appears continually to reinforce the distinction between specially commissioned/inspired prophets/apostles and the wider community of which they were a part, the inspiration of the former not extending to the latter but — quite the contrary — the latter often rejecting the inspired messages of the former. This, further, raises questions regarding the legitimacy of appeals to "conciliar consent" on the "premise that the Holy Spirit is guiding that consent"; Thomas C. Oden, *The Rebirth of Orthodoxy: Signs of New Life in Christianity*, 1st ed. (San Francisco: HarperSanFrancisco, 2003), 168. See further the discussion regarding appeals to the Spirit's guidance in chapter 4.

26. The NT authors themselves appear to base their claims on a "canonical" argument, specifically that their message is the legitimate continuation of the Tanakh (cf. Luke 24:27; Acts 18:28; Rom 1:2; 16:26; 1 Cor 15:3).

27. Thus, the canon's apparent claims to universal authority seem to be incompatible with any communitarian view that adopts the incommensurability of religious claims. As George

Perhaps one might posit that a later community, whether a community of a particular time and place or the collective early Christian community over some period of time, is authoritative to determine canonicity. Yet the same problems apply to later communities. On what grounds should one accept that a later community is more legitimate to determine canonicity? As was the case for the earliest Christian community, the "community" is not monolithic decades or even centuries later. There are now, and in ages past, numerous communities that differ regarding the scope of the canon. Examples range from early church times (the so-called canon of Marcion,[28] and Irenaeus's view of the Scriptures versus that of his gnostic opponents),[29] to the Middle Ages (the canon posited by the Council of Trent versus the Thirty-Nine Articles),[30] to recent times (the gospel revisions of the Jesus Seminar).[31] Hence, asserting

Lindbeck, *The Nature of Doctrine: Religion and Theology in a Postliberal Age* (Philadelphia: Westminster Press, 1984), 116, notes, "all the world's major faiths" have "relatively fixed canons of writings that they treat as exemplary or normative instantiations of their semiotic codes." For many, the positing of incommensurable religious systems is unproblematic and, perhaps, unavoidable. This does seem to present a problem for Christianity, however, given that Christ proclaims himself the truth, the life, and the way and makes unmistakably universal claims. Whereas no community can itself justify such claims because no community is neutral and each unavoidably operates from within its own cultural-linguistic context, God himself can make such claims and (according to the intrinsic canon model) it is his universal rulership that grounds the universal authority of the canon (whether or not it is recognized by a given community). As such, intrinsical canonical authority cannot be limited to intra-community regulative rules (see chapter 4) even if functional authority is, by definition, limited as such.

28. Marcion rejected the OT and, with the NT, accepted an edited version of Luke and ten letters of Paul, including Romans, Ephesians, Colossians, Galatians, 1–2 Corinthians, 1–2 Thessalonians, Philemon, Philippians, and the non-extant epistle to the Laodiceans, which appears to have been a forgery. See McDonald, *Biblical Canon*, 325. Notably, while Marcion has been cast as "the impelling force for the formation of the canon" (Helmut Koester, *Introduction to the New Testament*, vol. 2: *History and Literature of Early Christianity* [Philadelphia: Fortress, 2000], 8), "Marcion's role in the formation of the canon has been minimized in recent years" (Kruger, *Question*, 19; see John Barton, "Marcion Revisited," in *Canon Debate*, 341-54).

29. According to Irenaeus, the gnostics selectively used portions of the Scriptures, claiming some were corrupt, and they supplemented these with their own pseudepigraphal writings and secret oral traditions. See Irenaeus, *Against Heresies*, 3.2.1. Irenaeus responded with a multi-pronged argument that the authentic apostolic teachings had been preserved and passed down (*traditio*) in the Scriptures by the church (*Against Heresies*, 4.33.8; see chapter 5).

30. The Council of Trent, in its fourth session, April 8, 1546, officially included the OT Apocrypha (though earlier local councils accepted apocryphal books as early as the late fourth century), whereas the Thirty-Nine Articles of the Church of England of 1562/1571 excluded apocryphal books from doctrinal decisions but considered them useful for reading. See McDonald, *Biblical Canon*, 210.

31. The Jesus Seminar decided by consensus vote which deeds and sayings of Jesus are his-

that a later community might be authoritative to determine the canon likewise returns to the question, "which community?"

In order to overcome such problems, one might point to a particular historical community as the legitimate arbiter of canonicity. If so, one must be prepared to demonstrate what superiority of that community affords it the authority of canon determination over and against all others. Moreover, this demonstration, insofar as it attempts to uphold a community canon approach, must be accomplished without recourse to external standards, especially congruency with canonical revelation. As noted earlier, appeal to standards external to the community itself would deny the role of the community as arbiter. Appeal to the recognized canon itself would amount to the circular argument that the community is authoritative to *determine* the canon *because* they selected the right books.

In the absence of legitimate criteria by which one proposed community canon is superior to others, the door is left open to the objection that it is merely the historical dominance of a particular community (or communities) that ultimately carries the day.[32] If, after all, the canon is an arbitrary construct that depends upon merely the agreement of some human community, why adopt any canon at all? If the scope and authority of the canon are solely community-based, it appears that the canon would either be authoritative only for some communities and not others or it would remain in flux, ever shifting according to community opinion. In the former case, the canon has lost its claim to universal authority and thus much of its significance. In the latter case, the function of canon in its etymological sense of "rule" or "standard" appears to be nullified, or at least sterilized on the basis of the ideological dismissal of the very concept of an objectively authoritative canon in favor of the authority of community consensus.[33]

Thus, the community canon approach (1) leaves open the danger of the

---

torical, thus rejecting many deeds and sayings of Jesus contained in the canonical four gospels and favoring others from documents such as the *Gospel of Thomas* and the hypothetical Q. See Robert W. Funk and the Jesus Seminar, *The Gospel of Jesus: According to the Jesus Seminar* (Salem, OR: Polebridge, 1999).

32. See David L. Dungan's contention, *Constantine's Bible: Politics and the Making of the New Testament* (Minneapolis: Fortress, 2007), 133, that "the Christian *canonization* process involved a governmental intrusion into what had been a *scripture selection* process" (emphasis his).

33. Here, one would have doctrine that is descriptive of the community's religious views by which the community self-regulates (cf. the cultural-linguistic model of Lindbeck) but would be unable to claim the prescriptive validity of Christian doctrine for all peoples, which is precisely the claim that Christ makes.

rejection of radical community-opposed, but truly prophetic, voices; (2) requires a compelling and internally consistent rationale for the selection of the particular community that legitimately functions as canon arbiter; and (3) contradicts the biblical conception of propheticity, which posits that divinely appointed authority belongs to true prophets independent of the acceptance of any community.

The Role of the Community in Canon Recognition and Preservation

These problems with the community canon model, however, do not impinge upon the legitimate and crucial roles that the community plays regarding the canon. Whereas the community approach is inadequate for *determining* the canon, this does not mean that all communities inadequately recognize it. On the contrary, the community has been integral to preserving and passing down (*paradosis/traditio*) the canon to all future generations. From an intrinsic canon perspective, God guides willing members of the community throughout the ages to preserve and disseminate his canonical revelation. Thus, the intrinsic canon approach recognizes the community's painstaking preservation of information (i.e., the canon itself as well as relevant history) that affords the opportunity to recognize the canon.[34] It is not necessary to disparage the community's contribution in the history of the canon to concurrently recognize the community's inherent limitations regarding canon determination.

The community's role in the canon recognition process is essential to the *functional* authority of the canon within a given community. However, given the distinction between what something is (intrinsically) and what it is recognized to be, advocates of the intrinsic canon model do not believe the history of canon reception bears on the canonicity of the writings themselves. For instance, if what something *is* is relegated to what the community recognizes it to be, then Jesus Christ is divine only to the extent that he is recognized as such. For Christians, this would have the objectionable result that the nature of Jesus Christ is itself relative to community recognition, noting, of course, the failure of such recognition by the vast majority of Christ's contemporaries.[35]

---

34. I think here in particular of the dedicated scribes over the ages who so carefully copied the words of Scripture by hand.

35. Does the rejection of Christ by numerous communities have any bearing on the divinity of Christ *itself*? Conversely, does the Hindu belief that Brahman is the Supreme Being make it so? Are such claims simply incommensurable? The universal claims of Christ appear to require

Accordingly, the Christian community might recognize its own inadequacy to *determine* the canon and, accordingly, humbly seek to *discover* the scope of the canon as divinely intended. As such, divine revelation might reform the community as opposed to being re-formed thereby.

EARLY RECOGNITION OF A CANONICAL CORE

Although the variegated and complex history of canon recognition and function is not determinative regarding the intrinsic canon, it nevertheless holds important implications that appear to complement contemporary recognition of the sixty-six-book biblical canon. The history of canon recognition is notoriously murky, in part due to the limited amount of extant data. However, if the focus is placed on evidence regarding canon recognition among early Christians, apart from seeking to date a finally definitive canon list, even those who maintain a community canon approach might recognize strong evidence of rather early Christian recognition of at least an emerging core of functionally canonical writings.[36]

If the intrinsic canon is those writings that God commissioned as the rule or standard of Christianity, we might define the "functional canon" as those writings viewed and used by a given community as the rule or standard of Christianity. Given that different communities accept different writings as canonical, the intrinsic canon might differ from a given community's functional canon. Such variances are not surprising in light of the biblical history evidencing the fallibility of community recognition, including relative to the treatment of Christ himself (past and present).

When it comes to early canon recognition, we find evidence of functional canons of Scripture that correspond largely to the common canonical core of Scripture today, with variances regarding some books as might be expected.[37]

---

a conception of truth that transcends community acceptance or rejection. This does not require a naïve or uncritical realism, but it coheres with a critical (chastened) realism committed to God as the epistemological standard (see chapter 5).

36. For instance, Allert focuses on how "documents function[ed] in the church," and (employing Sundberg's distinction between Scripture and canon) concludes that "we can conceive of an authoritative body of Christian Scripture in the first century, but even into the fifth century, we cannot claim that this body of literature was closed" (*High View*, 51).

37. I will only mention a few highlights here. Those interested in a more developed survey should see Kruger's excellent studies, *The Question of Canon* and *Canon Revisited*. In this regard, Kruger notes, "early Christian communities had different functional canons" and, while

Indeed, by the first century AD, beyond the internal OT evidence (see chapter 2), there are a number of indications regarding the *functional* canonicity of the Law, Prophets, and Writings. For instance, the Prologue to Sirach (ca. 130–110 BC) mentions the Law, the Prophets, and "the others that followed them . . . the other books of our ancestors."[38] The "memoirs of Nehemiah" are mentioned in 2 Maccabees 2:13-14 (ca. 160 BC), where we also read that Nehemiah "founded a library and collected the books about the kings and prophets, and the writings of David" and that Judas Maccabeus made a similar collection, which might refer to the recognition of the Writings section.[39] Perhaps most strikingly, *b. Baba Bathra* 14.14b-15a identifies *by name* all of the twenty-four books of the OT and distinguishes between the Prophets and the Hagiographa (Writings). However, the dating of this passage is disputed, with opinions ranging from 164 BC to AD 200.

In any case, it appears there was an authoritative *functional* OT canon at least by ca. AD 70. Josephus mentions a three-part corpus of twenty-two "justly accredited" prophetic books from which "no one has ventured either to add or to remove, or to alter a syllable," which some scholars believe consists of the same writings as the twenty-four books of the Hebrew Bible today but numbered as twenty-two to correspond to the twenty-two letters of the Hebrew alphabet.[40] Around the same time, 4 Ezra 14:45 (also known as 2 Esdras) refers to "twenty-four books," presumably alluding to the OT corpus. Further, all the books of the OT, except Esther, were found at Qumran.[41] Fi-

---

there "was widespread agreement about the core canonical books," some "disagreement over the peripheral books was inevitable" (*Question*, 36).

38. The prologue was written by Ben Sira's grandson but many have pointed to evidence that Ben Sira himself held a similar OT collection. "Clearly, there was a biblical text that Ben Sira had before him that was similar to what was later viewed as canonical in Judaism" (Dempster, "Canons," 59, see also his discussion in 59-61).

39. Leiman holds that the collection of Judas Maccabeus (2 Macc 2:13-14) may "be a description of the closing of the Hagiographa, and with it the entire biblical canon" (*Canonization*, 29). For a similar argument see Beckwith, *Old Testament Canon*, 163-66, 436. See also Beckwith's case that the thirty-nine OT books (except Esther, Song of Songs, and Ruth) are demonstrably used as "canonical" in the intertestamental writings (*Old Testament Canon*, 76).

40. *Against Apion*, 1.8; following LCL 186:179, 181. He goes on, "it is an instinct with every Jew, from the day of his birth, to regard them as the decrees of God, to abide by them, and, if need be, cheerfully to die for them" (*Against Apion*, 1.8; following LCL 186:181). If this is not "canonical" authority, I am not sure what is. See also Stephen G. Dempster, "Torah, Torah, Torah: The Emergence of the Tripartite Canon," in *Exploring the Origins of the Bible: Canon Formation in Historical, Literary, and Theological Perspective*, ed. Craig A. Evans and Emanuel Tov (Grand Rapids: Baker, 2008), 87-127.

41. As Craig Blomberg, *Can We Still Believe the Bible?* (Grand Rapids: Brazos, 2014), 49,

nally, the witness of the NT regarding the OT (see chapter 2) and the way the earliest post-apostolic Christians utilize Scripture suggest a functional OT canon among Christians in the first century that likely corresponds to the thirty-nine-book OT canon.[42]

Regarding recognition of the NT, the words of Jesus were apparently functionally canonical from very early on (see chapter 2), including by early post-apostolic Christians.[43] Accordingly, the gospels appear to function as "canon" quite early.[44] Justin Martyr (AD 100–165) refers to gospel writings as the "memoirs of the apostles" (*First Apology*, ch. 67) and "indicates that they were used as Scripture in worship alongside the Old Testament during his day."[45] Further, Irenaeus (writing ca. AD 180) unequivocally asserts a fourfold gospel in *Against Heresies* 3.11.8.

Some corpus of Paul's letters also appears to have been functionally ca-

---

notes: "Given the fragmentary nature of so many of these [Dead Sea] Scrolls, it is quite possible that Esther was once present too; we just don't know." Bruce also notes this possibility and that, based on manner of usage in Qumran documents, "we might confidently say" that "the 'canon' of the Qumran community included [at least] the Pentateuch, the Prophets, the Psalms (possibly with a few supplementary psalms)," the "book of Daniel," and "probably Job" (*Canon*, 39). Blomberg emphasizes further that nearly "every book of the Hebrew canon has been found at Qumran" but "only three books of the Apocrypha are represented among the Qumran fragments" (*Can We Still Believe*, 49). Bruce believes that "it is probable, indeed, that by the beginning of the Christian era" the Qumran community was "in substantial agreement with the Pharisees and the Sadducees about the limits of Hebrew Scripture," contending that "the inter-party disagreements remembered in Jewish tradition have very little to do with the limits of the canon" (*Canon*, 40).

42. According to McDonald, the "notion that authority resided in what was later called the OT Scriptures was never doubted in the earlier Christian community" (*Formation*, 1). Eugene Ulrich, "The Notion and Definition of Canon," in *Canon Debate*, 30, affirms: "A collection of authoritative scriptures was certainly in existence and taken to be fundamental to the Jewish religion from sometime in the first half of the Second Temple period," but he views this as "a collection of authoritative books" rather than "an authoritative collection of books," utilizing "Metzger's distinction"; cf. Metzger, *Canon*, 283.

43. Cf. McDonald, *Formation*, 145

44. Here, it is important to note that a simple quotation of a text does not mean that it was considered Scripture (or "canonical"), nor should we assume that if one author considered a text Scripture that all others in the age did so. Cf. McDonald, *Formation*, 3. The manner of usage of a given text may, however, shed considerable light regarding how the text was viewed by some.

45. Kruger, *Question*, 202. Justin refers to "gospels" as "drawn up by His apostles and those who followed them" using "language [that] indicates (at least) two gospels written by apostles, and (at least) two written by apostolic companions," which "is most naturally understood as reference to our four canonical gospels" (*Question*, 170).

nonical quite early. For instance, Ignatius speaks of "every epistle" of Paul, expects his audience to be aware of some corpus thereof, and frequently refers to Pauline writings (*To the Ephesians*, 12:2 [ca. 110]; cf. 2 Pet 3:15-16; *1 Clement* [ca. 96]; Polycarp [ca. 110], *To the Philippians*, 3.2; 12.1).[46] As John Barton puts it, "astonishingly early, the great central core of the present New Testament was already being treated as the main authoritative source for Christians" with "little" suggestion of "any serious controversies about the synoptics, John, or the major Pauline epistles."[47] Milton Fisher even contends: "There is evidence that within thirty years of the apostle's [John's] death all the Gospels and Pauline letters were known and used."[48]

Further, Irenaeus extensively quotes from Scripture (OT and NT) in a manner suggesting that he knows (and expects his audience to know) which books are Scripture.[49] According to James Daniel Hernando, Irenaeus quotes from every NT book except Philemon and 3 John (in *Against Heresies* and *Fragments*) and his "writings contain quotations or verbal allusions to 77.9% (201 of 258) of the chapters in the canonical New Testament."[50] Hernando thus concludes that "*functionally* Irenaeus is operating with a New Testament canon of Scripture."[51]

Kruger notes that Irenaeus, the Muratorian Fragment (see below), Clement of Alexandria, and Theophilus of Antioch "already receive many of the New Testament books of Scripture" but, he believes, "this trend can be traced

46. Polycarp even appears to quote from Eph 4:26 in *To the Philippians*, 12.1. See the argument in Kruger, *Question*, 195-96. So also McDonald, *Biblical Canon*, 276.

47. John Barton, *Holy Writings, Sacred Text: The Canon in Early Christianity* (Louisville: Westminster John Knox, 1997), 18.

48. Milton Fisher, "The Canon of the New Testament," in *The Origin of the Bible*, ed. Philip Wesley Comfort (Wheaton, IL: Tyndale, 1992), 70. There are, however, various views in this regard, as might be expected given the paucity of extant evidence and various perspectives brought to the issue. Regarding Pauline letter collections see Stanley E. Porter, "When and How Was the Pauline Canon Compiled? An Assessment of Theories," in *The Pauline Canon*, ed. Stanley E. Porter (Leiden: Brill, 2004), 95-127. Some early fragments might also testify to widespread use, such as the fragment of John in Rylands Papyrus (P52), found in Egypt and believed to have been copied ca. AD 125. Also, Papyrus 46 (ca. AD 175-225) includes most of the Pauline epistles (including the final eight chapters of Romans, most of 1-2 Corinthians, two chapters of 1 Thessalonians, all of Ephesians, Galatians, Philippians, Colossians, and also Hebrews), breaking off in 1 Thessalonians (with many believing it originally included 2 Thessalonians and Philemon, and others believing the pastoral epistles were included as well).

49. See the discussion in chapter 5.

50. James Daniel Hernando, "Irenaeus and the Apostolic Fathers: An Inquiry into the Development of the New Testament Canon" (PhD diss., Drew University, 1990), 84.

51. Hernando, "Irenaeus," 84 (emphasis his). So also John Behr, "The Word of God in the Second Century," *ProEccl* 9/1 (2000): 95.

even further back into the second century."[52] In this regard, Kruger provides striking evidence that Papias, the *Epistle of Barnabas,* Ignatius, Polycarp, and *1 Clement* seemed to "regard a number of Christian writings as Scripture."[53] In Kruger's view, "Christians began to view their books as Scripture much earlier than Irenaeus — perhaps even by the turn of the century."[54]

Perhaps the earliest extant NT "canon" list, the Muratorian Fragment (which many scholars date ca. AD 180),[55] appears to identify twenty-three of

52. Kruger, *Question,* 202, see also 159-69. Notably, Kruger offers evidence that Clement of Alexandria (writing ca. 198) explicitly affirmed "only" the four "traditional" gospels and "received all thirteen Epistles of Paul, Hebrews, Acts, 1 Peter, 1 and 2 John, Jude and Revelation" and "viewed these books as having an ancient pedigree within the Christian church," being "'handed down' to the church from the apostles themselves" (*Question,* 167-68).

53. *Question,* 203, see also 176-202. Cf. 2 Pet 3:15-16; 1 Tim 5:18. For example, Kruger points to Ignatius (martyred ca. 110) as "a witness to the high authority early Christians attributed to the apostles and their teachings," which was "functionally indistinguishable from Scripture." Kruger lists 1 Corinthians, Ephesians, 1–2 Timothy, Matthew, John (and possibly Luke), Romans, Philippians, and Galatians as used by Ignatius without excluding that Ignatius might have known and used others as well (*Question,* 193).

54. *Question,* 203. Kruger draws from a broad range of sources from different regions and makes an impressive cumulative case, noting that while "any individual piece of evidence might be contested or questioned, it is the extent of the evidence that proves to be the compelling factor" (*Question,* 203).

55. The dating of the Muratorian Fragment is disputed, but it "is usually dated ca. AD 180–200"; Lee Martin McDonald and Stanley E. Porter, *Early Christianity and Its Sacred Literature* (Peabody, MA: Hendrickson, 2000), 619. While some have recently argued that it should be dated to the fourth century, due in large part to the putative absence of comparable canon lists before that time, the Muratorian Fragment itself supports a second-century date, stating in lines 73-76: "Hermas wrote the *Shepherd* very recently in our times, in the city of Rome" in the time of Pius, bishop of Rome (ca. 140–154). Moreover, "the heretics and heresies named by the Muratorianum [the Muratorian Fragment] all still belong to the second century"; Hans von Campenhausen, *The Formation of the Christian Bible* (Philadelphia: Augsburg Fortress, 1972), 244. See also Metzger, *Canon,* 193. Everett Ferguson, "Canon Muratori: Date and Provenance," StPatr 17/2 (1982): 681, in an article that Metzger thinks shattered Sundberg's theory (see Albert C. Sundberg, "Canon Muratori: A Fourth-Century List," HTR 66 [1973]: 1-41), presents compelling evidence for the earlier date of the Muratorian Fragment, writing, "Not only are the arguments for a fourth-century eastern setting so tenuous as to fail to carry conviction, but other considerations point strongly to an earlier western setting." See also Balla, "Evidence for an Early Christian Canon," 381; Childs, *New Testament,* 238; Kruger, *Question,* 163-64; Charles E. Hill, "The Debate over the Muratorian Fragment and the Development of the Canon," WTJ 57 (1995): 437-52. Conversely, see the arguments supporting Sundberg's late dating in McDonald, *Biblical Canon,* 369-78; McDonald and Porter, *Early Christianity,* 619-21; Geoffrey Mark Hahneman, "The Muratorian Fragment and the Origins of the New Testament Canon," in *Canon Debate,* 408.

the NT books as Scripture — the four gospels, Acts, thirteen Pauline epistles, Jude, 1–2 John (and likely 3 John), and Revelation.[56] The Muratorian Fragment, then, does not mention four or five books of the NT (Hebrews, James, 1–2 Peter, perhaps 3 John) and third- and fourth-century lists further mention some of the general epistles and Revelation as in a second category or "disputed."[57] That some of these writings were disputed itself suggests that early Christians took recognition of Scripture seriously, attempting to properly recognize genuinely apostolic books. Further, while extant NT lists are not uniform, they do appear to hold in common the majority of NT books, with only a handful of NT books omitted or disputed. While Athanasius is typically regarded as providing the first extant list of all twenty-seven NT books (*Festal Letter 39*, AD 367),[58] Origen's *Homilies on Joshua* appears to refer to all twenty-seven NT books over a century earlier (ca. 250).[59]

56. The extant fragment begins by listing Luke and John as the third and fourth gospels, leaving little doubt that Matthew and Mark appeared in the missing part of the fragment. The fragment also mentions the Wisdom of Solomon and the *Apocalypse of Peter*, but notes of the latter that "some of us are not willing for the latter to be read in church" (line 72) while also rejecting epistles to the Laodiceans and Alexandrians as forgeries and ruling out *Shepherd* because it was written "recently, in our times" (line 74). See Metzger, *Canon*, 305-7.

57. Eusebius of Caesarea (AD 265–340) provides a notable list of "recognized books" including the four gospels, Acts, Paul's epistles, 1 John, 1 Peter, and perhaps Revelation. He lists as "disputed writings, which are nevertheless recognized by many," James, Jude, 2 Peter, and 2–3 John. After mentioning a number of "rejected writings" (*Acts of Paul, Shepherd*, the *Apocalypse of Peter*, the alleged *Epistle of Barnabas*, and the so-called Teachings of the Apostles [*Didache*]), he notes that some "reject" and "others class with the accepted books" the "Apocalypse of John" and "among these some have placed also the Gospel according to the Hebrews, with which those of the Hebrews that have accepted Christ are especially delighted." Beyond these, he speaks of writings "cited by the heretics under the name of the apostles," including the Gospels of Peter, Thomas, Matthias, and others, the Acts of Andrew, John, and other apostles, "which no one belonging to the succession of ecclesiastical writers has deemed worthy of mention in his writings. And further, the character of the style is at variance with apostolic usage, and both the thoughts and the purpose of the things that are related in them are so completely out of accord with true orthodoxy that they clearly show themselves to be the fictions of heretics. Wherefore they are not to be placed even among the rejected writings, but are all of them to be cast aside as absurd and impious"; Eusebius, *Ecclesiastical History* 3.25 (*NPNF* 1:155-57). See, further, the surveys of other canon lists with some continued diversity into the sixth century, in McDonald, *Biblical Canon*, 445-51 and Metzger, *Canon*, 307-15.

58. Athanasius's list also includes the thirty-nine OT canonical books except Esther, numbered as twenty-two books while mentioning "Baruch" with Jeremiah and "the epistle" with Lamentations as one book. As not included in the canon but good for reading it lists the Wisdom of Solomon, Sirach, Esther, Judith, Tobit, the Teaching of the Apostles, and *Shepherd*.

59. Since the extant version was translated by Rufinus in the fourth century, some question

The history of canon reception is complicated and messy indeed and, while there appears to have been considerable agreement among the earliest post-apostolic Christians regarding a number of books (e.g., the gospels, some corpus of Paul's letters, and others), the extant evidence appears to be insufficient to settle debates regarding when the canon was *functionally* "closed," if at all. There is "exceptional difficulty in attempting to reconstruct the history of the New Testament canon" and this "arises not only from a critical paucity of primary sources but also from a superabundance of conflicting secondary literature."[60] Conclusions in this regard, then, must be emphatically tentative.

At minimum, however, the extant evidence suggests that, very early, Christians viewed some group of NT books as "Scripture" and thus as functionally "canonical." As Kruger puts it, early Christians were "able to say which books are (and are not) Scripture," which does not appear to be "materially different than saying which books are in (or not in) a [functional] canon."[61] Accordingly, Kruger rejects the oft-repeated claim that prior to the fourth century, Christians possessed a "boundless, living mass of heterogeneous" texts as at best "obscurant, and at worst misleading."[62] In his view, "early Christians did

---

whether there is some interpolation here, but there appears to be no evidence to support this claim. See Metzger, *Canon*, 139-40; Kruger, *Canon Revisited*, 284. Therein Origen mentions all twenty-seven NT books without mentioning any others or making any distinctions among them. See, further, Metzger's survey of Origen's writings (*Canon*, 135-41), in which he concludes that Origen accepted the four gospels, "fourteen Epistles of Paul, as well as Acts, 1 Peter, 1 John, Jude, and Revelation, but expressed reservation concerning James, 2 Peter, and 2 and 3 John" (*Canon*, 141).

60. Jonathan J. Armstrong, "From the κανὼν τῆς ἀληθείας to the κανὼν τῶν γραφῶν: The Role of the Rule of Faith in the Formation of the New Testament Canon," in *Tradition and the Rule of Faith in the Early Church*, ed. Ronnie J. Rombs and Alexander Y. Hwang (Washington, DC: Catholic University of America Press, 2010), 30. As Peter Balla puts it, "Due to the scarcity of evidence, one cannot firmly conclude when exactly and as a result of what development the early church came to possess a twenty-seven-book collection called the New Testament and a two-part collection that comprises our Bible of Old and New Testaments" ("Evidence," 372). Cf. Brevard Childs's view, "The Canon in Recent Biblical Studies: Reflections on an Era," in *Canon and Biblical Interpretation* (ed. Craig G. Bartholomew et al.; Grand Rapids: Zondervan, 2006), 36, that the interpretation of canon history is complex and oft-disputed since it necessarily includes speculation, being "left to a critical reconstruction of the process from indirect evidence."

61. Kruger, *Question*, 31. Cf. *Canon Revisited*, 36-38; Provan, "Canons to the Left of Him," 9-11; Barton, *Holy Writings*, 25.

62. Kruger, *Question*, 33. Kruger reacts specifically to Dungan's contention that "*scripture* is a boundless, living mass of heterogeneous sacred texts found in many religions of the world" (Dungan, *Constantine's Bible*, 132-33, emphasis his).

possess an authoritative corpus of books long before the fourth century, even if the edges were not entirely solidified."[63]

Given the historical circumstances in which Christianity arose and the limited extant evidence, the variegated history of canon recognition does not seem surprising, nor does it present a problem for the intrinsic canon model. Studies of the history of canon recognition provide significant information about the early *function* of canon, as well as some crucial information that might be utilized today in canon recognition. However, if "canonicity" is dependent on divine commission such that the canon is determined by God (as the intrinsic model supposes), then the history of canon recognition does not itself bear on canonicity as such. As Kevin Vanhoozer puts it: "History alone cannot answer the question of what the canon finally is; theology alone can do that."[64]

The Adequacy of the Intrinsic Canon Approach

We are now in a position to turn to the question: Is this intrinsic canon view indeed preferable to the community canon view? As seen above, the community canon approach (1) leaves open the danger of the rejection of radical community-opposed, but truly prophetic, voices; (2) requires a compelling and internally consistent rationale for the selection of the particular community that legitimately functions as canon arbiter; and (3) contradicts the biblical conception of propheticity, which posits that divinely appointed authority belongs to true prophets independent of the acceptance of any community. The intrinsic canon approach appears to avoid these problems. That is not to say, however, that the intrinsic canon approach is without its limitations.

The Theocentric Ground of the Intrinsic Canon Approach

In my view, the issue of canonicity in an intrinsic canon approach comes down to two fundamental questions:

1. Is there a divinely determined canon?
2. On what basis is the scope of that canon recognized?

63. Kruger, *Question*, 36.
64. Kevin Vanhoozer, *The Drama of Doctrine: A Canonical-Linguistic Approach to Christian Theology* (Louisville: Westminster John Knox, 2005), 146. See chapter 2.

These two questions highlight the limitations (but not defeaters) of the intrinsic canon approach. Most importantly, humans cannot prove with certainty that divine revelation exists.[65] Secondarily, even if they could, they could not prove with certainty the scope of the canon. With regard to both limitations, decisions of faith are required, which seems appropriate considering canonical exhortations to such faith. If one has decided to believe in a God who reveals himself to human beings via Scripture, it does not seem at all unreasonable also to believe that this same God provided means by which the community might correctly recognize that revelation as "canon."

One may, of course, reject the epistemological decisions of the intrinsic canon model to believe in and recognize such divine revelation, but that moves the discussion far beyond canonicity, to the question of theism itself. It seems to me, however, that theism of the type that undergirds the canon might best be engaged by seeking the theology (proper) of the canon itself. One might *procedurally* employ something like the canonical theological method explained later in this work prior to a commitment to Scripture as canon and, in so doing, uncover a theistic framework that undergirds belief in that biblical canon as divine revelation. Short of this, if one is willing to allow for the possibility of a minimal theism that expects recognizable divine revelation as canon, then the intrinsic canon model appears to provide a plausible avenue for further investigation.

Importantly, the internal coherence of the intrinsic canon approach may appeal to the intentions evidenced within the canon itself. The canonical writings evince the intention that they be read as canon in the minimal sense of "rule" or "standard."[66] Indeed, as seen in part earlier, an abundance of OT and NT evidence suggests the "canonical" nature of these writings.[67] Although the technical, contemporary meaning of "canon" may be anachronistic if applied univocally to the statements of biblical authors, the kernel of a collection of continuing, authoritative writings (divinely bestowed) is

---

65. The limitations regarding lack of certitude, however, do not cast reproach upon the intrinsic canon approach since postmodern epistemology has highlighted the requisite of choice underlying the starting point of any epistemology. In this manner, there is no ground for the supposition that a non-theistic approach to canon is somehow more objective. As Anthony Thiselton, "Canon, Community, and Theological Construction," in *Canon and Biblical Interpretation*, 4, points out, "Non-theism or positivism is no more value-free than *theism*."

66. Any proposed authority must cohere with its own doctrines as well as its own phenomena. The intention recognized in reading the Bible as canon does not itself prove its canonicity but does provide the necessary condition for a canonical approach.

67. See chapters 2 and 5.

evident in the text.[68] As such, the minimal concept of an authoritative intrinsic canon is not an external imposition upon the Bible.

From a theistic perspective, then, the intrinsic canon approach is internally coherent and plausible. To be sure, if one has ruled out *a priori* the possibility of a divinely determined canon, then one would not seek to discover and recognize the divinely intended scope of Scripture. On the other hand, once one has decided to allow for the possibility of a divinely determined canon, one can seek to recognize a canon of divinely appointed writings.

Conversely, if the biblical canon consists merely of books selected based on human whims and power structures (as some community canon model advocates suppose), why adopt such "canonical" texts instead of any others that might be popular or personally palatable? Indeed, why accept any writings as authoritative at all?

The Canon and Theological Function

I believe the intrinsic canon model presents a plausible, internally coherent approach to the issue of biblical canonicity over and against the common supposition that the biblical canon is merely a human construct. In doing so, the intrinsic canon approach impinges upon the larger question regarding the *foundational* authority and theological function of Scripture.

Whereas the intrinsic canon model naturally undergirds an approach to canon as the rule or standard for theology, some employ a community canon perspective in order to undergird the purported theological authority of the community (as normative interpretive arbiter or otherwise).[69] Some thus suggest that theology should operate according to a so-called "rule" or "canon of faith." This may entail a moving away from the canon of Scripture to a more fluid, community-based approach to theology.

Such an approach, however, gives rise to the question of the contemporary usefulness and functionality of the canon as "canon." This inquiry takes many forms. In one form, the canon is proposed as primarily a means of soteri-

---

68. Balla thus correctly argues, "the later use of the term 'canonical' should not prevent us from seeing an awareness in the authors of the New Testament of a connection between the writings of the 'Old Testament' and their own writings" ("Evidence," 373).

69. For example, Allert explicitly draws conclusions for "the argument that the early church appealed to the Bible and the Bible alone for its doctrine" (*High View*, 51). Cf. Franke, "Scripture," 202-5; D. H. Williams, *Retrieving the Tradition and Renewing Evangelicalism: A Primer for Suspicious Protestants* (Grand Rapids: Eerdmans, 1999), 231.

ological grace rather than epistemological meaning.[70] In another form, the removal of the constraints of the canon and the opening to a new, supposedly better, collection is anticipated.[71] In still another form, the explicit use of a "canon within the canon" that fits the beliefs of the community is accepted.[72] These related issues find support in various (but not all) kinds of community canon models.

Conversely, by recognizing the intrinsic canonicity bestowed by God upon the Bible, the intrinsic canon model can affirm the soteriological *and* epistemological function of Scripture. It rejects the possibility that any community-determined "canon" could supersede or replace the genuinely "canonical" revelation of God, and it does not need a canon within the canon because it takes seriously all canonical books. While the community canon model leaves a shifting *foundation* for theology because the canon, or the standard, changes according to the collective will of the community or tradition, the intrinsic canon model seeks to recognize the divinely commissioned canonical books as *the* theological foundation under God (cf. Matt 7:24).[73]

In this regard, the *function* of the canon as "canon" not only hinges upon decisions regarding whether to adopt a canon and, if so, which writings are taken to be properly "canonical," but whether and to what extent such "canonical" writings are *allowed to function* canonically. Although the canonical theological method explained later in this book can be (minimally) employed apart from commitments regarding the nature of the canon, one's view of the canon (if followed through methodologically) will set parameters of how the canon could possibly function theologically for and within Christian community.

---

70. For William J. Abraham, *Canon and Criterion in Christian Theology* (Oxford: Clarendon, 1998), the canon is to function primarily soteriologically rather than primarily epistemologically and may refer to all recognized lists of communities. He states, "I want, that is, to relocate the whole idea of canon within the arena of means of grace within the Church" (*Canon and Criterion*, 21).

71. Consider Robert Funk's call, "The Once and Future New Testament," in *Canon Debate*, 556–57, for a new Bible with a version to "include whatever traces of the original strangeness of Jesus and Paul we can isolate or reconstruct and eliminate everything else" and a second version that would "contain the current twenty-seven books plus others" in sections by dates, a massive book of literature in successive stages.

72. James D. G. Dunn, "Has the Canon a Continuing Function?" in *Canon Debate*, 559, claims that "no Christian church or group has treated the New Testament writings as uniformly canonical" but "*all Christians have operated with a canon within the canon*" (emphasis his). Thus, according to Dunn, the church should be "recognizing how *few* the essentials are and how *wide* must be the range of acceptable liberty" ("Has the Canon," 564).

73. This is not to be confused with *classical* or *strong* foundationalism (see chapter 5).

If the canon is *merely* a human construct, then it follows that the canon could not possess divinely commissioned theological authority. If the canon's authority is imposed by the community, then it follows that the community *might* possess authority to impose theological interpretations as normative. If the canon is determined by God and merely recognized by humans, then it follows that the canon holds a divinely commissioned authority independent of human recognition and intra-community functionality thereof.

CONCLUSION

This chapter has highlighted the logical tension between the concept of a community-determined canon (community canon model) and the possibility of the radically prophetic function of that canon. A brief survey of positions regarding the date of the closing of the canon, which hinge upon competing definitions regarding what qualifies as canonical function, highlighted the central question that faces community canon approaches: Which community is adequate to determine the canon?

In addition to the insoluble difficulties one encounters when answering this question, examination of selected cases wherein the community rejected a canonical prophet, including Jesus himself, suggests considerable problems for community-determined canonicity. First, it would seem that a community-determined canon might silence radical propheticity. Further, the nature of the prophetic office/gift seems to stand in contradiction to the concept of community-determined theological authority.

Although the intrinsic canon model also introduces challenging questions, a critical evaluation of apparent inconsistencies in the community canon approach to canon determination favors an intrinsic canon model wherein God determines the scope of the canon, which humans may adequately recognize. According to this view, the canon's authority is rooted in its nature as divine revelation, inspiration, and commission. If the canon of Scripture has a divine origin, it *is* the authoritative and trustworthy foundation for theology and practice, to be received not merely as "the word of men, but as it is in truth, the word of God" (1 Thess 2:13).

This conclusion holds significant implications that support, though do not necessarily require, a canonical theological method. In this and other ways, conclusions regarding the nature and proper function of the biblical canon impinge upon the crucial divide between communitarian and canonical approaches, to which we now turn.

CHAPTER 4

Communitarian Approaches to Theology

While disagreement about the history, nature, scope, and function of the canon continue, the sixty-six books of the Protestant canon are accepted by an overwhelming majority of self-described Christians.[1] However, among Christians who share this common canonical core, there are significant differences regarding the functional authority of the canon in theological method. In particular, there are crucial disagreements about how much doctrinal authority is invested in the canon and how much doctrinal authority, if any, is to be invested elsewhere. What is the proper relationship between canon and community, particularly when it comes to the understanding and articulation of doctrine? This question impinges on long-standing debates over the relationship between Scripture, Tradition, and the Church.

Relative to such divergences, one might distinguish between canonical and communitarian approaches to theological authority and method, akin to the differentiation between the intrinsic and community models of canonicity.[2] In brief, a canonical approach is one that views the biblical canon as the uniquely authoritative, sufficient source of theological doctrine, adopts the biblical canon as the rule of faith, and denies the positing of any normative extracanonical interpretive authority.[3] Conversely, communitarian approaches

---

1. Of course, a significant number of Christians accept more books, but very few Christians accept less than this common canonical core.

2. There is overlap between the implications of the canon debate and the divergence of canonical and communitarian approaches. But while the intrinsic canon model supports canonical theological method, one does not require the other.

3. Perhaps the most well-known canonical approach is that of Kevin Vanhoozer; see especially his *The Drama of Doctrine: A Canonical-Linguistic Approach to Christian Theology*, 1st ed.

typically posit the primacy of the biblical canon while emphasizing the theological authority of the community and adopting a community-determined extracanonical rule of faith or other normative interpreter for theological doctrine. As such, communitarian approaches afford a determinative theological role to the community (past and/or present). Whereas both canonical and communitarian approaches recognize important roles for the canon and the community in theological method, they hold divergent perspectives on the issue of the respective theological authority and functions of the canon and community.

This chapter introduces communitarian approaches to theological authority and method, focusing on the significant growth of communitarian approaches among Protestants in recent decades.[4] After briefly surveying the Roman Catholic and Orthodox communitarian approaches, this chapter introduces the wide spectrum of Protestant communitarian approaches by way of some prominent movements.[5] In doing so, the considerable contemporary conflict over the role of the community regarding the authority of doctrine comes to the fore, which directly impacts the meaning, nature, and practicability of the Protestant Scripture principle (*sola Scriptura*) in theological method.

(Louisville: Westminster John Knox, 2005). Canonical approaches to systematic theology may hold affinities with, but should not be confused with, canonical approaches in the discipline of biblical studies (see chapter 8). Further, some approaches to theology use the label "canonical" but may not fall under what I describe as canonical theology (e.g., canonical theism, that is, "the theism expressed in and through the canonical heritage of the church," which consists of "not just a canon of books in its Bible but also a canon of doctrine, a canon of saints, a canon of church fathers, a canon of theologians, a canon of liturgy, a canon of bishops, a canon of councils, a canon of ecclesial regulations, a canon of icons, and the like"; William J. Abraham, "Canonical Theism: Thirty Theses," in *Canonical Theism: A Proposal for Theology and the Church*, ed. William J. Abraham, Jason E. Vickers, and Natalie B. Van Kirk (Grand Rapids: Eerdmans, 2008), 2 (Thesis IX).

4. This chapter focuses specifically on the Protestant communitarian turn, which generally frames itself as moving beyond the conservative–liberal impasse.

5. Some thinkers that self-identify within these communitarian approaches might hold some views that are more amenable to a canonical approach. This grouping of movements is not intended to categorize each individual theologian who might work within such movements but to identify some leading thinkers therein that exemplify the increasingly influential communitarian trajectory.

THE COMMUNITARIAN APPROACHES OF
ROMAN CATHOLICISM AND THE ORTHODOX CHURCH

Roman Catholicism

Roman Catholicism is often categorized as positing a two-source theory of revelation with "extra-biblical oral tradition" as an additional source of revelation beyond Scripture.[6] However, Peter Kreeft explains, the "church as writer, canonizer, and interpreter of Scripture is not another source of revelation but the author and guardian and teacher of the one source, Scripture."[7] The "apostles entrusted the 'Sacred deposit' of the faith (*depositum fidei*), contained in Sacred Scripture and Tradition, to the whole of the Church."[8] The Church is, accordingly, entrusted with "the transmission and interpretation of Revelation" and "'does not derive her certainty about all revealed truths from the holy Scriptures alone. Both Scripture and Tradition must be accepted and honored with equal sentiments of devotion and reverence.'"[9]

Confusion in this regard is, however, historically rooted. According to many historians, the supplementary view (Tradition II) was at one time the *de facto* (if not the *de jure*) view of Catholicism, having grown out of the coincidence view (Tradition I) beginning with Basil, carried forward by Augustine, and gaining ground throughout the Middle Ages.[10] As Anthony Lane views it, once it became clear that "not all that the church taught was to be found in Scripture . . . tradition had to supplement it."[11] This view of the "formal and material insufficiency of Scripture" did not prevail earlier because "medieval writers had no difficulty in finding everything in Scripture, since their prin-

6. Craig D. Allert, "What Are We Trying to Conserve?: Evangelicalism and *Sola Scriptura*," *EvQ* 76/4 (2004): 333. See the discussion of Traditions 0, I, and II, in chapter 1 (pages 7-11).

7. Peter Kreeft, *Fundamentals of the Faith: Essays in Christian Apologetics* (San Francisco: Ignatius, 1988), 275. According to his view, *sola Scriptura* "separates Church and Scripture. But they are one" (*Fundamentals*, 274).

8. *Catechism of the Catholic Church*, 2nd ed. (Washington, DC: United States Catholic Conference, 2000), 27.

9. *Catechism*, 26, quoting from *Dei Verbum*, 9. However, the "great Tradition" must "be distinguished from" its "particular forms, adapted to different places and times," the latter of which may be "retained, modified or even abandoned under the guidance of the Church's magisterium" (*Catechism*, 26-27).

10. See, for example, Anthony N. S. Lane, "Scripture, Tradition and Church: An Historical Survey," *VE* 9 (1975): 41.

11. Lane, "Scripture," 41.

ciples of exegesis [e.g., allegory] provided them with the necessary means."[12] Later on, however, "an awareness of the insufficiency of the (early) tradition gave birth to" the "doctrine of implicit tradition," which means that "the tradition of the church is to be found at its richest in its most developed form — the present teaching of the church," such that "Pope Pius IX could say that he himself was the tradition."[13] According to this view, which Heiko Oberman labeled Tradition III, "not only Scripture, but now also Scripture and tradition taken together are materially insufficient to support by simple explication" some "authoritative definitions" of the Church such as the mariological dogmas of 1854 (the Immaculate Conception) and 1950 (the Assumption), leaving the "teaching office of the Church" as a "norm" that "takes on the function of the source."[14]

Gavin D'Costa notes that there is not yet any resolution to "the debate on the crucial Catholic question: Are there two 'sources' of revelation or one?"[15] He contends, however, that "scripture and tradition are intrinsically and necessarily related, without either making scripture subservient to tradition or the Magisterium, or swallowing it up into the tradition."[16] Thus "we should properly say *sola scriptura et ecclesia*."[17]

Whichever view one takes regarding the source(s) of revelation, the Church unmistakably identifies the Magisterium as the normative interpreter of Scrip-

---

12. Yves Congar, *Tradition and Traditions* (New York: Macmillan, 1966), 113. According to Anthony N. S. Lane, "Sola Scriptura? Making Sense of a Post-Reformation Slogan," in *A Pathway into the Holy Scripture*, ed. P. E. Satterthwaite and David F. Wright (Grand Rapids: Eerdmans, 1994), 315, the "ingenuity of medieval allegorists . . . caused Scripture to be described as a nose of wax."

13. Lane, "Scripture," 47.

14. Heiko A. Oberman, *The Dawn of the Reformation: Essays in Late Medieval and Early Reformation Thought* (Edinburgh: T&T Clark, 1986), 294-95. Cf. Keith A. Mathison, *The Shape of Sola Scriptura* (Moscow, ID: Canon, 2001), 183; Lane, "Sola Scriptura?" 318.

15. D'Costa, "Revelation, Scripture and Tradition: Some Comments on John Webster's Conception of 'Holy Scripture,'" *International Journal of Systematic Theology* 6/4 (2004): 343. There has been an ongoing debate regarding how to interpret the Council of Trent in this regard, which many took to posit two sources of revelation. See Lane, "Scripture," 45, 46. Some Catholic scholars (e.g. Joseph Geiselmann and Karl Rahner) have claimed that Scripture was materially but not formally sufficient, that is, "Scripture contains everything, but some things only implicitly" (D'Costa, "Revelation," 344). Conversely, the majority view (e.g., Benedict XVI) has been that "while scripture was materially sufficient, it was not exclusively so, and thus one must grant status to another 'source' of revelation: tradition, upon which dogma can be based." (D'Costa, "Revelation," 344; cf. Lane, "Sola Scriptura?" 316-18; Oberman, *Dawn*, 286).

16. D'Costa, "Revelation," 343.

17. D'Costa, "Revelation," 343.

ture and Tradition: "The task of authentically interpreting the word of God, whether written or handed on, has been entrusted exclusively to the living teaching office of the Church [the Magisterium], whose authority is exercised in the name of Jesus Christ."[18] Yet "this Magisterium is not superior to the Word of God, but is its servant. It teaches only what has been handed on to it" such that "divinely revealed" teaching "is drawn from this single deposit of faith."[19] On the other hand, "the entire body of the faithful, anointed as they are by the Holy One, cannot err in matters of belief. They manifest this special property by means of the whole people's supernatural discernment in matters of faith when 'from the Bishops down to the last of the lay faithful' they show universal agreement in matters of faith and morals."[20] The final theological authority thus appears to reside with the church universal, interpreted by the Magisterium.

The Orthodox Church

Orthodoxy presents a thoroughgoing communitarian approach to theology wherein "scripture, tradition and Church are viewed as a comprehensive unity with interdependent parts," but the Church provides the final normative interpretation.[21] It is "the Church" that "forms the very ground from which scripture and tradition emerge and together, in turn, make up a coherent source of revelation, the supreme norm for the life of the Church."[22] Whereas "the Orthodox tradition advocates the supreme authority and primacy of scripture," it does so on the "basis" that the "later Church Fathers" considered "the entire corpus of scripture" to be "directly inspired by God."[23] In other words, the "official evidence for the authority and primacy of scripture is its canoni-

18. *Dei Verbum*, 10. Cf. *Lumen Gentium*, 25.

19. *Catechism*, 27, quoting from *Dei Verbum*, 10.

20. *Lumen Gentium*, 12. With regard to infallibility, the proclamations of the Pope are infallible when the Pope speaks *ex cathedra* (which is a very rare occurrence). Although "individual bishops do not enjoy the prerogative of infallibility, they nevertheless proclaim Christ's doctrine infallibly" when they and the Pope "are in agreement on one position as definitively to be held" (*Lumen Gentium*, 25).

21. Theodore G. Stylianopoulos, "Scripture and Tradition in the Church," in *The Cambridge Companion to Orthodox Christian Theology*, ed. Mary Cunningham and Elizabeth Theokritoff (Cambridge: Cambridge University Press, 2008), 21.

22. Stylianopoulos, "Scripture," 21. As such, "the Church is the foundational reality behind both scripture and tradition" ("Scripture," 24).

23. Stylianopoulos, "Scripture," 21.

sation as a sacred corpus in the Church's tradition over the first four centuries of church life."[24]

Some have wondered "whether the slogan 'the Bible alone' (*sola scriptura*) ought to be replaced with the slogan 'tradition alone' (*sola traditio*)" in virtue of the "force" of the "communal memories and traditions" behind "the formation of the Bible."[25] However, "neither slogan is true because scripture and tradition are mutually interdependent."[26] Rather, it is "through community that God seeks to fulfill his purposes in history. In their mutual interdependence, scripture, tradition and Church cannot be played off against each other."[27] Nevertheless, by "its canonical status, scripture occupies the primacy among the Church's traditions" such that the "Bible as the supreme record of revelation is the indisputable norm of the Church's faith and practice."[28] The "scriptures thereby bear God's authority and challenge the Church, making it accountable to the revealed will of God."[29]

Formally, then, the "Bible constitutes the record of divine revelation and forms the measuring standard for the faith and practice of the Church."[30] As such, "nothing in the Church must therefore contradict the teaching and spirit of the Bible"; rather everything "must be in harmony with the scriptural witness."[31] Yet, "scripture belong[s] exclusively to the church"[32] and "in the end it is the Church, inspired by the same Spirit that moved the biblical authors, which has the final discernment and normative interpretation about what is historical and cultural and what is theological and binding in the scriptures."[33]

24. Stylianopoulos, "Scripture," 22.

25. Stylianopoulos, "Scripture," 24.

26. Stylianopoulos, "Scripture," 24. For a recent Orthodox treatment, see Edith Humphrey, *Scripture and Tradition: What the Bible Really Says* (Grand Rapids: Baker, 2013). Interestingly, the seventeenth-century Eastern Orthodox Patriarch Lucaris accepted something very much like the magisterial reformers' view of *sola Scriptura*. The Eastern Orthodox church, however, rejected this view as heretical soon after Lucaris's death in 1638, maintaining that the "church itself . . . enjoyed infallible spiritual authority equal to that of the Scriptures," whereas "unrestricted access to the Bible, they feared, would bring both heresy and chaos"; Randall Herbert Balmer, "*Sola Scriptura*: The Protestant Reformation and the Eastern Orthodox Church," *TJ* 3/1 (1982): 56.

27. Stylianopoulos, "Scripture," 25.

28. Stylianopoulos, "Scripture," 25.

29. Stylianopoulos, "Scripture," 25.

30. Stylianopoulos, "Scripture," 21.

31. Stylianopoulos, "Scripture," 25.

32. Stylianopoulos, "Scripture," 24.

33. Stylianopoulos, "Scripture," 24. Thus, whereas Stylianopoulos believes that "the Bible in places appears to teach straight predestination (Jn 12:39-40; Mk 4:11-12; Rom 8:29)," he reports

If the Church provides the normative interpretation of Scripture, however, it is difficult to see how Scripture *functions* as the "indisputable norm" in any way that could "challenge the Church."

Against individual interpretation, the Church's normative interpretation adheres to the "rule of faith" as "a doctrinal sense of clarity pertaining to foundational beliefs," which are considered to be "grounded in the apostolic tradition and the apostolic interpretation of the Old Testament heritage."[34] Accordingly, "the scope and content of the [Nicene–Constantinopolitan] Creed is" believed to be "an official theological manifesto, a normative doctrinal framework of the faith, based on the Bible and summing of the Church's binding teaching pertaining to God and salvation. Both the Creed and the theological tradition behind it constitute the substance of the Church's theology."[35]

Among the "interpretative principles" that Stylianopoulos gleans "from the patristic exegetical heritage," particularly notable for our purposes is what he describes as the "unwavering commitment" of "Orthodox scholars" to: (1) "the authority, primacy and unity of the scriptures according to God's inspiration and providence," (2) "the centrality of the mystery of Christ as the decisive criterion of interpretation," (3) "harmonious interdependence between scripture, tradition and church," (4) "the importance of the 'rule of faith' and the accompanying theological tradition in interpretation," (5) "creative use of available methodologies with emphasis on the spirit rather than the letter," and (6) "the ongoing living tradition as normative interpretative agent ultimately expressed through church councils and their reception by the whole Church."[36]

---

that "John Chrysostom called such instances 'idioms' of scripture which must not be taken at face value; otherwise ideas unworthy of God would accrue, presenting him as an arbitrary and cruel tyrant" ("Scripture," 23). See John Chrysostom, *Homily 16 on Romans* (Rom 9:20-21).

34. Stylianopoulos, "Scripture," 28. Stylianopoulos contends, however, that "the appeal to the Church Fathers or to the 'mind' of the Church is essentially an appeal to the authority of the Church's normative doctrinal tradition pertaining to core issues of the faith" and is "not intended to restrict scholarship and creativity" ("Scripture," 28). Accordingly, Orthodox theologians "engage in the whole array of critical methodologies" but "with a close eye on the patristic exegetical tradition" ("Scripture," 29). At the same time, Orthodox theologians share "disquiet over the disruptive impact of modern biblical studies" ("Scripture," 32).

35. Stylianopoulos, "Scripture," 28.

36. Stylianopoulos, "Scripture," 30-31. Yet he also notes the need "to establish a tradition of constructive scholarly conversation towards a commonly defined Orthodox hermeneutic" ("Scripture," 32).

The Protestant Turn to the Community

The communitarian approaches above are undergirded by their distinctive biblical canons and rejection of *sola Scriptura*. Whereas Protestants, conversely, hold to the common canonical core and many espouse *sola Scriptura* (variously defined), the past few decades have seen a significant communitarian turn among various Protestants, including evangelicals. As Peter Leithart puts it, "Evangelicalism is awash in the 3Rs: retrieval, renewal, and *ressourcement*."[37]

Ressourcement, also referred to under the label *la nouvelle théologie*, describes a renewal movement of Roman Catholic thinkers who called for a return to and renewed reading of the Tradition that was influential upon the ecumenical trajectory of Vatican II.[38] Moving beyond neo-Scholasticism (e.g., Vatican I), Henri de Lubac and others "emphasized a strategy of ressourcement, going back to the sources" of patristic theology and beyond.[39]

As early as the "1940s and 1950s, the *ressourcement* helped to liberate Protestants from tired liberalism or oppressive fundamentalism, while also freeing Catholics from neo-scholasticism."[40] Today, the ecumenical spirit and language of Vatican II appears regularly in Protestant works calling for retrieval and a renewed emphasis on the great Christian tradition toward the desideratum of a generous ecumenical orthodoxy.

For our purposes, we will survey a few significant movements that have embraced a communitarian turn (to various degrees). Such movements, however, are not monolithic. Scholars who self-identify within one movement might

---

37. Peter J. Leithart, "The Word and the Rule of Faith," *First Things* (2015): http://www.firstthings.com/web-exclusives/2015/01/the-word-and-the-rule-of-faith (accessed 1/30/15). D. H. Williams, editor of Baker's Evangelical Ressourcement Series, is among the most prominent evangelical advocates for *ressourcement*, which in his view is "a return to the ancient sources of the faith for their own sake"; *Retrieving the Tradition and Renewing Evangelicalism: A Primer for Suspicious Protestants* (Grand Rapids: Eerdmans, 1999), 229.

38. See, further, Gabriel Flynn and Paul D. Murray, eds., *Ressourcement: A Movement for Renewal in Twentieth-Century Catholic Theology* (Oxford: Oxford University Press, 2012). Cf. Hans Boersma, *Nouvelle Théologie and Sacramental Ontology: A Return to Mystery* (Oxford: Oxford University Press, 2009).

39. James K. A. Smith, *Introducing Radical Orthodoxy: Mapping a Post-Secular Theology* (Grand Rapids: Baker Academic, 2004), 44. Along with de Lubac, Yves Congar, Marie-Dominique Chenu, and Jean Daniélou are among the most influential proponents of this movement. Indeed, some consider Jean Daniélou's article, "Les orientations presents de la Pensée religieuse," *Études* 249 (1946): 1-21, to be the manifesto of this movement.

40. Gabriel Flynn, "*Ressourcement*, Ecumenism, and Pneumatology: The Contribution of Yves Congar to *Nouvelle Théologie*," in *Ressourcement*, 223-24.

nevertheless hold vastly divergent views, and some scholars overlap with more than one movement. This survey is not aimed at labeling or restricting individuals to one "camp" or another but at introducing the widespread nature of the communitarian turn in Protestant theology by letting selected exemplars speak for themselves.

Postliberalism

Postliberalism has been located "at the center of" a "resurgence of confessional Christianity," having led the way in seeking to address postmodernism via a communitarian turn.[41] The main features of this diverse movement include emphasis on culture as mediator of experience, doctrine as descriptive of the practices of a particular community and regulative within that community, ecumenically oriented communitarianism, and a renewed attention to Scripture calling for intratextuality and narrativity.[42] Due to the influence of George Lindbeck and Hans Frei (among others), postliberalism is sometimes referred to as the Yale school of theology.[43]

In his landmark work *The Nature of Doctrine* (1984), Lindbeck offered a cultural-linguistic approach to doctrine as a third way, between the modernistic cognitive-propositionalist and experiential-expressive approaches. Lindbeck depicted cognitive propositionalism as tending toward reducing religion to "a formally organized set of explicit statements," holding "prop-

41. Timothy R. Phillips and Dennis L. Okholm, "The Nature of Confession: Evangelicals & Postliberals," in *The Nature of Confession: Evangelicals & Postliberals in Conversation*, ed. Timothy R. Phillips and Dennis L. Okholm (Downers Grove, IL: InterVarsity, 1996), 11.

42. See George A. Lindbeck, *The Nature of Doctrine: Religion and Theology in a Postliberal Age* (Philadelphia: Westminster, 1984), 34, 135; Lindbeck, "A Panel Discussion: Lindbeck, Hunsinger, Mcgrath & Fackre," in *Nature of Confession*, 247.

43. George Lindbeck is perhaps the foremost exemplar of postliberalism while Hans Frei arguably made the largest scholarly contribution, particularly regarding narrative theology. See also David Kelsey's *The Uses of Scripture in Modern Theology* (Philadelphia: Fortress, 1973), which greatly influenced Lindbeck. Other prominent scholars associated with postliberalism include the Yale-educated George Hunsinger, William Placher, and Stanley Hauerwas, many of whom were significantly influenced by Karl Barth. In this regard, "taken literally, 'postliberal' implies a critique of modern liberalism — especially the kind that Karl Barth opposed in his theological critiques of Liberal Protestantism, but also those philosophical critiques of liberalism posed in different ways by Ludwig Wittgenstein, Gilbert Ryle and Alasdair MacIntyre, and the sociological and anthropological ones made by Peter Berger and Clifford Geertz"; C. C. Pecknold, *Transforming Postliberal Theology: George Lindbeck, Pragmatism and Scripture* (New York: T&T Clark International, 2005), 1.

ositional truth" to be the "decisive test of adequacy."[44] Propositionalism describes the "approach of traditional orthodoxies" as well as "the outlook on religion adopted by much modern Anglo-American analytic philosophy with its preoccupation with the cognitive or informational meaningfulness of religious utterances."[45]

Experiential expressivism, on the other hand, is committed to the "primacy of experience," representing the liberal correlationist appropriation of the Enlightenment quest for certain, indubitable, universal, necessary, and neutral epistemological foundations.[46] This approach "interprets doctrines as noninformative and nondiscursive symbols of inner feelings, attitudes, or existential orientations" and is "particularly congenial to the liberal theologies influenced by" Schleiermacher and others."[47]

Lindbeck emphasized that culture and language unavoidably shape all human thought and experience.[48] Accordingly, religion is a "kind of cultural and/or linguistic framework or medium that shapes the entirety of life and thought" rather than "primarily an array of beliefs about the true and the good" or "a symbolism expressive of basic [universal] attitudes, feelings, or sentiments."[49] There is no "single generic or universal experiential essence" of religion, as modernistic liberalism suggests; one can "no more be religious in general than one can speak language in general."[50] Thus, the cultural-linguistic model moves beyond both the cognitive-propositionalist emphasis on propositions and universal reason and the modern experiential-expressivist edifice built on purportedly universal and homogenous religious experience, focusing instead on doctrine as descriptive of "particular religions" in their own cultural-linguistic context.[51]

44. Lindbeck, *Nature of Doctrine*, 64, 113.

45. Lindbeck, *Nature of Doctrine*, 16.

46. Lindbeck, *Nature of Doctrine*, 113.

47. Lindbeck, *Nature of Doctrine*, 16.

48. Lindbeck, *Nature of Doctrine*, 23, 24.

49. Lindbeck, *Nature of Doctrine*, 33. For Lindbeck, religion is thus "not primarily a set of propositions to be believed, but is rather the medium in which one moves" (*Nature of Doctrine*, 35).

50. Lindbeck, *Nature of Doctrine*, 23.

51. Lindbeck, *Nature of Doctrine*, 23.

The Linguistic Turn and Antifoundationalism

Lindbeck plays off Ludwig Wittgenstein's concept of "language games," characterizing doctrines as the descriptive rules of discourse of the believing community, which function as rules of grammar do in language. Doctrine is thus "regulative," functioning as "communally authoritative rules of discourse, attitude, and action."[52] Hence, the "task of descriptive (dogmatic or systematic) theology is to give a normative explication of the meaning a religion has for its adherents."[53]

Being descriptive of a particular community's religion, it makes little sense to think of doctrines in terms of universal rationality or experience.[54] Doctrine is, rather, evaluated relative to its "intrasystematic" truth, that is, "the truth of coherence" with the community's "total pattern of speaking, thinking, feeling, and acting."[55] Some have criticized postliberalism at this juncture for its apparent insularity, suggesting "that theology ought to have external criteria, subject to public scrutiny, by which its validity can be tested."[56] The postliberal might, in turn, accuse those critics of operating on bygone modernistic epistemological grounds, not recognizing that "each type of theology is embedded

52. Lindbeck, *Nature of Doctrine*, 18. "Like a culture or language, it [religion] is a communal phenomenon that shapes the subjectivities of individuals" with its own "distinctive logic or grammar" (*Nature of Doctrine*, 33). Cf. Paul Holmer, *The Grammar of Faith* (San Francisco: Harper & Row, 1978).

53. Lindbeck, *Nature of Doctrine*, 113. Here, theology is "the scholarly activity of second-order reflection on the data of religion" (*Nature of Doctrine*, 10).

54. Lindbeck defines doctrines as "communally authoritative teachings regarding beliefs and practices" indicating "what constitutes faithful adherence to a community" (*Nature of Doctrine*, 74). Cf. Stanley Hauerwas's view of ethics as the study of a community's moral values in *A Community of Character: Toward a Constructive Christian Social Ethic* (Notre Dame: University of Notre Dame Press, 1981).

55. Lindbeck, *Nature of Doctrine*, 64. He distinguishes this from "ontological" truth, which is the "truth of correspondence to reality" (*Nature of Doctrine,* 64). Here, "just as grammar by itself affirms nothing either true or false regarding the world in which language is used, but only about language, so theology and doctrine, to the extent that they are second-order activities, assert nothing either true or false about God and his relation to creatures, but only speak about such assertions" (*Nature of Doctrine*, 69). Here, "postliberal theology" does not exclude "the possibility of metaphysical or ontological commitments" but encourages "'a certain pragmatic tentativeness' towards them" (Pecknold, *Transforming Postliberal Theology*, 8).

56. Alister E. McGrath, *Christian Theology: An Introduction*, 5th ed. (Malden, MA: Wiley-Blackwell, 2011), 94. For McGrath, "An Evangelical Evaluation of Postliberalism," in *Nature of Confession*, 36, this virtually reduces truth to "internal consistency."

in a conceptual framework so comprehensive that it shapes its own criteria of adequacy."[57]

Lindbeck describes his own epistemology as "postliberal antifoundation-alism," without meaning to "imply relativism or fideism," questioning "not whether there are universal norms of reasonableness, but whether these can be formulated in some neutral, framework-independent language."[58] He thus rejects classical foundationalism but without requiring "the rejection (or the acceptance) of the epistemological realism and correspondence theory of truth" or "propos[ing]" a "common framework . . . within which to compare religions," which are potentially "incommensurable."[59]

The Communitarian Turn

In light of the failure of the modernistic quest to ground doctrine in *universal* reason or experience, Lindbeck turns to the community, countering Descartes's turn to the subject. In this regard, postliberalism has been characterized as "an Anglo-American variation on" the *ressourcement* "theme of returning to sources." It advocates not only "a return to the scriptural narrative" but also a "'return to the tradition', allied in various ways with the *nouvelle théologie*" and its *ressourcement* "task of creative faithfulness to the tradition in the face of contemporary challenges."[60]

Postliberalism is thus highly "communitarian," appealing to "values, experiences, and language of a community" and "insist[ing] upon the importance of traditions and their associated historical communities in the shaping of experience and thought."[61] Here, "meaning is given within the praxis of the church."[62] This orientation dovetails with Alasdair MacIntyre's criticism of liberalism's attempted "repudiation of tradition" and his alternative notion of tradition-constituted and tradition-constitutive rationality — a theory of

57. Lindbeck, *Nature of Doctrine*, 113. Indeed, Lindbeck claims, "Theoretical frameworks shape perceptions of problems and their possible solutions in such a way that each framework is in itself irrefutable" and thus there can be no "decisive confirmation or disconfirmation" of any system (*Nature of Doctrine*, 11). Thus, "theological method" cannot be tested "apart from performance" (*Nature of Doctrine*, 134).

58. Lindbeck, *Nature of Doctrine*, 132, 128.

59. Lindbeck, *Nature of Doctrine*, 68-69, 49. Classical foundationalism (e.g., Descartes) posits that knowledge requires the indubitability, universality, and neutrality of basic beliefs that ground other beliefs with certainty (see chapter 5).

60. Pecknold, *Transforming Postliberal Theology*, 1, 2.

61. McGrath, *Christian Theology*, 92-93.

62. Phillips and Okholm, "Nature of Confession," 13.

communal rationality that contends that there is "no standing ground, no place for enquiry, no way to engage in the practices of advancing, evaluating, accepting, and rejecting reasoned argument apart from that which is provided by some particular tradition."[63]

The Source(s) of Doctrine

Within postliberalism, rather than in propositions purportedly derived from Scripture (cognitive propositionalism) or in universal religious experience (experiential expressivism), the meaning of the Christian faith is found in the practices of the believing community. "Meaning is constituted by the uses of a specific language" such that "what 'God' signifies" is determined by "examining how the word operates within a religion and thereby shapes reality and experience" and in this way "theological description in the cultural-linguistic sense is intrasemiotic or intratextual."[64]

Alongside this communitarian conception of theological meaning, postliberalism views Scripture as creating the Christian community's "only real world" and thus emphasizes intertextuality and a narrative approach to reading Scripture on its own terms (e.g., as realistic narrative).[65] Frei thus attempted to reverse "the great reversal [that] had taken place" in liberal biblical studies wherein "interpretation was a matter of fitting the biblical story into another world with another story rather than incorporating that world into the biblical story."[66] This complemented Yale scholar Brevard Childs's development of his influential canonical approach to biblical interpretation.[67]

Via a postcritical recovery of "premodern scriptural interpretation in contemporary form" that critically appropriates selected procedures of modern (liberal) biblical criticism, "postliberalism tries to divorce itself from the anti-ecclesial" and "the anti- or noncreedal ways of reading Scripture that have

---

63. Alasdair MacIntyre, *Whose Justice? Which Rationality?* (London: Duckworth, 1988), 349, 350, cf. 354-69.

64. Lindbeck, *Nature of Doctrine*, 114.

65. Phillips and Okholm, "Nature of Confession," 12; cf. Lindbeck, *Nature of Doctrine*, 122. See, especially, Hans W. Frei's groundbreaking *The Eclipse of Biblical Narrative* (New Haven: Yale University Press, 1974). Lindbeck also notes the significant influence of "Karl Barth's exegetical emphasis on narrative" (*Nature of Doctrine*, 135).

66. Frei, *Eclipse*, 130.

67. See chapter 8 for discussion of Childs's canonical approach to biblical studies in relationship to my canonical theology, which comport in some respects but significantly differ in others.

prevailed on the modern evangelical side."[68] Lindbeck posits the "uncondi-tionality and permanence of the ancient Trinitarian and Christological creeds" but not the "terminology and conceptuality in which they are formulated" or any supposed ontological reference thereof.[69] Such doctrines are regulative within "the concrete life and language of the community," to be obeyed as "a rule" rather than interpreted as "a truth" (contra propositionalism): "The theo-logian's task is to specify the circumstances, whether temporary or enduring, in which it applies."[70]

This raises the crucial question of "who or what can be appealed to as most nearly infallible in grammatical and, by transference, doctrinal matters."[71] Believing that the "Roman [Magisterium], Reformation [*sola Scriptura*], and Orthodox [Spirit-guided Church universal] positions" are presently irreconcilable, Lindbeck appeals to the "*consensus fidelium* or con-*sensus ecclesiae*."[72] He recognizes that this raises its own line of questions in "highly variegated religions such as Christianity," including: "Which claimants to the authentic Christian tongue should be heeded?"[73] Lind-beck's solution is to "delimit a mainstream of the religion" by drawing a "sample from as large a cross section, as wide a consensus, as is possible," therefore referring "to tradition, to magisterial pronouncements (as voices of the tradition and of consensus), and to the canonical writings as gener-ally accepted instances of genuinely Christian (or Islamic, or Buddhist, or Jewish) speech."[74] Thus, the "locus of infallibility" is "the whole community of competent speakers of a language," where competency requires (among other things) being "mainstream" and "ecumenical" rather than "in isolated backwaters or ingrown sects uninterested in communicating widely."[75] In

68. Lindbeck, "Panel Discussion," 246. This involves "acceptance of biblical criticism, but placing it in a very subordinate role as far as the theologically significant reading of Scripture is concerned" ("Panel Discussion," 247).

69. Lindbeck, *Nature of Doctrine*, 92. Here, there is "abiding doctrinal grammar" but "vari-able theological vocabulary" (*Nature of Doctrine*, 113).

70. Lindbeck, *Nature of Doctrine*, 107. Accordingly, Lindbeck focuses on praxis while repu-diating "the doctrinal relevance" of "metaphysically oriented speculation" (*Nature of Doctrine*, 107-8).

71. Lindbeck, *Nature of Doctrine*, 99.

72. Lindbeck, *Nature of Doctrine*, 104, 99.

73. Lindbeck, *Nature of Doctrine*, 99.

74. Lindbeck, *Nature of Doctrine*, 99-100.

75. Lindbeck, *Nature of Doctrine*, 102, 100. By "infallibility," he means "an empirically based confidence that the *consensus fidelium* cannot mortally err," the key modifier being "mortally" (*Nature of Doctrine*, 101).

all this, the "critical task" for Lindbeck was "to renew the ecumenical imperative for catholic unity."[76]

Postconservatism

Stanley Grenz and John Franke serve as the primary exemplars of postconservatism of the kind discussed here, which is postmodern, nonfoundationalist, trinitarian, communitarian, and eschatological.[77] Postconservatism frames itself as resisting the boundary setting of conservatism while maintaining its own critical posture toward (but not fear of) liberalism.[78] In this way, postconservatism seeks to engage postmodernism and offer its own third way beyond the modernistic "right–left dichotomy" of "the supposedly universal experience" posited by liberalism and the conservatives' "foundationalist theological method that appealed to an inerrant Bible" or a propositionalist traditionalism.[79]

---

76. Pecknold, *Transforming Postliberal Theology*, 1. See Lindbeck, *Nature of Doctrine*, 135.

77. Roger Olson has also been an influential communicator. See his *Reformed and Always Reforming: The Postconservative Approach to Evangelical Theology* (Grand Rapids: Baker Academic, 2007). On the pastoral side, see Brian D. McLaren, *A Generous Orthodoxy* (Grand Rapids: Zondervan, 2006). It should be noted, however, that thinkers might self-describe as "postconservative" and yet hold widely differing views regarding what that entails. For instance, Kevin Vanhoozer has self-identified as postconservative in some writings but holds a view quite different from the Grenz/Franke form surveyed here (cf. *Drama*, 278-91).

78. Roger E. Olson, "Reforming Evangelical Theology," in *Evangelical Futures: A Conversation on Theological Method*, ed. John G. Stackhouse, Jr. (Grand Rapids: Baker, 2000), 202-3. Olson sees conservatism as a bounded set and postconservatism as a centered set but rejects the view that postconservatism is "theologically 'left'" ("Reforming," 203). He identifies postconservatism as "reformist" in the sense of a "liberated evangelical theology" that "break[s] free with bold confidence from captivity to categories of 'right' and 'left,'" over and against evangelical conservative traditionalists of two types: biblicist and paleo-orthodox ("Reforming," 203; cf. Olson, *Reformed and Always Reforming*, 19-22). By "conservatism," Olson means "the style of doing theology that relies heavily on authoritative tradition and rejects or consciously neglects the critical and constructive tasks of theology" (*Reformed*, 19). Gerald McDermott, "Evangelicals Divided: The Battle Between Meliorists and Traditionalists to Define Evangelicalism," *First Things* (April 2011): http://www.firstthings.com/article/2011/04/evangelicals-divided (accessed 7/19/15), however, challenges Olson's categorization as misleading, or inaccurate, and labels both Grenz and Olson among what he calls meliorists.

79. Stanley J. Grenz, "Articulating the Christian Belief-Mosaic: Theological Method after the Demise of Foundationalism," in *Evangelical Futures*, 112. Cf. Stanley J. Grenz, *Renewing the Center: Evangelical Theology in a Post-Theological Era*, 2nd ed. (Grand Rapids: Baker, 2006), 197.

Nonfoundationalism and the Communitarian Turn

Echoing postliberalism's critique of modernism, Grenz proposes theology after the "demise" of the foundationalist "quest for complete epistemological certitude," often "termed 'strong' or 'classical' foundationalism."[80] He adopts nonfoundationalism and a coherentist theory of truth wherein "meaning and truth" are "an internal function of language" and "absolute justification of beliefs belongs to the realm of the ideal."[81] Grenz thus prefers the image of a "web of belief" or "mosaic," believing that "theology can no longer model itself after the foundationalist metaphor of constructing an edifice."[82]

This nonfoundationalist framework facilitates "the communitarian turn," which "returns theological reflection to its proper primary location within the believing community."[83] Here, theology is "an intellectual enterprise by and for the Christian community," which "seeks to understand, clarify and delineate

---

80. Grenz, *Renewing*, 110.

81. Grenz, *Renewing*, 203, 200. He uses nonfoundationalist and postfoundationalist terminology interchangeably. Cf. Grenz, "Articulating," 109.

82. Grenz, *Renewing*, 213, cf. 199. For Grenz, theology is an "interrelated, unified whole," a "belief-mosaic of the Christian community" with some pieces "more central to the 'picture'" and others "more peripheral" (*Renewing*, 213). Here Grenz relies heavily on his (questionable) understanding of Wittgenstein as the "means to overcome metaphysical realism" and the work of Nancey Murphy and W. V. Quine for the shift to "communal dimensions of truth pioneered by the coherentists and the pragmatists" (*Renewing*, 201-3). See Nancey Murphy's historicist holism *Beyond Liberalism and Fundamentalism: How Modern and Postmodern Philosophy Set the Theological Agenda* (Valley Forge, PA: Trinity Press International, 1996), 88, 94, 100-106; cf. W. V. Quine and J. S. Ullian, *The Web of Belief* (New York: Random House, 1970). Murphy speaks of the theologian as "contributing to the reweaving of the doctrinal web as it has been handed on to her"; the theologian is "responsible to the formative texts, understood in light of the long development of communal practices of interpretation" as well as "the boundary conditions provided by current experience," which "in the broad sense described" by Murphy is the "life of the church in the world" (*Beyond Liberalism*, 106). Grenz also favors Wolfhart Pannenberg's eschatological "coherentist/pragmatist approach," in which "truth is essentially historical" and "shows itself through the movement of time climaxing" eschatologically (Grenz, "Articulating," 117; cf. Grenz, *Renewing*, 203-5, 240-43). See Wolfhart Pannenberg, *Systematic Theology*, 3 vols. (Grand Rapids: Eerdmans, 1991), 1:21-22, 24-25. Grenz continues in this vein, "until the eschaton, truth will by its own nature always remain provisional and truth claims contestable" ("Articulating," 117). Cf. Stanley J. Grenz and John R. Franke, *Beyond Foundationalism: Shaping Theology in a Postmodern Context* (Louisville: Westminster John Knox, 2001), 28-54.

83. Grenz, "Articulating," 121.

the community's interpretive framework" in connection with the gospel and the biblically disclosed narrative of divine action.[84]

The Spirit-Appropriated Role of Scripture in Theological Method

Grenz's "evangelical theological method . . . seeks to take seriously the post-modern situation" by way of "a conversation involving Scripture, tradition, and culture."[85] Noting that "recent conversations between Catholics and Protestants about the relationship between Scripture and tradition have started to close the breach created in the sixteenth century," Franke adds that "significant differences still remain, such as the question, which has priority, Scripture or the church?"[86] In his view, this very question "rests on foundationalist understandings."[87] According to his "nonfoundationalist" perspective, conversely, "Scripture functions in an ongoing and dynamic relationship with the Christian tradition in ways that are at odds with the common evangelical conception of *sola scriptura*."[88] Indeed, "Scripture and tradition must function together" as "coinherent aspects of the ongoing ministry of the Spirit."[89]

Scripture as the "instrumentality of the Spirit" is the "primary voice in the [communitarian] theological conversation," *primarily* aimed at spiritual sustenance rather than doctrine.[90] However, the "authority of Scripture is not ultimately invested in any particular quality that inheres in the text itself" but "is based on the work of the Spirit who speaks in and through the text" as well as other media.[91] The "ultimate authority is the Spirit speaking through Scripture"[92] and "the same Spirit whose work accounts for the formation of

84. Grenz, "Articulating," 122.

85. Grenz, "Articulating," 109.

86. John R. Franke, "Scripture, Tradition, and Authority: Reconstructing the Evangelical Conception of *Sola Scriptura*," in *Evangelicals & Scripture*, 201.

87. Franke, "Scripture," 201.

88. Franke, "Scripture," 193. On their pneumatological–ecclesiological view of *sola Scriptura*, see Franke, "Scripture"; and Stanley J. Grenz, "Nurturing the Soul, Informing the Mind: The Genesis of the Evangelical Scripture Principle," in *Evangelicals & Scripture*.

89. Franke, "Scripture," 210.

90. Grenz, "Articulating," 125, 124. He adopts the narrative sketched by Gary Dorrien that seventeenth-century theologians, influenced by Enlightenment foundationalism, "transformed the doctrine of Scripture from an article of faith into the foundation of the entire systematic-theological program" (Grenz, "Nurturing," 28). See Dorrien, *The Remaking of Evangelical Theology* (Louisville: Westminster John Knox, 1998), 21-22.

91. Franke, "Scripture," 202, cf. 205; Grenz, "Articulating," 128.

92. Grenz, "Articulating," 127.

the Christian community also guides [and inspires] that community in the production and authorization of the biblical texts," pointing "toward an appropriate pneumatological–ecclesiological understanding of tradition."[93]

The Nature of Postconservative Theology

For Grenz, theology must be "trinitarian, communitarian, and eschatological."[94] First, "the confessions of the church suggest that any truly Christian theology must be trinitarian theology," with emphasis on the ongoing work of the Spirit.[95] Further, as the Trinity is "social or communal," so "theology is necessarily communitarian" as "the shared faith of the community."[96] Postconservatism thus emphasizes "reading within community" as part of "the one faith community that spans the ages," recognizing the "theological heritage — the tradition — within which we stand as contemporary readers of the text."[97] This embraces a "true evangelical 'ecumenism'" and seeks to "participate in a truly 'catholic' reading of the text, even in those instances when such a reading leads us to differ with past luminaries on certain theological issues."[98]

Moving from a "creed-based to spirituality-based" approach,[99] postconservatism is an "open confessional tradition," which views "all theological formulations" as "culturally embedded." Postconservatism therefore does not ascribe "defining authority to past confessional statements which demand complete subscription to these formulations" but seeks "to develop and adopt new confessions in accordance with shifting circumstances."[100] Franke's "non-foundationalist turn" aims to highlight the "Spirit-guided trajectory of Christian tradition," which "provides a hermeneutical trajectory for theology that

93. Franke, "Scripture," 202.
94. Grenz, "Articulating," 109.
95. Grenz, "Articulating," 131.
96. Grenz, "Articulating," 133.
97. Grenz, "Articulating," 126.
98. Grenz, "Articulating," 127. Here theology is not only descriptive but also prescriptive, seeking "to articulate what *ought* to be the interpretive framework of the Christian community" ("Articulating," 122).
99. Stanley J. Grenz, *Revisioning Evangelical Theology* (Downers Grove, IL: InterVarsity, 1993), 37.
100. Franke, "Scripture," 206-7. This stands over and against what Franke calls "closed confessional traditions" that "hold a particular statement of beliefs to be adequate for all times and places" ("Scripture," 207).

is open-ended, eschatologically directed and performatively operative," yet "without elevating [tradition] to a position of final authority."[101]

This pneumatological–ecclesiological approach points to the eschatological reality that is in the process of being created by the Spirit through the community. Accordingly, "the ultimate, highest, and final purpose of theology is to articulate the Christian belief-mosaic in accordance with the actual (that is, future) world God is fashioning."[102] This presupposes the "demise of realism" and adopts "social constructionist insight[s]" toward positing an "eschatological realism," which contends that as "God's determined will," "future reality" is "far more real — and hence far more objective, far more actual — than the present world, which is even now passing away" (1 Cor 7:31).[103] The "community of Christ" thus has "a divinely given mandate to be participants in constructing a world that reflects God's own will for creation."[104]

The Theological Interpretation of Scripture

Another approach with communitarian leanings has come to be known as the theological interpretation of Scripture (TIS), "a family of interpretive approaches that privileges theological readings of the Bible in due recognition of the theological nature of Scripture, its ultimate theological message, and/or the theological interests of its readers."[105] Although TIS includes a good deal of "variety and vagueness," in part due to the "'ecclesiastical breadth' of the scholars involved," Daniel J. Treier identifies the common themes of "canon, creed, and culture as the foci by which theological interpretation serves the church."[106]

101. Franke, "Scripture," 206, 207.
102. Grenz, "Articulating," 136.
103. Grenz, "Articulating," 130, 136.
104. Grenz, "Articulating," 136.
105. Gregg R. Allison, "Theological Interpretation of Scripture: An Introduction and Preliminary Evaluation," *Southern Baptist Journal of Theology* 14/2 (2010): 29. Daniel J. Treier, *Introducing Theological Interpretation of Scripture: Recovering a Christian Practice* (Grand Rapids: Baker Academic, 2008), 11, locates the beginnings of this movement in the 1990s and identifies Karl Barth as a "forerunner" of the "recovery" of theological interpretation.
106. Daniel J. Treier, "What Is Theological Interpretation? An Ecclesiological Reduction," *International Journal of Systematic Theology* 12/2 (2010): 156, 148.

Beyond Modern Reading: The Linguistic and Communitarian Turn

TIS aims at moving beyond modernistic approaches to Scripture that exclude reading the Bible as a distinctively theological text. That is, it "seeks to reverse the dominance of historical criticism over churchly reading of the Bible," with some embracing a postcritical retrieval of precritical exegetical procedures.[107] Over and against the modern expectation of "neutral objectivity, supposedly bracketing any creedal commitments out of interpretation," TIS recognizes the "impossibility of such neutrality" and that "Christian beliefs can be productive for biblical interpretation, helping us to see what the scriptural texts are really about."[108] Practitioners of TIS are particularly dissatisfied with any approach to Scripture that "brackets out a consideration of divine action."[109] In Francis Watson's words, "the claims of modern biblical scholarship are to be resisted insofar as they prove incompatible with the claims of the ecclesial community, its canon, and its interpretive tradition."[110]

In this regard, Lindbeck's cultural-linguistic model has influenced TIS to "focus on Christian community as a culture."[111] TIS further owes "much to

107. Treier, *Introducing Theological Interpretation*, 14. Cf. David C. Steinmetz, "The Superiority of Pre-Critical Exegesis," in *The Theological Interpretation of Scripture: Classic and Contemporary Readings*, ed. Stephen E. Fowl (Malden, MA: Blackwell, 1997), 26-38. Here again, there is diversity within TIS and it is unclear how many practitioners adopt the "medieval fourfold sense of Scripture," with some advocating what might be called postcritical exegesis (Treier, "What Is Theological Interpretation?" 149). Joel B. Green, *Practicing Theological Interpretation: Engaging Biblical Texts for Faith and Formation* (Grand Rapids: Baker Academic, 2011), 195, explains that theological interpretation is a form of "'interested' exegesis" within an "ecclesial location" but with "no particular methodological commitments"; cf. Joel B. Green, *Seized by Truth: Reading the Bible as Scripture* (Nashville: Abingdon, 2007), 140.

108. Treier, *Introducing Theological Interpretation*, 34.

109. Kevin .J. Vanhoozer, "Introduction: What Is Theological Interpretation of the Bible?" in *Dictionary for Theological Interpretation of the Bible*, ed. Kevin J. Vanhoozer (Grand Rapids: Baker Academic, 2005), 19-25, here 20; cf. Treier, *Introducing Theological Interpretation*, 14, 34, 199; Francis Watson, "Authors, Readers, Hermeneutics," in *Reading Scripture with the Church: Toward a Hermeneutic for Theological Interpretation* (Grand Rapids: Baker Academic, 2006), 120; Vanhoozer, "What Is Theological Interpretation?" 22; Green, *Practicing Theological Interpretation*, 46-48, 127.

110. Francis Watson, "Authors," 120. But TIS includes various approaches to the precanonical history of the text, the finer points of the doctrine of Scripture, general and special hermeneutics, and the relationship of theological interpretation to biblical theology. Cf. the discussion among four leading proponents in A. K. M. Adam, Stephen E. Fowl, Kevin J. Vanhoozer, and Francis Watson, *Reading Scripture with the Church*.

111. Treier, *Introducing Theological Interpretation*, 81.

Wittgenstein's concept of 'language games,' with a focus on how words have meaning only as they are used in particular contexts."[112] In light of the linguistic turn, "we must pay attention not only to the original contexts of the Bible's composition but also to the historical and contemporary contexts of its reading."[113] At the same time, some TIS advocates caution that interpreters past and present might be "insufficiently critical or aware of their own presuppositions and standpoints."[114]

The Theological Role of Scripture and Community

TIS is thus committed to what Vanhoozer calls "the ecumenical consensus of the church" that "the Bible should be read as a unity and as narrative testimony to" God.[115] However, advocates of TIS hold differing views regarding the relative priority given to that which is (1) behind the text (the precanonical history of the text), (2) in the text (the contents of the text itself), and (3) in front of the text (the way individuals and interpretive communities interpret the text).[116]

Regarding that which is in front of the text, TIS includes various proposals concerning the extent of authority of Christian tradition, creeds, and the contemporary community. Stephen Fowl's robust communitarianism emphasizes "the church as Scripture's interpretative community"[117] and argues that "theology and ecclesiology should drive scriptural hermeneutics, not the other way around."[118] For Fowl, "the reading of Scripture is not a private matter for Christian individuals but rather a public activity of the church" via practical reason.[119] Thus, "theological interpretation of scripture" is "reading aimed at

---

112. Treier, *Introducing Theological Interpretation*, 81.

113. Treier, *Introducing Theological Interpretation*, 81.

114. Vanhoozer, "What Is Theological Interpretation?" 19.

115. Vanhoozer, "What Is Theological Interpretation?" 19; cf. Treier, *Introducing Theological Interpretation*, 201. Thus, "theological exegesis" emphasizes the prime role to be played by the canon "as a word about God and from God" (*Introducing Theological Interpretation*, 36).

116. Cf. Vanhoozer, "What Is Theological Interpretation?" 19; Green, *Seized by Truth*, 105-22.

117. Treier, *Introducing Theological Interpretation*, 85-91.

118. Stephen E. Fowl, "The Importance of a Multivoiced Literal Sense of Scripture: The Example of Thomas Aquinas," in *Reading Scripture with the Church*, 37. See Stephen E. Fowl, *Engaging Scripture: A Model for Theological Interpretation*, Challenges in Contemporary Theology (Malden, MA: Blackwell, 1998); Stephen E. Fowl, *Theological Interpretation of Scripture* (Eugene, OR: Cascade, 2009).

119. Treier, *Introducing Theological Interpretation*, 88.

shaping and being shaped by a community's faith and practice."[120] Thus, Fowl advocates that "Christians learn from the best interpretive habits and practices of those who both clearly understood the purposes for which Christians interpret scripture, and were relatively adept at keeping convictions, practices, and scriptural interpretation together as part of a single, complex practice called theology."[121]

From another standpoint, Vanhoozer carefully criticizes what he sees as overemphasis on the role of the community in Lindbeck's cultural-linguistic approach, advocating his own "canonical-linguistic approach" that "locates normativity in the divine author's, not the interpretative community's, use of Scripture" while recognizing the church's role in "performance of the Scriptures."[122] Some practitioners of TIS are thus more communitarian and would have greater affinities with other communitarian approaches described in this chapter (e.g., Fowl), while others (particularly Vanhoozer) have been critical of some communitarian approaches, acknowledging a robust role for the community while attempting to safeguard the unique role of the canon.

Retrieving Ruled Reading in Community

Despite differences among various practitioners of TIS, they collectively appreciate the practices of: "(1) "recovering the past," (2) "reading within the Rule(s)," and (3) "reading with others."[123] These three common commitments move past modern, critical, and individualistic approaches to theology, tending toward a communitarian way of addressing the postmodern interpretative situation.[124] For Treier, ruled reading includes a move beyond the crucial affirmation of the "consistency" of Scripture as "ultimately one 'book'" to "find[ing] basically the same theological commitments throughout the

120. Stephen E. Fowl, "Introduction," in *The Theological Interpretation of Scripture*, ed. Stephen E. Fowl (Cambridge, MA: Blackwell, 1997), xix. In this and other ways it is "nonmodern" and loyal to community rather than "the academy" ("Introduction," xvi). Accordingly, "Christians must see themselves as part of an ongoing tradition extending down to the present" ("Introduction," xvii).

121. Fowl, *Engaging Scripture*, 9.

122. Vanhoozer, *Drama*, 181. Cf. Vanhoozer's distinction between Performance I, which he advocates, and Performance II, which he attributes to Fowl (*Drama*, 151-85).

123. Treier, "What Is Theological Interpretation?" 148-49; cf. Treier, *Introducing Theological Interpretation*, 39-100.

124. As Treier notes, "If we replace the ideal of neutral objectivity with constructively critical use of interpreters' presuppositions and perspectives, then Scripture study must not be the province of isolated individuals" (*Introducing Theological Interpretation*, 34).

church fathers."[125] Whereas "interpretation according to the Rule of Faith" includes "stretching ourselves to explore imaginatively the classic Christian consensus," a "truly 'Christian' understanding of Scripture occurs within the boundaries of the Rule of Faith," receiving "helpful guidance from Nicene orthodoxy."[126] By way of such retrieval of traditions, ruled reading, and reading in community, TIS aims at "discern[ing] how the Holy Spirit leads members of the Christian community to discover the meaning of Scripture" and "how different parts of the body of Christ connect with each other in that process."[127]

Consensual Orthodoxy

A number of Protestant thinkers have made an increasingly influential call to return to classical Christian orthodoxy and retrieve the great Christian tradition toward a "new ecumenism" that "is grounded in ancient ecumenism."[128] Thomas Oden refers to this movement as paleo-orthodoxy as well as "classic consensual ecumenical teaching" (*consensus fidelium*).[129] Classic consensual orthodoxy seeks to encourage Protestantism (especially evangelicalism) to retrieve the orthodox consensus of Christianity, particularly that of the patristic tradition. Oden sees this as a "rebirth of orthodoxy" wherein "Christians are quietly relearning how to think ecumenically in classic terms."[130]

After Modernism

Oden sets his approach against what he describes as his own former liberalism, which he came to reject in favor of the classic Christian tradition. Against the modern conception of the individual interpreter "as a value-free, autonomous observer," Oden shuns novelty and advocates strict "accountabil-

125. Treier, *Introducing Theological Interpretation*, 63. Here, he refers to Thomas Oden's claim along these lines.

126. Treier, *Introducing Theological Interpretation*, 63, 64. However, diversity within TIS is expected and welcomed given that "specific confessional rules of faith and so forth are ingredient to the practice of theological interpretation" (Treier, "What Is Theological Interpretation?" 159-60).

127. Treier, *Introducing Theological Interpretation*, 80.

128. Thomas C. Oden, *The Rebirth of Orthodoxy: Signs of New Life in Christianity*, 1st ed. (San Francisco: HarperSanFrancisco, 2003), 158.

129. Oden, *Rebirth*, 34; cf. Thomas C. Oden, *Classic Christianity* (San Francisco: HarperOne, 2009), xiii.

130. Oden, *Rebirth*, 156.

ity before God in the midst of a remembering community."[131] Further, Robert Webber suggests that "return to the Christian tradition" possesses "power to speak to a postmodern world" dissatisfied "with the modern version of evangelical faith and with current innovations that have no connection with the past." [132]

Scripture and the Vincentian Rule of Faith

For consensual orthodoxy, the content of classic Christianity is "orthodoxy," which is "nothing more or less than the ancient consensual tradition of Spirit-guided discernment of scripture."[133] However, "believers quote scripture with different meanings," so "who is to decide which interpretation is correct?"[134] A "reliable rule" is needed to "distinguish fraudulent expressions of faith from true faith."[135] To this end, Oden adopts the Vincentian rule of faith as "what has been believed everywhere, always, and by all."[136]

Accordingly, "orthodoxy" consists of the "integrated biblical teaching as interpreted in its most consensual classic period" (Christianity's first five centuries), during which Oden believes the Spirit-led church forged an ecumenical and apostolic consensus of classical Christianity.[137] Whereas "classic Christianity is most reliably defined textually by the New Testament itself," it is "most *concisely* summed up in a primitive baptismal confession that was entirely derived from scripture as salvation history in a nutshell. This doctrinal core is recalled in the three prototype summaries of faith: the Apostles' Creed,

131. Oden, *Rebirth*, 159. "I am dedicated to unoriginality" (Oden, *Classic Christianity*, 15).

132. Robert Webber, *Ancient-Future Faith: Rethinking Evangelicalism for a Postmodern World* (Grand Rapids: Baker, 1999), 29. Cf. Thomas C. Oden, *After Modernity . . . What? Agenda for Theology* (Grand Rapids: Zondervan, 1990); Oden, *Rebirth*, 2; Oden, *Turning Around the Mainline: How Renewal Movements Are Changing the Church* (Grand Rapids: Baker, 2006).

133. Oden, *Rebirth*, 31. By "tradition," Oden means "the faithful handing down from generation to generation of scripture interpretation consensually received worldwide and cross-culturally through two millennia" (*Rebirth*, 32).

134. Oden, *Rebirth*, 158. Since believers disagree "on what canonical scripture as a whole conclusively teaches," Oden concludes (with Vincent) that Scripture itself cannot function as that rule (*Rebirth*, 161). See chapter 5.

135. Oden, *Rebirth*, 161.

136. Oden, *Rebirth*, 162; cf. Oden, *Classic Christianity*, 743.

137. Oden, *Rebirth*, 129. The "time-period" for orthodox "teaching is generally assumed to be the first five centuries" (Oden, *Rebirth*, 129). Compare D. H. Williams's appeal, *Evangelicals and Tradition: The Formative Influence of the Early Church* (Grand Rapids: Baker Academic, 2005), 62, to the normative "canonical tradition of the patristic church."

the Nicene Creed, and the so-called Athanasian Creed (and their subsequent consensual confessions and interpretations)."[138]

Whereas "scripture [holds] primacy over tradition" and "nothing would be less orthodox than to assert a tradition that has no basis in scripture," the faithful recollection of Scripture is itself presumed to be the traditional "consensual reading" thereof.[139] Thus, "any teaching that polarizes tradition against scripture has already lost its orthodox equilibrium. The key balancing feature of classic ecumenical Christian tradition transmission is this: tradition is itself a memory of scripture interpretation consensually received."[140]

Williams thus maintains that "*sola scriptura* cannot be rightly and responsibly handled without reference to the historic Tradition of the church, and when it is, any heretical notion can arise taking sanction under a 'back to the Bible' platform."[141] For Williams, the "Bible is capable of being understood only in the midst of a disciplined community of believers whose practices embody the biblical story" under the guidance of "'spiritual masters,' namely, the venerable voices of the historical church."[142] Similarly, Oden calls for "think[ing] intergenerationally with the whole community of believers under the authority of scripture about the apostolic testimony."[143]

---

138. Oden, *Rebirth*, 31. He believes these creeds "have enjoyed the widest ecumenical consent over the longest period of time across the broadest span of geography" (*Rebirth*, 164).

139. Oden, *Rebirth*, 32-33.

140. Oden, *Rebirth*, 32-33. He suggests a "pyramid of sources, with scripture at the base, then the early Christian writers, first pre-Nicene then post-Nicene, as the central mass, then the best of medieval followed by centrist Reformation writers at the narrowing upper mass, and more recent interpreters at the smaller, tapering apex — but only those who grasp and express the prevailing mind of the believing historical church" (*Classic Christianity*, xxiv).

141. D. H. Williams, *Retrieving the Tradition and Renewing Evangelicalism: A Primer for Suspicious Protestants* (Grand Rapids: Eerdmans, 1999), 234. He further argues that "any search for a doctrine of *sola scriptura* in the writings of the Fathers fails to grasp how the early church understood apostolic authority and the reciprocal relation that necessarily existed between Scripture, Tradition and the church" (*Retrieving*, 234). Accordingly, some advocates of consensual orthodoxy avoid or reject the phrase *sola Scriptura* whereas others employ the phrase with the proviso that the first few centuries of tradition function as interpretatively normative; D. H. Williams, *Evangelicals and Tradition*, 96-102; Williams, *Retrieving*, 229-34; cf. Mathison, *Shape*; Allert, "What Are We Trying to Conserve?"

142. Williams, *Evangelicals*, 101.

143. Oden, *Rebirth*, 158.

Vincentian-Ruled Theological Method

Oden identifies Vincent of Lérins's *Commonitorium* (ca. 432) as the "decisive classic text for orthodox ancient ecumenical method."[144] The Vincentian method employs the criteria of "universality, apostolic antiquity, and conciliar consent,"[145] corresponding to the "three Latin words — *ubique, semper, omnibus* (everywhere, always, by all)."[146] Agreement at "all three" of these levels assures "reliable ecumenical truth."[147]

But which community provides the context for these three criteria? What would qualify as genuinely universal agreement? Oden avers that "by all" (*omnibus*) does not "require absolute unanimity" but "consent . . . must be reasonably firm."[148] When disagreements arise, however, "Christian truth-claims" should be sifted through the "four filters" of: universality, (apostolic) antiquity, conciliar consensus, and (if necessary) ecumenical exegetes. Here, (1) "the universal prevails over the particular," (2) the older apostolic witness prevails over the newer alleged general consent," (3) "conciliar actions and decisions prevail over faith-claims as yet untested by conciliar acts," and (4) "where no conciliar rule avails, the most reliable consensual ancient authorities prevail over those less consensual over the generations."[149] In this

144. Oden, *Rebirth*, 157. Little is known about Vincent, though Oden describes fifth-century Lérins as a "major center for ecumenical classic Christianity" where "the vital energies of Eastern monasticism were transmitted to the West" (*Rebirth*, 157).

145. Oden, *Rebirth*, 162.

146. Oden, *Rebirth*, 162. Cf. the *consensus quinquesaecularis* advocated by seventeenth-century Lutheran Georg Calixtus.

147. Oden, *Rebirth*, 163.

148. Oden, *Rebirth*, 163. Yet, what degree of unanimity is required?

149. Oden, *Rebirth*, 171-72. Ecumenical exegetes are *"the most reliable consensual teachers of the ancient Christian tradition"* (*Rebirth*, 169, emphasis his). According to his view, "Athanasius, Basil, Gregory of Nazianzus, and John Chrysostom" of the East and "Ambrose, Augustine, Jerome, and Gregory the Great" of the West have been identified by "the conciliar process" as "its most consensual interpreters" in that they, though not "infallible," are the most "frequently specified in the documents of the ecumenical councils and in subsequent decretals" (*Rebirth*, 170). Cf. canonical theism, which Paul L. Gavrilyuk, "Scripture and the *Regula Fidei*: Two Interlocking Components of the Canonical Heritage," in *Canonical Theism*, 27, characterizes as "a massive retrieval of the church's canonical heritage," which is "constituted by materials, practices, and persons that formally or informally have been adopted by the whole church as canonical." This movement, however, differentiates itself from Oden's "consensual theism" in that "it is skeptical of the claim that there exists a consensus across the patristic era, Roman Catholicism, magisterial Protestantism, evangelical orthodoxy, and the like" due to "very serious differences that challenge the claim of consensus." Canonical theism thus "focuses on the

manner, "Orthodox, Catholics, and Protestants can, despite diverse liturgical and cultural memories, find unexpected common ground ecumenically by returning to classic interpreters of scripture texts that still stand as authoritative for teaching today."[150]

Radical Orthodoxy

Since the publication of John Milbank's *Theology and Social Theory,* Radical Orthodoxy (RO) "has arguably become the most discussed and provocative tendency in Anglophone theology."[151] Far more than an approach to theology, however, RO is a broad, ecumenical, transdisciplinary research project that arose among English-language theologians in the 1990s (largely at Cambridge). RO aims to construct a radically Christian comprehensive alternative to secularity across the range of disciplines via "engagement with classical mediaeval, modern and later modern thought in order to read theologically the signs of our own times."[152] RO has produced a voluminous amount of material and has provoked a fair bit of response and criticism.[153]

Catherine Pickstock characterizes RO not as "an exclusive movement" or school of thought, but as a "loose tendency" with a "concrete ecumenical proposal," one "potentially embracing all those who espouse a basically orthodox theology, but do not regard themselves as simply ecclesiastical or political traditionalists."[154] RO is thus critical of "Protestant biblicism and post-tridentine Catholic positivist authoritarianism," viewing both as "aberrant results of theo-

---

public, canonical decisions of the church existing in space and time across the first millennium" (Abraham, "Canonical Theism," 2 [Thesis VIII]).

150. Oden, *Rebirth*, 186.

151. Simon Oliver, "Introducing Radical Orthodoxy: From Participation to Late Modernity," in *Radical Orthodoxy Reader*, ed. Simon Oliver and John Milbank (New York: Routledge, 2009), 3. See John Milbank, *Theology and Social Theory: Beyond Secular Reason* (Cambridge, MA: Blackwell, 1990). Some of the most prominent RO thinkers include John Milbank, Catherine Pickstock, and Graham Ward.

152. Oliver, "Introducing Radical Orthodoxy," 3.

153. See, for instance, the series Veritas (London: SCM), Interventions (Grand Rapids: Eerdmans), and Illuminations: Theory and Religion (Oxford: Wiley-Blackwell). For one example of a sustained criticism of RO, see W. J. Hankey and Douglas Hedley, eds., *Deconstructing Radical Orthodoxy: Postmodern Theology, Rhetoric, and Truth* (Burlington, VT: Ashgate, 2005). Cf. David F. Ford, "Radical Orthodoxy and the Future of British Theology," *SJT* 54 (2001): 385-404.

154. Catherine Pickstock, "Reply to David Ford and Guy Collins," *SJT* 54 (2001): 405, 407.

logical distortions" of modernity.[155] The "designation 'orthodox'" in RO thus signals "commitment to credal Christianity and the exemplarity of its patristic matrix" that yet "transcends confessional boundaries."[156] RO's ecumenical goal of "reformed catholicism" has found "many surprising sympathizers amongst Baptists, Methodists, Mennonites, Nazarenes, and others."[157]

The End of Secular Modernity

RO advances an unwaveringly post-secular outlook, viewing "the very notion of 'the secular' as a myth," and robustly critiques modernity/liberalism as a "flawed, imploding project."[158] For Milbank, the approaching "end of modernity" entails "the end of a single system of truth based on universal reason."[159] For RO, "secularism" is itself "an ideological distortion of theology" that attempted to divorce "facts of nature" from "*value or purpose*."[160] Modernism did not remove "theological consensus to reveal a neutral territory" but replaced "a certain view of God and creation with a different view which still makes theological claims" about "origins, purpose, and transcendence," the "assumptions and prejudices" of which "are no more objective or justifiable than those of the ancient and mediaeval philosophers and theologians."[161]

Moving beyond "the modern predicament of theology" then, RO "no longer has to measure up to accepted secular standards of scientific truth or normative rationality."[162] It offers instead a "*via media*," standing "equally against theology as an internal autistic idiolect" and "theology as an ad-

155. John Milbank, Catherine Pickstock, and Graham Ward, "Introduction," in *Radical Orthodoxy: A New Theology*, ed. John Milbank, Catherine Pickstock, and Graham Ward (New York: Routledge, 1999), 2.

156. Milbank, Pickstock, and Ward, "Introduction," 2.

157. Pickstock, "Reply to Ford and Collins," 408.

158. Smith, *Introducing Radical Orthodoxy*, 70, 74. As Milbank puts it: "Once, there was no 'secular'" (*Theology and Social Theory*, 9).

159. John Milbank, "'Postmodern Critical Augustinianism': A Short Summa in Forty-Two Responses to Unasked Questions," in *The Radical Orthodoxy Reader*, ed. Simon Oliver and John Milbank (New York: Routledge, 2009), 49.

160. Oliver, "Introducing Radical Orthodoxy," 5.

161. Oliver, "Introducing Radical Orthodoxy," 6. The "secular" is not what remains after "religion and theology" are dismissed but is itself "a positive ideology" ("Introducing Radical Orthodoxy," 6).

162. Milbank, "Postmodern Critical Augustinianism," 49.

aptation to unquestioned secular assumptions," viewing both as "in secret [modernistic] collusion."[163]

Rejecting the Enlightenment conception of "rationality" as neutral, universal, and dispassionate, RO returns to the earlier view of "participation in the reason — the *logos* — of God mediated through traditions and social practices."[164] Here, "there is not a single aspect of human existence or creation that can be properly understood or described apart from the insights of revelation."[165] Accordingly, RO "defers to no experts and engages in no dialogues [with secular disciplines] because it does not recognize other valid points of view outside the theological."[166] Rather, RO employs "the tools of critical reflexivity honed by continental thinking, taking on board the full implications" of the "linguistic turn" such that it "reads the contemporary world through the Christian tradition, weaving it into the narrative of that tradition."[167]

Utilizing an "Augustinian model" and "Platonic legacy," RO espouses a participatory ontology, or theological materialism, that is set over and against the postmodern ontology of "flatness and materialism that ultimately lead to nihilism."[168] Here, "nothing *is* autonomously or in itself but *is* only insofar as it participates in the gift of existence granted by God."[169] This allows no "reserve of created territory" that is "independent of God . . . while allowing finite things their own integrity," affirming divine transcendence understood via Aquinas's analogy of being contra Scotus's univocity.[170] As Milbank puts

163. John Milbank, "The Programme of Radical Orthodoxy," in *Radical Orthodoxy? A Catholic Enquiry,* ed, Laurence Paul Hemming (Burlington, VT: Ashgate, 2000), 33.

164. Oliver, "Introducing Radical Orthodoxy," 5. See Alasdair MacIntyre, *After Virtue* (London: Duckworth, 1984); Alasdair MacIntyre, *Whose Justice? Which Rationality?*

165. Smith, *Introducing Radical Orthodoxy,* 69-70.

166. "Radical Orthodoxy: Twenty-four Theses," thesis 5, unpublished document quoted in Smith, *Introducing Radical Orthodoxy,* 70.

167. Graham Ward, "Radical Orthodoxy and/as Cultural Politics," in *Radical Orthodoxy? A Catholic Enquiry,* 106 (emphasis his).

168. Smith, *Introducing Radical Orthodoxy,* 74. Notably, Pickstock's reading of Plato contrasts with those that devalue "the temporal and material in favor of the eternal and the intelligible" (Smith, *Introducing Radical Orthodoxy,* 105); see Catherine Pickstock, *After Writing: On the Liturgical Consummation of Philosophy* (Oxford: Blackwell, 1998), 14.

169. Smith, *Introducing Radical Orthodoxy,* 75 (emphasis his).

170. Milbank, Pickstock, and Ward, "Introduction," 3. Some RO thinkers understand Scotus's univocity to present God as not qualitatively but merely quantitatively different from creatures, devaluing embodiment and mediation, and undergirding the modern conception of reason as autonomous, ultimately leading to nihilism (Smith, *Introducing Radical Orthodoxy,* 97).

it, "although it opposes the modern, [RO] also seeks to save it. It espouses, not the pre-modern, but an alternative version of modernity."[171]

Radical Ressourcement

RO involves a decided turn to retrieval of orthodox Christian thought and practice to bring it to bear on postmodernism. Thus, RO "is devoted to what has become known as *ressourcement*, namely the renewed reading of the depths of the Christian tradition in order to inform a rigorous, critical and authentically theological reading of our own times."[172] This includes "a renewed appreciation for the liturgical or doxological character of creation and the role that liturgy [sacramentality/aesthetics] plays in leading us to the divine."[173]

Although seeking "to retrieve premodern resources for theological reflection," RO seeks not "a simplistic return to old paths" but "to rethink tradition as the very condition for theological reflection."[174] RO's retrieval of orthodox Christian thought thus involves what others sometimes view as radical reinterpretation. Some RO thinkers thus argue for a "minimal core orthodoxy" that avoids "a narrow orthodoxy."[175] For Ward, there is "not *one* Christian tradition" but "orthodoxies" such that "orthodoxy is broader than might at first be believed."[176] Whereas differences regarding the *filioque* or the Eucharist "are not grounds for heterodoxy," the divinity and resurrection of Jesus and the trinity are core essentials.[177] As John Milbank puts it, RO "perpetuates the *nouvelle théologie*" as "catholic" but not "specifically Roman Catholic" such that "it can equally be espoused by those who are formally 'protestant,' yet whose theory and practice essentially accords with the catholic vision of the Patristic period through to the high middle ages."[178]

RO is thus "a hermeneutic disposition and a style of metaphysical vision," a "task" more than a "thing."[179] It is thus "not a system, method or formula"

---

171. Milbank, "Programme of Radical Orthodoxy," 45.

172. *Radical Orthodoxy Reader*, xi.

173. Smith, *Introducing Radical Orthodoxy*, 77.

174. Smith, *Introducing Radical Orthodoxy*, 65.

175. Smith, *Introducing Radical Orthodoxy*, 64.

176. Ward, "Radical Orthodoxy and/as Cultural Politics," 106 (emphasis his).

177. Ward, "Radical Orthodoxy and/as Cultural Politics," 106.

178. Milbank, "Programme of Radical Orthodoxy," 36. Smith seeks to show how Reformed theology "resonates with this 'catholic' theology, while also offering a critical voice to it" (*Introducing Radical Orthodoxy*, 65 n. 6).

179. Pickstock, "Radical Orthodoxy and the Meditations of Time," in *Radical Orthodoxy: A Catholic Enquiry*, 63.

but is "orthodox insofar as it seeks to be unapologetically confessional and Christian" and "radical insofar as it seeks to critically retrieve premodern roots (*radix*)" toward articulating "a confessional theology" and account of all "human experience."[180]

ASSESSING COMMUNITARIAN APPROACHES

The Communitarian Turn in Light of Postmodernity

These Protestant communitarian approaches share a number of common emphases that revolve around a communitarian turn that is itself responsive to the postmodern context. Such approaches turn to a community-determined extracanonical normative interpretive arbiter (e.g., rule of faith) or consensus. The community is thus afforded a determinative theological role, raising significant questions regarding the evangelical understanding of *sola Scriptura*.

The proliferation of communitarian approaches, at times contradicting one another in significant ways, highlights the considerable complexity of the issues involved. Consider the divergence between what Franke calls "closed confessional traditions" that "hold a particular statement of beliefs to be adequate for all times and places" and an "open confessional tradition," which "understands its obligation to develop and adopt new confessions in accordance with shifting circumstances."[181] Similarly, some appeal to the community-guiding role of the Spirit to bolster confidence in the received tradition as it has been traditionally interpreted while others suggest that the Spirit continues to "inspire" the community and thus may lead in surprising new directions.[182]

In common, however, these approaches tend to frame the communitarian turn as a way of addressing the failure of modernity and the corresponding postmodern predicament.[183] The demise of classical foundationalism is perhaps the most frequently appealed to tenet characterizing this postmodern context. As Merold Westphal puts it, that "classical foundationalism" is "philosophically indefensible is so widely agreed that its demise is the closest thing to a philosophical consensus in decades."[184] In various ways, the turn to the

---

180. Smith, *Introducing Radical Orthodoxy*, 66, 73-74.

181. Franke, "Scripture," 206-7.

182. Franke speaks of a "broader concept of inspiration" that includes God's work in Christian communities, connecting "Spirit and tradition" ("Scripture," 203, 202).

183. See Grenz, "Articulating," 107, 129.

184. Merold Westphal, "A Reader's Guide to 'Reformed Epistemology,'" *Perspectives* 7/9

community is proposed as the means to ground doctrine in the absence of indubitable foundations, being offered by some as the key to assuage the epistemological and hermeneutical concerns raised by the failure of modernity.

The modern myths of universal reason and experience have now been repudiated, and it is increasingly recognized that each person is inevitably affected by his or her own cultural-linguistic background, tradition, and many other factors that render a neutral perspective impossible. In light of this, communitarianism claims the epistemic right to ground doctrine in community/tradition and that interpretation itself should thereby be governed by the collective wisdom of the community over and against modernistic individualism.[185]

Evaluating the Communitarian Turn in Protestant Theology

Much can be learned from these influential communitarian approaches. Perhaps most significant is the welcome emphasis that no theology is done in a vacuum and isolationism is detrimental both to the individual attempting to practice it and to other Christians. Further, the calls to humbly and charitably work within community offer an important reminder against proclivities toward reductionist *sola Scriptura*. Community plays a crucial role in Christianity and much is gained by sustained engagement with the Christian tradition, including being alerted thereby to "some of the pitfalls we should avoid."[186]

Further, given the failure of modernity, every movement must engage the postmodern predicament. Moving beyond the strictures of modernism, communitarian approaches advance some healthy correctives in light of the demise of *classical* foundationalism. Some astutely criticize modernistic biblical criticism. Treier notes that for quite some "time, historical criticism of the Bible seemed to involve criticism of everything except itself. Postmodernity extends modern suspicion to include such criticism of critical methods."[187] Last but

---

(November 1992): 11. Cf. Merold Westphal, *Whose Community? Which Interpretation? Philosophical Hermeneutics for the Church*, The Church and Postmodern Culture (Grand Rapids: Baker Academic, 2009).

185. See Stanley Hauerwas, "The Church's One Foundation Is Jesus Christ Her Lord; or, in a World without Foundations: All We Have Is the Church," in *Theology without Foundations*, ed. Stanley Hauerwas, Nancey Murphy, and Mark Nation (Nashville: Abingdon, 1994), 143-62.

186. Grenz, "Articulating," 126.

187. Treier, *Introducing Theological Interpretation*, 34.

certainly not least, the emphasis of many communitarian approaches on the role of the Holy Spirit is of critical importance.

Some communitarian emphases, however, raise critical questions for thinking through the theological role of the biblical canon in relation to that of the community. First, does the (correct) repudiation of classical foundationalism require theology without foundations? Does it require, as is sometimes suggested, that the biblical canon cannot function as theologically foundational? If so, how should the biblical canon function relative to the community? If an extracanonical normative arbiter is adopted, could the canon *functionally* hold theological primacy relative to the community?

In this regard, does the communitarian turn endanger the functional authority of the biblical canon *as* canon? Franke contends that "closed confessional traditions" risk "transforming their creeds . . . into de facto substitutes for Scripture."[188] Yet, open confessional traditions might do likewise insofar as the contemporary community is appealed to as normative. While community plays a crucial role, it is sometimes unclear just what that role is and how it *should* function theologically.

Related to this concern, communitarianism faces the crucial questions of which community and on whose interpretation. The question of "which community" is particularly troubling in our contemporary pluralistic context. If community itself is the standard of "intrasystematic" truth and ethics, might not any community's beliefs and actions be legitimated insofar as they are internally coherent within their community? Whereas Lindbeck judges the "crusader's battle cry 'Christus est Dominus'" as "false when used to authorize cleaving the skull of the infidel," is the violence of the Ku Klux Klan or ISIS authorized insofar as it is "intrasystematically" ethical within their particular subcommunities?[189] Which version of self-identified Christianity (or any other religion) is legitimate and on whose interpretation?

Which self-identified Christian thought is genuinely Christian? Whose tradition during what time and from what place should be retrieved/*ressourced*? Even with the adoption of some specified community (e.g., the patristics), the vital question remains, whose interpretation of the tradition of that community?[190] If, as in postliberalism for example, interpretations that serve "the

---

188. Franke, "Scripture," 206.
189. Lindbeck, *Nature of Doctrine*, 64.
190. What if the selected community offers no internally coherent tradition?

upbuilding of the church" are "preferred," the question must be asked, the upbuilding of which church?[191] That is, which community?

Some contend that Spirit-led consensus is the key standard. Yet this raises at least two crucial questions: which perceived consensus and who is led by the Spirit and in what manner? Regarding the first question, the recognition of any consensus itself already requires a selection of some delimited community from which the purported consensus arises or an interpretation of the tradition of those deemed to be within that community. It would seem that there might be various purported consensuses or a lack thereof, depending on differing interpretations or delimitations of community. Thus, "which consensus" appears to be integrally related to the question "which community," which itself is not easily separable from the question, "whose interpretation?"

In this regard, who is Spirit-led? So-called closed confessional traditions tend to claim that the consensual tradition itself was guided by the Spirit in such a way that, although fallible, it is a trustworthy standard of genuine Christianity. However, open confessional traditions worry that traditionalism might "hinder such a community from hearing the voice of the Spirit speaking in new ways through the biblical text."[192] In this way, postconservatives appeal to the Spirit not only to suggest that past communities were reliably guided by the Spirit but that the Spirit continues to work in similar fashion in the contemporary community. Thus, they appear to move the locus of trustworthiness, if not functional primacy, to the contemporary voice of the Spirit speaking through various media.[193] Yet, one wonders, how does one reliably identify and test (cf. 1 John 4:1) the purported voice and work of the Spirit?

What guards against one's own individual or community perspective from being mistakenly presumed to be the leading of the Spirit?[194] Do both open

191. Phillips and Okholm, "Nature of Confession," 13.

192. Franke, "Scripture," 206.

193. Yet, when is the Spirit appropriating any particular medium? For A. B. Caneday, "Is Theological Truth Functional or Propositional? Postconservatism's Use of Language Games and Speech-Act Theory," in *Reclaiming the Center: Confronting Evangelical Accommodation in Postmodern Times*, ed. Millard J. Erickson, Paul Kjoss Helseth, and Justin Taylor (Wheaton, IL: Crossway, 2004), 137, postconservatism identifies "the Spirit's contemporary use of Scripture rather than Scripture itself as that which regulates the community's theology."

194. One might say Scripture itself but, according to this view, Scripture is normatively interpreted by the purported Spirit-led consensus and thus *could not* challenge it. Importantly, Daniel J. Treier, "Canonical Unity and Commensurable Language: On Divine Action and Doctrine," in *Evangelicals & Scripture*, 214, points out that "if language use is not commensurable," Grenz's view faces the considerable problem "that his caution about the Spirit not speaking against the Bible is moot, because we cannot actually check."

and closed confessional traditions run the risk of mistakenly assuming that their tradition/community was and is led by the Holy Spirit in a way that keeps them from "mortal" error? What guards, then, against the deceptions of false prophets and false spirits that plagued biblical, presumably Spirit-led, communities (Jer 14:14; Luke 6:26; cf. chapter 3), and of which Christ himself warned (Matt 7:15; 24:11, 24; Mark 13:22; cf. 2 Pet 2:1; Rev 16:13-14)?

Further, various purportedly Spirit-led communities hold mutually exclusive doctrines. Even if the leading of the Spirit does guarantee correct doctrine, which one out of the sea of claimants (if any) is thus led by the Spirit? As seen previously, biblical history includes many examples of God's people following false prophecy and departing from sound doctrine and practice, suggesting that Spirit-led communities (corporately) are not thereby immune from error, even egregious error. Alternatively, perhaps at least some theologically divergent communities are Spirit-led but such leading does not guarantee correct doctrine and does not exclude such divergences.[195] In either case, it would appear that *appeals to* corporate Spiritual guidance do not provide the means to differentiate effectively between genuine and false doctrine. Indeed, would not any identification of a Spirit-led consensus itself hinge upon which interpretation is operative?

Thus we return to the questions, whose interpretation and of which community? Some appeal to a communitarian doctrinal or interpretive rule (of faith). But which rule? Beyond appeal to Spirit-led consensus generally, one might contend that there is a universal, apostolic, and conciliar *core* consensus (as with the Vincentian rule) that might function as such a rule, perhaps the patristic tradition itself as interpreted by consensual exegetes. However, if some *consensus fidelium* is the rule, does this not return us to the original questions? If one delimits the rule to "competent" interpreters, i.e., those who are "mainstream," "catholic," "orthodox," and "ecumenical," what qualifies as mainstream, universal, orthodox, and ecumenical?[196] Would Jesus and his first-century apostles themselves qualify as "mainstream" in relation to their wider contemporary community?

Perhaps one might appeal to a "minimal core orthodoxy" (as in Radical Orthodoxy) whether that be a specifically identifiable rule of faith or otherwise. It may be that, as the various critical issues above suggest, some rule or standard

195. Some of this hinges upon one's theology of divine providence and the operation of the Holy Spirit, which itself depends on which theological authorities are operative and in what manner. Even if a particular theology of the Spirit's operation is adopted, however, the question of how to recognize such remains.

196. See the earlier discussion of Lindbeck, *Nature of Doctrine*, 100.

is desirable, by which these and other matters might be adjudicated. Might an adequate approach to these (postmodern) theological concerns, then, itself depend on the viability of the overarching communitarian appeal to some normative rule of faith? If so, which rule of faith?

CONCLUSION

This chapter has offered an overview of communitarian approaches to theology, noting both some positive implications and critical open questions. Of crucial concern at this juncture is one's understanding regarding which community, consensus, or interpretation is valid, coupled with the relative plausibility and practicability of *sola Scriptura* in light of postmodernism. It also remains to address the broader question of whether there is a minimal core orthodoxy or viable rule of faith and, if so, how such might be accurately identified and implemented. Each of these issues will be further explored in subsequent chapters, beginning in the next chapter with a consideration of issues concerning the rule of faith.

CHAPTER 5

The Rule of Faith

Canonical and communitarian approaches sharply diverge regarding the roles of canon and community. Whereas the former denies any extracanonical normative interpretive authority, the latter affords the community a determinative theological role, which often entails adoption of some extracanonical rule of faith or procedure of ruled reading. This, however, raises at least two crucial questions for consideration: First, which rule? Second, is such an appeal to an extracanonical rule viable and practicable?

The answer to these questions hinges, in large part, on just what the adoption of a normative rule or ruled reading is supposed to achieve. The Protestant communitarian turn is (at least in part) aimed at finding a way to ground and interpret Christian faith after modernity. Regarding the latter, D. H. Williams contends that because "a Scripture-only principle" is "no guarantor of orthodox Christianity,"[1] an extracanonical "rule of faith or norm for interpretation is essential if orthodox faith is to be achieved."[2] Conversely, "where no interpreta-

---

1. D. H. Williams, *Retrieving the Tradition and Renewing Evangelicalism: A Primer for Suspicious Protestants* (Grand Rapids: Eerdmans, 1999), 234. Where Scripture is interpreted "apart from the church's Tradition," Williams contends, there is "scarce assurance that an orthodox Christian faith would be the result" (*Retrieving*, 98).

2. D. H. Williams, *Evangelicals and Tradition: The Formative Influence of the Early Church* (Grand Rapids: Baker Academic, 2005), 77. Similarly, Thomas C. Oden, *The Rebirth of Orthodoxy: Signs of New Life in Christianity*, 1st ed. (San Francisco: HarperSanFrancisco, 2003), 161, contends that because "key areas of disagreement remain on the particular interpretations of so many sacred texts," one must interpret "in accordance with some general [extracanonical] rule"; cf. Daniel J. Treier, *Introducing Theological Interpretation of Scripture: Recovering a Christian Practice* (Grand Rapids: Baker Academic, 2008), 64.

tive guide exists as a theological 'court of appeal,' hermeneutical fragmentation can be the only result."[3] The claim here, echoed by many others, is that some normative rule for interpretation will, to some preferable degree, address the problem of "hermeneutical fragmentation."[4] However, is any extracanonical rule of faith or ruled reading viable toward this end?

Toward addressing this question, we first engage Irenaeus's seminal appeal to apostolic tradition and the rule of faith in his polemic against the gnostics, which informs a brief survey of the widely varying conceptions of the "rule of faith" and a suggestion that the canon itself be recognized as the rule of faith.

IRENAEUS ON SCRIPTURE, TRADITION, THE CHURCH, AND THE *REGULA FIDEI*

The Authority and Interpretation of Scripture

Throughout his refutation of Gnosticism, Irenaeus adamantly affirms both the apostolic writings of the NT and the prophetic writings of the OT, employing Scripture frequently and dogmatically as theologically authoritative (i.e., "canonical" in the minimal sense described in chapters 2-3).[5] According to James Hernando, Irenaeus uses the words "Scripture" or "Scriptures" in *Against Heresies* to introduce citations from the OT sixty times, from the NT fourteen times, and from both the OT and NT fifty-five times.[6] Further, in *Against Heresies* and *Fragments*, Irenaeus quotes from "twenty-five of twenty-seven New Testament books (Philemon and 3 John excluded)" and his "writings contain quotations or verbal allusions to 77.9% (201 of 258) of the chapters in the canonical New Testament."[7] As John Lawson observes,

3. Williams, *Retrieving*, 97-98.

4. As Oden puts it, "not everyone fully concurs on what canonical scripture as a whole conclusively teaches" (*Rebirth*, 161).

5. Irenaeus often quotes Scripture to refute christological errors as well as other gnostic heresies and frequently addresses the proper interpretation of biblical passages (*Against Heresies*, 3.16.7; cf. 3.7.2; 4.16.1; 4.32.2).

6. James Daniel Hernando, "Irenaeus and the Apostolic Fathers: An Inquiry into the Development of the New Testament Canon," (PhD diss., Drew University, 1990), 75. He introduces noncanonical writings thusly only twice and in both cases there is reason to believe he uses "scripture" in a non-technical sense (see "Irenaeus," 76 n. 116).

7. Hernando, "Irenaeus," 84. Harvey notes 629 allusions or citations from the OT and 1,065 allusions or citations from the NT in *Against Heresies*; W. Wigan Harvey, ed., *Libros Quinque Adversus Haereses* (Cambridge: Typis Academicis, 1857), 513-23.

even the casual reader of Irenaeus "cannot fail to observe" the "extensive use made of Scripture. At times, chapter after chapter is nothing other than a mosaic of Biblical quotations."[8] Thus, whereas the scope of what Irenaeus considered to be Scripture is disputable, he speaks of and uses "Scripture" in a *functionally* canonical manner that suggests that he and his audience know its nature and contents.[9]

Of the foundational authority of Scripture, Irenaeus writes, "We have learned from none others the plan of our salvation, than from those through whom the Gospel has come down to us, which they did at one time proclaim in public, and, at a later period, by the will of God, handed down to us in the Scriptures, to be the ground and pillar of our faith."[10] Irenaeus further emphasizes the clarity of Scriptures, saying, "the entire Scriptures, the prophets, and the Gospels, can be clearly, unambiguously, and harmoniously understood by all."[11] Scripture, then, does not require a special interpretation such as the gnostics would suppose. Moreover, whereas "the Scriptures are indeed perfect, since they were spoken by the Word of God and His Spirit," we, "inasmuch as we are inferior to, and later in existence than, the Word of God and His Spirit, are on that very account destitute of the knowledge of His mysteries."[12] The Scriptures, then, are perfect due to their unique connection to Christ and the Spirit, which is not possessed by the later community.

Tradition according to Irenaeus

Irenaeus's view of the relationship of Scripture and tradition has been a matter of considerable dispute. Some scholars take "tradition" in Irenaeus to refer to an authoritative norm, along with Scripture, the "rule of faith," and the Church.[13] Yet many scholars note that Irenaeus's use of *traditio* (παράδοσις),

8. John Lawson, *The Biblical Theology of Saint Irenaeus* (London: Epworth, 1948), 23.

9. Hernando thus contends that "*functionally* Irenaeus is operating with a New Testament canon of Scripture" ("Irenaeus," 84, emphasis his). Similarly, John Behr, "The Word of God in the Second Century," *ProEccl* 9/1 (2000): 95, contends that, for Irenaeus, "the apostolic writings themselves are now accepted as canonical Scripture."

10. Irenaeus, *Against Heresies*, 3.1.1 (*ANF* 1:414); cf. Eph 2:20.

11. Irenaeus, *Against Heresies*, 2.27.2 (*ANF* 1:398). Believing Scripture is not ambiguous, Irenaeus opposes any method which stretches the meaning of Scripture beyond its clear intent.

12. Irenaeus, *Against Heresies*, 2.28.2 (*ANF* 1:399).

13. Williams believes that Irenaeus held a "three-legged stool" of "Scripture, Tradition and the church" (*Retrieving*, 90). Christopher A. Hall, "What Evangelicals and Liberals Can Learn from the Church Fathers," *JETS* 49/1 (2006): 88, believes that "tradition" is "more than the

which refers to either the act of handing something down or that which is handed down, indicates that when he speaks of *Christian* tradition he means the *transmission* and/or content of the original apostolic doctrine.[14] John Behr even believes that, for Irenaeus, "the content of tradition is nothing other than that which is also preserved in a written form, as Scripture — they are not two different sources"; Scripture and tradition are "identical" for Irenaeus.[15] In this regard, of the thirty-five instances of παράδοσις (or *traditio*) in *Against Heresies*, four instances refer to the gnostic tradition; one refers to a universal non-Christian tradition; nine refer to Christ's warnings regarding the tradition of the elders in Matt 15; and twenty-one refer to some form of Christian tradition, which Irenaeus relates specifically to the tradition of the apostles themselves.[16]

Some believe Irenaeus set up extrascriptural tradition as a rule to resolve disputes when he asks, "How should it be if the apostles themselves had not left us writings? Would it not be necessary, [in that case,] to follow the course of the tradition which they handed down to those to whom they did commit the Churches?"[17] Notice, however, that this question is set in the hypothetical absence of *written* Scriptures and appears to be aimed at the retrieval and defense of only the authentic teachings of the apostles.[18] Irenaeus argues that

---

apostolic canonical documents" including "the cluster of practices and beliefs contained in the Church's rule of faith (*regula fidei*)."

14. See Everett Ferguson, "*Paradosis* and *Traditio*: A Word Study," in *Tradition and the Rule of Faith in the Early Church*, ed. Ronnie J. Rombs and Alexander Y. Hwang (Washington, DC: Catholic University of America Press, 2010), 3-29. Cf. Einar Molland, "Irenaeus of Lugdunum and the Apostolic Succession," *JEH* 1/1 (1950): 15; Harvey, ed., *Libros Quinque*. Irenaeus, *Proof of the Apostolic Preaching*, trans. Joseph P. Smith, Ancient Christian Writers 16 (New York: Newman, 1952), 100, seemingly equates tradition with the apostolic witness when he describes "the tradition of the preaching, that is, the witness of the apostles."

15. Behr, "Word of God," 246. Irenaeus seems to view church tradition as the preservation of the same doctrine that is found in the Scriptures (coinherence/coincidence), leaving ambiguity regarding the relationship between Scripture and tradition. Philip J. Hefner, "Saint Irenaeus and the Hypothesis of Faith," *Dialog* 2 (1963): 303, notes, "At times, he [Irenaeus] speaks of the Scripture as part of the tradition, it contains the gospel which was handed on in various forms from Christ through the apostles to later generations within the church." André Benoit, "Ecriture et tradition chez Saint Irénée," *RHPR* 40/1 (1960): 36, believes that "Irenaeus is only interested in the problem of Tradition by relationship to his demonstration by Scripture. Tradition is only a secondary theme" (my translation).

16. Hernando, "Irenaeus," 33.

17. Irenaeus, *Against Heresies*, 3.4.1 (*ANF* 1:417).

18. Molland points out that because of this "controversy with the Gnostics Irenaeus is willing to meet them on their own basis by leaving the Scriptures out of consideration for a moment and arguing from tradition only" ("Irenaeus," 21; cf. Williams, *Retrieving*, 90).

the truth of the tradition received from "the prophets, the apostles, and all the disciples," which has been preserved by the church, is manifest in the unified beliefs of the Christian churches across widely diverse geographical regions, in direct contrast to Gnosticism.[19]

This tradition is unalterable. Even the "rulers in the Churches" are not to "teach doctrines different from these (for no one is greater than the Master)" or "inflict injury on the tradition." The "faith" is "ever one and the same" and even discourses on it of "great length" make no "addition to it."[20] It appears, then, that Irenaeus's high regard for "tradition" is directed at the unchanging teachings of the apostles via their unique relationship with the Master and that the authoritative "tradition" of which Irenaeus speaks is a closed "deposit" to which nothing could be added.

This appears to be reinforced in his statement:

> True knowledge is [that which consists in] the doctrine of the apostles, and the ancient constitution of the Church throughout all the world, and the distinctive manifestation of the body of Christ according to the successions of the bishops, by which they have handed down that Church which exists in every place, and has come even unto us, being guarded and preserved without any forging of Scriptures, by a very complete system of doctrine, and neither receiving addition nor [suffering] curtailment [in the truths which she believes]; and [it consists in] reading [the word of God] without falsification, and a lawful and diligent exposition in harmony with the Scriptures.[21]

Irenaeus thus claims that the genuine apostolic doctrine has been preserved in and by the Church, which has itself been handed down by the "succession of the bishops."

Irenaeus on Apostolic Succession

Irenaeus's much-noted treatment of "apostolic succession" appears within the context of argument over who possesses the genuinely apostolic tradition. The gnostics claimed to possess the legitimate but secret apostolic tradition.

---

19. Irenaeus, *Against Heresies*, 3.24.1 (*ANF* 1:458).
20. Irenaeus, *Against Heresies*, 1.10.2 (*ANF* 1:331).
21. Irenaeus, *Against Heresies*, 4.33.8 (*ANF* 1:508).

Arguing against this, Irenaeus presents evidence of the historical connection between the churches and the apostles themselves in order to demonstrate that the church, not the gnostics, possesses the authentic teachings of the apostles:[22]

> It is within the power of all, therefore, in every Church, who may wish to see the truth, to contemplate clearly the tradition of the apostles manifested throughout the whole world; and we are in a position to reckon up those who were by the apostles instituted bishops in the Churches, and [to demonstrate] the succession of these men to our own times; those who neither taught nor knew of anything like what these [heretics] rave about. For if the apostles had known hidden mysteries, which they were in the habit of imparting to 'the perfect' apart and privily from the rest, they would have delivered them especially to those to whom they were also committing the Churches themselves.[23]

Irenaeus further lays out an account of the brief succession of bishops from Peter and Paul at Rome to his time (ca. AD 180) in order to support his argument that, had any "secret" knowledge been transmitted by the apostles, it would have been entrusted to those whom the apostles appointed as church leaders.[24] However, the apostolic tradition is not secret but "manifested

---

22. Much earlier, Clement of Rome had "base[d] the rights of the officeholder on the idea that this office derives from the apostles, and is to be respected for that reason"; Hans von Campenhausen, *Ecclesiastical Authority and Spiritual Power in the Church of the First Three Centuries* (Peabody, MA: Hendrickson, 1997), 156. Cf. Tertullian's similar move in *Prescription Against Heretics*.

23. Irenaeus, *Against Heresies*, 3.3.1 (*ANF* 1:415).

24. Irenaeus selects the church of Rome because "it would be very tedious, in such a volume as this, to reckon up the successions of all the Churches." After noting that the apostolic faith "comes down to our time by means of the successions of the bishops," he adds, "it is a matter of necessity that every Church should agree with this Church, on account of its preeminent authority, that is, the faithful everywhere, inasmuch as the apostolical tradition has been preserved continuously by those [faithful men] who exist everywhere" (*Against Heresies*, 3.3.2 [*ANF* 1:415-16]). It is important to recognize that Irenaeus refers not just to the church at Rome, but also to those at Smyrna and at Ephesus. These all preserve the apostolic witness. The succession is a device to help prove the truth of the teachings of these churches (Irenaeus, *Against Heresies*, 3.3.4 [*ANF* 1:416]). Scholars disagree over whether the Latin phrase *hanc ecclesiam*, or "this church" that everyone must agree with (in 3.32), belongs with the preceding clause and refers to the "church of Rome" or to the following reference to the "faithful everywhere." For the traditional reading see Irenaeus, *Contre Les Hérésies*, Sources Chrétiennes (Paris: Cerf, 1969). For the non-Roman interpretation see Luise Abramowski, "Irenaeus, Adv Haer III 3,2: Ecclesia Romana and Omnis Ecclesia; and Ibid 3,3: Anacletus

throughout the whole world."[25] This, coupled with Irenaeus's view that apostolic tradition is unalterably "ever one and the same" such that even the highest leader cannot "teach doctrines different from these," appears to exclude any secret authoritative apostolic content.[26] However, does Irenaeus think that such successors nevertheless possess normative interpretive authority?

The Question of Interpretive Authority

Irenaeus states, "it is incumbent to obey the presbyters who are in the Church — those who, as I have shown, possess the succession from the apostles; those who, together with the succession of the episcopate, have received the certain gift of truth, according to the good pleasure of the Father."[27] Further, Irenaeus avers that "every word" shall "seem consistent to" those who "diligently read the Scriptures in company with those who are presbyters in the Church, among whom is the apostolic doctrine."[28] Does this suggest that presbyters possess normative interpretive authority?

---

of Rome," *JTS* 28 (1977): 101-4. Cf. Pierre Nautin, "Irénée, Adv haer, III 3,2: Eglise de Rome ou église universelle?" *RHR* 151 (1957): 37-78.

25. He adds, "But surely if Luke, who always preached in company with Paul, and is called by him 'the beloved,' and with him performed the work of an evangelist, and was entrusted to hand down to us a Gospel, learned nothing different from him (Paul), as has been pointed out from his words, how can these men [gnostics] who were never attached to Paul, boast that they have learned hidden and unspeakable mysteries?" (Irenaeus, *Against Heresies*, 3.14.1 [*ANF* 1:438]).

26. Irenaeus, *Against Heresies*, 1.10.2 (*ANF* 1:331). As Williams notes, "Irenaeus's appeal to the sufficiency of Tradition alone [if we had no written Scriptures], or to the vindication of apostolicity by tracing episcopal succession, were polemical tactics he used when pushed to the extreme" (*Retrieving*, 90). Irenaeus was not attempting to "forge a theory of ecclesiology" but to put forward "an authoritative means by which Christians could be sure of the truth of their salvation in the face of competing schemes" (*Retrieving*, 90).

27. Irenaeus, *Against Heresies*, 4.26.2 (*ANF* 1:497). Elsewhere, Irenaeus cautions against those "who desert the preaching of the Church" and thus "call in question the knowledge of the holy presbyters, not taking into consideration of how much greater consequence is a religious man, even in a private station, than a blasphemous and impudent sophist" (*Against Heresies*, 5.20.2 [*ANF* 1:548]).

28. Irenaeus, *Against Heresies*, 4.32.1 (*ANF* 1:506). Beyond this, Irenaeus refers in 4.26.2 to a "certain charism of truth" (*charisma veritatis certum*). As Francis A. Sullivan, *From Apostles to Bishops: The Development of the Episcopacy in the Early Church* (New York: The Newman Press, 2001), 150, notes, "Some have understood this as a 'charismatic gift' by which bishops would be assured of holding the truth. Others, though, think Irenaeus was describing the gospel truth itself as the *charisma certum* or 'assured gift,' which the successors of

While the presbyters "among whom is the apostolic doctrine" should be obeyed, Irenaeus indicates that ecclesial office alone does not guarantee orthodoxy or authority. Regarding some who "are believed to be presbyters by many" but are "puffed up with the pride of holding the chief seat, and work evil deeds in secret," he cautions, "from all such persons, therefore, it behoves us to keep aloof, but to adhere to those who, as I have already observed, do hold the doctrine of the apostles, and who, together with the order of priesthood (*presbyterii ordine*), display sound speech and blameless conduct for the confirmation and correction of others."[29]

As Molland notes, "the holders of this office cannot claim their authority merely because they have received their office lawfully and in this way are within the succession from the Apostles. They lose their authority when they become schismatics or heretics or display a conduct which deprives them of confidence."[30] The authority of the presbyter is thus contingent upon whether or not his doctrine and practice is in harmony with the authoritative apostolic teachings. As such, presbyters could not themselves be final or normative authorities, interpretive or otherwise.

Further, of Jesus's statement regarding the "traditions of the elders" that they made "void the word of God by reason of [their] tradition" (Matt 15:3), Irenaeus comments, "the tradition of the elders themselves, which they pretended to observe from the law, was contrary to the law given by Moses."[31] If the Levitical succession of priesthood did not preserve truth via their traditions, how could succession by itself be sufficient to ensure true doctrine?

Irenaeus was well aware that there could be disagreements even among genuine successors, in the midst of which he emphasized unity in spite of some disagreements, particularly where such disagreements were about matters he considered nonessential.[32] For example, Victor, bishop of Rome, admonished

---

the apostles were handing on in the church." Von Campenhausen contends that this refers to "not any special official 'charisma' but the traditional doctrine itself" (*Ecclesiastical Authority*, 172). He goes on to state that "Irenaeus does not contemplate a special sacramental 'character' of the episcopate, nor does he ever stress the authority of the bishops as opposed to that of the laity." For an enlightening study of the "charisma veritatis" that was linked to official appointment and the fact that Irenaeus taught that "the office in itself did not insure the trustworthiness of the official, whether presbyter or bishop," see Donald James Brash, "Pastoral Authority in the Churches of the First and Second Centuries" (PhD diss., Drew University, 1987), 190-201.

29. Irenaeus, *Against Heresies*, 4.26.3-4 (*ANF* 1:497).

30. Molland, "Irenaeus," 23.

31. Irenaeus, *Against Heresies*, 4.12.1 (*ANF* 1:475), cf. 4.9.3.

32. Denis Minns, *Irenaeus* (Washington, DC: Georgetown University Press, 1994), 11, notes

those who celebrated Easter on Passover, the fourteenth of Nisan, to relent and celebrate Easter on a Sunday or face the breaking of fellowship. Irenaeus, however, wrote to Victor claiming that "such uniformity was unnecessary; Victor's predecessors had not required it, nor should Victor."[33] In his letter, Irenaeus recounts an earlier disagreement between Polycarp (bishop of Smyrna) and Anicetus (bishop of Rome) wherein, despite differing traditions regarding the Eucharist, "Anicetus conceded to Polycarp" for the sake of unity.[34] Succession, it seems, did not guarantee correctness and, further, neither Polycarp not Irenaeus considered the bishop of Rome to be beyond correction.[35]

Apostolic "successors" apparently function here not as normative interpreters but as witnesses and transmitters of the genuine apostolic teachings. This also seems to be the case when Irenaeus recounts listening to Polycarp "speak of his familiar intercourse with John" the apostle, who, "having thus received from the eyewitnesses of the Word of life, would recount them all in harmony with the Scriptures."[36] In this regard, Irenaeus uses the evidence that the Church possesses the genuine apostolic *traditio* to point to the authority of Scripture itself: "Since, therefore, the tradition from the apostles does thus exist in the Church, and is permanent among us, let us revert to the Scriptural proof furnished by those apostles who did also write the Gospel."[37]

Here and elsewhere, Irenaeus does not seem to advance any authority to compete with that of Scripture, interpretively or otherwise. Accordingly, Hefner questions whether "Irenaeus subordinates Scripture to tradition as a hermeneutical key," as "some have held," believing "tradition as such possesses whatever interpretive authority it has by virtue of the Faith or 'hypothesis' which it transmits."[38]

---

that "there was a plurality and diversity of views even within communities which Irenaeus would have regarded as belonging to the authentic Church." Cf. Williams, *Evangelicals*, 23.

33. Sullivan, *From Apostles to Bishops*, 153. See Eusebius, *Ecclesiastical History*, 5.23-24.

34. Irenaeus, *Fragments*, 3 (*ANF* 1:569). Irenaeus thus suggests allowable diversity regarding ecclesial practice.

35. Williams rightly points out that "acknowledging such diversity within early Christianity is not antithetical to positing a central axis of faithful self-awareness that functioned within the unfolding of sacramental activities and intellectual exchange of living communities" (*Evangelicals*, 23).

36. Irenaeus, *Fragments*, 2 (*ANF* 1:568). Recall, also, that Polycarp (like others) distinguished his authority from that of the apostles (*Phil.* 3.2).

37. *Against Heresies*, 3.5.1 (*ANF* 1:417). Irenaeus does not here make any substantive arguments from tradition but establishes the church as the possessor of apostolic truth, then proceeds to exposit that truth from Scripture.

38. Hefner, "Saint Irenaeus," 306. Regarding the "hypothesis," see the discussion of the rule of faith below.

If this interpretation of Irenaeus is correct, what is to be made of his appeals to tradition and the rule of faith? The situation that Irenaeus was countering sheds significant light.

The Polemic Context

According to Irenaeus, the gnostics selectively used Scripture, supplemented these with their own writings, argued that many of the apostolic writings were incorrect or corrupted, and claimed that the true teachings of Christ resided in their secret oral tradition.[39] "When, however, they [the gnostics] are confuted from the Scriptures, they turn round and accuse these same Scriptures, as if they were not correct, nor of authority, and [assert] that they are ambiguous, and that the truth cannot be extracted from them by those who are ignorant of tradition. For [they allege] that the truth was not delivered by means of written documents, but *vivâ voce*."[40] Notice that Irenaeus depicts the gnostics' argument as the one promoting hermeneutical ambiguity and the consequent need for oral tradition.[41]

Further, "when we refer them to that tradition which originates from the apostles, which is preserved by means of the succession of presbyters in the Churches, they object to tradition, saying that they themselves are wiser not merely than the presbyters, but even than the apostles, because they have discovered the unadulterated truth."[42] As Irenaeus describes it, Gnosticism put forth a multifaceted attack, sometimes arguing from the accepted Scriptures, at other times arguing from other, nonapostolic writings, and at still other

39. Although Marcion's influence may have been exaggerated by some, he is a well-known example of one who selectively used the Scriptures claiming, among other things, that many of the NT books were corrupted by Judaizers. See Henry Chadwick, *The Early Church* (London: Penguin, 1993), 40.

40. Irenaeus, *Against Heresies*, 3.2.1 (*ANF* 1:415).

41. While Irenaeus's presentation of Gnosticism has been called into question, for our purposes it is sufficient to deal with Irenaeus's arguments within the context of his expressed views regarding his opponents. For an introduction to Gnosticism see Christoph Markschies, *Gnosis: An Introduction* (London: T&T Clark, 2003).

42. Irenaeus, *Against Heresies*, 3.2.2 (*ANF* 1:415). The gnostics had their own tradition of "secret" teachings and the Valentinians, at least, "claimed to be able to supplement the writings of the apostles with secret unwritten traditions and with several additional gospels" (Chadwick, *Early Church*, 81). They "boasted of possessing a secret tradition revealed mystically to them in parables by Christ," which "they alone are qualified to understand"; Hamilton Timothy, *The Early Christian Apologists and Greek Philosophy* (Assen: Van Gorcum, 1973), 24.

times appealing to a "secret" tradition that only they could interpret.[43] Again, it was the gnostics who first appealed to an extrascriptural tradition and interpretation as the true teaching. Irenaeus's argument seems to be a direct and proportionate response to this claim.

Irenaeus thus argued that, although the first generation of apostles was gone, there remained living witnesses (successors) that could testify that the Church possessed the teachings of the apostles, being only a couple of generations removed from them. An appeal to tradition and apostolic succession would not necessarily suffice to settle a disagreement within the church, as seen earlier, but is appropriate to counter gnostic claims of an alternative secret and normative tradition.

The Rule of Faith

In this context, Irenaeus appeals to the rule of faith: "Lest the like befall us, we must keep strictly, without deviation, the rule of faith, and carry out the commands of God."[44] He employs it specifically against his opponents' use and interpretation of Scripture, claiming that they use "their own peculiar assertions" and "disregard the order and the connection of the Scriptures" and thus incorrectly interpret Scripture.[45] He likens gnostic interpretation to taking a Homeric poem and rearranging its words and phrases to form a new non-Homeric story, or rearranging the mosaic pieces of a king's portrait into a poor representation of a dog or fox.[46] Conversely, the one

---

43. Chadwick adds, "The Valentinian appeal to unwritten tradition Irenaeus answered by appealing to the churches of apostolic foundation" (*Early Church*, 81). Von Campenhausen states, "Such an appeal in confirmation of one's own tradition corresponds exactly to the gnostic methods of proof against which it is used," though it is used to bolster "far better and more trustworthy evidence" in "favour of the true tradition" (*Ecclesiastical Authority*, 163).

44. Irenaeus, *Proof of the Apostolic Preaching*, 49. Irenaeus is the first extant writer to refer to the rule of faith, sometimes as the "canon of faith," the "rule of truth," the "hypothesis," etc. (Chadwick, *Early Church*, 45).

45. Irenaeus, *Against Heresies*, 1.8.1 (*ANF* 1:326).

46. Irenaeus, *Against Heresies*, 1.9.4; 1.8.1 (*ANF* 1:330, 326). Cf. Tertullian, *Prescription against Heretics*, 39. Treier explains, "Heretics such as the gnostics would arrange the verses of the Bible in a manner that set the New Testament against the Old Testament, and the God revealed in Jesus Christ against the God of Israel, thus, by analogy, making the mosaic resemble a dog or fox" (*Introducing Theological Interpretation*, 57).

who retains unchangeable in his heart the rule [κανών] of the truth which he received by means of baptism, will doubtless recognise the names, the expressions, and the parables taken from the Scriptures, but will by no means acknowledge the blasphemous use which these men make of them. For, though he will acknowledge the gems, he will certainly not receive the fox instead of the likeness of the king. But when he has restored every one of the expressions quoted to its proper position, and has fitted it to the body of the truth, he will lay bare, and prove to be without any foundation, the figment of these heretics.[47]

Irenaeus thus contends that the gnostics "imposed an alien pattern upon Scripture," arbitrarily rearranging pieces of Scripture into an entirely different picture than what Irenaeus sees as Scripture's unambiguous intent.[48] Conversely, he argues that, contra the gnostics' foreign hypothesis, Scripture should be interpreted in accordance with a hypothesis that encapsulates the scriptural story and intent. For him, "proofs [of the things which are] contained in the Scriptures cannot be shown except from the Scriptures themselves."[49] It may be, then, that for Irenaeus the rule of faith is not an addition to the teachings of Scripture but consists of Christian essentials distilled from Scripture.[50]

In a number of instances, Irenaeus refers to the rule. In one representative instance, Irenaeus writes:

47. Irenaeus, *Against Heresies*, 1.9.4 (*ANF* 1:330).

48. Hefner, "Saint Irenaeus," 301. Recall Irenaeus's earlier contention that "the entire Scriptures, the prophets, and the Gospels, can be clearly, unambiguously, and harmoniously understood by all" (*Against Heresies*, 2.27.2 [*ANF* 1:398]).

49. Irenaeus, *Against Heresies*, 3.12.9 (*ANF* 1:434).

50. Richard A. Norris, "Theology and Language in Irenaeus of Lyon," *AThR* 73/3 (1994): 291, 295, comments: "What marks this *hupothesis* out as the truthful one — as 'the rule of truth' — is the fact that it is not independently derived." Thus, Irenaeus "locate[s] his *hupothesis* or 'rule' on a level with what it immediately interprets: i.e., he wants a reliable study guide, and not a discourse which explains the catechesis in other terms." Kathryn Greene-McCreight, "Rule of Faith," in *Dictionary for Theological Interpretation of the Bible*, ed. Kevin J. Vanhoozer (Grand Rapids: Baker Academic, 2005), 703, comments: "In the ancient world, unassembled mosaics were shipped with the plan or key (hypothesis) according to which they were to be arranged. The Rule of Faith is like the key, he says, which explains how the Scriptures are to be arranged, to render the portrait of the King." However, in *Against Heresies* 1.8.1, Irenaeus refers to an *already assembled* image of a king that is taken apart and then rearranged by the gnostics into an image of a dog or fox.

The Church, though dispersed throughout the whole world, even to the ends of the earth, has received from the apostles and their disciples this faith: [She believes] in one God, the Father Almighty, Maker of heaven and earth, and the sea, and all things that are in them; and in one Christ Jesus, the Son of God, who became incarnate for our salvation; and in the Holy Spirit, who proclaimed through the prophets the dispensations of God, and the advents, and the birth from a virgin, and the passion, and the resurrection from the dead, and the ascension into heaven . . . and His [future] manifestation from heaven in the glory of the Father.[51]

However, it is not clear whether such summary statements themselves *are* the rule or a distillation of the rule. Such ambiguity is magnified by the fact that the statements are not identical.

Thus, just what the rule of faith consists of for Irenaeus is unclear. Many scholars recognize that it closely relates to Scripture, while offering various views on the nature of the relationship.[52] Of particular note here is the contention that it was likely an extracanonical hermeneutical arbiter because such was needed to counter the gnostics.[53] Regarding the similar situation that

---

51. Irenaeus, Against Heresies 1.10.1 (*ANF* 1:330).

52. For instance, Heinz Ohme, *Kanon ekklesiastikos: Die Bedeutung des altkirchlichen Kanonbegriffs* (Berlin: de Gruyter, 1998), 68, contends that for Irenaeus, Scripture can be called the κανὼν τῆς ἀληθείας and is understandable by itself. Robert M. Grant, *Irenaeus of Lyons* (New York: Routledge, 1996), 49, states that "Irenaeus' rule of faith or truth is the same as the *hypothesis* of the scriptures." Gérard Vallée, *A Study in Anti-Gnostic Polemics: Irenaeus, Hippolytus, and Epiphanius* (Waterloo, Ontario: Wilfrid Laurier University Press, 1981), 17, states of the rule that "taught by the Lord, delivered by the apostle; it is derived from scripture and also serves to expound scripture; it resides in the community through tradition; it is summarized in creedlike statements and can be expounded by reason." Williams contends that Irenaeus and Tertullian "believed the rule was the ratio or 'scope' of scriptural revelation." That is, it was "the purport of scriptural teaching" (*Retrieving*, 96). Joseph F. Mitros, "The Norm of Faith in the Patristic Age," in *Orthodoxy, Heresy, and Schism in Early Christianity*, ed. Everett Ferguson (New York: Garland, 1993), 89, believes that if asked what the final rule was, Irenaeus would say "the answer would be: both Scripture and tradition." Molland contends that "*regula veritas* and the tradition of the Church are not an addition to the contents of the Scriptures. The apostolic doctrine is found in the Scriptures, and this doctrine is preached by the Church" ("Irenaeus," 20).

53. For Williams, "Scripture was not sufficient alone for the refutation of heretical groups"; a hermeneutical arbiter was needed (*Retrieving*, 93). Jonathan J. Armstrong, "From the κανὼν τῆς ἀληθείας to the κανὼν τῶν γραφῶν: The Role of the Rule of Faith in the Formation of the New Testament Canon," in *Tradition and the Rule of Faith*, 40, believes that "the rule of faith served as a hermeneutical principle for Irenaeus, and therefore it would seem incorrect to

Tertullian faced, Williams avers that "because scriptural interpretation was so often at issue between catholics (or 'mainline' Christians) and various forms of gnosticism, it became clear to Tertullian that any appeal to the Bible alone for maintaining pure doctrine was impossible."[54] Williams maintains that "no aspersion is being cast on the eminence of Scripture, but it was necessary to bypass it for the authority of the church's historical teaching because Scripture was itself the point of contention."[55] That is, "taken strictly on its own, 'arguments about Scripture achieve nothing but a stomach-ache or a headache' since the Bible can be used to support any doctrine whatsoever."[56]

However, the authority of the church's teaching and its interpretation of Scripture *was also a point of contention.* As Williams himself notes, the gnostics "were busy proliferating a gospel Tradition based on a gnostic hermeneutic of Scripture — in effect, another structure of authority allegedly based on divine revelation."[57] If one could not effectively appeal to Scripture because it was a point of contention, presumably one also could not effectively appeal to church authority or interpretation since both were also points of contention.

Given this context, how could any extrascriptural rule of faith resolve the gnostic problem faced by Tertullian, Irenaeus, and others? After all, what would prevent *any* extrascriptural rule of faith or tradition from itself being misinterpreted and reorganized in a similar fashion to the gnostic misinterpretation of the Scriptures themselves (e.g., via an allegorical or mystical reading)?[58] To be sure, Scripture can be (and has been) treated like a wax nose. Yet why should one think that tradition itself, including a rule of faith, might also not be treated thus?

Whereas Irenaeus contends that the Scriptures are to be "the ground and pillar of our faith" and that "the entire Scriptures . . . can be clearly, unambiguously, and harmoniously understood by all," he depicts the gnostics as the

---

conclude that for Irenaeus the rule of faith represents the Scriptures themselves." According to Greene-McCreight, "the Rule of Faith functions as a hermeneutical key for the interpretation of Scripture" ("Rule of Faith," 703).

54. Williams, *Retrieving*, 91; cf. Tertullian, *Prescription against Heretics*, 19. For Tertullian, wherever "the true Christian rule and faith shall be, there will likewise be the true Scriptures and expositions thereof, and all the Christian traditions" (*Prescription against Heretics* 19 [*ANF* 3:251-52]).

55. Williams, *Retrieving*, 91.

56. Williams, *Retrieving*, 92. He adds: "Tradition could not be alleged as an authority in anything that was ruled out by Scripture" (*Retrieving*, 92).

57. Williams, *Retrieving*, 91. Further, he recognizes that the gnostics "agree with neither" Scripture or Tradition (*Retrieving*, 88).

58. Anything can be misinterpreted, especially if misinterpretation is intentional.

ones who claim the Scriptures are "ambiguous" and "that the truth cannot be extracted from them by those who are ignorant of tradition," and thus advance their secret tradition as the normative interpretation.[59] It is the gnostics who allege that "the truth was not delivered by means of written documents, but *vivâ voce*" and that one must appeal to extrascriptural tradition in order to understand the truth.[60] For Irenaeus, conversely, the "proofs [of the things which are] contained in the Scriptures cannot be shown except from the Scriptures themselves."[61]

Given this situation, it is difficult to see how an appeal to the church or any extracanonical rule of faith would be any more effective than Scripture itself in countering the gnostic claims. Any apologetic appeal to a rule of faith would require the prior identification of the genuinely apostolic *traditio*, submission to its authority, *and* interpretation of the rule itself.

Whatever might be said of Irenaeus's prescriptions in this regard, Irenaeus held a very high view of Scripture and used it extensively and authoritatively to refute Gnosticism. Irenaeus's *functionally* canonical use of Scripture complements his crucial affirmation that: (1) Scripture is not so interpretively ambiguous (when read on its own terms) as to leave room for a revolutionary conception such as that of Gnosticism; and (2) interpretation of Scripture should meet the standard of being in harmony with Scripture.

59. Irenaeus, *Against Heresies*, 3.1.1; 2.27.2; 3.2.1 (*ANF* 1:414, 398, 415). Accordingly, Williams comments, the "idea that there existed an authentic apostolic Tradition which was orally transmitted within the church yet never mentioned in Scripture or supported by the basic rule was unknown to the early church" (*Retrieving*, 96). R. P. C. Hanson, "The Church and Tradition in the Pre-Nicene Fathers," *SJT* 12 (1959): 27, contends that the "rule of faith" of Irenaeus, Tertullian, and Origen "cannot possibly be regarded as an extra-Scriptural tradition in any significant sense of the phrase" but "is Scriptural doctrine loosely summarized into articles, that is all."

60. Irenaeus, *Against Heresies*, 3.2.1 (*ANF* 1:415).

61. Irenaeus, *Against Heresies*, 3.12.9 (*ANF* 1:433). Thus, "insofar as Irenaeus maintains the Scriptures to be complete and comprehensible in and of themselves, it is clear that the canon of Scripture and the rule of faith are very closely associated for Irenaeus" (Armstrong, "From the κανὼν τῆς ἀληθείας," 40). Cf. Christoph Markschies, *Kaiserzeitliche christliche Theologie und ihre Institutionen: Prolegomena zu einer Geschichte der antiken christlichen Theologie* (Tübingen: Mohr Siebeck, 2009), 238.

WHICH RULE? WHOSE INTERPRETATION?

Identifying the Rule

Ambiguity regarding the proper identification and function of the rule of faith is not unique to Irenaeus or his interpreters. Historically and contemporarily, the rule of faith is notoriously difficult to define with precision. The historical data includes diversity regarding terminology, content, and function and is diversely interpreted by historians. Upon surveying late-nineteenth- to early-twentieth-century scholarship regarding the rule of faith in early Christian literature, Jonathan Armstrong notes that "scholars examining essentially the same textual evidence came to entirely contradictory conclusions" and since then, "opinions have become ever more diverse."[62]

A number of scholars have contended that the rule of faith "must be either the Scriptures or the main content of the Scriptures."[63] Beyond possible indications by Irenaeus, some point to Tertullian's statement that the "action" of "the Christ who is come must be examined by being placed side by side with the rule of the Scriptures [*scripturarum regulam*]."[64] Others highlight Origen's perhaps synonymous use of *regula scripturarum* (apparently of the Scriptures) and *regula christianae veritatis*.[65] These and other instances are by no means conclusive, however, as still other quotations might be read as suggesting that Scripture (or part thereof) is not the rule. Whatever else might be said, Armstrong concludes, the "rule of faith and the Scriptures were intimately associated from earliest times."[66]

Many scholars believe that, for early Christians, the "rule" consisted of an extracanonical formula or summary of doctrine. Some hold that "the rule of faith" was "the baptismal confession of the ancient church."[67] Others have con-

---

62. Armstrong, "From the κανὼν τῆς ἀληθείας," 43.

63. Valdemar Ammundsen, "The Rule of Truth in Irenaeus," *JTS* 13 (1911): 575. He points to Irenaeus, *Against Heresies*, 2.25.1; 2.27.1; 2.28.1 and concludes that "the Rule of Truth is the main, unambiguous content of the Scriptures" ("Rule," 576; cf. Ohme, *Kanon ekklesiastikos*, 68).

64. Tertullian, *Against the Jews*, 9 (*ANF* 3:164). Here, Tertullian "appears to equate the rule with the Scriptures" (Armstrong, "From the κανὼν τῆς ἀληθείας," 40).

65. *De Principiis* 5.3.3. See Henri de Lubac, *History and Spirit: The Understanding of Scripture according to Origen* (San Francisco: Ignatius, 2007), 68 n. 105.

66. Armstrong, "From the κανὼν τῆς ἀληθείας," 40. Armstrong himself believes that the canon or rule of truth (κανὼν τῆς ἀληθείας) was "a direct antecedent" to the biblical canon and "served as the primary standard of orthodoxy during the era preceding the final emergence" thereof ("From the κανὼν τῆς ἀληθείας," 47).

67. "From the κανὼν τῆς ἀληθείας," 32-33. Theodor Zahn put forward this view in 1881

tended that the frequent references to the rule in early Christian literature as an antiheresy polemic suggest that it should not be identified with the baptismal formula.[68] Bridging hypotheses regarding the rule's liturgical and polemical functions in various contexts, Kathryn Greene-McCreight views the rule of faith as "a confession of faith for public use in worship, in particular for use in baptism," which "outlines the authoritative articles of faith."[69]

Complicating things further, we possess only a few written specimens that *might* be examples of the rule or a distillation thereof, each of which is "uniquely worded."[70] Williams believes that "the dozen or so citations of the rule reveal that it was an elastic summary of the fundamental doctrines of Christianity" rather than a creed or fixed formula.[71] Thus, he maintains, "the canon or rule of faith was not as static or as fixed as the early apologists might have us believe. There was no one rule of faith but rules, and when placed together they show a fluidity of wording and style."[72] Thus, the rule should not "be confused with

---

and "deeply influenced subsequent scholarship" (Armstrong, "From the κανὼν τῆς ἀληθείας," 32). In this regard, some appeal to Tertullian's statement: "When entering the water, we make profession of the Christian faith in the words of its rule" (*The Shows*, 4 [*ANF* 3:81]; cf. Irenaeus, *Against Heresies*, 1.9.4).

68. See the discussion in Armstrong, "From the κανὼν τῆς ἀληθείας," 39.

69. Greene-McCreight, "Rule of Faith," 703; cf. Williams, *Retrieving*, 88; Williams, *Evangelicals*, 155-56.

70. Armstrong, "From the κανὼν τῆς ἀληθείας," 33. R. P. C. Hanson, *Tradition in the Early Church* (London: SCM, 1962), 93, suggests that the rule was "closely associated with Scripture, and often proved from Scripture" but not "in form precisely the same as Scripture" and "not a creed" or "a mere list of proof-texts." Rather, he considers it a subject-divided account "of the content of the preaching and teaching of the Church contemporary with the writer who mentions" it, perhaps explaining "why the rule never during this period quite becomes a fixed and stereotyped formula."

71. Williams, *Evangelicals*, 155; cf. Williams, *Retrieving*, 91. As such, it seems the rule was "adaptable to the given didactic or polemical circumstances at hand" (*Retrieving*, 92; cf. Williams, *Evangelicals*, 155, 156). In Williams's view, the rule was "something distinct but not separate from or in addition to the Bible" (*Retrieving*, 96). That is, the rule was "a condensed version of the Christian faith that existed alongside the Scripture as an extension of its teaching and as its chief hermeneutic," a "distillation of the Tradition" that was "deemed to be synonymous with the apostolic faith itself" (*Retrieving*, 98, 92). For J. Todd Billings, *The Word of God for the People of God: An Entryway to the Theological Interpretation of Scripture* (Grand Rapids: Eerdmans, 2010), 22, similarly, the rule of faith is "a distillation of core Christian teaching that can help unveil the inherent patterns of Scripture"; cf. Treier's view that "the Rule not only defines and defends parameters for proper interpretation but also derives from Scripture itself" (*Introducing Theological Interpretation*, 58). Yet if the rule is itself derived from Scripture, did not its very derivation from Scripture require interpretation without the distilled rule?

72. Williams, *Evangelicals*, 157. It is uncertain whether writers intended to convey the rule

the creeds, which scholars now believe had an interrelated but separate orig-ination in the life of the ancient church."[73] There appears to be, then, no fixed content of the rule of faith identifiable in early Christian literature, adding to the ambiguous nature of contemporary appeals to the rule of faith.

Consensually Selecting a Rule

What, then, might function as the contemporary rule of faith, which is pur-portedly essential to assuage hermeneutical diversity and achieve ortho-doxy? Williams advocates the "normative status of the patristic tradition represented in the Nicene faith" (i.e., consensual orthodoxy; see chapter 4).[74] In his view, "like the Rule of faith," the "great ecumenical creeds" were later "products of the life of the church and its faith as the very purport of Scripture," being "formulated and defended as an extension of biblical teaching."[75] Similarly, Thomas Oden adopts for contemporary theological method the Vincentian rule: "What has been believed everywhere, always, and by all," the doctrinal core of which is "recalled in the three prototype summaries of faith: the Apostles' Creed, the Nicene Creed, and the so-

---

itself in such distillations. Nevertheless, Williams notes that the "various manifestations con-tain evidence of the shared essentials of the church's tradition, revealing a fairly cohesive platform of doctrinal norms to which one could appeal" (*Evangelicals*, 157). Greene-McCreight likewise contends that the "understanding can be expressed in different words, but the content remains the same: a trinitarian creedal affirmation that later develops into the fixed forms like the Apostles' Creed and the Nicene Creed" ("Rule of Faith," 703).

73. Williams, *Retrieving*, 88. Williams takes the fourth- and fifth-century ecumenical creeds to "represent the activity of the early church more universally than the varied instances of the rule of faith" (Williams, *Evangelicals*, 65-66).

74. Williams, *Evangelicals*, 66. Compare the Eastern Orthodox view that "in scope and content the [Nicene-Constantinopolitan] Creed is but an official theological manifesto, a nor-mative doctrinal framework of the faith, based on the Bible and summing up the Church's binding teaching pertaining to God and salvation. Both the Creed and the theological tradition behind it constitute the substance of the Church's theology"; Theodore. G. Stylianopoulos, "Scripture and Tradition in the Church," in *The Cambridge Companion to Orthodox Christian Theology*, ed. Mary Cunningham and Elizabeth Theokritoff (Cambridge: Cambridge University Press, 2008), 28.

75. Williams, *Retrieving*, 99. He explains that after "the mid-third century we hear little more about the ongoing existence of the Rule as an oral body of truth distinguished from Scripture," and "any appeal to an oral-only tradition becomes strictly limited to matters of local church practice" (*Retrieving*, 99).

called Athanasian Creed (and their subsequent consensual confessions and interpretations)."[76]

It is difficult to see, however, why introducing a huge amount of additional material (five centuries of consensual tradition) that itself requires interpretation, and which is recognized to be less reliable than Scripture, should be expected to reduce hermeneutical diversity and lead to greater consensus, absent some other unifying factors. Far from resolving the problem of interpretive diversity, application of the Vincentian rule (like other ruled readings) itself requires interpretation at nearly every turn (e.g., whose interpretation of what is universal, of what is apostolic, of which councils, and which ecumenical exegetes).[77] Further, does not any appeal to consensus require interpretive decisions regarding *which* consensus and on *whose* interpretation?[78]

In this regard, some offer the contemporary Spirit-led community consensus as the standard, whereas others who agree that contemporary Christian theology should utilize a rule or ruled reading consisting of Christian tradition are not agreed upon which traditions should be utilized and in what manner. For example, Michael Allen and Scott Swain's call to "Reformed catholicity" appeals to Reformed and Lutheran confessions.[79] In this regard, Leithart asks:

---

76. Oden, *Rebirth*, 162, 31. Williams speaks of Oden's approach as a "'steady-state' theory of orthodoxy" that leaves "a number of interpretative problems which still need to be addressed" (*Retrieving*, 32-33). He further cautions that "the Vincentian canon of faith" includes both "continuity and change" and is not a "static equation of petrified orthodoxy" (*Retrieving*, 38; cf. Williams, *Evangelicals*, 77).

77. Questions arise not just regarding identifying which consensus of which group but which point of consensus (e.g., asceticism, slavery, or the role of women for instance).

78. Cf. George Lindbeck's appeal, *The Nature of Doctrine: Religion and Theology in a Postliberal Age*, 1st ed. (Philadelphia: Westminster Press, 1984), 99, 102, 100, to the "competent interpreters" who are "mainstream," "orthodox," "catholic," and "ecumenical." Do not most communities consider their own teachers to be at least competent and (intracommunally) orthodox?

79. Michael Allen and Scott R. Swain, *Reformed Catholicity: The Promise of Retrieval for Theology and Biblical Interpretation* (Grand Rapids: Baker, 2015), 96, argue "for a 'ruled reading' of Holy Scripture on the basis of Reformed theological and ecclesiological principles" and characterize "Reformed catholicity" as "an exercise in Reformed ressourcement," in "theological remembrance and retrieval" (cf. 64-68). This includes "a certain receptivity," particularly of the church's "normative creedal and confessional deliverances" (*Reformed Catholicity*, 18). Here, the "rule of faith" is a "normative" summary of biblical doctrine (*Reformed Catholicity*, 107). Cf. David Buschart and Kent D. Eilers, *Theology as Retrieval: Receiving the Past, Renewing the Church* (Downers Grove, IL: IVP Academic, 2015), 75-77; Keith A. Mathison, *The Shape of Sola Scriptura* (Moscow, ID: Canon, 2001), 275-79; Paul L. Gavrilyuk, "Scripture and the *Regula Fidei*: Two Interlocking Components of the Canonical Heritage," in *Canonical Theism: A Pro-*

"Doesn't the decision to erect specifically Protestant principles as "ancient landmarks" militate against the catholic aim of retrieving an early Christian consensus? Can Scripture unify if each church reads as seems right in its own eyes?"[80] The communitarian appeal to consensus, then, itself lacks consensus.

THE FUNCTIONALITY OF A COMMUNITARIAN RULE OF FAITH

We have seen that there is no fixed view regarding the content of the rule of faith identifiable in early Christian literature. Competent scholars have proposed widely diverging options for what the rule of faith was in the early church and for what it should be today. Given this ambiguity regarding the nature and content of the rule of faith, is appeal to an extracanonical rule or ruled reading viable and practicable, particularly as a functional interpretive key? How could an extracanonical rule *function* toward guarding (consensual) orthodoxy when there is no consensus on the rule itself?

Suppose, however, that all Christians universally agreed with Allen and Swain's characterization of the rule of faith as "any shorthand summary" of Christian faith, typically focused on the Trinity and the gospel story. Such "Church dogmas provide" a "divinely authorized interpretive key for unlocking the treasures of God's word."[81] First, how should one adjudicate between different summaries that fit such a description?[82] Second, even if there were

---

posal for *Theology and the Church*, ed. William J. Abraham, Jason E. Vickers, and Natalie B. Van Kirk (Grand Rapids: Eerdmans, 2008), 27-42.

80. Peter J. Leithart, "The Word and the Rule of Faith," *First Things* (2015): http://www.firstthings.com/web-exclusives/2015/01/the-word-and-the-rule-of-faith (accessed 1/30/15).

81. Allen and Swain, *Reformed Catholicity*, 108, 109, 113. Compare Treier's view of the rule of faith as "a Trinitarian summary of the structure of the Bible's story that is reflected in creeds such as the Apostles' and the Nicene" (*Introducing Theological Interpretation*, 34). Depictions of the rule of faith in this rather underdetermined fashion are not uncommon. Leithart wonders, however, "about the adequacy of a *precis* of the Bible that never mentions Abraham or Israel, skipping 75 percent of the book it's supposed to summarize" ("Word").

82. R. R. Reno, "Series Preface," in Jaroslav Pelikan, *Acts*, Brazos Theological Commentary on the Bible (Grand Rapids: Brazos, 2005), 13, 14, states that while "dogma clarifies rather than obscures," the "Nicene tradition does not provide a set formula for the solution of exegetical problems" and "the rule of faith cannot be limited to a specific set of words, sentences, and creeds. It is instead a pervasive habit of thought." For Allen and Swain, the "church can and has erred in its confession" such that "various expressions of the rule of faith are always subject to revision and reform in light of the clear teaching of Holy Scripture, which remains 'the supreme judge.'" Yet "the rule of faith is" not "open to endless revision" and "Church dogma" is "an ancient landmark that should not be moved" (*Reformed Catholicity*, 111-12). But if the rule

universal consensus on the precise wording of a singular shorthand summary (e.g., the Nicene Creed), how could any shorthand summary function as a unifying hermeneutical key? That is, how could a pithy summary arbitrate between a plethora of controversial theological issues, many of which could not be addressed in such a summary?

Williams points out that whereas "a Baptist" and "a Methodist" both "claim to believe what the Bible says," they do not "agree on what it is that the Bible says." This supports his claim that some "rule of faith or norm for interpretation is essential if orthodox faith is to be achieved."[83] However, could any plausibly ecumenical consensual rule adequately adjudicate between the different interpretations of Baptists and Methodists? It seems that any such summary might, at best, function as a delimitation of a broadly Christian reading.

Yet, what would prevent various Christians from divergently interpreting any rule or summary of Christian doctrine? Indeed, what is to be made of the fact that Tertullian could seemingly quote or summarize the rule and, yet, defend Montanism? In this regard, Williams describes Tertullian as an "eccentric controversialist" who took "certain freedoms" when he cited "the Rule" in "order to accommodate it to a polemical agenda or to his Montanism."[84] If one agrees with the majority of Christians that Montanism was heretical, does Tertullian's case itself not suggest the insufficiency of the rule of his day to fulfill the function as interpretive norm toward excluding heresy? Indeed, the second- and third-century use of the rule of faith provided "no consensus in the beginning of the fourth century" regarding central issues of the Trinity doctrine.[85] Further, as successful as the later ecumenical creeds were in many ways, they still have not removed significant hermeneutical diversity regarding the Trinity doctrine (see chapter 7).

The persistence of hermeneutical diversity is no fault of the Nicene Creed or any other summary.[86] *Any* rule of faith (or tradition more generally) would require interpretation and thus not be capable of removing significant herme-

---

is a "divinely authorized interpretive key," how could the rule be revised in light of Scripture and what are the limits of acceptable revision?

83. Williams, *Retrieving*, 99. Similarly, Greene-McCreight believes the rule "circumscribes a potential set of interpretations while disallowing others" ("Rule of Faith," 704).

84. Williams, *Retrieving*, 93.

85. Williams, *Evangelicals*, 66.

86. This does not detract from the importance and historical usefulness of such creeds and earlier "rules" of faith, which (among other things) testify that the diversity in early Christianity was not nearly as great as some would have us believe. See Andreas J. Köstenberger and Michael J. Kruger, *The Heresy of Orthodoxy* (Wheaton, IL: Crossway, 2010).

neutical diversity.[87] This recognition, however, undercuts the communitarian rationale, which posits the fact that Scripture may be variously interpreted as the impetus for retrieval of extracanonical tradition as hermeneutical arbiter in the first place. Yet, *any* rule of faith would be no more capable of self-interpretation than is the content of the biblical canon. One might appeal at this juncture to some *vivâ voce* as normative interpreter, perhaps an extracanonical individual or group.[88] However, since *all* communication requires interpretation, even direct speech can be variously interpreted (see chapters 6 and 7).

Perhaps, then, we should simply give up the quixotic quest for some "rule" or standard that will be sufficient to "guarantee" faithful interpretation and exclude what is deemed by some to be unacceptable hermeneutical diversity among self-professing Christians. Perhaps, alongside recognition of the demise of classical or strong foundationalism and the attendant futility of seeking an indubitable and neutral foundation, we might likewise recognize the futility of seeking any human source that might effectively resolve the "problem" of hermeneutical diversity.

This might open the way for a renewed recognition of the canon itself as rule of faith, which neither rests on the assumption of an indubitable, indefeasible, universal, neutral foundation nor expects the canon itself to be able to remove hermeneutical diversity, and (I will argue) is preferable even on the central tenets of communitarian approaches.

THE BIBLICAL CANON AS THE RULE OF FAITH

I believe the triune God is the foundation of doctrine and, indeed, of everything else. I recognize the canon, by virtue of its divine commission, as the

87. Consider the disagreement of Prosper of Aquitane, John Cassian, and Vincent of Lérins regarding the orthodoxy of Augustine's teaching on grace, with each holding different understandings of what constituted tradition (e.g., located in the pontiffs or the entire consensus). See Alexander Y. Hwang, "Prosper, Cassian, and Vincent: The Rule of Faith in the Augustinian Controversy," in *Tradition and the Rule of Faith*, 68-87.

88. This might consist of the Magisterium, the entire body of believers, or appeal to a Spirit-led community (see chapter 4). Mathison comments: "Unless we wish to fall into the same question-begging circular argumentation that Rome and Orthodoxy fall into, we cannot simply assert that our communion is the correct branch because our communion's interpretation of Scripture comes closest to our communion's interpretation of Scripture. Rome's aberrations must be measured against the ancient rule of faith to which she claims adherence" (*Shape of Sola Scriptura*, 334). Yet who does such measuring and on whose interpretation of the rule and the doctrines of various communities?

rule of faith. The canon, then, is the "supreme authority of Scripture in matters of doctrine" under God.[89]

The notion of "canon" in the limited sense of "rule" or "standard" appears often in Scripture, including the concept of canonically ruled understanding.[90] Perhaps the capstone OT statement appears in Isaiah 8:20, which suggests that the law and the testimony are to function as a rule or standard against which teachings are to be measured (cf. v. 16). In this regard, as has been seen in chapter 2, the OT writers are divinely commissioned to write down teachings and laws that are to function as their covenantal rule of faith and practice,[91] the NT writers treat the "Scriptures of the prophets" as a "rule" or "standard" (i.e., as "canonical" in the minimal sense),[92] and the apostles present their teachings as a divinely commissioned, and thus authoritative, rule or standard.[93] Further, the NT evinces the function of prophetic and apostolic teachings as a rule or standard (in the minimal sense) in the nascent Christian community. The early Christians were "continually devoting themselves to the apostles' teaching" (Acts 2:42; cf. Tit 3:8) and the Bereans were commended for testing teachings by comparison to the Scriptures (Acts 17:11; cf. 1 Thess 2:13).

In this vein, insofar as the canon is properly recognized as divinely commissioned covenantally prophetic and apostolic writings, it *is* the "rule" (κανών) of all faith and practice over which there can be no other normative rule, interpretive or otherwise.[94] Indeed, what could be a more trustworthy "canon" or "rule"?

This view of Scripture appears to cohere with the spirit of Irenaeus, wherein

---

89. Alister E. McGrath, "Engaging the Great Tradition: Evangelical Theology and the Role of Tradition," in *Evangelical Futures: A Conversation on Theological Method*, ed. John G. Stackhouse, Jr. (Grand Rapids: Baker, 2000), 151.

90. I mention only a few representative texts here, each of which warrant thorough exegetical and canonical investigation, which cannot be reproduced here.

91. See, e.g., Exod 17:14; Deut 6:4-8; 11:22; 31:9, 12; Josh 1:8; 22:5; 23:6; 1 Kgs 2:3; Neh 8:8-18; 9:3; Jer 30:2.

92. See, e.g., Rom 16:25-26. See also Matt 4:4-10; 11:10; 26:24; Mark 12:10; Luke 4:21; 10:26; 24:27, 44; John 7:42; 10:35; Acts 24:14; Rom 4:3; 2 Tim 3:16.

93. For instance, Paul exhorts, "Retain the standards of sound words which you have heard from me" (2 Tim 1:13; cf. Gal 6:16; 2 Thess 2:15; 3:14; Tit 1:9; 2 John 9-10; Jude 3). See, further, Gal 1:8-12; 2 Cor 11:2-4; 2 Thess 3:6; Rev 22:18.

94. Compare Kevin Vanhoozer's view, "The Voice and the Actor: A Dramatic Proposal about the Ministry and Minstrelsy of Theology," in *Evangelical Futures*, 81, that "the Scripture principle" sets "critical parameters," the "fence around the gospel" such that "the whole canonical dialogue; the dialogue of diverse biblical voices is itself the measuring rod for Christian theology."

the authority of *traditio* correlates directly with its (putative) apostolicity. Given the apostles' Christ-commissioned status and their direct relationship with him, the original apostolic faith of these unrepeatable witnesses trumps any successors. As Oden puts it, "Only a dozen apostolic votes of duly elected original eyewitnesses to revelation easily override a gazillion opinions of those who were not eyewitnesses to revelation."[95] Thus, insofar as the original teachings of the apostles can be ascertained, they are authoritative for those who would follow Jesus today and rule out any teachings that do not accord with them. Such a view not only appears to cohere with intracanonical principles (Isa 8:20) but this appears to have been the view of apostolicity held by early Christians (see chapter 3). The question, then, is where do we find the most trustworthy deposit of apostolic *traditio*?

A strong case can be made that the most accurate record of the genuinely apostolic *traditio* is found in the NT canon, which itself testifies to the authority of the OT canon. The meticulous preservation of NT writings is well-attested in scholarship and I am confident, along with the vast majority of Christians, that the NT Scriptures contain the accurate teachings of the apostles and of their teacher, Jesus.[96] Whereas it made sense for Irenaeus to appeal to the witness of successors only two generations removed from the apostles to ground the *traditio*, it seems to me that the extant textual evidence is itself the best available historical witness now that roughly two millennia have passed.

Moreover, it seems to me that the supposition of an extracanonical normative arbiter would not advance the concerns of Irenaeus or cohere with the canon's own claims (cf. Isa 8:20). If the biblical canon is correctly recognized as the unequaled rule of faith and practice, then it follows that Scripture should *function* as the norming norm (or rule of faith) that is not normed by anything else (*norma normans non normata*). Insofar as any extracanonical "norm" determines the understanding of Scripture, Scripture itself cannot *function* as the *norma normans* because it would already be interpretively normed by some other norm.

Far from being antitraditional or ahistorical, recognition of the canon

95. Oden, *Rebirth*, 167. On this line of thought, however, would not first-generation apostolic witness trump postapostolic consensus? If so, wouldn't the canon itself trump postapostolic consensus, especially given the fact that the common canonical core itself might enjoy the broadest "ecumenical" consensus?

96. For an overview of the transmission of the NT see Bruce M. Metzger, *The Text of the New Testament: Its Transmission, Corruption, and Restoration*, 3rd ed. (New York: Oxford University Press, 1992).

itself as the unequaled rule coheres with some robust Christian traditions. The sixteenth-century Formula of Concord teaches that "the only rule and norm, according to which all dogmas and all doctors ought to be esteemed and judged, is no other whatever than the prophetic and apostolic writings of both the Old and of the New Testament." All "other writings, whether of the fathers or the moderns, with whatever name they come, are in nowise to be equaled to the Holy Scriptures, but are all to be esteemed inferior to them."[97] Thus, "Holy Scripture alone is acknowledged as the [only] judge, norm, and rule, according to which, as by the [only] touchstone, all doctrines are to be examined and judged."[98] Similarly, the Westminster Confession of Faith lists the sixty-six-book canon as all "given by inspiration of God, to be the rule of faith and life."[99] Thus, the "infallible rule of interpretation of Scripture is the Scripture itself."[100]

Far earlier, Augustine states: "As regards our writings, which are not a rule of faith or practice, but only a help to edification, we may suppose that they contain some things falling short of the truth." He posits "a distinct boundary line separating all productions subsequent to apostolic times from the authoritative canonical books of the Old and New Testaments. The authority of these books has come down to us from the apostles through the successions of bishops and the extension of the Church, and, from a position of lofty supremacy, claims the submission of every faithful and pious mind." Thus, "in consequence of the distinctive peculiarity of the sacred writings, we are

---

97. The Formula of Concord, Epitome of the Articles I in Philip Schaff, ed., *The Creeds of Christendom* (New York: Harper & Brothers, 1882), 3:93-94.

98. The Formula of Concord, Epitome of the Articles III in Schaff, *Creeds*, 3:96. Note the formula's crucial distinction between "Scripture alone" as the "rule" and the Apostles', Nicene, and Athanasian Creeds. Whereas doctrine should conform to the latter, such creeds "do not possess the authority of a judge — for this dignity belongs to Holy Scripture alone; but merely give testimony to our religion," particularly how the "Scriptures have been understood and explained in the Church of God" (Epitome III in Schaff, *Creeds*, 3:97). If I understand these parts of the formula correctly, they cohere with the canonical approach offered here, which also recognizes that extracanonical writings might provide internal statements of faith and doctrine regarding how a community reads and interprets Scripture, and even set down such as requisites of membership. But they are not normative interpretive authorities which Scripture may not challenge. Rather, they are believed because they are viewed to be proper interpretations of Scripture rather than ruling the reading of Scripture itself.

99. Westminster Confession of Faith 1.2, in Schaff, *Creeds*, 3:602.

100. Westminster Confession of Faith 1.2, in Schaff, *Creeds*, 3:605. It goes on to mention the analogy of Scripture and "the Holy Spirit speaking in the Scripture" as the "Supreme Judge" by which all controversies, creeds, etc. "are to be examined" (Westminster Confession of Faith 1.2, in Schaff, *Creeds*, 3:605-6).

bound to receive as true whatever the canon shows to have been said by even one prophet, or apostle, or evangelist."[101] Whereas extracanonical books offer "merely a profitable study," one owes "unhesitating assent to nothing but the canonical Scriptures."[102] Thus, the "reasonings" of "Catholics" of "high reputation" are "not to be treated by us in the same way as the canonical Scriptures are treated. We are at liberty, without doing any violence to the respect which these men deserve, to condemn and reject anything in their writings" if they are found to be untrue. "I deal thus with the writings of others, and I wish my intelligent readers to deal thus with mine."[103]

Undoubtedly, one might marshal interpretations of these and other quotations from Augustine that oppose the canonical approach offered in this book.[104] Yet such passages raise critical questions regarding whether and to what extent Augustine himself would endorse Oden's appeal to consensual exegetes or other normative interpreters of the canon. In this and other regards, Augustine's writings themselves are subject to interpretation. Any purported interpretive arbiter must also be interpreted, *ad infinitum*.

Why not, then, give up the futile quest for an interpretive arbiter capable of resolving hermeneutical diversity and recognize the canon as the rule of faith? The practitioner of canonical *sola Scriptura* posits the canon itself as rule not because she naively thinks the canon requires no interpretation but because she does not believe *any* rule or normative interpreter (other than God) could actually eliminate hermeneutical diversity. According to this view, the canon functions as the standard against which all theological proposals are measured, without expecting to eliminate hermeneutical diversity.

In this regard, no reading of Scripture is deemed perfectly adequate and that is why the canon is never bypassed or replaced by any other standard. For those who believe the canon is infallible, then, it makes sense to reserve for it the unique role of rule in virtue of its being an infallibly reliable criterion

---

101. Augustine, *Against Faustus the Manichaean*, 11.5 (*NPNF* 4:180). Of course, Augustine favored the Apocrypha.

102. Augustine, *Against Faustus the Manichaean*, 11.8 (*NPNF* 4:183); *Nature and Grace*, 71 (*NPNF* 5:146). Notably, Augustine accuses the Manichees of arbitrary use of some Scriptures, asking, "Are you, then, the rule of truth?" (*Against Faustus the Manichaean*, 11.2 [*NPNF* 4:178]). See the further discussion of these statements and of similar statements by Cyril of Jerusalem and Basil of Caesarea noted in Armstrong, "From the κανὼν τῆς ἀληθείας," 46.

103. Augustine, *Letters*, 148.4.15 (*NPNF* 1:502). See also the discussion in chapter 3 of early Christians differentiating their authority from that of Scripture.

104. Notably, Heiko Oberman, *The Harvest of Medieval Theology* (Grand Rapids: Eerdmans, 1967), 370, views Irenaeus as condemning "extrascriptural tradition" but interprets Augustine as mentioning "an *authoritative* extrascriptural oral tradition" (emphasis his).

of theological truth claims, even though we must continually and intentionally recognize that our interpretation of it is not infallible (individually or collectively).

Some communitarians might believe that the canon functions in this manner within their theological method, albeit alongside an extracanonical interpretive norm. However, as much as I do not wish to exclude any who posit the canon as the unequaled rule of theology along these lines, the fundamental question is whether the canon itself is allowed to *function* as the unequaled norm not only formally (*de jure*) but in actual practice (*de facto*). Such function appears to be impossible alongside an extracanonical normative interpreter because Scripture would be ruled out *a priori* from challenging the normative interpreter.

That is, if the community (past or present) itself is or provides from within itself the normative interpretive authority, how could there be any prophetic voice that challenges the community consensus?[105] As Vanhoozer puts it, "we should resist locating interpretative authority in community consensus, for even believing communities, as we know from the Old Testament narratives, often get it badly wrong, and to locate authority in the community itself is to forgo the possibility of prophetic critique."[106] Thus, as McGrath contends, we must be careful to avoid "plac[ing] the authority of an interpreter of Scripture over that of Scripture itself. The priority of Scripture over all other sources and norms, including its interpreters, must be vigorously maintained." Otherwise, "it is not Scripture that is infallible but a specific interpretation of Scripture."[107]

Why, then, should any who view the Scriptures as infallible (as I do) appeal to any extracanonical authority or arbiter that lacks the quality of being infallibly inspired by the Holy Spirit?[108] Why not, instead, agree that the common canonical core itself is the rule that is not ruled (interpretively or otherwise) by any other? Even if one does not share belief in Scripture's infallibility, on Lindbeck's communitarian procedure of "draw[ing] a sample from as large a

---

105. Not all communitarian approaches suffer from this shortcoming to the same degree, of course.

106. Vanhoozer, "Voice," 80. Vanhoozer nevertheless believes the Vincentian rule is "not bad as a rule of thumb" ("Voice," 80).

107. McGrath, "Engaging," 151.

108. As Williams notes, the "patristic tradition was not and is not infallible. None of the creeds that originated from that age is inerrant. Even the staunchest defender of the contemporary relevance of patristic resources will admit that not everything the patristic fathers taught is true or even valuable" (*Evangelicals*, 78). Who, then, determines what is correct and incorrect in this tradition and on whose interpretation? If the canon is infallible but the tradition is not, why should the latter provide the normative interpretation of the former?

cross section, as wide a consensus, as is possible," what fares better than the common canonical core itself?[109] Even on communitarian grounds, that is, what has enjoyed a wider consensus? The common canonical core is by far the most attested; it has received the most attention by interpreters and enjoys nearly universal reverence and primacy among Christians. It appears, then, to be the most "consensually" recognized rule.

THE CANONICAL FOUNDATION

Some might worry that recognizing the canon as the rule of faith itself rests on a failed foundationalist epistemology. But while communitarian approaches rightly recognize the demise of *classical* or *strong* foundationalism, it does not follow from this that one should not posit any kind of theological foundation.

In this regard, Franke's contention that the question — "which has priority, Scripture or the church?" — is "ultimately unhelpful in that it rests on foundationalist understandings," appears to result from confusion regarding the meaning of "foundationalist."[110] As Grenz himself notes, "nearly every thinker is in some sense a foundationalist," at least in the broad sense of recognizing and operating on "the seemingly obvious observation that not all beliefs (or assertions) are on the same level; some beliefs (or assertions) anchor others" and "certain beliefs (or assertions) receive their support from other beliefs (or assertions) that are more 'basic' or 'foundational.'"[111] In other words, positing something upon which another point or body of knowledge rests does not require adherence to classical/modernistic foundationalism. Accordingly, adoption of the canon as theological anchor does not entail any commitment to classical or strong foundationalism and, indeed, does not require commitment to any particular theory of epistemic justification.

Notably, whereas in epistemological circles foundationalism simply "refers to a family of theories about what kinds of grounds constitute justification for belief" and entails no commitment to *classical* or *strong* foundationalism, the naked term "foundationalism" has often been used to refer to classical/

109. Lindbeck, *Nature of Doctrine*, 99.

110. John R. Franke, "Scripture, Tradition, and Authority: Reconstructing the Evangelical Conception of Sola Scriptura," in *Evangelicals & Scripture: Tradition, Authority, and Hermeneutics*, ed. Vincent Bacote, Laura C. Miguélez, and Dennis L. Okholm (Downers Grove, IL: InterVarsity, 2004), 201.

111. Stanley J. Grenz, "Articulating the Christian Belief-Mosaic: Theological Method after the Demise of Foundationalism," in *Evangelical Futures*, 110.

modernistic foundationalism.[112] However, "modest foundationalism," which does not posit "indubitability" or "certainty [as] a necessary condition of knowledge," is (in various forms) a prevalent position among "contemporary epistemologists."[113] Whether or not modest foundationalism is correct, the "failure of classical foundationalism" does not entail that "*no* form of foundationalism can succeed."[114] The point here is not to argue for any particular contemporary epistemological theory, all of which will likely either be rejected or significantly improved in the future, but to highlight that adopting the canon as *foundational* does not require naïve commitment to an already defeated conception of *classical* or *strong* foundationalism. Indeed, it may cohere with prevalent contemporary epistemological perspectives (though it does not hinge upon them).[115]

112. J. P. Moreland and Garrett DeWeese, "The Premature Report of Foundationalism's Demise," in *Reclaiming the Center: Confronting Evangelical Accommodation in Postmodern Times*, ed. Millard J. Erickson, Paul Kjoss Helseth, and Justin Taylor (Wheaton, IL: Crossway, 2004), 83. David K. Clark, "Relativism, Fideism & the Promise of Postliberalism," in *The Nature of Confession: Evangelicals & Postliberals in Conversation*, ed. Timothy R. Phillips and Dennis L. Okholm (Downers Grove, IL: InterVarsity, 1996), 120, correctly points out that much recent "discussion of these issues suffers from semantical problems," explaining that "opposing foundationalism *without giving nuanced qualification* as to the form of foundationalism one is rejecting will mislead all but unusually careful and honest readers" (emphasis his); cf. David K. Clark, *To Know and Love God* (Wheaton, IL: Crossway, 2003), 120-31. Potential confusion in this regard is exacerbated by the various (sometimes overlapping and sometimes contradictory) definitions and usages of terms such as antifoundationalism, nonfoundationalism, and postfoundationalism, which are often not clearly defined and (unsurprisingly) variously understood.

113. Moreland and DeWeese, "Premature Report," 83-84.

114. Moreland and DeWeese, "Premature Report," 84. Moreland and DeWeese contend that "the rejection of foundationalist epistemology is a serious mistake" and set forth a robust version of modest foundationalism ("Premature Report," 81). Cf. Stephen J. Wellum's contention, "Postconservatism, Biblical Authority, and Recent Proposals for Re-Doing Evangelical Theology: A Critical Analysis," in *Reclaiming the Center*, 186, that "to fail to distinguish a 'biblical foundationalism' from a classical, Enlightenment one is simply a mistake of gigantic proportions." In this regard, William Abraham's experience might be instructive. He describes himself as initially "deeply drawn to coherentism, in that it fitted with the attraction of cumulative case arguments and with the clear character of historical reasoning. However, it became all too clear over time that I was generalizing too quickly from the critical place of judgment in certain areas of inquiry and failing to distinguish between classical and moderate forms of foundationalism. I had confused the discovery of cumulative case arguments with coherentism and have since abandoned it as a global theory"; "The Emergence of Canonical Theism," in *Canonical Theism*, 145-46.

115. I do not mean to diminish the important work of epistemologists, in which I am quite interested, but I do mean to recognize the fallibility of epistemological theories. I am commit-

Whereas some are uneasy with edifice metaphors, such metaphors might be helpful and appropriate as long as they are not saddled with the baggage of classical or strong foundationalism. Jesus himself explicitly depicted his words as foundational, likening those who heed his words to the one who builds on the rock (Matt 7:24-26; cf. Luke 6:47-49). Further, Ephesians 2:19-20 describes "God's household" as "built on the foundation of the apostles and prophets, Christ Jesus Himself being the corner *stone*" (cf. 1 Cor 3:10-12). If the biblical canon is correctly recognized as the inscripturation of covenantal prophetic and apostolic testimony of Christ, it seems that the canon should be recognized as a divinely commissioned theological foundation.

Whereas edifice metaphors themselves are not problematic, the idea of a static, completed construction prior to the eschaton is. A canonical approach to systematic theology, however, does not aim to (and indeed cannot) arrive at a completed once-for-all system but always points back to, and requires further investigation of, the canon itself.

According to this view, the canon *is* the divinely commissioned rule of faith and therefore the norm of theology over and alongside which there can be no other (non-divine) norm (interpretive or otherwise). Such recognition of the canon as theological foundation rests on a decision of faith in Scripture but does not thereby give license to overconfidence in one's interpretation. On the contrary, canonically ruled reading recognizes that all human interpretations are fallible, requiring vigilance to guard against simplistic reading and private interpretation on the one hand and an overconfidence in the views of others on the other, humbly making use of the best available resources at one's disposal and doing so within nonisolationistic Christian community in dialogue with the wider academy.

This canonical approach to doing systematic theology will be laid out further in chapters 8–10 but, first, questions remain regarding whether canonical

---

ted to a minimal conception of critical realism, meaning that there is a real world independent of one's beliefs, about which one can have true knowledge, alongside the crucial recognition that human knowledge is fallible, theory-laden, and historically and culturally conditioned. Therefore, we can know but we know only in part (cf. 1 Cor 13:9-12) and thus should maintain humility regarding the extent and accuracy of our knowledge, without retreating from rigorous application of our God-given faculties toward knowing Him and our world as accurately as possible. This critical realism is itself open to and seeks correction from the canon insofar as it might reveal the nature of human knowledge. This commitment itself operates on the view that truth is that which God knows and God has sufficiently revealed theological knowledge via the canon.

sola Scriptura is defensible (chapter 6) and whether it is indeed preferable when applied to an issue such as the doctrine of the Trinity (chapter 7).

CONCLUSION

This chapter has engaged the complex issue of which rule of faith should be adopted for theology, approached by engaging the seminal view of Irenaeus and a survey of the various perspectives regarding what the rule of faith was in earliest Christianity and what it should be today. Whereas many communitarian approaches advocate that some extracanonical rule or ruled reading is essential to orthodoxy and assuaging unwanted hermeneutical diversity, there is considerable ambiguity and disagreement regarding which rule should be employed and on whose interpretation. In the latter regard, whatever rule one adopts would itself require interpretation and in the former regard, there is no more consensually recognized "rule" or standard than the common canonical core itself. One might, then, adopt the biblical canon as the rule of faith and foundation of theology without expecting that doing so will assuage hermeneutical diversity. The implications of such a move for canonical theological method will be taken up in the following chapters, beginning with a working model of canonical *sola Scriptura* in chapter 6.

CHAPTER 6

Sola Scriptura: reductio ad absurdum?

The *sola Scriptura* principle has long been the subject of criticism, including the oft-repeated claim that *sola Scriptura* inevitably reduces to absurdity as "self-referentially inconsistent," among other things.[1] Defenders of *sola Scriptura* are divided in how to understand the principle and, consequently, how to respond to this and other criticisms. Much criticism of *sola Scriptura* portrays the principle in a reductionist form (so-called solo *Scriptura*), where Scripture alone is the "rule" to be read in isolation, uninfluenced by any tradition, philosophy, or experience. Many defenders of *sola Scriptura* correctly reject reductionist *sola Scriptura* as impossible to implement and in other ways not viable. Instead they advocate a communitarian *sola Scriptura*, which contends that a normative extracanonical interpretive arbiter of Scripture must be adopted in order to produce and maintain sound Christian theology and mitigate the deleterious results of individualism and rampant hermeneutical diversity. Canonical theology, however, posits another option beyond reductionism on the one hand and communitarianism on the other, contending that reductionist *sola Scriptura* should be rejected yet *without* adopting a community-determined, extracanonical normative interpreter of Scripture.

This chapter outlines a working model of canonical *sola Scriptura*, carefully defining what the principle means and does not mean toward advancing the discussion beyond simplistic reductionism. In doing so, it addresses

---

1. Philip Blosser, "What Are the Philosophical and Practical Problems with Sola Scriptura?" in *Not by Scripture Alone: A Catholic Critique of the Protestant Doctrine of Sola Scriptura*, ed. Robert A. Sungenis (Santa Barbara: Queenship, 1997), 50.

some of the most important and prominent criticisms of *sola Scriptura*, including the charges that it: (1) is self-defeating — as itself unbiblical or the product of circular reasoning; (2) isolates Scripture to the exclusion of any other revelation, the proper use of reason and scholarship, and interpretive communities past and present; and (3) leads to subjectivism and hyperpluralism. Engagement with these (and related) criticisms leads to the conclusion that, whereas such criticisms effectively defeat reductionist *sola Scriptura*, none of them defeat the canonical *sola Scriptura* principle. Rather, the sufficiency and epistemological primacy of Scripture relative to theological doctrine is logically consistent and practicable toward canonical systematic theology.

A WORKING MODEL OF CANONICAL *SOLA SCRIPTURA*

Defining *Sola Scriptura*

The meaning of the phrase *sola Scriptura* varies considerably depending upon who is using it. Accordingly, it is necessary to begin with a working model that carefully defines what the principle means and does not mean.[2] Suppose, then, that canonical *sola Scriptura* means that: (1) Scripture is the uniquely infallible source of divine revelation that is available to contemporary humans collectively; (2) Scripture alone provides a sufficient and fully trustworthy basis of theology; and (3) Scripture is the uniquely authoritative and final norm of theological interpretation that norms all others.[3]

Four integral corollaries of canonical *sola Scriptura* guard against various misapplications: (1) *tota Scriptura* holds that all of Scripture together functions as the infallible source of revelation, sufficient basis of theology, and authoritative and final norm of theological interpretation (2 Tim 3:16; cf. Matt 4:4); (2) *analogia Scriptura* means that Scripture is internally coherent,

2. This working model is restricted to the meaning of *sola Scriptura* for theological method rather than the related issues of how *sola Scriptura* relates to ecclesial authority within the church (e.g., church discipline, intrachurch authority of clergy, etc.).

3. "Infallible" here means that Scripture is unfailingly accurate with regard to all that it affirms. Intrinsic to the infallibility of Scripture is the belief that divine revelation was accurately inscripturated via divine inspiration — "God-breathed" (cf. 2 Tim 3:16; 2 Pet 1:20-21). For a model of revelation–inspiration attentive to the doctrine and phenomena of Scripture, see Fernando Canale, *Back to Revelation–Inspiration: Searching for the Cognitive Foundation of Christian Theology in a Postmodern World* (Lanham, MD: University Press of America, 2001).

thus any Scriptural text should be understood in light of the biblical canon as a whole (Isa 8:20; Luke 24:27, 44-45); (3) Spiritual Things Are Spiritually Discerned (1 Cor 2:11-14) teaches that the Holy Spirit should be sought for illumination of all biblical interpretation; and (4) the primacy of Scripture recognizes that, although Scripture is the uniquely infallible source of revelation that is collectively available, it is not the only source of revelation (cf. Rom 1:18-23; 1 Cor 14:29).[4]

This canonical *sola Scriptura* approach, then, suggests that the canon *qua* canon is the rule of faith but neither excludes other factors nor implies that the canon requires no interpretation or should be subjected to private interpretation. In this way, canonical *sola Scriptura* should *not* be understood to mean that: (1) Scripture is the only source of knowledge; (2) Scripture excludes reason, requires no interpretation, or is subject to private interpretation; (3) interpretive communities and traditions past and present should be ignored or dismissed; or (4) all theological doctrine requires a direct biblical statement (or statements).[5]

First, Scripture is not the only source of knowledge generally or of revelation in particular.[6] Scripture itself recognizes general revelation (Rom 1:18-23), extracanonical prophecy (Acts 2:17; 1 Cor 14:29), and the apostolic tradition of the first generation (2 Thess 3:6).[7] However, whereas the Trinity is the source of all legitimate revelation, the canon of Scripture is the uniquely infallible medium of revelation collectively available today and is thus the

---

4. Each of these corollaries is canonically derived. The application of 2 Tim 3:16 as representative of *tota Scriptura* presupposes the correct identification of the scope of Scripture (i.e., canon) and suggests that, although the NT Scriptures were still in the process of writing when this verse was written, Paul's affirmation of existing Scripture in this instance lends itself to an application of all Scripture that can be correctly identified as such (cf. 1 Tim 5:18; 2 Pet 3:16, and the discussion in chapter 2).

5. I distinguish private interpretation, which purports to exclude all other factors and thus results in isolationism, from individual interpretation, which does not attempt to interpret Scripture in isolation from the community but recognizes that each individual's interpretation cannot be bypassed.

6. Accordingly, *sola Scriptura* does not suggest that only the Bible should be read but advocates the full development of one's mind in accordance with biblical principles, learning from and engaging the best scholarship without "uncritical absorption"; see Anthony N. S. Lane, "*Sola Scriptura*? Making Sense of a Post-Reformation Slogan," in *A Pathway into the Holy Scripture*, ed. P. E. Satterthwaite and David F. Wright (Grand Rapids: Eerdmans, 1994), 302.

7. Regarding general revelation, this approach holds that nature, properly understood, does not contradict Scripture (Ps 19:1-6). At the same time, post-Fall nature includes much that does not reveal God (Gen 3:17-18; Rom 8:20).

prime revelation by which any other purported source of theological data must be judged.[8]

Second, Scripture cannot even be read, much less properly interpreted, without reason. Scripture advocates the careful use of human reason (e.g., Isa 1:18; Acts 17:2; 18:4), though it is imperative to recognize that every person has cognitive shortcomings and is subject to presuppositions, idiosyncrasies, and blind spots. Thus, the sufficiency of Scripture with regard to theological doctrine does not entail the sufficiency of individual, or collective, interpretation of Scripture. This complements the third point: interpretive communities and traditions past and present (historical and contemporary theology) should be valued and respected. Although extracanonical voices must not *determine* doctrine, there is no place for "historical amnesia" as if one could interpret Scripture in a vacuum.[9]

Finally, *sola Scriptura* does not require a direct biblical statement for every point of doctrine or practice.[10] Theological doctrine should be derived from Scripture directly or by sound induction or deduction that discernibly and defensibly corresponds to the canon as a whole.[11] Scripture thus provides the authoritative data of theology and by Scripture all theological interpretation is to be tested. Whereas Scripture may be illuminated by extracanonical factors, it should never be subjected to or judged by any external standard.

---

8. God (Father, Son, and Spirit) is the living source of infallible revelation, from whom the authority of Scripture derives. Yet the Spirit does not supersede Scripture. Believers are to "test the spirits" (1 John 4:1) and thus the Spirit-inspired canon functions as the collectively available standard by which all other factors may be measured.

9. Craig D. Allert, "What Are We Trying to Conserve? Evangelicalism and *Sola Scriptura*," *EvQ* 76/4 (2004): 347.

10. As John Frame, "In Defense of Something Close to Biblicism: Reflections on *Sola Scriptura* and History in Theological Method," *WTJ* 59 (1997): 275, states, an idea "may be based on a general principle rather than a specific text" but should nevertheless be able to "be shown to be exemplified in particular texts."

11. According to this working model, ecclesial policy and practice has a wider range of acceptable derivation than theological doctrine, in consideration of the fact that Scripture is selective in that which it addresses. Whereas one should not be too quick to assume that Scripture does not lay down either a principle or a policy that applies to a specific matter of ecclesial practice, where one or both is absent the church has a degree of authority within the sphere of intrachurch policy and governance (1 Thess 5:12; Tit 1:5-9) and a duty to contextualize the practice and communication of the faith appropriately (without compromising biblically derived theological doctrine). Further, a given church's doctrinal statements may possess ministerial authority within a particular community but are themselves subject to disconfirmation by Scripture.

Descriptive vs. Prescriptive *Sola Scriptura*

Prescriptively, then, this model of *sola Scriptura* proposes that all extracanonical factors and presuppositions regarding doctrine should be intentionally and consciously judged by the uniquely authoritative canon of infallible Scripture, insofar as this is possible. Descriptively, however, it is crucial to recognize that every interpreter and interpretive community is influenced (for good or ill) by various factors and/or presuppositions including the use of reason, experiences, particular traditions, and others.[12] Yet in much the same way that the incapability of the human mind to fully understand God does not render theology void, the fact that one will not achieve a perfectly biblical theology should not deter from the effort to maximize correspondence to the canon.

Is *sola Scriptura*, then, unworkable in practice?[13] The inability to implement

---

12. As Kevin Vanhoozer, *The Drama of Doctrine: A Canonical-Linguistic Approach to Christian Theology* (Louisville: Westminster John Knox, 2005), 158, notes, "all rational thought presupposes a shared context of intellectual commitments and assumptions, in short, an intellectual tradition." Woodrow Whidden, "*Sola Scriptura*, Inerrantist Fundamentalism, and the Wesleyan Quadrilateral: Is 'No Creed but the Bible' a Workable Solution?" *Andrews University Seminary Studies* 35/2 (1997): 219-20, further comments that "all Christians are using tradition, reason, and experience as vigorous *formative* components in their conceptual development." He exhorts that this should be honestly recognized while maintaining the "conservative Protestant concern for the *normative* finality of biblical authority" ("*Sola Scriptura*," 217). The model of canonical *sola Scriptura* recognizes the influence of extracanonical factors descriptively but prescribes that, since each of these factors can positively or negatively affect doctrinal conclusions, the recognizable influences of each factor should be subjected to Scripture. Colin Brown, "Evangelical Tradition," *Evangel*, Spring 2007, 1-2, contends in this regard that, although postmodernism "suggests that it is impossible to escape from the consequences of our situatedness" such "that we are all victims of our interpretive communities," evangelicals "cannot be content with such a conclusion." We should recognize that our personalities and personal history "shape all that we are" and "how we respond" and "think and articulate" and that "we are all 'situated' by our fallenness" and thus "see through a glass darkly" while remaining "committed to *Sola Scriptura*" in fellowship with others but "skeptical of all human authorities . . . including my own" — because only "God and his Word is infallible."

13. See Christian Smith's criticism, *The Bible Made Impossible: Why Biblicism Is Not a Truly Evangelical Reading of Scripture* (Grand Rapids: Brazos, 2011), 3, of the "'biblicism' that pervades much of American evangelicalism," which he claims is "literally impossible, at least when attempted consistently on its own terms." The view he criticizes, however, is an extreme one. For example, canonical *sola Scriptura* does not suggest that Scripture "represents the totality of God's communication to and will for humanity" or that "any reasonably intelligent person can read" and correctly understand "the Bible in his or her own language" without taking into account the "literary, cultural, and historical contexts," among other extremes (Smith, *Bible Made Impossible*, 4-5).

sola Scriptura perfectly is not due to the concept itself. It is the result of the inescapable hermeneutical circle that is common to all interpretation. In order to subject other factors to Scripture, this hermeneutical circle must be recognized and intentionally addressed via a hermeneutic of suspicion wherein all identifiable relevant presuppositions and factors should be tabled for scrutiny, as far as possible, pending a thorough investigation of the canon as a whole, on the basis of which those presuppositions and factors might be accepted, rejected, or reformed. This process is ongoing, avoiding vicious circularity by proceeding in a hermeneutical spiral such that the interpreter attempts to subject ever more presuppositions and factors to the canonical data at each opportunity. This requires honest self-criticism and epistemic and interpretive humility and should be undertaken in dialogue with interpretive communities past and present. The interpreter must be willing to submit unreservedly to the claims of canon while recognizing that perfect interpretive correspondence to the canon is unattainable. As Lane puts it, while it is impossible (and not desirable) "to approach the Bible with a mind empty of all Christian tradition" or other presuppositions, "prior understanding is certainly open to correction."[14] Thus, all factors but Scripture alone are subject to a hermeneutic of suspicion, including one's own interpretation (cf. 2 Cor 10:5).

With this working model in mind, we now turn attention to three prominent criticisms: Is *sola Scriptura* (1) self-defeating, (2) isolationist, or (3) responsible for hyperpluralism?

IS *SOLA SCRIPTURA* SELF-DEFEATING?

Is *Sola Scriptura* Unbiblical?

Critics such as Robert Sungenis argue that any conception of *sola Scriptura* is invalid because "no statement in Scripture defines *sola scriptura*."[15] Peter Kreeft adds that *sola Scriptura* "is self-contradictory, for it says we should believe only Scripture, but Scripture never says this! If we believe only what Scripture teaches, we will not believe *sola scriptura*, for Scripture does not

---

14. Lane, *"Sola Scriptura?"* 310-11.
15. Robert A. Sungenis, "Point/Counterpoint: Protestant Objections and Catholic Answers," in *Not by Scripture Alone*, 212. Patrick Madrid, *"Sola Scriptura*: A Blueprint for Anarchy," in *Not by Scripture Alone*, 19, likewise claims that the "fatal flaw of *sola scriptura* is that it is not taught in Scripture" and "the Bible contains no evidence to support it."

teach *sola scriptura*."[16] Does the principle of *sola Scriptura* itself derive from a *sola Scriptura* approach?

The words *sola Scriptura* are not found in Scripture. As noted earlier, however, canonical *sola Scriptura* does not require that all theological beliefs must be stated in Scripture verbatim. As the Westminster Confession of Faith puts it, doctrine must be "either expressly set down in Scripture, or by good and necessary consequence may be deduced from Scripture."[17] In order for this objection to be defeated, then, one need only show that canonical *sola Scriptura* is properly derived from Scripture itself.[18]

That Scripture claims doctrinal authority is generally accepted by Christians and demonstrable via texts such as 2 Tim 3:16: "All Scripture is inspired by God and profitable for teaching, for reproof, for correction, for training in righteousness" (cf. 2 Pet 1:20-21; 1 Thess 2:13). Scripture further proclaims its own trustworthiness (infallibility) in statements such as "the Scripture cannot be broken" (John 10:35). The dispute among Christians, however, resides primarily with regard to the *sola* of *sola Scriptura*.

Since canonical *sola Scriptura* departs from the reductionist view of *sola* that excludes all other factors, all that is necessary to undergird the *sola* of the canonical approach is evidence that Scripture claims unique authority over all other factors. Here the three categories that encompass other possible sources of theology — reason, experience, and tradition — are not excluded as factors but are explicitly subordinated to the unique authority of Scripture.[19]

First, while humans should make careful and appropriate use of reason and experience (cf. Isa 1:18), the reliability of human reason and experience is

16. Peter Kreeft, *Fundamentals of the Faith* (San Francisco: Ignatius, 1988), 275. D. H. Williams, "The Search for *Sola Scriptura* in the Early Church," *Int* 52/4 (1998): 364, concurs, "it is too often forgotten that the teaching of *sola scriptura* is itself not in the Bible."

17. Westminster Confession of Faith, 1.6. As Alister McGrath, *Reformation Thought: An Introduction*, 3rd ed. (Malden, MA: Blackwell, 2001), 101, explains, the mainline reformers endorsed those beliefs that were "explicitly stated in the Bible" or those that "may reasonably be inferred from those that are thus stated." Thus, appeals to the need for "extrabiblical theological concepts" like the Trinity or creation *ex nihilo* miss the point (e.g., Smith, *Bible Made Impossible*, 82), since these concepts, though expressed by extracanonical terms, describe canonical concepts (on the former, see chapter 7). The inclusion of careful deductions and inferences from Scripture is a practice testified to in the intracanonical use of Scripture.

18. While by no means exhaustive, the few examples here suggest that the minimal form of this principle is indeed properly derived from Scripture.

19. Scripture suggests that extracanonical prophecy, which falls under a broader category of special revelation rather than fitting neatly into the three categories here, also should be tested by (among other things) Scripture (Isa 8:20; cf. 1 John 4:1; 1 Cor 14:37-38; 1 Thess 5:19-21).

explicitly undermined throughout the Bible, especially in light of the Fall (Ps 14:1-3; Rom 1:21; 3:11). To take just a few of the many examples: 1 Cor 3:19-20 contends that "the wisdom of this world is foolishness before God" and "the Lord knows the reasonings of the wise, that they are useless" (cf. 1 Cor 2:1-16; 1 Tim 6:20).[20] Proverbs 28:26 adds, "He who trusts in his own heart is a fool" (cf. Job 11:7; Prov 14:12; Isa 55:8-9; Rom 11:3; 1 Cor 2:16). Human experience is thus to be tested by God's word (Matt 24:24-26; cf. 2 Cor 11:3-4; Gal 1:8) because, as Jeremiah 17:9 explains, "the heart is more deceitful than all else and is desperately sick; who can understand it?" These and other texts prescribe that human reason and experience are to be subject to Scripture because they are fallible and, thus, at least partially unreliable.[21]

With regard to religious authority, Christ criticizes those who "invalidated the word of God" and transgressed "the commandment of God for the sake of your tradition" (Matt 15:6, 3; cf. Mark 7:5-13; Col 2:8).[22] Peter's response to the high priest's command (religious authority) is equally clear: "We must obey God rather than men" (Acts 5:29), the apostolic message itself being not merely "the word of men" but "the word of God" (1 Thess 2:13).[23] Here and elsewhere, the traditions of the contemporary religious community, by which the OT was written and to whom it was entrusted for centuries, are explicitly challenged and subordinated to the word of God. These and other biblical texts do not reject all tradition (cf. 2 Thess 3:6) but they do suggest that Scripture is the sole arbiter of doctrinal orthodoxy.

Expecting the writers of Scripture to state *sola Scriptura* more explicitly than they have fails to properly recognize the historical context. It would have been premature for a biblical author to proclaim, or appeal to, Scripture alone in so many words because, while the canon remained in process, the inspired spoken word of legitimate, divinely commissioned prophets and apostles was likewise authoritative, some of which was yet to be inscripturated.[24] The authors of the NT were thus situated in a unique, unrepeatable era, writing as

---

20. This does not exclude reason but requires that human reason be subjected to the wisdom of God and illuminated by the Holy Spirit (cf. 1 Cor 2:1-16).

21. See also Rom 1:21; 2 Cor 3:14-15; 4:4; Rom 1:26-27; Gal 5:24; 1 Tim 3:2-4.

22. Christ here challenges not only the content of the particular tradition but also the interpretive authority of community leaders.

23. This text applies not only to the oral statements of apostles but to the NT itself insofar as it reliably inscripturates apostolic testimony.

24. Even the prophets and apostles were not infallible in everything they said and did (2 Sam 7:3-5; Gal 2:11). Accordingly, even recognized inspired apostles were to have their teachings tested against verified past revelation (cf. Gal 1:8).

firsthand apostolic witnesses to the incarnate and risen Christ, who was himself the ultimate revelation of God and promised the apostles that the Spirit "will teach you all things, and bring to your remembrance all that I said to you" (John 14:26) and "guide you into all truth" (John 16:13; cf. 8:31; Jude 3).[25]

Notice, however, that the apostles expected their message to be ratified or rejected on the basis of existing Scripture. The Bereans confirmed "the word of God" that was "proclaimed by Paul" by "examining the Scriptures daily to see whether these things were so" (Acts 17:11, 13), thus exemplifying the apostolic principle, "test the spirits to see whether they are from God, because many false prophets have gone into the world" (1 John 4:1). Isaiah 8:20 had set the standard for such testing before: "To the law and to the testimony! If they do not speak according to this word, it is because they have no dawn." Paul likewise exhorts the Corinthians "not to exceed what is written" (1 Cor 4:6; cf. 14:37). This principle of appeal to the final authority of existing Scripture was implemented repeatedly by Christ and others in statements such as those that begin with the words "it is written" (Matt 4:4-10; cf. Acts 23:5; Rom 3:4, 10).[26] Thus, the contemporary proclamation of even those whose writings would become Scripture was to first be tested by existing Scripture (John 5:45-47; 17:8; cf. Matt 22:29).

As such, if the canon has been correctly recognized as genuinely prophetic/apostolic, the burden of proof is on those who wish to assert an additional source or sources in twenty-first-century practice and beyond. Consider, in this regard, Paul's prescription that "even if we, or an angel from heaven, should preach to you a gospel contrary to what we have preached to you, he is to be accursed!" (Gal 1:8; cf. 2 Cor 11:2-4). Likewise, John exhorts: "If anyone comes to you and does not bring this teaching, do not receive him into your house, and do not give him a greeting" (2 John 10; cf. Rev 22:18). Application of these instructions in the twenty-first century requires appeal to the NT writings. In other words, to implement these exhortations properly today is to apply *sola Scriptura* as the test of any gospel proclamation. In all this, canonical *sola Scriptura* is properly derived from Scripture itself.

---

25. These promises of the Spirit testify to the full sufficiency of Scripture.

26. Inner-biblical interpretation is itself key since Satan himself can quote Scripture and preface it with "it is written" (Luke 4:10-11) while twisting its meaning. Christ answers Satan's misuse, however, by appealing to other Scriptures (Luke 4:12), exemplifying *analogia Scriptura*.

Is *Sola Scriptura* Viciously Circular?

Is *sola Scriptura*, then, a product of circular reasoning? To be sure, the one who advocates *sola Scriptura* has already come to a decision of faith in Scripture. However, it is widely recognized that every epistemological starting point requires a decision to believe something.[27] It is crucial to recognize, then, that the charge of circularity is not a problem for canonical *sola Scriptura* specifically but a universal epistemological issue.[28] The one who claims that tradition is needed to get beyond the circularity of canonical *sola Scriptura* merely adds another epistemological circle, since tradition itself would require some ground for its acceptance. However, it appears that any basis or authority that might be appealed to in order to ground tradition could also be appealed to in order to ground Scripture directly.[29] Ultimately, however, canonical *sola Scriptura* proclaims that the canon is self-authenticating (cf. John 17:17) while at the same time recognizing the appropriateness of taking into account the wider evidence in favor of Scripture.[30] Accordingly, there is no logical fallacy in choosing to accept Scripture's own claims and thus adopting Scripture as the basis of theology.

What about the Canon?

Sola Scriptura is inextricably linked to questions about the nature and scope of the biblical canon. Blosser contends that "*sola scriptura* is self-referentially

27. As John Frame states, "circularity of a kind is inevitable when we are seeking to justify our ultimate standard of truth and falsity" ("In Defense," 272). Blosser is aware of this kind of response but inexplicably rejects it, stating: "'The Bible means what the Church says it means' is not circular" in the way that *sola Scriptura* is "since the Church's interpretation is not closed off from history, but empirically testable for fidelity and coherence both against Scripture and other traditions of the Church." ("What Are the Philosophical and Practical Problems," 59-60).

28. Cf. Oden's Vincentian rule, which posits consensus while also purportedly derived from consensus.

29. The Scriptures are ratified by Christ directly so there is no "tradition" necessary to ground Scripture save the first-century apostolic *traditio* itself, which has been reliably inscripturated and preserved.

30. Because Scripture is afforded theological primacy by divine commission alone, there is no witness adequate to ground this primacy except God, whom we come to know through the Scriptures. Requiring further grounding goes beyond what is possible or necessary for any epistemological system. This is not to say that all beliefs are equally warranted. In this regard, consider the work of Alvin Plantinga, *Warranted Christian Belief* (New York: Oxford University Press, 2000).

inconsistent because the Bible contains no inspired index of its own contents and cannot even be identified as a divine revelation except on extrabiblical grounds of tradition — but in violation of the *sola scriptura* principle."[31] This criticism rests on the assumption that the biblical canon is, as Robert Jenson puts it, "a dogmatic decision of the church. If we will allow no final authority to churchly dogma, or to the organs by which the church can enunciate dogma, there can be no canon of scripture. The slogan *sola scriptura*, if by that is meant 'apart from creed, teaching office, or authoritative liturgy,' is an oxymoron."[32] Thus, one "can't say with any authority exactly what Scripture is" without appealing to tradition or ecclesial authority.[33]

However, canonical *sola Scriptura* operates on the intrinsic canon approach, wherein God *determines* the canon, which is thereafter *recognized* by humans.[34] Since *sola Scriptura* affirms general revelation and does not reject the use of history or other tools for general knowledge, there is no problem with affirming the functional necessity that some community preserve and recognize the canon or with utilizing historical information to recognize the canon's proper contents.[35] Notably, the criteria by which one might recognize canonicity are

31. Blosser, "What Are the Philosophical and Practical Problems," 51. Likewise Madrid comments that there is "'no inspired table of contents' in Scripture" but "that information comes to us from outside Scripture" ("*Sola Scriptura*," 22). Cf. Gavin D'Costa, "Revelation, Scripture and Tradition: Some Comments on John Webster's Conception of 'Holy Scripture,'" *International Journal of Systematic Theology* 6/4 (2004): 346-50.

32. Robert W. Jenson, *Systematic Theology*, 2 vols. (New York: Oxford University Press, 1997), 1:27-28.

33. See the discussion in Keith A. Mathison, *The Shape of Sola Scriptura* (Moscow, ID: Canon, 2001), 314-15.

34. Kreeft argues: "The Church (the apostles) wrote Scripture" and "the bishops of the Church, decided on the canon. . . . If Scripture is infallible, then its cause, the Church, must be infallible" (*Fundamentals*, 275). However, according to an intrinsic canon perspective, God is the cause of Scripture (cf. 2 Tim 3:16). Mathison further points out that if one "asserts that an infallible New Testament requires an infallible Church" then "an infallible Old Testament requires an infallible Israel" (cf. Rom 3:2), contra the Church's claims (*Shape*, 294).

35. The complex history of canon recognition, which was necessary to the functional (but not intrinsic) authority of the canon, in no way contradicts canonical *sola Scriptura* because, on the intrinsic canon approach, the books of Scripture do not become "canon" when they are recognized but are intrinsically canonical from the time of their writing. Thus, claims like that of Allert that, since "the Bible could not function as the rule of faith for Tertullian 'because he has no 'Bible' to which he may appeal" (which, Allert admits, assumes that Tertullian "did not know of a closed canon") only present an issue if one assumes that the canon does not exist until its scope is determined by the church ("What Are We Trying to Conserve?" 344). That it necessarily takes time for humans to recognize the canonical writings and for them to be widely available need not subvert their intrinsic canonicity.

apparent in Scripture itself (e.g., propheticity/apostolicity, 2 Pet 3:1-2; cf. Luke 11:49; Eph 2:20).[36] Ultimately, the canonical books are self-authenticating and authoritative because of God's action, whether it is recognized as such or not.[37]

IS *SOLA SCRIPTURA* ISOLATIONIST?

This brings us to the second prominent question: Does *sola Scriptura* isolate Scripture to the exclusion of other revelation, experience, the proper use of reason and scholarship, or interpretive communities past and present? Canonical *sola Scriptura* does not advocate isolationism or anti-intellectualism but contends that the very best scholarship in all areas should be engaged and appropriately utilized. As previously mentioned, this approach does not exclude reason or experience but also does not uncritically admit either as adequate sources or arbiters of theology due to their fallibility (cf. Jer 17:9). When Scripture appears to conflict with reason or experience, the one committed to *sola Scriptura* will question one's own reasoning or experience rather than Scripture (cf. Rom 11:33). In this way, experience, reason, and interpretive communities (past and present) are each intentionally subordinated to the unique epistemological primacy and authority of the canon. However, the role of tradition warrants further elaboration.

The Role of Tradition

Many Christians advocate an authoritative doctrinal role for the church or tradition (of various degrees), some viewing one or both of these as integral to a proper understanding of *sola Scriptura*.[38] These communitarian *sola Scriptura*

36. Likewise, the need for consistency with past revelation is apparent in Isa 8:20 (cf. Deut 13:1-5) and self-authentication to those willing to believe appears in John 7:17 (cf. 10:4-5). See chapter 2.

37. As Geoffrey Bromiley, "The Church Fathers and Holy Scripture," in *Scripture and Truth*, ed. D. A. Carson and John D. Woodbridge (Grand Rapids: Zondervan, 1983), 203, states, "the early church had to deal with the fact of a New Testament as well as an Old Testament canon because it had no real power — and it realized that it had no real power — either to make or to unmake the canon. Irrespective of its judgment, the writings that came down in and to it were either apostolic or not."

38. See chapters 1 and 4. In this regard, Richard Bauckham, "Tradition in Relation to Scripture and Reason," in *Scripture, Tradition, and Reason: A Study in the Criteria of Christian Doctrine*, ed. Richard Bauckham and Benjamin Drewery (New York: T&T Clark, 2004), 125,

views, however, must adequately address two questions: (1) which tradition or church, and (2) whose interpretation of that tradition or church teaching?

An advocate of a communitarian position might answer the former question by appealing to the "universal" Christian tradition of the first few centuries as the valid guide and arbiter of biblical interpretation.[39] However, even a cursory reading of the church fathers shows that there was no monolithic, universal Christian tradition, raising the question: which of the traditions of the first few centuries of Christianity?[40]

One cannot coherently adopt all the traditions that labeled themselves as Christian because some are mutually exclusive. Further, it is inadequate to claim that we should accept only the teachings of "true" Christians, for this assumes that we already know what true Christianity is, the necessary identification of which is precisely the rationale for appealing to tradition or community as a source or arbiter of interpretation in the first place.

Perhaps appeal to the ecumenical creeds could provide the necessary delimitation of acceptable tradition or ecclesial communities.[41] However, why

states, "there has been a narrowing of the rift between Catholic and Protestant views of the relationship between Scripture and tradition, such that some scholars have spoken of an 'ecumenical convergence.'"

39. In Vincentian fashion, D. H. Williams, *Tradition, Scripture, and Interpretation* (Grand Rapids: Baker Academic, 2006), 24, contends, "In real and tangible ways," the patristic "period has functioned like a 'canon' of Christian theology" such that "the apostolic and patristic legacies are foundational to the Christian faith in *normative* ways that no other period of the church's history can claim." Mark Saucy, "Canon as Tradition: The New Covenant and the Hermeneutical Question," *Them* 36/2 (2011): 235-36, responds: "Privileging the early patristic tradition as some kind of 'hermeneutical ground zero' or as *necessary* for evangelicals to stay orthodox" actually "neglects the hermeneutical norm the canonical writers employed in the new-covenant Story." The "canonical script" was the apostles' "hermeneutical lens for the gospel that founded the church" and "the Protestant Reformers intended under the maxim of *sola scriptura*."

40. As Anthony N. S. Lane, "Scripture, Tradition and Church: An Historical Survey," *VE* 9 (1975): 46, explains, "it became clear that tradition had changed over the years and it seemed to have been plainly erroneous at times." D. H. Williams, *Evangelicals and Tradition: The Formative Influence of the Early Church* (Grand Rapids: Baker Academic, 2005), 62, notes that what he describes as "the canonical tradition of the patristic church" is like "a coat of many colors. It has different shades and hues that portray a composite, sometimes contrasting, garment of faith."

41. Mathison, for instance, advocates a communitarian *sola Scriptura* view of Tradition I wherein "the true interpretation of Scripture is found only in the Church" (*Shape*, 319). "Scripture is to be interpreted by the church within the hermeneutical context of the *regula fidei* or rule of faith," expressed "in the ecumenical creeds," Nicene and Chalcedon being "the creedal confessions of all orthodox Christians" that "serve as the doctrinal boundaries of orthodox Christianity" (*Shape*, 337). In his view, though "Scripture alone is inherently infallible" and

should these (or any) creeds be accepted? If they are accepted because of the authority of the church, we are back to the original question (which church?). If they are accepted because they are biblical (as in Protestantism) we would have to first know what is biblical to make this determination, requiring the interpretation of Scripture prior to a creed's adoption. The suggestion that only the "universal" creeds be accepted does not suffice because no creed has been *universally* accepted by all who self-identify as Christians, requiring once again prior identification of true Christians or authentically Christian beliefs.[42] As Lane puts it, the creeds and confessions "have a value as representing the wisdom of the church and presenting the teachings of Scripture. But they have no independent authority and are not to be accepted if contrary to Scripture at any point."[43]

So, which church or tradition?[44] Acceptance of a particular tradition or church merely *because* that tradition or church claims to be the true one

---

"has the absolute and final authority of God Himself," the "ecumenical creedal statements are without error," though their authority is "derivative" as "summaries of the Word of God" and the church is fallible (*Shape*, 338). Conversely, Torsten Löfstedt, "In Defence of the Scripture Principle: An Evangelical Reply to A. S. Khomiakov," *EvQ* 83/1 (2011): 68, comments: "It would be nice to have the apostolic tradition clearly written out, and reconstructed in the same way as the Greek New Testament. But we don't. Evangelicals accept certain creeds because they find they are consistent with Scripture. There is no reason for us to make a special exception for the Nicene Creed."

42. Thomas Oden, *The Rebirth of Orthodoxy* (San Francisco: HarperSanFrancisco, 2003), 163, avers that "by all" (*omnibus*) does not "require absolute unanimity" but that "consent" must "be reasonably firm." What degree of "unanimity," then, is "reasonably firm," and among whom?

43. Lane, "*Sola Scriptura*?" 324. He nevertheless chastises those who "take their adherence to *sola Scriptura* to the point of rejecting all creeds" ("*Sola Scriptura*?" 311). D. H. Williams, *Retrieving the Tradition and Renewing Evangelicalism: A Primer for Suspicious Protestants* (Grand Rapids: Eerdmans, 1999), 234, however, contends that while this "is fair enough," the "reverse is also true. Scripture can never stand completely independent of the ancient consensus of the church's teaching without serious hermeneutical difficulties." Cf. Williams, "Search for *Sola Scriptura*," 363. Without rejecting statements of faith, however, Frame helpfully cautions against "emphasizing Confessions and traditions as if they were equal to Scripture in authority," "equating *sola Scriptura* with acceptance of confessional traditions," and "failing to encourage self-criticism within our particular denominational, theological, and confessional communities" ("In Defense," 290).

44. All positions accept some traditions and reject others. The question is, for what reason? Vanhoozer contends that "Church tradition accorded supreme authority to Scripture" and thus the "irony" is "that many of those today who speak up for tradition turn a deaf ear to what tradition has actually handed down concerning the supremacy of Scripture" (*Drama of Doctrine*, 164-65).

amounts to the circularity that appeal to tradition or ecclesial authority is purported to avoid. Some appeal instead to the widest consensus, but this raises questions regarding which consensus within which self-identifying Christian community and about whether a majority community perspective is legitimate simply in virtue of being predominant (and, if so, what of community rejection of Jesus himself?). If, on the other hand, a tradition or church is authoritative insofar as it is in consonance with Scripture, such an approach first requires the primacy and interpretation of Scripture (requiring that the community is not itself authoritative in biblical interpretation).[45]

In this regard, some communitarians advocate the "'single-source' theory of Tradition (Tradition I)" with a "traditional way of interpreting scripture within the community of faith," while maintaining that "Scripture has final authority."[46] Yet, how can Scripture have final authority if its correct interpre-

---

45. Mathison partially recognizes the problem with his view: In "Tradition I, the true interpretation of Scripture is found only in the Church. Yet the true Church is identified largely by its adherence to the true interpretation of Scripture. How then do we identify the Church when there are numerous communions claiming to be the Church" without "falling into radical subjectivism or logical circularity?" (*Shape*, 319). He claims that we might "identify the Christian churches" by "their adherence to the apostolic *regula fidei*," thus "identify[ing] the fragments of the true visible Church by their acceptance of the common testimony of the Holy Spirit in the rule of faith, especially as expressed in written form in the ecumenical creeds of Nicea and Chalcedon" (*Shape*, 321). Yet why that "rule of faith" and whose interpretation of it? He suggests it is because the "Holy Spirit has borne a miraculously unanimous witness to a common fundamental creed throughout this same Christendom" (*Shape*, 321). Yet some who self-identify as Christians have rejected these creeds so this once again assumes that one already knows who the true Christians are, which is the very point at issue. How, then, does this get beyond the vicious circularity or radical subjectivity that Mathison wants to avoid? Cf. the similar problems faced by Oden's consensual orthodoxy and Lindbeck's appeal to the *consensus fidelium*. Further, even if one were to accept the content of ecumenical creeds as the rule, how would that help to resolve the denominational fragmentation over the host of issues that are not addressed in such creeds? See the following chapter.

46. Allert, "What Are We Trying to Conserve?" 333. N. Clayton Croy, *Prima Scriptura: An Introduction to New Testament Interpretation* (Grand Rapids: Baker Academic, 2011), 133, argues for adopting "*prima scriptura* in lieu of *sola scriptura*" wherein "Scripture is still the primary authority for Christian faith and life" and "if ever there is a conflict between Scripture and tradition, Scripture must have priority." He further notes that "it is an encouraging sign that Christians of different stripes [especially since Vatican II] are beginning to recognize the need for both Scripture and tradition" since "surely the two should be inseparable" (*Prima Scriptura*, 133). He thus rejects "no creed but the Bible" in favor of a Wesleyan Quadrilateral (*Prima Scriptura*, 134; cf. Whidden, "*Sola Scriptura*," 216). Both Croy and Whidden rightly seek to avoid isolationism and private interpretation and other misunderstandings/misapplications of *sola Scriptura*. However, *prima Scriptura* (by itself) is also prone to unfortunate

tation is determined by an external standard?[47] Moreover, does not tradition itself require interpretation?[48] An infallible interpreter of Scripture would be needed with this approach because, once *final* interpretive authority is granted (or recognized), no rightful basis for departure from that interpretive arbiter would remain.

For instance, such a view would condemn the action of reformers like Martin Luther. Allert claims that Luther's *sola scriptura* meant to reject "contemporary church authority" but not "tradition."[49] He contends that, only because the sixteenth-century Roman Catholic church had strayed so far from

---

misunderstandings and problems, including its use by some to posit Scripture as merely the first among equals, limiting the authority of Scripture to the realm of value rather than fact. Edith Humphrey, *Scripture and Tradition: What the Bible Really Says* (Grand Rapids: Baker, 2013), 14, notes that the Wesleyan Quadrilateral has been "widely misconstrued" (in the words of Albert Outler, who coined the phrase) as in the "radical tendency" of some "revisionist theologians" who "make the fourth member of the Quadrilateral, experience, the trump card or the arbiter in" debates. How, then, should we "arbitrate between criteria when Scripture, tradition, reason, and (personal) experience seemingly collide?" (Humphrey, *Scripture*, 15). It seems to me that it is far better to promote a proper understanding of canonical *sola Scriptura* that does not boil down to either "sterile 'traditionalism' or naïve 'biblicism'" (Whidden, "*Sola Scriptura*," 217) and yet upholds the unique (*sola*) infallibility, sufficiency, and interpretive normativity that properly belongs to Scripture as canon.

47. As John Frame affirms, "*Sola Scriptura* is the doctrine that Scripture, and only Scripture, has the final word on everything, all our doctrine, and all our life. Thus it has the final word even on our interpretation of Scripture, even in our theological method" ("In Defense," 272).

48. Kevin Vanhoozer, *First Theology: God, Scripture & Hermeneutics* (Downers Grove, IL: InterVarsity, 2002), 222, cautions in this regard, "To replace *sola Scriptura* with 'Scripture in tradition' — which is to say, with community conventions — is to use the wrong strategy at the worst time. . . . There is a real danger in tying the fate of the literal sense too closely to community consensus." Elsewhere, he lays out three concerns with any "decision to take tradition as the authoritative interpretative framework for reading Scripture and as the criterion for deciding which readings are acceptable." First, "some of what passes for tradition is more akin to invention than discovery." Second, "traditions are susceptible, like individuals, to prideful self-glorification. Belonging to a particular tradition, then, is no more guarantee of the truth of one's interpretations than were the 'dreams of Cartesian orphans' who thought they could obtain objectivity as individuals. Third, it is not clear how tradition can be criticized given the presumption of coincidence, that is, the notion that tradition is Scripture rightly interpreted" (Vanhoozer, *The Drama of Doctrine*, 162).

49. Allert, "What Are We Trying to Conserve?" 338. Lane adds, "The prime enemy was not tradition, not even supplementary tradition, but the teaching of the contemporary (Roman) church" ("Scripture, Tradition and Church," 42). Najeeb George Awad, "Should We Dispense with *Sola Scriptura*? Scripture, Tradition and Postmodern Theology," *Di* 47/1 (2008): 69, 75, believes Luther would have agreed with the view that an interpretative tradition sharing Scripture's authority is necessary.

Scripture, the "teaching authority of the church had to be soundly rejected. But this did not mean that the individual had the right to interpret [Scripture] as he or she saw fit."[50] Yet, how can one break from the teaching authority of the church without breaking from tradition? Allert explains that "Luther could not argue for a return to Tradition I because the church had corrupted that. But this did not mean that Luther rejected tradition — he was calling for a return for Scripture to be the final arbiter, not the church."[51] Thus, by breaking from Rome, Luther in fact rejected major aspects of the contemporary tradition of his church.[52] Yet, apart from the teaching authority of the church, how did Luther know which traditions and interpretations to accept and which to reject? Torsten Löfstedt asks, in this regard, since "Luther had identified" the Pope as the Antichrist and it "was apparent that teachings of the Church contradicted each other; on what basis could the Reformers argue that one theologian's writings were more reliable than another's, or that the decisions taken by an ecumenical council were infallible?"[53] By rejecting the teaching

50. Allert, "What Are We Trying to Conserve?" 338. McGrath comments that magisterial reformers were theologically conservative and "painfully aware of the threat of individualism, and attempted to avoid this threat by stressing the church's traditional interpretation of Scripture where this traditional interpretation was regarded as correct" (*Reformation Thought*, 101). However, though "keenly aware of the threat of individualism," the "hermeneutical principle" was not to "be found in the individual" but "in Scripture itself"; Heiko A. Oberman, *The Dawn of the Reformation: Essays in Late Medieval and Early Reformation Thought* (Edinburgh: T&T Clark, 1986), 285. Cf. Lane, "Scripture, Tradition and Church," 44.

51. Allert, "What Are We Trying to Conserve?" 339. He contends that many evangelicals incorrectly interpret Luther's view of *sola Scriptura* as a rejection of tradition by mistakenly relying on Luther's pre-1522 writings, which "show a decided emphasis on the authority of the Bible over papal decisions." Many appeal to Luther's famous "Here I Stand" speech at the Diet of Worms, where Luther contended that he could not submit his faith to the pope or councils because they have erred and contradicted one another. Allert argues, however, that this "makes perfect sense if Luther is understood as rejecting the authority of the contemporary church and not as rejecting tradition per se" ("What Are We Trying to Conserve?" 338). He further contends that "Luther more precisely defined what the *sola scriptura* principle should look like" when "the radical wing of the Reformation started to rise" ("What Are We Trying to Conserve?" 338). Is it not possible, then, that Luther might have implemented a more radical view of *sola Scriptura* when he sparked the reformation than he was willing to allow for the radical reformers?

52. Lane states, "while the Reformers did not despise tradition they only accepted it if it was scriptural, Scripture remaining the final arbiter" ("Scripture, Tradition and Church," 43).

53. Löfstedt, "In Defence," 53. He notes that John Calvin pointed to the erring "general council of the Old Testament church" when it "unanimously condemned Micaiah'" (1 Kgs 22:26-27). "Why should one assume that later Church councils have been prevented from erring? Indeed, whole councils have been declared errant, for example the second council

authority of his church Luther must have finally decided for himself, based on his own (nonisolationist) interpretation, which traditions he viewed as valid.[54] Accordingly, tradition could not have itself functioned as his final interpretive arbiter.[55] "It was because Luther and other reformers used their private judgment in interpreting Scripture that the reformation was possible."[56]

So, which tradition or community? Absent arbitrary assent, one's answer to this question requires that one has used one's own faculties (though not necessarily in isolation) to interpret something (Scripture, tradition, or contemporary church teachings) on the basis of which a community or tradition might be embraced. Individual interpretation thus plays an unavoidable and crucial role, though it need not amount to private interpretation (see below).[57] As Lane puts it, "Scripture needs to be interpreted, but it does not need a normative interpretation."[58]

What, then, is the proper theological role for tradition and interpretive communities? Does canonical *sola Scriptura* isolate against interpretive communities past and present, ignoring history, tradition, and contemporary the-

---

of Ephesus (AD 449)" (Löfstedt, "In Defence," 70). Appeal to the ecumenical creeds is of no help here on two counts. First, the "reformers accepted the creeds only because they believed them to be scriptural" (Allert, "What Are We Trying to Conserve?" 337). But in order to know whether a creed was scriptural they must have first *interpreted* Scripture. Second, the ecumenical creeds gave no basis upon which Luther's departure from Rome could be arbitrated because Luther's break was over issues that fell outside the ecumenical creeds.

54. As Allert comments, the magisterial "reformers did not reject tradition, but neither did they accept it without judging it against the final arbiter of Scripture." Thus, "tradition was not a normative interpretation of Scripture" ("What Are We Trying to Conserve?" 337). Rather, Scripture was to be "the norm for identification of true tradition, rather than tradition the norm for interpretation of Scripture" ("What Are We Trying to Conserve?" 337).

55. As Brad Gregory, *The Unintended Reformation: How a Religious Revolution Secularized Society* (Cambridge, MA: Belknap, 2012), 96, comments, the "distinctions between what in the church's tradition was acceptable and unacceptable were themselves a function" of "understandings of the Bible, which was of course the underlying bone of contention in the first place."

56. Löfstedt, "In Defence," 66.

57. Even if there were some legitimate argument for an identifiable tradition or a particular community as interpretive arbiter, by what mechanism should one come to recognize that particular tradition or community, especially if one is already part of a community with a differing tradition (perhaps itself teaching *sola Scriptura*)?

58. Lane, "*Sola Scriptura?*" 326. Christians can recognize "the role that the church necessarily and properly plays in the development and testing of doctrine" without according "the church a normative or infallible role" (Lane, "*Sola Scriptura?*" 50). Bromiley adds, "although Christianity cannot abandon its constitutive understanding of Scripture without abandoning itself, no agreed interpretation, however ancient or assured, can be described as definitive" ("Church Fathers," 219).

ology? Certainly not. Scripture itself recognizes the authoritative "tradition" of the OT prophets and first-generation apostles, some of which was transmitted orally (1 Cor 11:2; 2 Thess 2:15; 3:6). On the other hand, Scripture strongly cautions against the "tradition of men" (Col 2:8) and any religious "tradition" that invalidates "the word of God" (Mark 7:13; cf. Matt 15:2-3, 6; Mark 7:3, 5, 8-9; Gal 1:14-16). Which traditions, then, should be accepted today and on what basis?

Many traditions, oral and written, have claimed to be apostolic (e.g., Gnosticism). However, we possess no extant extracanonical writings that can be confidently identified as having come down to us from the prophets or apostles themselves and oral traditions provide no record that can be traced historically, especially after so many generations have passed.[59] Conversely, the biblical canon itself contains the genuine written tradition of the prophets and apostles, for which there is abundant historical and textual witness.[60] The only infallible, authoritative contemporary rule of faith, then, is the canon itself (all of it), by which any extracanonical tradition must be tested.[61]

At the same time, we should engage and learn from individual and community interpretations past and present. Many errors could be avoided by

59. Indeed, Lane states, "it has often been noted that the content of Papias' traditions [such as his millenarian tradition] is a clear indication that by the year AD 150 oral tradition was already bankrupt and consisted as much of legend as of reliable information," and by "the middle of the third century such oral tradition had died out" ("Scripture, Tradition and Church," 39). Further, some written "traditions came to be [seen as] apostolic within a few years of their fourth-century origin" ("Scripture, Tradition and Church," 39). Cf. R. P. C. Hanson, *Tradition in the Early Church* (London: SCM, 1962), 35-46, 57. Yet, even if some extracanonical tradition, such as the Apostles' Creed, could be confirmed as apostolic, its content is insufficient to settle doctrinal disputes between denominations. Further, contemporary appeal to apostolic succession is unhelpful because multiple mutually exclusive communities claim apostolic succession.

60. Already, during the time of that first-generation apostolic witness, Christian doctrine was to be tested by the apostles' tradition (e.g., Gal 1:8-9; 2 Thess 3:6). Even more so, then, after the first generation passed away, any further traditions, oral or written, should be checked against the inscripturated first-generation apostolic tradition (cf. 1 Cor 4:6), which appropriately came to be recognized as the NT canon. To be sure, "in some sense, the synoptic Gospels, Acts and Paul's letters, and certainly many other parts of the NT rely on tradition." Yet "since this tradition was incorporated into the NT, and can now only be reconstructed on the basis of our NT, there is no point in demanding allegiance to it rather than to the NT. The authority of this tradition is theoretical" (Löfstedt, "In Defence," 56). Written texts can be used to "judge the reliability of other (oral) traditions, because we can be reasonably sure of the age and authenticity of the written texts" (Löfstedt, "In Defence," 58).

61. Vanhoozer thus contends that "the Rule [of Faith] is the canon 'rightly understood.'" It "protects us from eccentric exegesis, yet it remains open, in principle, to correction from Scripture." Thus, the "ultimate purpose of the Rule is to let Scripture interpret Scripture" (*Drama of Doctrine*, 207).

seriously engaging the history of Christian thought. Accordingly, the serious theologian should listen carefully (but not uncritically) to historical and contemporary Christian voices.[62] We can stand on the shoulders of theological giants without accepting those giants as doctrinal authorities in themselves. We can treasure the tradition surrounding, and the preservation of, the word of God without subscribing to either the doctrinal infallibility or the final interpretative authority of postapostolic traditions or communities.

Is SOLA SCRIPTURA Culpable for Theological Subjectivism and Hyperpluralism?

Private Interpretation?

Stanley Hauerwas contends that *sola Scriptura* is the "sin of the Reformation," exposing Scripture to subjective interpretation by assuming "that the text of the Scripture makes sense separate from the Church that gives it sense."[63] In this way, it is claimed, "no creed but the Bible" lacks an objective means to interpret Scripture and thus leads to extreme individualism.[64] Clark Carlton further argues that "the idea that the Scriptures are self-interpreting is patently absurd. It assumes a degree of absolute objectivity that would make the most ardent positivist cringe with embarrassment. . . .Texts do not exist in the abstract. Yet, this is exactly what the doctrine of *sola Scriptura* assumes: a bare text that somehow imposes its meaning on the reader."[65]

Canonical *sola Scriptura* does not advocate such a naïve approach to

---

62. As Alister McGrath, "Engaging the Great Tradition: Evangelical Theology and the Role of Tradition," in *Evangelical Futures: A Conversation on Theological Method*, ed. John G. Stackhouse, Jr. (Grand Rapids: Baker, 2000), 151, puts it: "Evangelicalism must see tradition as its servant, not its master. To affirm the supreme authority of Scripture in matters of doctrine should not prevent us from paying attention to what others who have gone before us have found in their engagement with Scripture."

63. Stanley Hauerwas, *Unleashing the Scripture: Freeing the Bible from Captivity to America* (Nashville: Abingdon, 1993), 155.

64. As Allert puts it, the "*sola scriptura* principle guided by Tradition 0 allows for many different interpretations. How, in this kind of situation, is the determination made as to the orthodox interpretation?" ("What Are We Trying to Conserve?" 342). "Too often," he claims, "the Bible is posited as the 'rule of faith' for Evangelicals" ("What Are We Trying to Conserve?" 343; cf. Williams, "The Search for *Sola Scriptura*," 358).

65. Clark Carlton, *The Way: What Every Protestant Should Know about the Orthodox Church* (Salisbury, MA: Regina Orthodox Press, 1997), 90.

hermeneutics. Moreover, Carlton's criticism might similarly apply to tradition or church-provided dogma because they too require interpretation. Traditions and contemporary interpretations do not bypass individual interpretation and "impose" their meaning on their reader or hearer any more than Scripture does. All communication requires interpretation such that some degree of individual interpretation by the receptor is unavoidable (the hermeneutical circle).

The proper reading of Scripture (and any other text), then, includes recognition that no one interprets in a vacuum. Far from nullifying the analogy of Scripture, however, this very recognition highlights its crucial interpretive role. First, the oft-repeated and misunderstood dictum that "Scripture interprets itself" need not be taken to mean that Scripture requires no interpretation. The thrust of the analogy of Scripture as understood by this approach is that particular passages should be understood in light of other passages, extending to the entire canon (cf. Isa 8:20; Luke 24:44).[66] In this way, the analogy of Scripture is intended to safeguard against eisegesis and private, idiosyncratic interpretations of Scripture.

According to this approach, the canon is the objective rule or standard to which interpretation should discernibly correspond. Private interpretation (including any canon within the canon) is to be intentionally offset by conscientious submission to the claims of Scripture as a whole (*tota Scriptura*). This, of course, cannot be accomplished mechanically and, thus, the possibility of one's idiosyncratic private interpretation subverting the meaning in the text is ever present. However, the danger of private interpretation cannot be avoided by granting authority to a past or present interpretive community because each individual may decide for oneself which tradition or church to accept as authoritative. Individual interpretation, then, cannot be bypassed altogether or entirely handed over to the authority of others.

Nevertheless, as Whidden rightly emphasizes, "the alternative [to recognition of the value of interpretive communities past and present] has all too often been highly individualistic persons with a very autocratic sense of their exclusivist stranglehold on truth."[67] One need not choose, however, between granting final interpretive doctrinal authority to a tradition or community and the total rejection of learning from and participating in interpretive com-

66. Vanhoozer thus suggests that "we must read the Bible canonically, as one book"; the "canon is the primary context that enables us to discern and to describe what God is doing as author with the biblical texts," whereas the church is only a secondary, albeit helpful, context (*Drama of Doctrine*, 178).

67. Whidden, "*Sola Scriptura*," 226.

munities past and present. No one should develop one's theology privately, in isolation from Christian community (cf. Heb 10:23-25). Isolationism and historical amnesia only make one more susceptible to unrecognized historical influences and philosophical presuppositions.[68] Both historical and contemporary theology should thus be earnestly engaged, without making either determinative. Any tradition that agrees with Scripture might be affirmed, but such affirmation requires the careful interpretation of Scripture. Within this process, one must remain cognizant of the potential for personal or collective misinterpretation of Scripture, which might require rejection of some traditions that were previously accepted. As John Stackhouse reminds us, "the Bible is God's Word written, but our interpretations of it are not."[69] This calls for a humble approach to Scripture (see chapter 9).

Canonical *sola Scriptura*, then, rejects an isolationist approach to biblical interpretation while maintaining that all interpretations (individual or corporate) must be intentionally subjected to the uniquely authoritative standard of Scripture. The Bible is not to be subjected to private interpretation. On the other hand, no individual should give up one's own conscientious duty to wrestle with Scripture while participating in Christian community. *Sola Scriptura*, then, safeguards against private interpretation not only by paying attention to the historical and contemporary interpretive community but by subjecting all interpretations to the analogy of Scripture.

Hermeneutical Diversity

This brings us to the final issue of this chapter: Is *sola Scriptura* at fault for the fragmentation of Christianity? Many have blamed *sola Scriptura* for hermeneutical diversity and hyperpluralism. Brad Gregory, for example, has recently claimed that the *sola Scriptura* principle is the "most important, distant historical source of Western hyperpluralism."[70] Blosser contends that, "as a result of

---

68. Indeed, one who overlooks or denies "the influence of tradition in the act of interpretation" might be "enslaved by interpretive patterns that are allowed to function uncritically, precisely because they are unacknowledged"; John R. Franke, "Scripture, Tradition, and Authority: Reconstructing the Evangelical Conception of *Sola Scriptura*," in *Evangelicals & Scripture: Tradition, Authority, and Hermeneutics*, ed. Vincent Bacote, Laura C. Miguélez, and Dennis L. Okholm (Downers Grove, IL: InterVarsity, 2004), 201.

69. John G. Stackhouse, Jr., "Evangelical Theology Should Be Evangelical," in *Evangelical Futures*, 47.

70. Gregory, *Unintended Reformation*, 92. Christian Smith refers to the "major problem"

its hermeneutical anarchy, *sola scriptura* has splintered into denominational factionalism" by the thousands.[71] Whidden is more reserved in his suggestion that "the bewildering array of doctrinal options that have arisen among groups that strenuously profess fidelity to the Bible as their sole authority" is a "historical trend which makes the practical application of *sola Scriptura* questionable."[72]

In this regard, Patrick Madrid seeks to defeat *sola Scriptura* via a pragmatic test, asking for even one example "of *sola scriptura* actually working, functioning in such a way that it brings about doctrinal certitude and unity of doctrine among Christians."[73] However, the premise of Madrid's argument is invalid, at least with reference to this canonical approach, since *sola Scriptura* does not entail any claim to provide "doctrinal certitude" or "unity of doctrine" and thus is not defeated by the lack thereof. Conversely, what approach has accomplished this feat? If the standard is unity, then all denominations (indeed all worldviews) have failed. As Ronald Rittgers correctly notes, Protestants "separated from a medieval church that was itself in schism with the Christian East. If unity of theological truth is the ideal, then one must conclude that medieval Christendom failed long before Protestants were on the scene — and not just at the level of praxis."[74] It is thus historically demonstrable that the

---

of "pervasive interpretive pluralism," ascribing it to "failure to come to terms with the multivocality and polysemy of scripture." If this were "correct, we would not have anything like the disagreement, conflict, and division that we in fact do have in Christianity today — especially among Evangelical biblicists" (*Bible Made Impossible*, 17, 173).

71. Blosser, "What Are the Philosophical and Practical Problems," 93. Kreeft states, "private interpretation leads to denominationalism. Let five hundred people interpret the Bible without Church authority and there will soon be five hundred denominations. But denominationalism is an intolerable scandal by scriptural standards — see John 17:20-23 and 1 Corinthians 1:10-17" (*Fundamentals*, 275).

72. Whidden, "*Sola Scriptura*," 214. Whidden here refers to *sola Scriptura* where it is falsely understood or applied. Consider, further, N. T. Wright's statement, "How Can the Bible Be Authoritative?" *VE* 21 (1991): 13, "It seems to be the case that the more you insist that you are based on the Bible, the more fissiparous you become; the church splits up into more and more little groups, each thinking that they have got biblical truth right." Mathison contends that "as long as solo *scriptura* is held by the majority of Protestants, whether under the guise of liberalism or fundamentalism, Protestantism will continue to divide and create" a "public scandal" (*Shape*, 306).

73. Madrid, "*Sola Scriptura*," 26.

74. Ronald K. Rittgers, "Blame It on Luther," *ChrCent* 130/2 (2013): 29. Beyond the break with the Eastern Church in 1054, Nico Vorster points to the Great Schism (1378–1418). In further response to Gregory's claims, Vorster, "*Sola Scriptura* and Western Hyperpluralism: A Critical Response to Brad Gregory's *Unintended Reformation*," *Review of European Studies*

sola Scriptura principle is not responsible for de-unifying Christianity. One wonders if any approach could bring about *doctrinally certain* hermeneutical unity in a fallen world such as ours.[75]

Hermeneutical diversity presents genuine ecclesiological and hermeneutical problems, but they are not problems for (or derived from) *sola Scriptura* qua *sola Scriptura*. In my view, hermeneutical diversity stems from the fact of disparate human minds, none of which works perfectly and all of which are temporarily and partially separated from the authoritative interpreter — the Holy Spirit — because of the Fall. Simply put, the historical failure fallacy could be applied to any worldview because humans inevitably fail.[76] Even if we somehow enjoyed perfect ecclesial and hermeneutical harmony, such that we all believed identically, it is very likely that we would all nevertheless be wrong together about a great many things.

That is, while many individuals incorrectly interpret Scripture, do not many communities also come to erroneous interpretations? As Vanhoozer aptly comments, "I see no reason that cognitive malfunction could not be corporate as well as individual."[77] The many examples of the misuse of human cognitive and religious freedom to choose whom we will serve (Josh

---

5/1 (2013): 52, notes that "late medieval Europe was not a unified institutionalised society as Gregory suggests" but was "characterised by doctrinal controversy, power struggles with the church and social discord" such that it is "incorrect to regard the *sola scriptura* principle as the main historical origin of the fragmentation of Western society." Rather, "widespread religious plurality already existed within medieval Christianity" (Vorster, "*Sola Scriptura*," 58). Vorster points to the major role of the eleventh- through fifteenth-century intellectual revolutions, the rise of universities, the printing press, and questions about the reliability of the Vulgate as key factors. The "*sola scriptura* principle was a partial phenomenon within this much larger intellectual environment"; thus, he considers Gregory's view to be "a highly artificial and reductionist argument" ("*Sola Scriptura*," 52). Vorster points to the many doctrinal controversies and fragmentation already present within Catholicism in the centuries prior to the Reformation, such as Dominicans vs. Franciscans, Thomistic realism vs. Ockhamistic nominalism, etc. (Vorster, *Sola Scriptura*, 57). Alister McGrath, *The Intellectual Origins of the European Reformation*, 2nd ed. (Malden, MA: Blackwell, 2004), 16, 18, similarly refers to the "astonishing doctrinal diversity of the 14th and 15th centuries" and many doctrinal controversies "characteristic" of late medieval Catholicism.

75. Claims or expectations of doctrinal certitude reveal a lack of epistemic humility and, perhaps, ignorance of well-known epistemological issues.

76. "It was not this or that theological method that brought about religious diversity, but human frailty. Plurality always was and will be a feature of human reality" (Vorster, "*Sola Scriptura*," 62).

77. Vanhoozer, *First Theology*, 223. As Lane puts it, "*sola Scriptura* is the statement that the church can err" ("*Sola Scriptura*?" 324).

24:15) should caution us against overconfidence in our interpretation of Scripture and dissuade us from any tendencies to isolationism, historical or contemporary ignorance, and the like, but it is not an appropriate or compelling counterargument to freedom of belief generally (which requires freedom of interpretation) or *sola Scriptura* specifically.[78] As Vanhoozer states, the "interpreter has, it is true, an elder brother, the Christian tradition," and "individuals always read in some interpretive community." But "elder brothers, as everyone knows, can occasionally be bullies."[79] Despite the importance of the community, Vanhoozer contends, "the supreme norm for church practice is Scripture itself: not Scripture as used by the church but Scripture as used by God, even, or perhaps especially, when such use is *over against* the church."[80]

This canonical *sola Scriptura* approach, then, advocates far-reaching epistemic humility, recognizing that both the interpretations of individuals (including ourselves) and communities are fallible. As such, the individual and collective task of Christians is to seek to bring our interpretations into ever-greater conformity to the canon. This task might be advanced via a rigorous process of theological interpretation that applies a canonical approach wherein a hermeneutical spiral is continuously employed to bring interpretations closer and closer in line with, and in full submission to, all of Scripture (see chapter 8).[81]

78. For example, Allert contends that "Arius's interpretations based on Scripture alone seem to throw a wrench into" the view of the radical reformers and others ("What Are We Trying to Conserve?" 344; cf. Mathison, *Shape*, 340). But the theological aberrations of Arius (and others) are not logical consequences of *sola Scriptura*. Criticism of the radical Reformation on the basis of some extremists (who, it could be argued, did not actually follow *sola Scriptura*) seems unfair to the broader radical reformed tradition.

79. Vanhoozer, *First Theology*, 223. He further notes, "the believing community is all too often portrayed in Scripture as unbelieving or confused, and subsequent church history has not been reassuring either" (*First Theology*, 219).

80. Vanhoozer, *Drama of Doctrine*, 16. While recognizing the importance of the community, he rejects the postliberal "cultural-linguistic turn" in which "the Bible only becomes canonical Scripture in the context of the church's practice" such that "Scripture cannot function as canon apart from church tradition, its hermeneutical key" (*Drama of Doctrine*, 142).

81. As John Webster, "Principles of Systematic Theology," *International Journal of Systematic Theology* 11/1 (2009): 70, puts it, "Scripture must be the *terminus ad quem* of systematic theological analysis, not merely its *terminus a quo*," that is, the goal and final limit and not merely the origination point of theology.

Conclusion

Canonical *sola Scriptura*, understood to mean that Scripture is the uniquely infallible source of divine revelation that is collectively available, the sufficient and fully trustworthy basis of theology, and the final norm of theological interpretation, does not inevitably reduce to absurdity. This *sola Scriptura* approach rejects isolationism, anti-intellectualism, elevation of private interpretation, and ignorance of past and present wisdom of other Christians while subjecting extracanonical factors (e.g., reason, experience, tradition) to Scripture.

As such, canonical *sola Scriptura* is not self-defeating, isolationist, or culpable for theological subjectivism or pluralism. It is appropriately derived from Scripture itself and advocates the proper use of reason and scholarship and engagement with interpretive communities past and present over and against private interpretation, all of which are subordinated to Scripture. The unique sufficiency and epistemological primacy of Scripture with regard to theological doctrine are thus logically consistent and practicable toward a canonical systematic theology.

Building on the working approach to canonical *sola Scriptura* laid out in this chapter, chapter 7 follows up on the practicability of this canonical *sola Scriptura* approach in comparison to communitarian approaches by engaging one of the most prominent issues raised by those who reject reductionist *sola Scriptura* and hold communitarian *sola Scriptura*, the Trinity doctrine.

CHAPTER 7

Sola Scriptura and the Theology of the Trinity:
A Case Study

Many recent evangelical publications have been devoted to ongoing controversies over the Trinity doctrine, claiming that some are tampering with, or
reinventing, the Trinity.[1] In this vein, Stephen Holmes contends that the recent
"explosion of theological work claiming to recapture the doctrine of the Trinity" actually "misunderstands and distorts the traditional doctrine so badly
that it is unrecognizable."[2] Concerned about the continued proliferation of
theological controversy over such a foundational doctrine, some have placed
significant blame on a perceived lack of regard for Christian tradition. Advocates of communitarian approaches frequently appeal to the Trinity doctrine
as a prime example of the need for some form of extracanonical normative
arbiter.[3] The argument typically goes something like this: the Trinity doc-

---

1. See, for example, Kevin Giles, *Jesus and the Father: Modern Evangelicals Reinvent the
Doctrine of the Trinity* (Grand Rapids: Zondervan, 2006); Millard J. Erickson, *Who's Tamper-
ing with the Trinity? An Assessment of the Subordination Debate* (Grand Rapids: Kregel Aca-
demic, 2009); Bruce Ware, "Tampering with the Trinity: Does the Son Submit to His Father?"
Journal for Biblical Manhood and Womanhood 6/1 (2001); Gilbert Bilezikian, "Hermeneutical
Bungee-Jumping: Subordination in the Godhead," *JETS* 40/1 (1997): 58; Phillip Cary, "The New
Evangelical Subordinationism: Reading Inequality into the Trinity," in *The New Evangelical
Subordinationism? Perspectives on the Equality of God the Father and God the Son*, ed. Dennis
W. Jowers and H. Wayne House (Eugene, OR: Pickwick, 2012).

2. Stephen R. Holmes, *The Quest for the Trinity: The Doctrine of God in Scripture, History,
and Modernity* (Downers Grove, IL: IVP Academic, 2012), xv.

3. This claim extends far beyond legitimate intrachurch doctrinal authority, which includes
the right of any communal body to draft and expect members to abide by certain beliefs and
practices, distinguishing between "church traditions" and "the tradition" and claiming a universal authority for the latter; Kevin Giles, "The Authority of the Bible and the Authority of

trine is not sufficiently grounded or adequately clear in Scripture itself and, thus, tradition broadly or an external rule of faith more narrowly (e.g., the Nicene Creed) is needed to provide the sufficient ground or clarification of the doctrine.

This chapter introduces both of these claims in succession and then proceeds to evaluate their combined force with regard to the Trinity doctrine in light of the crucial and decisive question: Does a community approach succeed in overcoming the problems that its proponents (and others) attribute to (reductionist) *sola Scriptura*? This question is critical because the rationale for communitarian approaches depends upon their ability to supplement Scripture in a way that meets objections to *sola Scriptura*. However, examination of some contemporary Trinitarian debates within mainstream evangelicalism over social vs. Latin understandings of the Trinity, the eternal functional subordination of the Son, eternal generation, and the proper understanding of the tradition itself, raises crucial questions regarding the effectiveness of communitarian approaches to theological method.

Two Community Claims:
Insufficiency of Canon and Sufficiency of Creed

Claim 1: Scripture Is Insufficient for the Trinity Doctrine

Proponents of the claim that Scripture is insufficient to adequately ground or articulate the Trinity doctrine often appeal to two subsidiary claims as evidence. First, the Bible must be interpreted (that is, it does not actually interpret itself) and, second, Scripture can be (and has been) interpreted in a myriad of ways, especially in relation to the issues pertinent to the Trinity doctrine. As Kevin Giles explains, "the Bible can often be read in more than one way, even on important matters. This comment is uncontroversial because it is undeniable. History gives innumerable examples of learned and devout theologians who have differed from others in their interpretation of the Bible on almost every doctrine or ethical question imaginable," including "the doctrine of the Trinity."[4] Thus, hermeneutical diversity is offered as evidence of the insuffi-

---

the Theological Tradition," *The Priscilla Papers* 27/4 (2013): 16. Giles explains that "doctrine or theology is always an expression of the mind of the church. It is a communal belief" of "consensus" that is then called "the tradition" ("Authority of the Bible," 17).

4. Kevin Giles, *The Trinity and Subordinationism: The Doctrine of God and the Contemporary Gender Debate* (Downers Grove, IL: InterVarsity, 2002), 8-9. He goes on: "Quoting biblical

ciency of the canon, which lays the groundwork for the corresponding claim that elevates community.

Craig Allert likewise contends that those holding a reductionist view of *sola Scriptura* "could easily appeal to the Bible to reject essential Christian truths like the Trinity."[5] Allert points to both the Arian controversy and the anti-Trinitarian beliefs of some radical reformers as examples of heretical beliefs that were purported to be grounded in Scripture, thus exhibiting "the danger in this kind of understanding of the relationship between Scripture and tradition."[6] Recognizing that this "may be an extreme view of the *sola scriptura* principle" he contends that such examples illustrate "just how far it may be taken when the right of private judgment is retained at the expense of tradition as a tool to help understand scripture."[7] Allert's "point here is that a *sola scriptura* principle guided by Tradition 0 allows for many different interpretations. How, in this kind of situation, is the determination made as to the orthodox interpretation?"[8] Further, he claims, "Arius's interpretations based on Scripture alone seem to throw a wrench into" the "seemingly perspicuous schema" of those who defend Scripture as the rule of faith.[9] Thus, since "the Bible needs to be interpreted and determination must be made as to the proper interpretation," the "the only way to know which [interpretations] are proper and which are not is to appeal to the [extracanonical] rule of faith."[10]

---

texts and giving one's interpretation of them cannot resolve complex theological disputes." He claims this approach "had to be abandoned" in the "fourth century" and "should also be abandoned today because it always leads to a 'text-jam'" (*Trinity*, 3). Notably, Giles appeals to Scripture more prominently in some later works but without departing from this fundamental approach; see Giles, *Jesus and the Father*; "Authority of the Bible."

5. Craig D. Allert, "What Are We Trying to Conserve? Evangelicalism and *Sola Scriptura*," *EvQ* 76/4 (2004): 342.

6. Allert, "What Are We Trying to Conserve?" 340. "Clearly, the charge that Arius was 'sinfully misusing' Scripture is true here. But what is the standard against which this sinful misuse is measured? If it is the Bible alone we are simply talking in circles" ("What Are We Trying to Conserve?" 343). Giles and Mathison similarly point to the Arian controversy; Giles, *Trinity*, 3; Keith A. Mathison, *The Shape of Sola Scriptura* (Moscow, ID: Canon, 2001), 340. Allert further cites the radical reformer Sebastian Franck (ca. 1499–1542) and his rejection of the "Nicene understanding of the Holy Trinity" ("What Are We Trying to Conserve?" 341). To his credit, Allert does qualify such examples: "I am not saying that *all* radical reformers rejected the Nicene doctrine of the Trinity. Nor do I want to group all radicals in the same category as Franck or Muntzer" ("What Are We Trying to Conserve?" 342).

7. Allert, "What Are We Trying to Conserve?" 340.

8. Allert, "What Are We Trying to Conserve?" 342.

9. Allert, "What Are We Trying to Conserve?" 344.

10. Allert, "What Are We Trying to Conserve?" 342, 344. For Mathison, whereas Scripture is

This dovetails with the recognition that every text requires interpretation and the interpreter will inevitably contribute to the resulting interpretation (the hermeneutical circle). Giles thus notes that words "are only symbols on a page until a human agent gives them meaning. The interpreting agent . . . always reads through the 'spectacles' given by the presuppositions she or he holds or takes for granted."[11] Thus, "*Context contributes to meaning*" and, therefore, "one can no longer think of the Bible as a set of timeless, transcultural rulings or as propositions that speak in every age with one voice."[12] According to communitarian proponents, then, the recognition that reading Scripture requires interpretation coupled with claims of widespread misinterpretation of Scripture grounds the claim that an extracanonical arbiter is needed.

Claim 2: Tradition Is Sufficient for the Trinity Doctrine

Because, it is claimed, Scripture alone is inadequate to ground or clearly articulate the Trinity doctrine, some community, tradition, or creed is necessary to arbitrate theological interpretation. This claim, however, rests on the assumption that community resources (e.g., tradition or creeds) sufficiently ground or articulate the Trinity doctrine in a way that mitigates the deficiencies attributed to Scripture alone.

This perspective thus affords special authority to tradition, particularly the ecumenical creeds. Accordingly, Kevin Giles follows up on his aforementioned point regarding the diverse interpretations of Scripture throughout history by averring that, regarding the Trinity doctrine, "tradition should prescribe the correct reading. This is claimed because this tradition is the fruit of deep and prolonged reflection by the best and most respected theologians across the

---

"the sole source of revelation" and "the only infallible, final and authoritative norm of doctrine and practice; it is to be interpreted in and by the Church; and it is to be interpreted according to the *regula fidei*" (Mathison, *Shape*, 281).

11. Giles, *Trinity*, 10. However, does tradition not also consist of symbols?

12. Giles, *Trinity*, 11 (emphasis his). Wayne A. Grudem, *Evangelical Feminism and Biblical Truth: An Analysis of More Than One Hundred Disputed Questions* (Sisters, OR: Multnomah, 2004), 426, on the other hand, strongly critiques this point, asserting that "Scripture can have no effect in his [Giles's] system. He can just reply, 'Yes, the Bible can be read that way, but other readings are possible,'" and thus "God's Word is effectively silenced." Craig Keener, "Subordination within the Trinity: John 5:18 and 1 Cor 15:28," in *New Evangelical Subordinationism*, 55, responds: "I acknowledge Kevin's noteworthy competence in the creeds, but I believe that Scripture is ultimately more authoritative than creeds and need not be conformed to the creeds (which, like Scripture, may be subject to interpretation)."

centuries on what the Bible teaches on the Trinity, and their conclusions are now codified in the creeds and Reformation confessions of faith."[13] Likewise, Keith Mathison asserts that "the ecumenical creeds represent the hermeneutical consensus already reached by the Church. They declare the basic essential truths which have been confessed by all Christians from the first days of the Church until today."[14] As such, the "ecumenical creeds of Nicea and Chalcedon" are the special "written form" of "the common testimony of the Holy Spirit in the rule of faith."[15] Thus, those that "reject the common Christian creed" may be "immediately recognize[d]" as counterfeit.[16]

This does not assert merely that tradition can be helpful to theological understanding and interpretation. Such a claim would also be accepted by the canonical approach, which also rejects any theological approach that is anti-intellectual, antihistorical, or promotes private interpretation to the exclusion of the Christian community. The communitarian approach makes the broader and stronger claim that community resources can remedy that which is purported to be lacking in Scripture alone. According to this claim, the communitarian approach to the Trinity doctrine should be able to overcome (or at least mitigate) the very problems it raises against Scripture alone.

Is the Community Approach Preferable in the Case of the Trinity?

We have seen the two complementary claims that Scripture is insufficient to ground or articulate the Trinity doctrine and, therefore, that an extracanonical rule of faith such as the Nicene Creed is needed to arbitrate and set the parameters of the orthodox doctrine of the Trinity. We now turn to evaluation of

13. Giles, *Trinity*, 8-9. Notably, Giles elsewhere qualifies that tradition need not always be followed. See below.

14. Mathison, *Shape*, 280. He goes on: "They [the ecumenical creeds] represent that which the entire Church has seen in Scripture." Denying this "consensus of faith" is "in effect a denial of Scripture itself" because, "if the entire Church for thousands of years confesses to being taught by the Spirit the same essential truths in Scripture, then it follows that those truths are what Scripture says" (*Shape*, 280). This is a dubious claim indeed. What about the supposed consensus prior to the East–West Schism? On what basis could Mathison, a Protestant, depart from that long-standing consensus?

15. Mathison, *Shape*, 321.

16. Mathison, *Shape*, 322. He goes on to refer to "liberal churches and teachers who use the words of the Christian creed but deliberately change their meaning." Notice that this requires interpretation of the meaning of the creed itself, however.

these overarching claims via the question: Is the community approach preferable in the case of the Trinity? The rationale for supplementing the canon with community resources entails that the community approach provides some considerable advantage (on balance) toward resolving the very concerns and worries that are brought against reductionist *sola Scriptura*.

The remainder of this chapter will suggest that the community approach's claim that some extracanonical tradition should function as the rule of faith is not preferable to a canonical approach in addressing the issue of the Trinity for the following four reasons:

1. Tradition is insufficient to settle contemporary Trinity disputes because, in many cases, it does not provide sufficient material to address the disputes.
2. Tradition cannot function as the doctrinally or interpretively authoritative rule of faith because many Christians, including some mainstream evangelical scholars, depart on the basis of Scripture from various particulars that appear in the Christian tradition.
3. Tradition is not preferable as a rule or interpretive authority because different scholars interpret it differently.
4. The elevation of tradition or other community resources fails to adequately answer the questions: Which tradition and on whose interpretation? How does an individual come to know which tradition and on whose interpretation?

CONTEMPORARY TRINITY DEBATES

The claim that the communitarian approach is preferable to Scripture alone in addressing the Trinity doctrine may be tested by a brief investigation of whether and how such an approach might constructively address some of the Trinity debates currently prominent in evangelical literature. This investigation will bring forth evidence that grounds the four aforementioned claims against the preferability of communitarian approaches.

Social vs. Latin Conceptions of the Trinity

The long-standing dispute over the Eastern and Western views of the Trinity has become a particular point of contention in light of the recent revival of

Trinitarian theology. It has become customary to posit a distinction between the Eastern (Greek) and Western (Latin) views of the Trinity whereby the West (e.g., Augustine) is supposed to have started with and emphasized the unity of nature in the Trinity (oneness) and then exposited how the one God could be Father, Son, and Spirit, whereas the East (e.g., the Cappadocian fathers) is supposed to have begun with and emphasized the plurality of the persons (threeness) of the Trinity and worked to explain how they could yet be one.[17]

However, Stephen Holmes's recent work, *The Quest for the Trinity*, challenges this "de Régnon thesis," seeking to "demonstrate that the patristic inheritance, East and West, essentially spoke with one voice."[18] Holmes maintains: "A statement of the doctrine was settled in the fourth century, and was then maintained, with only very minor disagreement or development, by all strands of the church — West and East, Protestant and Catholic — until the modern period."[19] According to his view, "the doctrine of the Trinity received from the fourth century" contains "no fundamental difference between East and West."[20] This common patristic inheritance, he suggests, includes the simplicity of the divine nature, "three divine hypostases that are instantiations of the divine nature." The three members exist "really, eternally, and necessarily," and "are distinguished by eternal relations of origin — begetting and proceeding — and not otherwise," such that other than language referring to such "relations of origin," everything "that is spoken of God . . . is spoken of the one life the three share, and so is indivisibly spoken of all three."[21]

Holmes thus highlights the understanding of divine personality as a cru-

17. See, for example, Adolf von Harnack, *History of Dogma*, 7 vols. (New York: Dover, 1961), 4:127-29.

18. Holmes, *Quest*, 144. The "de Régnon thesis" or "paradigm" is believed to stem from the work of Théodore de Régnon in his *Études de théologie positive sur la Sainte Trinité* (1892). Although de Régnon's influence is detected in many English histories of the Trinity, it has seldom been cited until recently and, according to much recent scholarship, de Régnon's own views have been neglected and mishandled. See Kristin Hennessy, "An Answer to de Régnon's Accusers: Why We Should Not Speak of 'His' Paradigm," *HTR* 100/2 (2007); Michael René Barnes, "De Régnon Reconsidered," *AugStud* 26 (1995): 51-79.

19. Holmes, *Quest*, xv. According to his view, the works that arise from the twentieth-century "sense" that the Trinity doctrine "stood in need of recovery" are "generally thoroughgoing departures from the older tradition, rather than revivals of it" (*Quest*, xv).

20. Holmes, *Quest*, 146. Holmes notes, however, that this conception "that made sense of" early church practices such as the worship of Jesus took "centuries to work out" (*Quest*, 55).

21. Holmes, *Quest*, 146. Embedded in his summary of "patristic Trinitarianism," Holmes includes the inexact and trophic nature of language that is nevertheless adequate (i.e., analogical rather than univocal). See chapter 9.

cial factor in the perception of division between East and West.[22] Whereas according to the de Régnon thesis, "Augustine thought differently from the Cappadocians" regarding personality, Holmes contends that just as "Augustine locates all that is truly 'personal' (knowledge, volition, action . . .) in the ineffable divine nature, not severally in the hypostases," so also do the Cappadocians such that "East and West alike are united in insisting on the unity of the divine will and knowledge."[23]

Accordingly, Holmes views the tripersonal understanding of the Trinity as a deviation from the Christian tradition: "The practice of speaking of three 'persons' in this sense [of three centers of consciousness, reason, and will] in the divine life, of asserting a 'social doctrine of the Trinity', a 'divine community' or an 'ontology of persons in relationship' can only ever be, as far as I can see, a simple departure from . . . the unified witness of the entire theological tradition."[24] Thus, Holmes rejects the widespread interpretation "offered by Zizioulas, Gunton, and others . . . that Augustine, and with him the Western tradition, failed to understand the basic reorientation of ontology in a personalist direction that was the chief achievement of the Cappadocian fathers."[25] Holmes thus opposes many recent and popular Trinitarian theologies, specifically those that hold "an unshakeable belief in the full personality, in the modern sense, of the three divine persons."[26]

22. Holmes notes that "by 'personality' in the modern sense, I assume that we mean the possession of self-determination, and so volition, and of self-awareness, and so cognition" (*Quest*, 144).

23. Holmes, *Quest*, 144.

24. Holmes, *Quest*, 195. Phillip Cary similarly claims that, in Nicene orthodoxy, there "is only one will in God" and the Son and Father "have but one will as they have but one being. Otherwise they would not be one God. Such are the logical consequences of Nicaea, which orthodox trinitarianism understands but evangelical subordinationists do not" ("New Evangelical Subordinationism," 6).

25. Holmes, *Quest*, 144. "God's knowledge, being perfect, is not discursive but complete and immediate" such that "God in one instant act of apprehension perceives all things, and all relations between them, perfectly. Already, it seems to me, the contemporary definition of 'personhood' is being stretched to, or beyond, breaking point by this single example," because, he says, the "discursive nature of my intellect is intrinsic to my being personal in this sense." He continues, "Far better, if the term must be used, to borrow coinages such as 'suprapersonal'" (*Quest*, 195). Holmes rejects the modern concept of personhood as "crudely anthropomorphic," which in application to God would amount to taking "an aspect of our own experience — a nexus of self-awareness, possession of volition, and ratiocination — and assert that it is necessary for God to be like this" (*Quest*, 194).

26. Holmes, *Quest*, 199. This is one of a number of common themes he attributes to the position he rejects; the others include "a focus on the gospel narratives, largely to the exclu-

This excludes a wide spectrum of Trinitarian theologians, including a number that many would consider faithfully evangelical. Millard Erickson and Thomas McCall stand as two notable exemplars who affirm the tripersonality of the Trinity. With Erickson's view of the Trinity "there are three wills [not one collective will] but the three, in the pattern known as perichoresis, always agree."[27] McCall strongly claims, "Trinitarian theology should insist on an understanding of persons that is consistent with the New Testament portrayal of the divine persons, that is, as distinct centers of consciousness and will who exist together in loving relationships of mutual dependence."[28] Moreover, McCall pushes back against the claim that such a view "merely imports a distinctly modern and foreign notion of 'person' into the doctrine of the Trinity." He notes, conversely, that "whatever exactly a 'modern' notion of personhood is, many contemporary Trinitarian theologians are

---

sion of other biblical data, particularly of the Old Testament; . . . a commitment to univocal language applying to the divine; and a willingness to entangle God's life with the history of the world" (*Quest*, 32). This last point is particularly telling as it relates to the conceptualization of the God–world relationship. See chapters 9 and 10.

27. Erickson, *Who's Tampering*, 254. Erickson believes the Father, Son, and Spirit "all had jointly decided that he [Christ] would go" in the incarnation (*Who's Tampering*, 135).

28. Thomas H. McCall, *Which Trinity? Whose Monotheism? Philosophical and Systematic Theologians on the Metaphysics of Trinitarian Theology* (Grand Rapids: Eerdmans, 2010), 236. McCall further states, "Future work on the doctrine of the Trinity should hold to an understanding of 'person' according to which to be a person (at least a divine person) is to be a distinct center of consciousness and will who subsists in relation to others (*Which Trinity?* 233). He believes this is required by the NT data: "If the Son is not an 'I' in relation to the Father from whom he is distinct as a 'Thou,' then we are left to wonder how we are to make sense of the claims that the Son obeys, glorifies, and loves the Father"; Thomas H. McCall and Michael C. Rea, "Theologians, Philosophers, and the Doctrine of the Trinity," in *Philosophical and Theological Essays on the Trinity*, ed. Thomas H. McCall and Michael C. Rea (New York: Oxford University Press, 2009), 338; cf. McCall, *Which Trinity?* 239-40; Peter Van Inwagen, *God, Knowledge & Mystery* (Ithaca: Cornell University Press, 1995), 265-67. For his part, McCall's commitment to tripersonality excludes Latin models of the Trinity (e.g., that of Brian Leftow) and he sees too many unresolved issues in the relative Trinitarianism model. He thus suggests that either a modified social model of the Trinity or the recently proposed constitution model present the most viable options going forward (though questions remain). Each seems to be able to "cohere with the NT portrayal of the distinct personhood of Father, Son, and Holy Spirit" while being consistent with "the monotheism of Paul, John, and other biblical authors," avoiding modalism and Arianism, and not "trespass[ing] the boundaries of the ancient ecumenical councils" (McCall, *Which Trinity?* 243-44). For the former see Keith Yandell, "How Many Times Does Three Go into One?" in *Philosophical and Theological Essays on the Trinity*, 151-69. For the latter see Jeffrey E. Brower and Michael C. Rea, "Material Constitution and the Trinity," in *Philosophical and Theological Essays on the Trinity*, 262-82.

actually working to counter it with a distinctly theological understanding of personhood."[29] Moreover, "I think it is important to retain continuity with the Christian tradition, but I am not at all convinced that conceiving of the divine persons in the robust sense of person that I have outlined here loses continuity with the tradition."[30]

Thus, among evangelicals, there exist fundamentally different and competing understandings of personhood, which substantially impact the nature and operation of the Trinity in salvation history.[31] In this context, does appeal to tradition hold promise for adequately addressing such differences?

Perhaps acceptance of a particular interpretation of the tradition (e.g., that of Holmes) would serve to arbitrate this debate. But interpretation of the tradition regarding the Trinity is itself disputed. Many of those who advocate the tripersonal view find support for it in their interpretation of the so-called Eastern view. Thus, Erickson affirms along with many others: "There was a difference of emphasis between the Eastern church, where subordination was taught, and the Western church, which more closely identified the acts of members of the Trinity as the acts of all three members together."[32] Holmes, on the other hand, argues: "The one who claims an East–West division, on any issue other than the narrow one of the *filioque*, is claiming something that the tradition never saw, and it is incumbent on him or her to specify the precise division, to demonstrate that it did in fact divide, and to account for the failure of generations of acute and holy theologians to perceive it."[33]

One who takes the opposite view of the tradition might likewise ask Holmes to account for the purported "failures" of many otherwise acute theologians past and present, including a major branch of Christianity, to recognize his

29. McCall, *Which Trinity?* 237. Cf. Cornelius Plantinga, Jr., "Social Trinity and Tritheism," in *Trinity, Incarnation, and Atonement: Philosophical and Theological Essays*, ed. Cornelius Plantinga, Jr. and Ronald J. Feenstra (Notre Dame: University of Notre Dame Press, 1989), 37.

30. McCall, *Which Trinity?* 238.

31. For some other accounts of the view that the persons of the Trinity each possess a distinct center of consciousness, see Cornelius Plantinga, Jr., "Social Trinity and Tritheism," 22; J. P. Moreland and William Lane Craig, *Philosophical Foundations for a Christian Worldview* (Downers Grove, IL: InterVarsity, 2003), 593-95; William Lane Craig, "Toward a Tenable Social Trinitarianism," in *Philosophical and Theological Essays on the Trinity*, 89-99.

32. Erickson, *Who's Tampering*, 166. He also qualifies that "in recent years the differences between the two traditions [Eastern and Western] have become less" (*Who's Tampering*, 168).

33. Holmes, *Quest*, 145. The *filioque* debate refers to dispute over whether the Holy Spirit proceeds from the Father alone or from the Father and the Son. The words "and from the Son" were added by the West to the Nicene Creed to say that the Spirit "proceeds from the Father *and from the Son.*"

view that the *filioque* is actually a "narrow" issue.[34] In this vein, one might further ask Holmes to provide a compelling account of the "failures" of many recent generations of "acute" theologians to "perceive" what he claims is the commonality of the East and West regarding the Trinity doctrine more broadly. Holmes attempts just such an account by appealing to the influence of, among other things, Romanticism and the modern concept of "personality," which he considers to be foreign to the patristic tradition and thereby misapplied.[35] Yet while doing so he challenges the so-called Hellenization hypothesis, which claims that the "theological tradition . . . became profoundly infected by Greek metaphysics in the patristic period," as lacking sufficient grounding in reliable historical research.[36] Any claim that the Trinity doctrine posited by those early church fathers is incorrect simply because of its purported roots in Greek philosophy exemplifies the genetic fallacy. However, would not the genetic fallacy likewise apply to the claim (implicit or explicit) that recent Trinitarian

34. Many have understood the *filioque* controversy to reflect a considerable division between East and West that itself entails a more robust conception of the "personalities" of the Trinity (e.g., in the Cappadocians) than Holmes's interpretation of the patristic tradition allows. So, whose interpretation is correct? Note the statement of Gregory of Nazianzus: "Either He [the Holy Spirit] is altogether Unbegotten, or else He is Begotten. If He is Unbegotten, there are two Unoriginates. If He is Begotten, you must make a further subdivision. He is so either by the Father or by the Son. And if by the Father, there are two Sons, and they are Brothers. . . . But if by the Son, then such a one will say, we get a glimpse of a Grandson God, than which nothing could be more absurd" (*Orations* 31.7, quoted in Erickson, *Who's Tampering*, 224).

35. Holmes writes: "I have suggested elsewhere that the influence of the Romantic movement was key," wherein personhood "understood as being fundamentally about self-determination, and so about volition, and so expressed primarily in spontaneous emotional reaction, became the highest good," leading to "enormous cultural pressure to" apply this "to God also." Consider also the "equivalent demands of personalism or existentialism" (*Quest*, 194).

36. Holmes, *Quest*, 195. He believes the more recent Trinitarian theologies were "too convinced of the rightness of some of the [historically inadequate] nineteenth-century criticisms and positions" that claimed "Hellenistic distortion of Christian theology" such that "doctrine of God, in particular, was shifted away from biblical presentations to an embracing of some Greek metaphysical ideas — notably simplicity, impassibility, eternity, and the like — which are alien to the Bible and have led to a distorted doctrine." In response, "we wanted to involve God in history, and believed a story, however vague, of Hellenistic infestation" (*Quest*, 197, 198). At the same time, he notes that the "development of the doctrine of the Trinity took place in the context of an intellectual culture that was shaped by Greek philosophy, and it could be argued that this became determinative. However, the argument needs to be made; as far as I am aware it has not really been seriously essayed since von Harnack, even if it has been regularly assumed" (*Quest*, 198). He considers it easier "to believe that the concepts were forced to fit the shape of Scripture than vice versa, and this was certainly the belief of those involved; an argument to the contrary at least needs credible evidence" (*Quest*, 198).

theologies are in error simply because they *may* have been influenced by Romanticism or Personalism?

There is thus considerable disagreement over how to understand the Trinity, which includes significant conflicts over the correct interpretation of the tradition. How, then, can the tradition itself mediate or arbitrate regarding the proper interpretation of the Trinity doctrine?[37]

Eternal Functional Subordination

Recently, the functional subordination of the Son and Spirit to the Father has been the subject of considerable debate.[38] A number of evangelicals (e.g., Bruce Ware and Wayne Grudem) claim that, while all of the persons of the Trinity are ontologically equal, Christ and the Spirit are eternally functionally subordinate to the Father.[39] According to this view, there is an eternal functional hierarchy within the Trinitarian relations wherein the Son and Spirit submit to the Father's commands.[40] On the other hand, many others (e.g., Millard Erickson, Kevin Giles, Gilbert Bilezikian) argue that the Father, Son, and Spirit are ontologically equal and also share equal authority such that submission of the Son and Spirit are temporary and functional "for the purpose of executing a specific mission of the triune God."[41]

37. A similar question can be asked of Scripture. See the discussion below.

38. This dispute typically aligns with the dispute over women in ministry.

39. See Ware, "Tampering"; Bruce A. Ware, *Father, Son, and Holy Spirit: Relationships, Roles, and Relevance* (Wheaton, IL: Crossway, 2005); Wayne A. Grudem, *Systematic Theology* (Grand Rapids: Zondervan, 1994); Grudem, *Evangelical Feminism*; Robert Letham, *The Holy Trinity: In Scripture, History, Theology, and Worship* (Phillipsburg, NJ: Presbyterian and Reformed, 2004); Bruce A. Ware, "Equal in Essence, Distinct in Roles: Eternal Functional Authority and Submission among the Essentially Equal Divine Persons of the Godhead," in *New Evangelical Subordinationism*; Wayne A. Grudem, "Biblical Evidence for the Eternal Submission of the Son to the Father," in *New Evangelical Subordinationism*.

40. The view of those who support eternal functional subordination (like those who oppose it) is not monolithic, however. Some affirm eternal generation whereas some deny it. Moreover, some (e.g., J. Scott Horrell and Bruce Ware) believe that prayer is rightly directed only to the Father while Grudem contends that one may correctly pray to any person of the Trinity. See Erickson, *Who's Tampering*, 54. Some avoid speaking of the gradation in ontological terms whereas some believe the gradation to be essential (and thus ontological), while paradoxically maintaining that the persons are ontologically equal.

41. Erickson, *Who's Tampering*, 20. Bilezikian states, "If we must talk of subordination it is only a functional or economic subordination that pertains exclusively to Christ's role in relation to human history" ("Hermeneutical Bungee-Jumping," 60). Cf. Giles, *Trinity*; Giles, *Jesus*

Many who reject eternal functional subordination believe that it logically implies heterodoxy and "contains an implicit ontological subordination."[42] Giles even suggests that this view tends toward Arianism and thus "implicitly contradict[s] . . . the ETS statement of faith."[43] Nevertheless, Erickson allows that each of the two competing views "falls within the boundaries of traditional orthodoxy. Neither view has ever been condemned by an official body of the church."[44] Both sides claim that the other is tampering with the Trinity doctrine.[45] Both sides claim that the other misinterprets Scripture, and both sides claim that tradition is on their side. How, then, can tradition mediate the dispute? On one hand, Bilezikian states: "Except for occasional and predictable deviations, this [temporary functional subordination] is the historical Biblical trinitarian doctrine that has been defined in the creeds and generally defended by the Church, at least the western Church, throughout the centuries."[46] Conversely, Grudem claims that eternal functional subordination "has been the historic doctrine of the church" and thus "egalitarians" not only lack the "basis of arguments from Scripture" but "should also have the honesty and courtesy to explain to readers why they now feel it necessary to differ with the historic doctrine of the church as expressed in its major creeds."[47]

Confusion over the proper interpretation of historical theology on this point relates to the debate discussed in the previous section. Erickson contends: "In general, the gradational view more closely resembles the traditional Eastern view of the Trinity, and the equivalence view is a variety of the Western

and the Father; Giles, *The Eternal Generation of the Son: Maintaining Orthodoxy in Trinitarian Theology* (Downers Grove, IL: IVP Academic, 2012); Giles, "The Trinity without Tiers," in *New Evangelical Subordinationism*; McCall, *Which Trinity*, 175-88.

42. Erickson, *Who's Tampering*, 257. He states, "If one member always and everywhere is functionally superior to the other, then there must be an ontological basis for this difference" (*Who's Tampering*, 257). Gilbert Bilezikian likewise believes that "a subordination that extends into eternity cannot remain only functional" but is "*ipso facto* an ontological reality" ("Hermeneutical Bungee-Jumping," 63).

43. Kevin Giles, "The Evangelical Theological Society and the Doctrine of the Trinity," *EvQ* 80/4 (2008): 323. Cf. Bilezikian, "Hermeneutical Bungee-Jumping," 57-58. On the other hand, see Robert Letham, "Reply to Kevin Giles," *EvQ* 80/4 (2008).

44. Erickson, *Who's Tampering*, 257.

45. See, for example, Giles, *Jesus and the Father*; Erickson, *Who's Tampering*; Ware, "Tampering"; Bilezikian, "Hermeneutical Bungee-Jumping," 58.

46. Bilezikian, "Hermeneutical Bungee-Jumping," 60. Likewise, for Erickson, the "view of the eternal equality of authority of the three persons has been the dominant view of church theologians of the past" (*Who's Tampering*, 81).

47. Grudem, *Evangelical Feminism*, 422.

approach to the doctrine."[48] On the other hand, Holmes (as has been seen) rejects the East–West dichotomy on this point and suggests that both conceptions are, therefore, incorrect: "Is it the case that, either, the Cappadocian fathers insist on the sole monarchy of the Father, or that developed Trinitarianism refuses the sole monarchy in a proto-democratic impulse? Neither is true."[49]

In this regard, the very concept of a subordination of the Son's (divine) will to the Father's will depends upon the presupposition that the Father, Son, and Spirit each possess a will that might be subordinated to the other's command. That is, a tripersonal conception of the Trinity is required by the view that the Son's will is eternally *or* temporarily subordinate and obedient to the Father's will.[50] Thus, Holmes's interpretation of the tradition rules out both views (conceived in this fashion) as ontologically impossible, because Holmes rejects tripersonality (and thus multiple wills) within the Trinity, meaning that "the monarchy is the shared possession of the three hypostases" and "is therefore not to be simply linked to the Father."[51]

48. Erickson, *Who's Tampering*, 257.

49. Holmes, *Quest*, 145.

50. At times, Erickson might be taken to refer to a singular divine will, such as when he states, "The Father's will, which the Son obeys, is actually the will of all three members of the Trinity, administered on their behalf by the Father" (*Who's Tampering*, 248). However, it is apparent from Erickson's explanation elsewhere that "will" here refers not to a shared faculty but to a unified harmonious will that the three "wills" share in the sense of agreement. Thus, "the sending of the Son to earth was done by the Father but on behalf of the Trinity. In a very real sense, all of them sent the Son, and all had jointly decided that he would go" (*Who's Tampering*, 135). He notes that Giles "believes that the gradational view of three wills leads to tritheism" but notes "that the word will is somewhat ambiguous, and that tritheism can be avoided by a view in which there are three wills but the three, in the pattern known as perichoresis, always agree" (*Who's Tampering*, 254).

51. Holmes, *Quest*, 146. Since Holmes considers the Trinity to have one shared (simple) faculty of will, it is impossible that one divine person could obey the will of another. Any obedience of the Son to the Father would have to be restricted to the human will in the incarnation. The issue of divine simplicity is itself much disputed. Bruce Ware, William Lane Craig, and others have explicitly rejected divine simplicity. Moreland and Craig state, "Nothing in Scripture warrants us in thinking that God is simple and that each person of the Trinity is identical to the whole Trinity" (*Philosophical Foundations*, 593). Cf. Alvin Plantinga, *Does God Have a Nature?* (Milwaukee: Marquette University Press, 1980); Cornelius Plantinga, Jr., "Social Trinity and Tritheism," 39. However, many evangelicals still advocate divine simplicity. So Grudem, *Systematic Theology*, 177-80; Millard J. Erickson, *God the Father Almighty: A Contemporary Exploration of the Divine Attributes* (Grand Rapids: Baker, 1998), 210-32; Dennis W. Jowers, "The Inconceivability of Subordination within a Simple God," in *New Evangelical Subordinationism*; James E. Dolezal, *God without Parts: Divine Simplicity and the Metaphysics of*

Adding to the disagreements over the proper interpretation of the tradition, many of the statements drawn from tradition to support eternal functional subordination appear to refer to eternal generation and thus may not address the issue of subordination at all.[52] It is a matter of protracted dispute whether eternal generation broadly or such statements narrowly entail subordination (ontological or functional).[53] Moreover, while "many of the historical references that" Ware and Grudem "cite as support for a historical belief in [eternal] functional subordination actually rest upon this idea of eternal generation," Ware rejects eternal generation and Grudem appears to reinterpret it (see below).[54] Thus, Erickson critiques: "If Ware and Grudem do not hold this view [of eternal generation], they cannot cite these earlier sources in support of their own view [of eternal functional subordination]."[55] This overlap between the debates over eternal functional subordination and the eternal generation of the Son further highlights the extent of interpretive disagreement since there are some who affirm and deny eternal generation on both sides of the

God's Absoluteness (Eugene, OR: Pickwick, 2011); Stephen R. Holmes, Listening to the Past: The Place of Tradition in Theology (Grand Rapids: Baker Academic, 2002), 50-67. McCall contends that, in this regard, those convinced of "the Latin theological tradition will" be "suspicious of anything that threatens to compromise the doctrine of divine simplicity" (Which Trinity? 221). For a critical response to Holmes see R. T. Mullins, "Simply Impossible: A Case against Divine Simplicity," Journal of Reformed Theology 7/2 (2013).

52. Grudem, for example, claims that the "great, historic creeds affirm that there is an eternal difference between the Father and Son, not in their being (for they are equal in all attributes and the three persons are just one 'being' or 'substance'), but in the way they relate to one another" (Evangelical Feminism, 415). He thus appeals to the "eternal generation of the son," which "found expression in the Nicene Creed," as well as language of eternal generation from the Chalcedonian and Athanasian Creeds, the Thirty-Nine Articles of the Church of England, the Westminster Confession of Faith, and numerous theologians (Evangelical Feminism, 415-22).

53. For example, while Giles accepts eternal generation he believes that it does not entail subordination, either ontological or functional (Jesus and the Father, 240; cf. Giles, Eternal Generation). Erickson, on the other hand, denies eternal generation (see below) but believes that the Nicene, Niceno–Constantinopolitan, and Chalcedonian Creeds express the eternal generation of the Son. He allows that some who affirm functional subordination take it as "an inference drawn from eternal generation," but he argues that "nothing is said [in these or the Apostles' Creed] about subordination or relative authority" (Who's Tampering, 146). At the same time, Erickson suggests that eternal generation entails subordination (Who's Tampering, 184, 251). Paul Helm, "Of God, and of the Holy Trinity: A Response to Dr. Beckwith," The Churchman 115/4 (2001): 350, further maintains that "if the word 'begotten' is to retain any meaning then it must carry the implications that the Father caused the Son to be," which implies "in some undeniable sense the Son is subordinate to the Father." See the discussion below.

54. Erickson, Who's Tampering, 184.

55. Erickson, Who's Tampering, 184.

functional subordination issue.[56] To this ongoing debate regarding eternal generation we now turn.

Eternal Generation

The Nicene Creed is widely taken to assert the traditional doctrine of the eternal generation of the Son.[57] In this regard, Stephen Holmes identifies eternal generation as an essential element of what he contends is unified patristic Trinitarianism.[58] Numerous evangelical theologians, however, reject eternal generation and thus reject this part of the Nicene Creed. For example, Ware purports that "both the 'eternal begetting of the Son' and 'eternal procession of the Spirit' seem to me highly speculative and not grounded in biblical teaching."[59] Erickson also rejects the doctrine of eternal generation: "It appears to me that the concept of eternal generation does not have biblical warrant and does not make sense philosophically. As such, we should eliminate it from theological discussions of the Trinity."[60] Similarly, John Feinberg rejects the "doctrines of eternal generation and procession."[61] Paul Helm adds, "Do these claims [regarding eternal generation] not take us far from the New Testament, and give rise to unnecessary

---

56. For example, Kevin Giles (TFS = temporary functional subordination) and Robert Letham (EFS = eternal functional subordination) affirm eternal generation while Millard Erickson (TFS) and Bruce Ware (EFS) deny it. Erickson, however, contends that it was earlier gradationists who grounded EFS in eternal generation, whereas "more recent gradationists tend to avoid these terms and particularly regard the term *monogenēs* as meaning 'one and only' rather than 'only begotten'" (*Who's Tampering*, 53). Further, most who accept the equivalence view (TFS) are reluctant "to take literally the idea of eternal generation. . . . There is no idea that the Son and the Spirit derive their being or their personhood from the Father" (*Who's Tampering*, 81).

57. There exist various versions and translations of the Nicene Creed, but they all are typically understood to teach the eternal (that is, timeless) generation of the Son (e.g., "light from light" and "begotten, not made"). Eternal generation also appears in other creeds (e.g., Athanasian, Chalcedonian) and the teachings of various church fathers. Erickson thus states, "The creeds of the church, including those arising from the ecumenical councils, quite uniformly reflect the idea of the eternal begetting of the Son by the Father" (except the Apostles' Creed) (*Who's Tampering*, 166).

58. Holmes, *Quest*, 146.

59. Ware, *Father, Son, and Holy Spirit*, 162 n. 3.

60. Erickson, *Who's Tampering*, 251.

61. John S. Feinberg, *No One like Him: The Doctrine of God* (Wheaton, IL: Crossway, 2001), 492.

speculation?"[62] J. P. Moreland and William Lane Craig contend, "Although creedally affirmed, the doctrine of the generation of the Son (and the procession of the Spirit) is a relic of Logos Christology which finds virtually no warrant in the biblical text and introduces a subordinationism into the Godhead which anyone who affirms the full deity of Christ ought to find very troubling."[63]

Grudem, however, appears to avoid explicit rejection of the Nicene Creed on this point by reinterpreting the traditional language of "'paternity' (or 'generation') for the Father, 'begottenness' (or 'filiation') for the Son, and 'procession' (or 'spiration') for the Holy Spirit" as labels that "do not mean anything more than 'relating as a Father,' and 'relating as a Son,' and 'relating as Spirit.'"[64] He claims, however, that "it would be more helpful if the language of 'eternal begetting of the Son' (also called the 'eternal generation of the Son') were not retained in any modern theological formulations."[65] Kevin Giles, on the other hand, characterizes Grudem's interpretation as a "doctrinally dangerous" move that "reject[s] a theological idea enshrined in the creeds and confessions" and seeks "to replace it with another idea — the eternal subordination of the Son in authority — as the primary basis for differentiation, with no historical support at all, or any theological merit."[66]

There is, then, considerable controversy among evangelicals over eternal generation, functional subordination, and social vs. Latin conceptions of the Trinity, and such disagreements include fundamentally different interpretations of the Christian tradition. It is difficult to see how the tradition itself could, then, function as interpretive authority. In light of this brief survey of significant contemporary conflicts over the Trinity in evangelical literature, we now return to discuss each of the four ways in which the community approach does not appear to be preferable.

62. Helm, "Of God," 351. "There is no question but those who formulated the doctrine of the Trinity in terms of the begetting of the Son and the processing of the Spirit were influenced by Neoplatonism, particularly by the idea that from the One emanated Mind and Soul," with the crucial difference that the "Son and Spirit are hypostases in their own right" ("Of God," 351).

63. Moreland and Craig, *Philosophical Foundations*, 594.

64. Grudem, *Systematic Theology*, 254 n. 38. Grudem believes the biblical term *monogenēs* should be translated "only," claiming it would have been *monogennētos* if "only begotten" was intended (*Systematic Theology*, 1233).

65. Grudem, *Systematic Theology*, 1234.

66. Giles, *Jesus and the Father*, 240. Giles recognizes that the "biblical support is not strong" for "differentiating the Father, Son, and Spirit on the basis of origination" (*Jesus and the Father*, 239 n. 166). He thus relies heavily on the tradition as "the key" to the "meaning" of the Trinity (*Eternal Generation*, 37).

The Inadequacy of Community Resources to Arbitrate the Trinity Debates

Inadequate to Arbitrate the Debates

First, extracanonical tradition is insufficient to helpfully address these contemporary Trinity disputes because, in many cases, it does not provide sufficient material to do so. There is no universally applicable extracanonical tradition that adequately arbitrates these debates. Both sides often claim tradition is on their side, but they may take different approaches to which parts of tradition are theologically acceptable, they widely vary in their interpretations of that tradition, and they offer mutually exclusive claims regarding its application.[67]

Conversely, one might rightly point out that Scripture alone also does not settle these debates, as evidenced by the fact that the debates continue among Bible-believing Christians. However, the canonical *sola Scriptura* approach does not expect Scripture to settle such disputes because of its fundamental (descriptive) recognition of the universal hermeneutical context within which different human interpreters (individual or collective) inevitably contribute to the result of interpretation, leading to unavoidable hermeneutical diversity. It is the communitarian criticism that presumes that Scripture ought to settle such disputes and, if it does not, Scripture must therefore be supplemented with community resources (e.g., extracanonical tradition). The canonical *sola Scriptura* approach holds, rather, that *no* approach is adequate to settle all interpretive disagreements.[68]

Inadequate to Be the Rule of Faith

This brings us to the second point: Tradition cannot function as the doctrinally or interpretively authoritative rule of faith because many Christians, including some mainstream evangelical scholars, depart (on purportedly Scriptural bases) from various particulars that appear in the Christian tradition. The Nicene Creed appears to present the most promising test case since it is identi-

---

67. The points of conflict that the creeds and tradition do address can also be (at least as adequately) addressed by Scripture.

68. Even the "settling" of all such disagreements by force would not remove the possibility of private, unspoken disagreements.

fied by communitarians as representative of the Church's "hermeneutical consensus" and containing the "basic essential truths which have been confessed by all Christians from the first days of the Church until today."[69]

In order to implement the authority of the Nicene Creed, however, one must first determine which form should function as the rule of faith.[70] That is, should the Eastern or Western (*filioque*) wording of the Creed be adopted? This is no small question, as is shown by the repercussions that still divide major branches of Christianity. Neither the "ecumenical" creeds specifically nor the tradition more broadly appears to be able to settle this debate. Indeed, the debate itself is over which tradition and whose interpretation are correct.[71] John Feinberg thus asks whether such a debate should have been pursued in the first place: "If my rejection of the doctrines of eternal generation and eternal procession are correct, then there are really no grounds for a controversy over whether the Spirit proceeds just from the Father or from Father and Son. To the extent that the split between the Eastern and Western churches resulted from this dispute, the split was totally unnecessary."[72] Whether or not one agrees with Feinberg, this raises significant questions about the practicability and wisdom of adopting any creed as the rule of faith. In the case of the *filioque*, differing interpretations led to dispute over the particular wording of the Creed, contributing to a controversy greater than any in the previous thousand years of Christian history.

Even if one sidesteps the *filioque* controversy, as informative and helpful as the Nicene Creed and its history have been, the Creed is not universally accepted. Consider the debate over eternal generation, a doctrine widely considered to be essential to the Nicene Creed but variously interpreted and even rejected by many evangelicals (e.g., Erickson, Feinberg, Helm, Ware, and Craig). How, then, could the Creed function as the delimiter of evangelical orthodoxy or as interpretive authority?[73]

This problem is not limited to contemporary evangelical debates. In fact, many have claimed that John Calvin was an advocate of eternal generation

69. Mathison, *Shape*, 280. However, while Nicea stands as an important testament to the fact that the full divinity of Christ was not the result of a vote but was already the overwhelming majority view, it does not present a *universal* view.

70. Of course, this is an issue common to all ancient texts.

71. Recall, conversely, that the canonical approach does not expect to be able to settle debates but suggests a common rule (the common canonical core) for dialogue.

72. Feinberg, *No One like Him*, 492.

73. A creed or confession legitimately functions as delimiter within a community who adopts it, but how could any creed do so "universally"?

(e.g., Gregg Allison),[74] others that he rejected the doctrine (e.g., Loraine Boettner), and still others that he did not think it "worth defending" (e.g., Millard Erickson).[75] Representative of this apparent ambiguity, Calvin states: "I felt that I would be better advised not to touch upon many things that would profit but little, and would burden my readers with useless trouble. For what is the point in disputing whether the Father always begets? Indeed, it is foolish to imagine a continuous act of begetting, since it is clear that three persons have subsisted in God from eternity."[76] At best, this shows the considerable complexity of interpreting past theologians and the ambiguity that often arises in historical theological interpretation. At worst, Calvin might be among those excluded from orthodoxy on the view that the Nicene Creed functions as the rule of faith. One's conclusion in this regard is, as always, a matter of interpretation.[77]

Mathison believes that, because "heretics are liars," the "creeds are necessary to detect and remove them from the Church. Solo *Scriptura* cannot even begin to accomplish this necessary task."[78] However, is evangelicalism prepared to exclude or repudiate anyone who rejects eternal generation and, if

74. Gregg R. Allison, "Theological Interpretation of Scripture: An Introduction and Preliminary Evaluation," *Southern Baptist Journal of Theology* 14/2 (2010): 33 n. 3, claims to follow Calvin in affirming eternal generation. For example, Calvin affirms: "We confess that the Son, since he is God, exists of himself, but not in respect of his person; indeed, since he is the Son, we say that he exists from the Father. Thus his essence is without beginning; while the beginning of his person is God himself" (*Institutes*, 1.13.25; cf. *Institutes*, 1.13.18).

75. Erickson, *Who's Tampering*, 184. Loraine Boettner, *Studies in Theology* (Philadelphia: P&R, 1964), 122, claims to follow Calvin when he insists that if the Father "is the *Fons Trinitatis* — the fountain or source of the Trinity — from whom both the Son and the Spirit are derived, it seems that in spite of all else we may say we have made the Son and the Spirit dependent upon another as their principal cause, and have destroyed the true and essential equality between the Persons of the Trinity." He prefers to say "that within the essential life of the Trinity no one person is prior to, nor generated by, nor proceeds from, another" (*Studies*, 123). Notably, Calvin does refer to the Father as "the fountain and wellspring of all things," but this may be in reference only to created things (*Institutes*, 1.13.18).

76. *Institutes* 1.13.29. Erickson believes this comment suggests "that he did not personally espouse the doctrine or consider it to make any sense" (*Who's Tampering*, 163).

77. This calls into question the felicitous claim that "the magisterial reformers' understanding of tradition allowed them to agree with the Roman Catholic Church on the essential doctrine of the Holy Trinity as understood at Nicaea and Constantinople — it was, in other words, part of the Tradition" (Allert, "What Are We Trying to Conserve?" 341). Responding to Holmes, Jon Mackenzie, "A Double-Headed Luther? A Lutheran Response to *The Holy Trinity* by Stephen R. Holmes," *EvQ* 86/1 (2014): 46, questions the "feasibility of his [Holmes's] presentation of Luther" as "read into the paradigmatic Trinitarianism of the fourth century."

78. Mathison, *Shape*, 340.

so, on whose interpretation? Moreover, what about the myriad other complex disputes among evangelicals over momentous issues of divine ontology and the God–world relationship (e.g., divine simplicity, timelessness, and impassibility) that appear to hinge upon one's acceptance or rejection of various metaphysical presuppositions entailed by eternal generation?

In all this, how can one distinguish between heresy and the true doctrine of the Trinity? If the orthodox view of the Trinity is that held by Christians universally, then the orthodox view either does not include eternal generation because some Christians reject it or those who reject eternal generation are not truly Christians. This kind of creedal approach faces numerous seemingly insoluble difficulties in adequately answering questions like: Which creed and on whose interpretation? If the creeds get their authority from a community, the appeal to creeds with regard to who is or is not an orthodox Christian begs the question. In other words, to say that creeds derive authority from the genuinely Christian community is circular because the very identification of who is genuinely Christian rests on the creeds themselves.

The more modest claim of the canon itself as "rule" appears to hold considerable advantages because, with an intrinsic canon approach, no appeal is made to the community to determine the canon or to provide the final interpretation thereof (though the community should be utilized as a resource in the process of interpretation). What one could say, then, is that any statement of faith is valid and possesses canonically derived (ministerial) authority insofar as it agrees with Scripture. This is precisely what the canonical approach's working model of *sola Scriptura* claims.

Inadequate as Interpretive Authority

This brings us to the third problem with the communitarian approach relative to the contemporary Trinity debates: Tradition is not a sufficient rule or interpretive authority because different scholars interpret it differently. In fact, hermeneutical diversity may be a greater problem within communitarian approaches, which add diverse interpretation of Christian tradition to that of Scripture. Many evangelicals believe that tradition itself (broadly conceived) is inadequate because it contains mutually exclusive interpretations of Scripture and mutually exclusive explanations regarding doctrines, including self-identified disputes between theologians in the tradition.[79] The presence and

---

79. Of course, critics of Scripture perceive numerous contradictions in the canon. However,

extent of contradictions in the tradition is itself contended and is (like every other claim) subject to interpretation.

For example, Origen's theology seems to have heavily influenced the doctrine and language of eternal generation in the Nicene Creed (e.g., "light from light"). However, many consider Origen to be a heretical church father whose teachings include subordinationism, which would contradict other claims regarding the full ontological equality of Father, Son, and Spirit.[80] Holmes suggests, however, that it is "certainly not logically necessary" that Origen's "assertions of origin and dependence" imply subordination, and he thinks this was "probably not intended by Origen."[81] Yet, if Holmes's interpretation is right, then the interpretation of many other historical theologians (past and present) is wrong. Who decides, then, whether Origen's theology is properly interpreted as subordinationist or not and, perhaps more consequentially, whether the Nicene Creed itself entails subordinationism?

The question for our purposes is not whether the interpretations of Holmes or other theologians are correct, as important as that is. The question is, in light of the far-reaching interpretive disagreements among highly qualified and respected theologians, how could tradition itself function as an interpretive authority? Whether or not one adopts the broader claims made by many evangelicals that tradition includes insoluble contradictions, it seems undeniable that informed and proficient historical theologians differ in their historical interpretations. As seen earlier, Holmes laments the recent "explosion of theological work" on the Trinity that, he claims, "misunderstands and distorts the traditional doctrine so badly that it is un-

---

most evangelicals recognize tensions but not theological contradictions within Scripture and the traditional view itself is a high view.

80. Other notables that are often considered to adopt some form of subordinationism include Justin Martyr and Hilary of Poitiers; both, however, are variously interpreted.

81. Holmes, *Quest*, 79 n. 73. Holmes thus departs from J. A. Lyons's reading of Origen's "assertions of origin and dependence as implying subordination" (*Quest*, 79). Cf. J. A. Lyons, *The Cosmic Christ in Origen and Teilhard de Chardin: A Comparative Study* (New York: Oxford University Press, 1982), 111-15. Holmes recognizes that "Origen struggled to find an adequate expression of the relationship of the Son to the Father," seeing the Son as a mediator who "bridges" the "ontological gap between the perfect being of the Father" and creatures (maintaining the "Platonic hierarchy of being"). As such, the Son "is located ontologically below the Father but above the creatures" (*Quest*, 79). Origen thus "seemingly finds it impossible to speak of God's activity in the creation without lapsing [perhaps unintentionally, Holmes suggests] into subordinationist language" (*Quest*, 80). He adds, "Origen's theology works, until the troubling question of the economy [the God–world relationship] is brought into play" (*Quest*, 81).

recognizable."[82] Some reputable theologians accept and make use of the de Régnon thesis while others reject it as a misinterpretation of the tradition. Some contend that the Trinity is tripersonal and find support for this in their interpretation of the so-called Eastern view, while others reject the idea of three wills in the Trinity, claiming the Trinity possesses one simple collective will. Some contend that the tradition supports eternal functional subordination whereas others deny eternal subordination altogether. Some reject eternal generation whereas others consider it to be an essential mark of orthodoxy. Each of these disputes depicts mutually exclusive positions held by evangelical scholars who possess the support of some community and (often) claim that tradition is on their side.[83]

Thus, like Scripture, tradition also requires interpretation and is interpreted in various ways by evangelicals. Perhaps, then, the addition of tradition as an authoritative source or hermeneutical key or "rule" actually exacerbates the issue of hermeneutical diversity, providing more fodder for interpretive disagreement and theological conflict. This severely undercuts the communitarian claim that because Scripture requires interpretation and has been interpreted in various mutually exclusive ways regarding the Trinity doctrine, the addition of community resources (e.g., tradition, creeds) is advisable.[84] Tradition itself (like every other communication) requires interpretation and has been interpreted in widely divergent ways by respected evangelicals. Who, then, decides which interpretation of historical theology (if any) is correct?[85] If the tradition is itself interpreted in such widely divergent ways, how can tradition itself become a hermeneutically authoritative interpretive tool?

82. Holmes, *Quest*, xv. He goes on, "It may be that recent writers are right in their accounts of the content and use of Trinitarian doctrine, but if so, we need to conclude that the majority of the Christian tradition has been wrong in what it has claimed about the eternal life of God" (*Quest*, 2). This assumes that Holmes's own interpretation of the "majority of the Christian tradition" is correct, which is by no means clear. For Holmes's communitarian approach, see Holmes, *Listening to the Past*.

83. With regard to the functional subordination debate, for example, Erickson comments that each side "claims that it has the support of history — indeed that it is the view that has always been held by the church" Erickson, (*Who's Tampering*, 20).

84. See Allert, "What Are We Trying to Conserve?" 342; Giles, *Trinity*, 9; Giles, *Jesus and the Father*, 70.

85. Moreover, who decides which traditional data is admissible? This presents no problem for a canonical approach due to the common canonical core.

Inadequate to Answer:
Which Tradition and on Whose Interpretation?

This brings us to the final claim against the communitarian approach: The elevation of tradition or other community resources fails to adequately answer the questions: Which tradition and on whose interpretation? Giles himself recognizes that, while tradition should prescribe the correct interpretation, "sometimes it needs to be corrected or rejected," such as when the Reformers departed from "the traditional way Scripture had been read" because "it supported ideas and practices excluded by clear biblical teaching."[86] Yet if tradition itself prescribes the correct interpretation, how could one come to reject that tradition? That is, how does one know when the tradition is wrong if the tradition itself provides the correct understanding?[87]

As Millard Erickson puts it, claiming that some "community is the arbiter of what is truth . . . does not solve the problem; it only shifts it."[88] Indeed, every one of the ongoing Trinitarian disputes among evangelicals in this chapter is "held by a group of persons who constitute its community of validation. The problem then is, which community shall be the one whose judgment of validation I accept?"[89] Even with communitarian approaches, individual interpretation that informs the decision of where one will place faith (or not) is unavoidable. As such, the community itself cannot adequately function as the arbiter of truth.

On the other hand, the canonical approach recognizes that, whereas any individual or community interpretation may be incorrect, Scripture itself is uniquely infallible and thus uniquely adequate to function as the rule. This highlights the central and crucial difference between Scripture and tradition. Whereas tradition is sometimes wrong (as even communitarian advocates recognize), Scripture is fully sufficient and infallibly trustworthy. Whereas my interpretation of *both* Scripture and tradition may be wrong, one is best served to employ efforts to interpret Scripture itself on account of its infallibility (using, without giving hermeneutical normativity to, extracanonical resources).

---

86. Giles, *Trinity*, 5.

87. Giles suggests that tradition regarding the issue of slavery or the status of women in the church was "not the product of prolonged theological debate, and it was never endorsed by a universal church council, creed or confession" (*Trinity*, 5). Further, what about the departures of the Reformers?

88. Erickson, *Who's Tampering*, 84.

89. Erickson, *Who's Tampering*, 84. As such, "it is still the individual who must choose" and, to choose, must interpret (*Who's Tampering*, 84).

In this way, the canonical approach faces no difficulties in relation to the questions regarding which community or tradition is adequate because the canonical approach denies that any community, tradition, or creed should operate as a hermeneutically authoritative rule in biblical or theological interpretation. Moreover, the canonical approach maintains that each individual has a right to religious freedom and a duty to engage and interpret Scripture and theology in accordance with the individual's own conscience. The question regarding which community of faith one should be a part of, then, is left to each individual's decision. Everyone must ultimately choose which religious beliefs to accept (if any) and which community most closely allies with those beliefs. With a canonical approach, the question becomes which community of faith possesses a system that appears to best correspond to the canon, with internal consistency.

The Adequacy of Canonical *Sola Scriptura* for the Trinity Doctrine

Evangelicals on both sides of the debate typically accept the claim, which I believe to be true, that the Trinity doctrine is grounded in Scripture, at least in its essential elements.[90] The suggestion of this canonical approach is that such minimal grounding is sufficient for a canonical systematic theology. This does not entail anything resembling the naïve view that the Nicene Creed is derivable directly from Scripture.[91] Nor should anything in this book be

90. I take this claim to be uncontroversial among evangelicals (though it is not so with others). As Fred Sanders, "Redefining Progress in Trinitarian Theology: Stephen R. Holmes on the Trinity," *EvQ* 86/1 (2014): 9, puts it, "The doctrine of the Trinity is in fact well grounded in the gospel and well attested in the scriptures" apart from "any new arguments from the theological journals. Considered in itself, the doctrine is already credible and biblical." McCall adds, "Christians have been Trinitarians because they have been convinced that the revelation of God in Jesus Christ demands it" (*Which Trinity?* 231). Indeed, "so far as I can see, the only reason for Christians to believe in the doctrine of the Trinity at all is on the basis of God's revelation in Jesus Christ as seen in Scripture," though McCall does believe theologians should work within the constraints of the ecumenical creeds and "go as far as possible toward coherence with the Latin creeds and various confessional statements" (*Which Trinity?* 231, 233). Although coming to a different conclusion regarding the nature of the Trinity, Holmes similarly notes the "remarkable level of continuity in the exegetical appeals made by developers and defenders of Trinitarian doctrine from the patristic period down to (conservative) defenders of the doctrine of the Trinity today" (*Quest*, 51). He adds, "Any standard account of biblical authority will affirm, whatever else is also affirmed, that the propositional claims concerning God's life made or necessarily implied by biblical texts are adequate guides to the truth of God's life" (*Quest*, 51).

91. As Holmes sees it, the fourth century's "technical terminology" that was unavailable

taken to mean that community or historical theology is unhelpful or should be ignored. The canonical approach recognizes that the Christian tradition has informed and shaped the conversation, with great benefits but also some apparent shortcomings. Yet as Fred Sanders puts it, we can no "longer afford to displace the weight of this burden onto a temporary resting place like tradition or the consent of all the faithful, lest that prop suffer the strains of bearing what it was never intended to support."[92] We need to "render the doctrine of the Trinity with unprecedented clarity as a biblical doctrine."[93]

My suggestion that the minimal yet rigorously clear grounding of the Trinity doctrine in the canon itself is sufficient for a canonical systematic theology is motivated by an approach to theology that operates as a continuous (never fully or finally complete) construction of models that aim to derive from, correspond to, and make sense of the entire canonical data without doing injury to any of it. With this kind of canonical approach, the theologian is continually driven back to the text for further explanation and the resulting (humble) theological system is more like the traveling wilderness sanctuary than a cathedral. This does not mean that communities operating on such a canonical approach cannot construct a serious, detailed, and beautiful systematic theology in the form of models, but it does mean that no such models should be taken too seriously. Rather, taking seriously the claim that interpreters (individually and collectively) inevitably bring something to theological interpretation, the canonical approach expects that theology will never stop "reforming" and thus urges restraint from going beyond the limits of canonical revelation or running

earlier gave "firm intellectual grounding to an idea that is so deeply engraved in Christian devotion and confession as to be inescapable. The early Christians worshiped the Trinity from the first; the tale of the development of Trinitarian theology is an account of how they came to find a satisfying way of speaking of the One they worshipped" (*Quest*, 57-58). Thus, the fourth-century dogma says more than the tradition up to that point. Is it not possible, then, that the fourth-century language that served so well in its time to meet the Arian heresy might not be the best language to convey the Trinity doctrine as derived from the canon today? Might twenty-first-century tools unavailable to fourth-century Christians contribute to further understanding?

92. Sanders, "Redefining Progress," 8. At the same time, Sanders agrees with Holmes's perspective that "we should take the patristic consensus [including eternal generation and simplicity] as a normative baseline for getting Scripture right, and then take up and read the Bible with a retrieved and revived doctrine of God" ("Redefining Progress," 8).

93. Sanders, "Redefining Progress," 8. Thus, "systematic work on the doctrine of the Trinity will need to give more attention than usual to exegesis and hermeneutics. This is not something that can be outsourced to the biblical studies department anymore; for theologians of the Trinity, the exegetical questions must now be handled as part of the systematic task" ("Redefining Progress," 8).

too far ahead in constructing models that purport to adequately correspond to it. In this way, theological models based on a canonical approach remain open to the further insights of broad and systematic as well as deep and close study of the canon such that any statements of beliefs, models, or systematic theologies are continually subject to revision. No extracanonical resource can, therefore, be finally determinative. While being open to such change, even radical change if deemed necessary, one should neither ignore nor be too hasty to discard the interpretations of predecessors or contemporaries. Theological method will not lead to theological unity, but movement toward common canonical theological method can lead to productive dialogue that includes listening to and learning from one another.

With the essence of this approach in mind, we may briefly revisit the four ways I have claimed in this chapter that the community approach is not preferable, by asking whether and to what extent the same might apply to the canonical approach. Before doing so, notice that even if the claims applied equally against *sola Scriptura*, this would not be sufficient reason to add uninspired extracanonical resources that continue (and perhaps exacerbate) the issues at hand. Recall that the overarching claim of the community approach laid out at the beginning of this chapter was that tradition is needed to remedy (in some significant way) the supposed shortcomings of Scripture alone. As shall be seen, however, I believe the canonical approach does adequately meet each of the communitarian objections.

Nevertheless, one might offer the four parallel arguments against Scripture alone that: (1) Scriptural data is also not sufficient to address Trinitarian debates (evident since they are ongoing), (2) Scripture cannot function as its own "rule," (3) different scholars also interpret Scripture in vastly different ways, and (4) Scripture itself cannot arbitrate between differing interpretations.

First, the canonical approach claims that Scripture is sufficient and adequate to function as the "rule" in addressing the Trinity debates (and all others) without claiming to be able to settle them universally. Indeed, the canonical *sola Scriptura* approach holds that no approach is adequate to settle all interpretive disagreements.

Second, the canonical approach has none of the difficulties that the community approach has regarding the determination of a sufficient and adequate rule of faith. The canon itself is the rule of faith and holds the practical advantages of already being accepted by evangelicals and consisting of a common canonical core that is accepted by the vast majority of self-identifying Christians. Whereas many evangelical scholars reject particular aspects of the Christian tradition (including even elements of the Nicene Creed), I know of no evangelical scholar who rejects the canon of Scripture and the sixty-six books of the canon that are nearly universally affirmed by Christians. Although, with the intrinsic canon approach, such broad support does not itself ground (or determine) the canon, the functional authority of the canon is already in place and, as suggested in the discussion of adequate canon recognition in chapters 2–3, there appear to be sufficiently good reasons for personally and collectively ratifying the recognition of the sixty-six books of the Protestant canon.

In this regard, adopting the canon as the rule for theology is at least as co-herent on communitarian grounds alone as the adoption of any extracanonical normative interpreter. Indeed, if one is seeking the widest consensus possi-ble, what has enjoyed a wider consensus than the common canonical core it-self?[94] In this regard, communitarian approaches may recognize the epistemic rights and internal coherence of Christians (in community) recognizing the common canonical core as "foundational." Further, one could even argue for a very particular "community," that of the uniquely commissioned and Spirit-inspired prophets in the Hebrew Bible (OT), ratified by Christ, and the Christ-commissioned first-century apostolic community (rather than the entire com-munity of Israel or first-century Christians, for instance) as the determinative and prescriptive community through which the Holy Spirit worked in a unique, unrepeatable, and "foundational" manner (cf. Eph 2:20).

Third, the canonical approach recognizes that Scripture does require in-terpretation but also that all communication requires interpretation. It sim-ply does not follow that because Scripture is often misinterpreted, Scripture is therefore doctrinally insufficient — unless sufficiency is taken to require universal uniformity of interpretation, which seems unattainable.[95] Herme-neutical diversity inevitably results from the fact that interpreters (individual or collective) always and unavoidably bring something that contributes to the resulting interpretation. This is not a problem with Scripture *per se,* but simply a universal reality. Hermeneutical diversity, then, does not provide grounds to dissuade one from a canonical approach. Instead, it magnifies the recognition that we (individually and collectively) are unavoidably prone to biased read-ings such that a pure, unadulterated, presuppositionless interpretation is un-attainable. This recognition requires the rejection of any approach that naïvely

94. Some communities accept more books but nearly all accept at least the common ca-nonical core.

95. It is striking, then, that Mathison suggests that Scripture is inadequate to function as its own rule of faith because there are so many mutually exclusive interpretations of Scripture, but at the same time refers to those "liberal churches and teachers who use the words of the Christian creed but deliberately change their meaning" (*Shape,* 322).

suggests that either the canon alone or the canon plus community resources will come to some final interpretation that settles matters for all Christians. This kind of self-critical awareness (individually and collectively) coupled with a high view of Scripture should only elevate the primacy of Scripture over all other resources. The thoughtful recognition of the inevitable defects in human interpretation may thus motivate the adoption of a minimal and humble theological approach that continually returns to the canon without either ignoring the bountiful resources of the community past and present or granting final theological or interpretive authority to any extracanonical factor.

Finally, the fourth issue is met by the recognition that the canonical approach does not claim to arbitrate between differing interpretations but claims simply to be the rule ("canon") to which all interpretations seek to correspond and against which all interpretations should be evaluated (individually and collectively). This requires that any interpretation be continually subjected back to the canon to see how it measures up to the "rule" and thereby be continually reformed and corrected in an ongoing hermeneutical spiral (see chapter 8). Each of the above ways in which the canonical approach appears to be preferable to communitarian approaches depends upon and flows from the claim that Scripture is canon ("rule") such that the canonical *sola Scriptura* approach complements the traditional evangelical affirmation that Scripture is sufficient for doctrine.

Conclusion

This chapter has presented and evaluated two fundamental communitarian claims: (1) that Scripture is not sufficient by itself to ground the Trinity doctrine; and (2) because theologians have come to innumerable interpretations of Scripture, "tradition should prescribe the correct reading" for the Trinity doctrine.[96] Regarding the Trinity, such claims seem ultimately to weigh against the community approach.

First, Scripture is not insufficient to ground or articulate the Trinity doctrine. Various interpretations and misinterpretations do not entail insufficiency. Even if they did, the community approach would be at least equally insufficient because of the myriad differences within tradition and mutually exclusive interpretations of tradition (including the Nicene Creed itself).

Second, this chapter presented four ways in which the community approach

96. Giles, *Trinity*, 9.

is significantly disadvantageous in comparison to the canonical approach, as evidenced by ongoing debates about the Trinity doctrine among evangelicals. Put simply, the community approach is inadequate to address contemporary debates over the Trinity, to be the rule of faith, as interpretive authority, and to answer the questions: Which tradition and on whose interpretation?

Finally, the canonical approach is preferable with regard to each of these four problems, itself calling for a humble approach to theological interpretation that adopts the canon as rule but does not claim thereby to be able to settle all debates. The canonical approach embraces the reality that all communication requires interpretation and therefore expects continuous canonical reform and improvement as each theological model and interpretation is intentionally and continually tested and informed by comparison to, and study of, the "rule" of the canon of Scripture itself. In this vein, the next chapter turns to a further explanation of this canonical approach to theological method by revisiting the analogy of Scripture.

CHAPTER 8

The Canonical Approach to Systematic Theology: Revisiting the Analogy of Scripture

The relationship between biblical and systematic theology has been tenuous in recent times, with both disciplines seeming to be in continual flux. Even the definitions of what constitutes biblical and systematic theology, respectively, have been matters of considerable dispute. Without reductionist conflation of these disciplines, this chapter outlines a canonical theological method that is akin to the analogy of Scripture, positing that Scripture as canon (*tota Scriptura*) may be employed as the rule that guides and sets the parameters for systematic theology in a way that is viable in light of contemporary issues regarding philosophical hermeneutics, exegetical methodology, biblical theology, and systematic theology.[1]

This canonical theological method encompasses two related sets of hermeneutical circles. The first consists of the interplay between the horizon of the text and that of the reader or interpreter. The second consists of the relation of the parts to the whole and vice versa in biblical hermeneutics. Before turning to these hermeneutical circles, however, we must first address the nature of this final-form canonical approach.

---

1. The analogy of Scripture has become a hallmark of Protestant interpretation. The Westminster Confession of Faith states, "The infallible rule of interpretation of Scripture is the Scripture itself: and therefore, when there is a question about the true and full sense of any Scripture (which is not manifold, but one), it must be searched and known by other places that speak more clearly" (1.9; cf. 2 Pet. 1:20-21; Acts 15:15-16). This complements the primacy of the canon and belief in its internal coherence and interdependence.

The Final-Form Canon as Basis of Theology

Whereas Christian theologians widely affirm the primacy of Scripture, the precise methodological function of Scripture varies considerably. The final-form canonical approach posited here recognizes the common canonical core as the divinely commissioned basis and rule of Christian doctrine. This recognition is admittedly a methodological presupposition, the justification of which is beyond the scope of this work. However, given the now-widespread recognition that every system requires the adoption of a starting point (which is not to say all are equally viable),[2] it seems appropriate to accept the biblical canon as basis of Christian doctrine given Scripture's own claims and its historical role within Christianity.[3] In this regard, however, one's view of the canon itself and just what is meant by "canonical approach" holds considerable implications.[4]

2. Kevin Vanhoozer, *Is There A Meaning in This Text?* (Grand Rapids: Zondervan, 1998), 19, notes: "Instead of making robust claims to absolute knowledge, even natural scientists now view their theories as interpretations." Cf. Fernando Canale, *Back to Revelation–Inspiration: Searching for the Cognitive Foundation of Christian Theology in a Postmodern World* (Lanham, MD: University Press of America, 2001), 9.

3. The canon itself gives numerous examples suggesting something like a canonical approach. While an implicit intention in the Bible to be read as "canon" does not itself prove the legitimacy of its canonicity, it does provide the necessary condition for a canonical approach. We have already seen that the notion of canon in the limited sense of "rule" or "standard" appears often in Scripture and it is worth recalling Christ's use of Moses, the Prophets, and the Psalms to explain "the things concerning Himself in all the Scriptures" (Luke 24:27, 44). Vanhoozer, *The Drama of Doctrine: A Canonical-Linguistic Approach to Christian Theology* (Louisville: Westminster John Knox, 2005), 120, further, makes a case that Philip, in "using Scripture to explain the event of Christ" (cf. Acts 8:27-35), may have been "initiating his Ethiopian inquirer into" just such "a 'canonical' practice initiated by Jesus Christ, abetted by the Spirit, and instantiated by the rest of the New Testament."

4. This canonical approach should not be confused or conflated with other "canonical" approaches as each holds differing presuppositions about the nature of the text (see below), particular nuances about the implementation of the canon within a given discipline, and differing perspectives regarding the role of the community. For instance, Paul McGlasson's postliberal "canonical" approach, *Invitation to Dogmatic Theology: A Canonical Approach* (Grand Rapids: Brazos, 2006), 54, 73-74, 130-37, attributes considerable importance to the community in canon determination and theological construction, adopting historical-critical tools and embracing "tradition I" as granting sole authority to Scripture but with the stipulation that Scripture must be interpreted in *and by* the community.

Canonical Approaches in Competition

Various canonical approaches have garnered considerable attention in recent years, particularly in discussions regarding the nature of biblical theology but also in systematics, with numerous scholars promoting "canon" as the foundation of doctrine.[5] Such diverse canonical approaches are known by many different names including canonical hermeneutics, canonical criticism, and canonical theology. Such monikers may be grouped loosely under the rubric of canonical approaches but one should not assume that such canonical approaches are identical or in every respect complementary.[6] The essential similarity is their common focus on canon as the object of study; yet even the meaning of "canon" varies among them.

James Sanders and Brevard Childs led the way in elevating the issue of canon to prominence in recent decades. Sanders's canonical criticism focuses on the community process of canon (its writing, redaction, collation, preservation, and determination) and community-canonical hermeneutics (meaning hermeneutics as defined by the contemporary community).[7] Here, the canon is fluid, consisting of community input and tradition from every stage of its history with the current community continuing to function as canon arbiter. Childs, conversely, promotes the primacy of the final canonical form, in which the "entire history of Israel's interaction with its traditions is reflected in the final text."[8] While Sanders's canonical criticism explicitly denies the primacy of the final form, shifting greater weight to the historical shaping as well as ongoing tradition and community input, Childs's thoroughly text-focused approach redirects attention to the final form of the canon as object of interpretation,

5. McGlasson believes that the "future of dogmatic theology" depends on "the issue of canon" (*Invitation to Dogmatic Theology*, 15). Kevin Vanhoozer likewise suggests that the fuller meaning of Scripture "emerges only at the level of the whole canon" (*Is There a Meaning*, 264). Cf. Charles J. Scalise, *From Scripture to Theology: A Canonical Journey into Hermeneutics* (Downers Grove, IL: InterVarsity, 1996), 81.

6. Considerable variety exists. See Anthony C. Thiselton, "Canon, Community, and Theological Construction," in *Canon and Biblical Interpretation*, ed. Craig G. Bartholomew et al. (Grand Rapids: Zondervan, 2006), 4; Christopher Seitz, "The Canonical Approach and Theological Interpretation," in *Canon and Biblical Interpretation*, 58.

7. James A. Sanders, *Canon and Community: A Guide to Canonical Criticism* (Philadelphia: Fortress, 1984), 21. See also James A. Sanders, *Torah and Canon* (Philadelphia: Fortress, 1972), 17-20; cf. James D. G. Dunn, *Unity and Diversity in the New Testament: An Inquiry into the Character of Earliest Christianity* (London: SCM, 1990).

8. Brevard S. Childs, *Introduction to the Old Testament as Scripture* (Philadelphia: Fortress, 1980), 54.

allowing him to emphasize the interrelationship of the parts and the whole of the canon as a unified document.[9] This difference seems to stem from the underlying perspective on the final form of "canon," on the one hand Sanders's community-formed and continuously determined canon and, on the other, Childs's community-shaped final-form canon that is received and recognized as canonical by later Christian communities.[10]

The Nature and Function of Canon

Two important issues arise not just regarding the differences between the seminal approaches of Sanders and Childs but also for canonical theological method: the scope and the "final form" of the biblical canon. With regard to the former, whereas Sanders's community canon approach supports the ongoing authority of the community to determine the scope of the canon such that there can be no "final form," my canonical approach recognizes the common canonical core of sixty-six books as divinely commissioned and thus intrinsically canonical and, accordingly, attempts to reserve both formal *and functional* primacy for the sixty-six-book canon.[11] According to this view,

---

9. Sanders, *Canon and Community*, 31. Further, Sanders has serious problems with Childs's synchronic view of the text (*Canon and Community*, 35). See Brevard S. Childs, "*Sensus Literalis* of Scripture: An Ancient and Modern Problem," in *Beiträge zur Alttestamentlichen Theologie: Festschrift für Walther Zimmerli* (Göttingen: Vandenhoeck & Ruprecht, 1977), 80-93; Brevard S. Childs, *Biblical Theology in Crisis* (Philadelphia: Westminster, 1970), 189-91.

10. Childs sees canon as something shaped by biblical communities but recognized, not imposed, by the church, while Sanders's definition of canon is a continuously community-determined corpus (Childs, *Biblical Theology*, 105; Sanders, *Canon and Community*, 15).

11. While neither the view of Sanders nor that of Childs matches the intrinsic canon view, Childs comes closer than Sanders in that he treats the canon as recognized rather than determined by a later ecclesial community (while giving more credence than I do to the purported communitarian shaping of the contents of the canon in biblical times). Moreover, my canonical approach comports in some respects with that of Childs in the realm of biblical studies, particularly regarding the treatment of the canon as a unified corpus in the task of interpretation. However, my view significantly differs regarding the conclusions of historical-critical approaches relative to the history of the text, which Childs criticizes (particularly rejecting the antisupernaturalism inherent in some such approaches) yet appropriates in significant ways. Whereas Childs tends to accept many conclusions of historical-critical scholarship (e.g., of source, form, tradition, and redaction criticism), he goes beyond them by taking the results of the shaping and redaction process to be "canonical," thus elevating the final form of the text and emphasizing the interpretation of that final form as a corpus in its own right. My view, conversely, accepts the self-testimony of Scripture regarding its origin and history. Thus,

the "canonical" *traditio*, which entails the importance of the community as receptor and preserver, is built into the final-form canon itself.

With regard to the latter, Sanders contends that a "final-form" approach is mistaken in that "there were numerous 'final' forms."[12] To be sure, the question of the final form of the canonical text includes a great deal of complexity, requiring considerable care. As a working approach it seems reasonable to approach the canonical text in the extant form(s) that we have, admitting the lack of access to a complete, original, final form.[13] This final-form approach thus utilizes the most attested findings of textual criticism wherever such bear on the canonical meaning of the text. However, canonical theology does not divert attention to non-manuscript-based reconstruction of the text based on form, source, or tradition criticism because of the unavoidably conjectural nature of such undertakings.[14] Rather, attention is focused on the received corpus of canonical texts and the study thereof, focusing on textual and intertextual hermeneutics regarding the final form of the sixty-six-book canon without neglecting textual issues that pertain to extant texts from this canon.

My approach to the canon includes three notable commitments regarding the nature of Scripture: (1) a high view of the revelation–inspiration of the canon, (2) the dual authorship (divine and human) of the canonical text, and (3) the grammatical-historical procedures of exegesis. Although readers need not subscribe to these commitments in order to practice the procedures of this canonical approach, a basic explanation of these commitments illuminates the rationale undergirding particular methodological decisions.

First, I hold a high view of the revelation and inspiration of the biblical canon as infallible, meaning that the canon is fully trustworthy and unfailingly accurate in all that it affirms. Accordingly, I believe that divine revelation was

---

whereas one might adopt something like Childs's canonical approach and appreciate much of the methodology of my canonical approach to systematics, I am operating with particular hermeneutical commitments to the revelation–inspiration and dual authorship of the canon as well as the adoption of grammatical-historical procedures. In light of these, I do not view the role of community in canon history in the same way that Childs does and I accordingly depart from his canonical approach in certain ways.

12. Sanders, *Canon and Community*, 25.

13. McGlasson notes, "The process of shaping is now unrecoverable historically, but the effect of shaping on the literature is precise and comprehensive" in the final form (*Invitation to Dogmatic Theology*, 41). Cf. Christopher Seitz, "Canonical Approach," in *Dictionary for Theological Interpretation of the Bible*, ed. Kevin J. Vanhoozer (Grand Rapids: Baker Academic, 2005), 102.

14. Consider the critical questions raised in Meir Weiss, *The Bible from Within: The Method of Total Interpretation* (Jerusalem: Magnes, 1984), especially 47-73.

accurately inscripturated in the canon via divine inspiration (2 Tim 3:16; 2 Pet 1:20-21) in such a way that the words written by the human authors are the word of God (cf. 1 Thess 2:13).[15] As Vanhoozer puts it, the "canon" is "Christ's Spirit-borne commissioned testimony to himself."[16] As such, the canonical text holds undiluted priority, including relative to that which is "in front of the text" such that traditional or contemporary community voices are valued as commentary but are not themselves determinative (interpretively or otherwise).

Second, I approach the canon as a text with dual authorship (divine and human) that is rendered harmonious via divine revelation and inspiration, being neither self-contradictory nor monolithic in its rich variety.[17] As such, there is a "properly theological unity implicit in the idea that God is the

15. Without pretending to be able to explicate the precise manner of God's agency and operation in revelation–inspiration, I subscribe in large part to Fernando Canale's sophisticated and complex historical-cognitive (linguistic) model; see his *Back to Revelation–Inspiration*, 127-60. This model affirms Scripture's claims to being divinely revealed and inspired (the doctrine of Scripture) while also carefully attending to the rich, multifaceted variety (yet not incongruity) in the canon (the phenomena of Scripture). Here, God condescends to "utilize the modes, characteristics, and limitations of human cognition and language" via various means of revelation such as theophanic (Exod 3:1-15; John 1:1-14), written (Exod 31:18), prophetic (spoken; Exod 20:1), visual (Isa 6:1-3; Acts 10:9-17), historical (Isa 43:18-19), and existential/ sapiential (cf. Prov 1:7) (*Back to Revelation–Inspiration*, 148, 134). The process of inspiration whereby revelation is inscripturated in the biblical canon consists of the human author "writing [according to each's background, personality, location, and literary style] while the divine author supervises the entirety of the process" (*Back to Revelation–Inspiration*, 147). The diverse phenomena of Scripture are thus accounted for by a "general historical supervisional pattern of God's inspiration" that "represents a nonintrusive, yet direct, overview of the entire process of the writing of Scripture," with an "occasional direct-remedial-corrective pattern" that ensures the trustworthiness of the entirety of Scripture as "historically constituted" (rather than historically conditioned) but does not "divinize Scripture into an otherworldly level of perfection and accuracy" (*Back to Revelation–Inspiration*, 145, 142, 147). Divine action in revelation–inspiration is thus not reduced to one pattern (and certainly does not correspond to mechanical dictation) but recognizes various patterns and diverse divine activities alongside the distinctive contributions and limitations of human authors, all of which "account for the richness and manifoldness of biblical revelation" (*Back to Revelation–Inspiration*, 134). Cf. Vanhoozer's view that the "doctrine of inspiration is what justifies the canonical practice of reading the Bible to hear the Word of God," wherein "inspiration is a matter of the Spirit speaking in and through the canonical Scriptures, coordinating the various human voices," while "each of the individual authors contributes, in his own way, to the guiding of the whole" such that, "together, they articulate the theo-drama." Here, "speaking of inspiration does not specify the exact process [or mode of guidance] but emphasizes the result" (*Drama*, 230, 231).

16. Vanhoozer, *Drama*, 194.

17. This does not, however, support a naïve view regarding the retrieval of authorial intention (i.e., the intentional fallacy). See below.

ultimate communicative agent speaking in Scripture," the "divine author" of the canon.[18] My reading of the canon as a unified and internally congruent corpus is undergirded by this view of the Holy Spirit's superintendence of the writing process, including the trustworthy conveyance of the history and conceptual framework that is presented in the text.[19] I agree with Vanhoozer that "we must read the Bible canonically, as one book. Each part has meaning in light of the whole (and in light of its center, Jesus Christ)."[20] Accordingly, the canonical text is the most trustworthy source of theological data such that

18. Vanhoozer, *Drama*, 177, 181. Cf. Nicholas Wolterstorff's proposal regarding the divine authorship of Scripture in *Divine Discourse: Philosophical Reflections on the Claim That God Speaks* (Cambridge: Cambridge University Press, 1995). Gerhard Maier, *Biblical Hermeneutics* (Wheaton, IL: Crossway, 1994), 22, contends that "biblical writers seek consciously to recede into the background. They point away from themselves to *God as the author*" (emphasis his).

19. In the words of David Yeago, "The Bible: The Spirit, the Church, and the Scriptures," in *Knowing the Triune God*, ed. David Yeago and James Buckley (Grand Rapids: Eerdmans, 2001), 70, recognizing "the biblical canon as inspired Scripture" means to approach "the texts as the discourse of the Holy Spirit, the discourse therefore of one single speaker, despite the plurality of their human authors" such that "the church receives the canon, in all its diversity, as nonetheless a *single* body of discourse." Cf. Daniel J. Treier's description, *Introducing Theological Interpretation of Scripture: Recovering a Christian Practice* (Grand Rapids: Baker Academic, 2008), 201, that theological "interpreters are not shy about relating particular passages to the larger context of the entire Bible. We need not ignore the historical development of words and concepts, engaging in simplistic synthetic connections that obscure the particularities of any given text. But neither should we operate as prisoners of alien standards imposed by academic guilds that tend to reject the unity of Scripture or allow passages to relate only on the narrowest criteria."

20. Vanhoozer, *Drama*, 178. Indeed, "that God speaks and acts in the canonical Scriptures that testify to him" is a "core 'evangelical' conviction" (*Drama*, 26). However, one who does not subscribe to this conviction might nevertheless approximate some procedures of this approach by way of something like a new literary criticism approach to the final-form canon as a unified literary work or the view that the final-form canon was redacted in a way that the community perceived to be sufficiently internally congruent. Yeago, "Bible," 71, contends that "there is no reason why a purely literary analysis could not take seriously a biblical canon, Jewish or Christian, as a unified whole, received as such by an important community of readers," and "no rational imperative" exists to "regard the formation of the canon as less significant than, say, the redaction of the Pentateuch; if the latter can be taken seriously as the composition of a single literary work out of diverse pre-existing parts, so too can the former." Cf. David Noel Freedman's "Master Weaver" hypothesis. In this regard, Paul R. Noble, *The Canonical Approach: A Critical Reconstruction of the Hermeneutics of Brevard S. Childs* (Leiden: Brill, 1995), 340, suggests that "Childs' Canonical Principle of interpretation (i.e., that the meaning of each text should be found through interpreting it in the context of the completed canon) is formally equivalent to believing that the Bible is so inspired as to be ultimately the work of a single Author."

claims that are properly derived from the canon are taken as theologically significant.[21]

Third, canonical theology as I practice it utilizes grammatical-historical procedures of exegesis canonically.[22] Here, among other things, one attempts to interpret the text in accordance with internal textual indicators.[23] Accordingly, biblical texts are taken in accordance with their textually indicated genre and thus are not treated as allegorical or mythological unless there is an internal textual indication thereof.[24] Further, I take the claims made in the text (carefully interpreted exegetically) to be accurate and historical.[25] This ap-

21. Compare Vanhoozer's canonical-linguistic approach wherein the supremely normative "canon — the final form of 'Holy Scripture'" is, among other things, "the charter document of the covenant that stands at the heart of the relationship of God and humankind" (*Drama*, 141). As "divine canonical discourse," Scripture is "not merely a record of revelation" but "itself a revelatory and redemptive word-act of the triune God" (*Drama*, 179, 177).

22. For an excellent introduction to grammatical-historical exegetical procedures see Douglas K. Stuart, *Old Testament Exegesis: A Handbook for Students and Pastors* (Louisville: Westminster John Knox, 2008). See also the treatment in Grant Osborne's masterful compendium, *The Hermeneutical Spiral: A Comprehensive Introduction to Biblical Interpretation*, 2nd ed. (Downers Grove, IL: InterVarsity, 2006). While I embrace and employ grammatical-historical procedures, I depart from the separation of disciplines that appears to be assumed in some iterations of the historical-grammatical method, itself fostering a somewhat atomistic approach to biblical interpretation. The canonical approach seeks to employ the procedures of grammatical-historical investigation while bringing to bear the exegesis of the parts of the text as canon to bear on the whole and vice versa without injury to the exegetical deliverances of any part thereof.

23. For a brief exposition of the procedures of grammatical-historical interpretation and how they derive from and are congruent with the internal contents of the canon, see Richard M. Davidson, "Interpreting Scripture: An Hermeneutical 'Decalogue,'" *Journal of the Adventist Theological Society* 4/2 (1993): 95-114.

24. Although scholarly disputes are ongoing in this regard, in my view, a given text should be read according to the internal indications thereof and I take this to be one upshot of ethical reading and a prerequisite of canonically ruled theology. Accordingly, I believe this is in congruence with Scripture's internal use of other Scripture (see Davidson, "Interpreting Scripture," 101-2). D. H. Williams, *Evangelicals and Tradition: The Formative Influence of the Early Church* (Grand Rapids: Baker Academic, 2005), 106, however, contends that the Reformers' rejection "of the mystical character of the text" was a mistake, claiming that "allegorical interpretation" might be employed and "reined in by the rule of faith." Yet, what prevents any rule itself from being read and applied allegorically and thus being treated as a "wax nose"?

25. Excepting, of course, those views that are depicted in the canon as themselves false (e.g., the views of Job's friends regarding his suffering). One who questions, however, whether the canon accurately depicts history might suspend judgment in this regard or take a realistic narrative approach (cf. Hans Frei) and ask what kind of claims (historical and otherwise) the text itself presents and to what theological conceptions such claims lead. Conversely, I take

proach does not look "behind" the text to a reconstructed precanonical history but focuses on the text's own claims as they appear in the final-form canon.[26] Taking the canon to accurately represent its own history, this approach engages relevant *extant* historical materials (e.g., other ancient literature, artifacts) while reserving priority for the canonical text.[27] Thus, this canonical

it to be within my epistemic rights to abandon the strictures of modern biblical criticism as themselves ideological and thereby critically question the procedures and results of interpretations that presuppose antisupernatural bias, a fragmentary view of the text, etc. In this regard, I am in agreement with the criticisms of some historical-critical methodologies offered by many of the communitarian approaches (see chapter 4). Whereas those who wish to adopt the tradition of modernistic biblical criticism have every right to do so, I believe those who reject that ideological tradition (in part or in whole) should also be afforded the right to privilege a distinctively theological approach.

26. Compare the way Richard M. Davidson frames his excellent study, *Flame of Yahweh: Sexuality in the Old Testament* (Grand Rapids: Baker, 2007), 2-3, as analyzing "the theology of the final canonical form of the OT. It utilizes insights from such widely accepted synchronic methodologies as the new literary criticism and the new biblical theology, which focus upon the final form of the OT text. It will not inquire about the possible precanonical history of the text but seek to understand the overriding theological thrust of Scripture wholistically as it now presents itself in the biblical canon. This canonical, close-reading approach does not ignore, however, the unique settings and theological emphases of different sections of the canonical OT. By focusing upon the final form of the OT text, I believe it is possible that the interests of both liberal-critical and evangelical OT scholarship may merge in seeking to understand what constitutes the canonical theological message of the OT regarding human sexuality." Consider also Vanhoozer's "canonical approach" that "has nothing to do with an ahistorical approach that takes the Bible as a free-floating 'text,' nor with a historicist approach that focuses on the events behind the text," but "takes the whole canon as the interpretative framework for understanding God, the world, oneself, and others" by reading "individual passages and books as elements within the divine drama of redemption" (*Drama*, 149). Joel B. Green, *Practicing Theological Interpretation* (Grand Rapids: Baker, 2011), 127, further points to the "aim of historical work" shifting "from the discovery of meaning embedded in or behind the text to hearing the robust voice of the text as a subject (rather than an object) in theological discourse." Thus, in Green's view, "theological interpretation of Christian Scripture concerns itself with interpretation of the biblical texts in their final form, not as they might be reconstructed by means of historical-critical sensibilities (i.e., Historical Criticism₁)" (*Practicing*, 49).

27. The historical context of a passage, as far as is ascertainable, may make vital contributions to understanding. However, canonical theology is wary of taking, for example, an ancient Near Eastern parallel and reading it into the biblical text. Consider treatments of ancient Near Eastern parallels regarding so-called "covenant love," wherein the supposed meaning of the cognates of the primary OT word for love (אהב) in ancient Near Eastern covenant contexts was imposed upon similar forms in the biblical text only to later have many scholars question the supposed meaning in comparative contexts and reject the view that the meaning of such cognates in the ancient Near Eastern texts requires a similar meaning in biblical contexts. See John C. Peckham, *The Love of God: A Canonical Model* (Downers Grove, IL: IVP Academic,

approach is interested in historical context to the extent that it is relevant to the canonical context, while avoiding theological conclusions based on decisions between speculative reconstructions of tradition history.[28]

Furthermore, this canonical text-based emphasis entails caution against the tendency to synthetically harmonize texts and flatten their meaning.[29] The primacy of the canon as rule and object of interpretation entails a high regard for the details included in that canon. The canonical approach is thus a text-based *and* text-controlled approach, which examines the canonical text to exposit its meaning faithfully. Yet, emphasis on the text does not merely amount to an annotated exegetical outline. Rather, the systematic theologian

---

2015), chapter 3; cf. the extended discussion in John C. Peckham, *The Concept of Divine Love in the Context of the God–World Relationship* (New York: Peter Lang, 2014), 197-201. Extrabiblical extant texts and artifacts shed considerable light on the interpretive options of the text but are themselves not determinative for the interpretation of the text because (among other reasons): (1) they themselves must be interpreted and are often underdeterminative with regard to meaning in their own context (we may know considerably less about the extracanonical text/artifact and its context than we know about the biblical text that it is used to interpret); (2) historical correspondence depends upon the dating and authorship of the biblical texts, which may be disputed and holds implications regarding whether reuse of a text is present and, if so, which text is reusing the other; and (3) the relationship between the text/artifact and the canonical text, if any, is often unknown. For instance, if a biblical writer is indeed writing after the supposed parallel (which is sometimes unclear), the biblical writer may be aware of and interacting with the extracanonical text/artifact (or with the trajectory of the view therein as it has impacted the writer's horizon) but the writer may be intentionally utilizing but changing (or correcting) the trajectory of that text/paradigm. Simply because ostensible contemporaries of biblical authors held a view or interpreted an issue in a particular way (to the extent we understand their view, itself questionable), it does not follow that the biblical authors shared that view or used overlapping material as their contemporaries did. This may seem like a rather obvious point but it holds considerable implications about how the extant historical materials should be used in interpreting biblical texts. Conclusions regarding such matters are often unclear and this approach therefore urges caution while affording priority to the canonical text.

28. This is not intended to frame the historical disciplines in a pejorative light but to recognize the fluidity of theories that remain in a high level of flux and uncertainty (cf. Osborne, *Hermeneutical Spiral*, 359). Nevertheless, emphasis on the final form need not entail neglect of the canon's diachronic elements. Cf. the concept of epigenetic growth in Walter C. Kaiser, Jr., *Toward an Old Testament Theology* (Grand Rapids: Zondervan, 2001), 8.

29. A method of analogy "can lead to an overemphasis on the unity of biblical texts," resulting in "'artificial conformity' that ignores the diversity of expression and emphasis between divergent statements in the Bible"; D. A. Carson and John D. Woodbridge, *Scripture and Truth* (Grand Rapids: Zondervan, 1983), 361. At the same time, doctrinal reading need not result in reductionism or worse. Cf. Daniel J. Treier, "Scripture, Unity of," in *Dictionary for Theological Interpretation of the Bible*, ed. Kevin J. Vanhoozer (Grand Rapids: Baker Academic, 2005), 733.

plays a vital role in asking questions of the text, while deliberately requiring justifiable and discernible answers from the text. With the broad contours of this canonical approach in mind, let us turn attention to its application to systematic theology.

A Canonical Systematic Approach

"System," in this approach, minimally refers to a collection of working parts that contribute to and complement the whole. A canonical "system" looks beyond (without overlooking) the limits of individual texts and passages, viewing its parts in light of the whole and its whole in light of its parts without imposing one upon the other.[30] It thus transcends those exegetical methodologies and biblical theologies that are restricted to a mere compilation or summary of fragmentary parts.[31] A canonical systematic approach looks for the patterns and inner logic of the *texts* in relation to the whole canonical *text*, rejecting any dichotomy between limited pericope and broad overarching reading, embracing both in mutual reciprocity such that "system" is not sought at the expense of the particular complexity and variety of individual texts.

As systematic, this approach utilizes some of the questions and analytical tools of philosophy while intentionally moving the grounding of system away from the answers provided by philosophical traditions and back toward the canon itself.[32] Consequently, a canonical system seeks to draw its content and answers from Scripture, requiring the product of exegesis (biblical data) as material condition of the system. However, it also goes beyond the typical exegetical delimitations to try to ascertain (via another level of exegesis) the undergirding suppositions that form the context for the passage and to uncover the implied presuppositions that structure the conceptual framework of the canonical system. At all times, however, the conceptual framework that the interpreter attempts to derive from the text remains open to criticism. The system should never be permitted to overbear the texts and must consciously avoid the imposition of a canon within the canon, engaging the entire canon

30. That is, the whole should not be understood in light of a single isolated text and an individual text/passage should not be imposed upon by the aggregate.

31. Biblical theology is variously defined and, by some definitions, closely complements what I call here canonical theology.

32. Childs notes, "For systematic theologians the overarching categories are frequently philosophical. The same is often the case for biblical scholars even when cloaked under the guise of a theory of history" (*Biblical Theology*, 158; cf. Canale, *Back to Revelation–Inspiration*, 53).

descriptively without dogmatic discrimination. Toward doing so, this approach aims at two criteria of adequacy: canonical correspondence and coherence.

Canonical Coherence

Canonical coherence seeks systematic internal consistency, methodologically subscribing to the canon's own claims to internal coherence and thus entailing a sympathetic reading of the canon.[33] Such a reading seeks congruity among diverse texts without injury to any text, expecting internal consistency (but not simplistic identity) without dismissing or glossing over apparent tension.[34] The canon is thus approached as a unified corpus while recognizing its diversity stemming from various human authors and historical contexts.

Whereas some maintain that the canon contains irreconcilable incongruities and contradictions,[35] others have pointed out that the considerable diversity and polyphony in the canon does not necessarily amount to a disharmonious cacophony of voices. Even where "the same vocabulary" and in-

---

33. Because mutually exclusive systems might at least appear to be equally coherent, coherence is treated as a necessary but not sufficient criterion of adequacy. Cf. Grant Osborne's "criteria of coherence, comprehensiveness, adequacy, and consistency," and "durability" (*Hermeneutical Spiral*, 398).

34. See Vanhoozer's application of Paul Ricoeur's distinctions (regarding personal identity) between *idem* as a "self-sameness" or "'hard identity,' where hard connotes immutability and permanence" and *ipse* identity, and "'soft' identity" as a "kind of sameness" that "partakes more of narrative than of numeric identity" (*Drama*, 127). Vanhoozer proposes that, as divinely authored but not dictated, the canon exhibits a unity of *ipse* identity, which allows for "development" and "growth" and is thus "entirely, and especially, compatible with the pattern of promise and fulfillment" one sees in OT and NT (e.g., the unity without uniformity that is manifest in the NT typological use of the OT) (*Drama*, 128).

35. Sanders contends, "Consistency is a mark of small minds. It can also be a manipulative tool in the hands of those who insist that the Bible is totally harmonious, and that they alone sing the tune!" (*Canon and Community*, 46). Conversely, Osborne notes that "critical scholarship" is "often more 'literalistic' than are conservative scholars in that it often assumes that any so-called contradiction or difference between biblical writers removes the basis for a deeper theological unity between them" (*Hermeneutical Spiral*, 350). Without indefeasibly presupposing that the canon is incongruous or congruous, one might methodologically seek to read the text *as* a unified, internally consistent corpus without glossing over tensions, suspending overall judgment in order to engage the canonical text as a literary corpus. This makes sense even given a skeptical view because the ultimate coherence of the canon could not be properly evaluated apart from a consideration of the canon and its component parts, which is precisely what this method aims to undertake.

tertextual allusions are used "in markedly different ways" (e.g., Romans 4 and James 2 of Gen 15:6), "if each addresses different questions, it is plausible that their voices are complementary rather than contradictory."[36] As such, *apparent* tensions do not rule out undergirding theological consistency.[37] Although tensions appear among broad themes of Scripture as well as isolated texts, further study and reflection may witness perceived contradiction give way to a more complex, even beautiful, underlying harmony.[38] Indeed, faithful attention to the diversity in Scripture itself points the interpreter back to the text to seek understanding that progressively expands in depth and breadth. This entails the refusal to gloss over or smooth out seemingly incongruent parts, attempting to let the text of the canon speak (as far as possible) in all its diversity, toward steadily illuminating the goal of theology proper, the never-ending quest to know God.[39]

The view that canonical texts were written from within a canonical stream of thought provides a historical rationale for approaching the canon as internally consistent. The canonical context itself constitutes an aspect of historical context insofar as earlier parts of the canon provided the framework and con-

---

36. Treier, "Scripture, Unity of," 733.

37. As I. Howard Marshall, *New Testament Theology: Many Witnesses, One Gospel* (Downers Grove, IL: InterVarsity, 2004), 30, comments, where tensions arise there might be an "underlying unity" despite a "different level of perception."

38. David Noel Freedman's hypothesis of a "master weaver" who has woven a coherent message (amidst significant diversity) into Israel's history presents a recent example of finding congruity behind and beyond formerly suggested discontinuity in the OT canon. Freedman, *The Unity of the Hebrew Bible* (Ann Arbor: University of Michigan Press, 1991), 73, exposits "demonstrable links" pointing to "the intricate and interlocking character of the Hebrew Bible," which "supports the view that a single mind or compatible group [a Master Weaver or Editor] was at work in collecting, compiling, organizing, and arranging the component parts into a coherent whole." Cf. Stephen G. Dempster, *Dominion and Dynasty: A Biblical Theology of the Hebrew Bible* (Downers Grove, IL: InterVarsity, 2003); Walter C. Kaiser, Jr., *Recovering the Unity of the Bible: One Continuous Story, Plan, and Purpose* (Grand Rapids: Zondervan, 2009). Consider also Hans Frei's seminal proposal of the unity of narrative, which gathers Scripture as part of an overarching realistic narrative, in *The Eclipse of Biblical Narrative* (New Haven: Yale University Press, 1974). Cf. Meir Sternberg, *The Poetics of Biblical Narrative* (Bloomington: Indiana University Press, 1985); Robert Alter, *The Art of Biblical Narrative* (New York: Basic, 1981). Consider also Robert Jenson's aim, *Systematic Theology* (New York: Oxford University Press, 1997), 1:57, 58, to interpret "the God identified by the biblical narrative," thus "follow[ing] the one biblical narrative, to identify the one biblical God" such that the "unity of Scripture" is "construe[d]" by "the identity of this God."

39. Hasty harmonization may obscure the larger picture that might emerge given a patient, close reading of the text as canon (see chapter 10).

tributed to the shaping of later parts of the canon such that successive human authors consciously intended faithfulness to preceding canonical testimony (e.g., Isa 8:20). As Anthony Thiselton comments, "Intertextual resonances form part of the hermeneutic of the biblical traditions themselves."[40] While authorial intentions and claims do not guarantee that congruity obtains in the midst of diversity and multivalency, they do support the legitimacy of looking for coherence in the canon.

The interpreter, then, might attempt to humbly (but not hastily) look for discernible, demonstrable, and defensible ways that the various parts of the text speak in harmony. However, this should be done with great caution to avoid altering the upshot of the text to fabricate harmony; the text must be allowed to speak for itself insofar as possible. With regard to these and other kinds of questions asked of the text, potential answers (interpretations) are submitted to, and circumscribed by, the range of meaning allowed by the text. In this way, the interpreter may look first for potential coherence in the text as canon and where coherence is elusive it should be forthrightly noted, admitting the various options that cannot, as of yet, be confidently ruled in or out. The criterion of coherence thus looks for congruity among the canonical texts while conscientiously dealing with areas of perceived or apparent tension.

Canonical Correspondence

Canonical correspondence is particularly crucial given that systematic theologians sometimes neglect exegetical research, isolating their theological construction from exegetical considerations. Without due consideration to biblical exegesis, however, systematic theology cannot be ruled by the canon. Conversely, some exegetes tend to neglect a systematic view of the text, which may leave them unwittingly beholden to systematic presuppositions that unduly affect their interpretation. A canonical system seeks to avoid both pitfalls by integrating exegesis and systematics under the primacy of canon.

Ideally, one would prefer perfect correspondence to the canon. However, recognition of the limitations and fallibility of any human interpreter requires the more attainable goal of discernible, demonstrable, and defensible correspondence to the canonical text. Thus, while acknowledging the ever-present

40. Thiselton, "Canon, Community, and Theological Construction," 5.

limitations of human subjectivity, canonical theological method seeks the maximum achievable correspondence to the text.[41]

Yet this raises questions regarding the nature of the text itself, particularly regarding the intentionality thereof. Should interpretation correspond to authorial intention or to something else? Some deconstructionist perspectives locate meaning in the interpreter or interpretive community as opposed to in the text itself.[42] Some more moderate hermeneutical approaches locate meaning in a "fusion" of the textual and interpreter's horizons. Such approaches recognize a hermeneutical circle wherein both text and interpreter bring content to the interpretation such that *meaning* extends far beyond that of the elusive authorial intention.[43] A third, more conservative approach maintains the emphasis on determinate meaning corresponding to authorial intention.[44] This third approach tends to suppose that the "author's original meaning" is unchanging, whereas significance changes over time.[45]

Although a full engagement with the complexities of these influential hermeneutical perspectives is beyond the scope of this work, canonical theological method seeks to properly recognize the limitations and impact of the unavoidable hermeneutical circle. It does so by aiming at the recognizably (but not fully) determinate intention in the text while acknowledging that human

41. As such, while competent interpreters may hold differing interpretations, they might nevertheless "come together and check one another against the standard of the Scripture"; D. A. Carson, "The Role of Exegesis in Systematic Theology," in *Doing Theology in Today's World: Essays in Honor of Kenneth S. Kantzer*, ed. J. D. Woodbridge and T. E. McComiskey (Grand Rapids: Zondervan, 1991), 53-54.

42. See Stanley Fish's reader-response criticism in his *Is There a Text in This Class? The Authority of Interpretive Communities* (Cambridge, MA: Harvard University Press, 1980).

43. See Hans-Georg Gadamer, *Truth and Method*, trans. Joel Weinsheimer and Donald G. Marshall (New York: Continuum, 2004). Gadamer considers it impossible that the reader fully recover the meaning of the text objectively since the horizon of the interpreter always contributes to the interpretation due to one's historically affected consciousness (*wirkungsgeschichtliches Bewußtsein*). Cf. Paul Ricœur, *Interpretation Theory: Discourse and the Surplus of Meaning* (Fort Worth: Texas Christian University Press, 1976), 30.

44. See E. D. Hirsch, *Validity in Interpretation* (New Haven: Yale University Press, 1967). Hirsch contends that the text always has a determinate meaning based on the author's intent. More recently, Walter C. Kaiser, Jr., *Toward an Exegetical Theology: Biblical Exegesis for Preaching and Teaching* (Grand Rapids: Baker Academic, 1998) 33, 47, posits that "the *author's* intended meaning is what a text means" and thus the sole task of the expositor is to clearly, accurately, and adequately (though not necessarily perfectly) describe authorial intent.

45. For Kaiser, significance "does and must change since interests, questions, and the times in which the interpreter lives also change. But an author's original meaning *cannot* change — not even for himself!" (*Toward an Exegetical Theology*, 32).

interpretations entail an inescapable degree of indeterminacy (in this and other regards).[46] According to this view, the intention *in* the text is the effect of the author's intention (cause) in writing that text. Accordingly, the text inscripturates, to some degree, authorial intention, but no human author exhaustively conveys intended meaning. Thus, the text itself is not identical to the complexity and fullness of the intention in the author's consciousness at the precise time of writing.[47] Given the inaccessibility of the author's consciousness at the moment of writing (the fullness of which is lost even to the author in subsequent moments), appeal to intent *beyond* or *behind* the text is speculative and, perhaps, counterproductive. The text itself is thus the object of interpretation.

Nevertheless, the text should be read with the recognition that the author is the unquestioned cause of the text, which was written for some purpose.[48] There is a determinate meaning that the author intended to convey in the text, notwithstanding the fact that the interpreter is incapable of capturing the entirety of that intended meaning. It is thus the task of the interpreter to ascertain the intent that is preserved and discernible in the text and thereby interpret the meaning *in* the text, insofar as possible, in keeping with the textual controls that delimit the justifiable scope of interpretation.[49] Thus, as Christopher Seitz

---

46. By "underdetermined," here and elsewhere, I mean simply that the available data might be insufficient to confidently identify what belief or interpretation should be adopted. See chapter 9.

47. As Jean Grondin, *Introduction to Philosophical Hermeneutics* (New Haven: Yale University Press, 1994), 73, states, "It is entirely pointless to try to reconstruct the unconscious process of thought production that occurs in composition." Nevertheless, as Christopher M. Tuckett, *Reading the New Testament: Methods of Interpretation* (Philadelphia: Fortress, 1987), 160, notes, one must at least know the intended language in order to know the meaning, for example, of "pain" whether in English or French.

48. As Vanhoozer, *Is There a Meaning*, 109, contends, pebbles formed by waves into words would not be considered text by anyone. Text requires an ordering agent, an author. "The author is the historical cause of a textual effect; his or her intention is the cause of the text being the way it is. No other explanation adequately accounts for the intelligibility of texts" (*Is There a Meaning*, 44).

49. While this canonical approach recognizes that one's interpretation is always more than the determinate intention in the text due to the horizon of the interpreter (cf. Gadamer's fusion), it insists that the interpreter's horizon should continually be subjected to the canonical text, as far as possible. Here, however, it must be recognized that Scripture "has its *own* horizon, we have *our* horizon, and there have been many, many horizons in between"; Bruce Ellis Benson, "'Now I Would Not Have You Ignorant': Derrida, Gadamer, Hirsch and Husserl on Authors' Intentions," in *Evangelicals & Scripture: Tradition, Authority, and Hermeneutics*, ed. Vincent Bacote, Laura C. Miguélez, and Dennis L. Okholm (Downers Grove, IL: InterVarsity, 2004), 186.

explains, a canonical reading "shares a concern for the objective reality of the text and for its intentional direction and ruled character."[50]

In this regard, I adopt hermeneutical (critical) realism such that determinate meaning exists in the text prior to and independent of interpretation while recognizing that the interpreter brings his or her own horizon to the text such that explicating the meaning in the text is an imperfect, complex, and continual process.[51] Thus, while there is an objective standard (the text), the interpreter may never attain that standard perfectly in interpretation. This highlights the importance of the hermeneutical spiral between text and reader/ interpreter, within which the interpreter should continually subject his or her horizon to that of the canonical text.[52]

THE HERMENEUTICS OF A CANONICAL SYSTEMATIC APPROACH

Microhermeneutical and Macrophenomenological Exegesis

This hermeneutical spiral, which continually subjects the interpreter's horizon to criticism and correction by the text, advances Fernando Canale's crucial distinction between [micro]hermeneutical and [macro]phenomenological exegesis.[53]

---

50. Seitz, "Canonical Approach," 100. See also Vanhoozer's approach to the text as a communicative act, based on the speech-act theory of Austin and Searle, in which "the sense of the text" is logically inseparable from "the intention of the author" as ordering agent (*Is There A Meaning*, 109).

51. See the discussion in Vanhoozer, *Is There a Meaning*, 26. Cf. Anthony C. Thiselton, *Hermeneutics: An Introduction* (Grand Rapids: Eerdmans, 2009), 306-26. Consider also Bruce Ellis Benson's treatment of these issues, which he concludes by saying: "I believe that there are authors, that they have intentions, that words express intentions and that readers and listeners are able to discern those intentions." ("Now I Would Not Have You Ignorant," 191). See the further discussion in chapter 9.

52. Here and elsewhere, I use the term "spiral" to refer to the process of going back and forth between various components (e.g., text and context, interpreter's horizon and text's horizon) toward better understanding, avoiding vicious circularity while moving ever closer to the intended meaning *in* the text. Thus, "continuous interaction between text and system forms a spiral upward to theological truth" (Osborne, *Hermeneutical Spiral*, 392). As Grondin states, "The goal of understanding better, conceived in terms of an unreachable *telos* and the impossibility of complete understanding, bears witness to the fact that the endeavor to interpret more deeply is always worthwhile" (*Introduction to Philosophical Hermeneutics*, 71).

53. Canale, *Back to Revelation–Inspiration*, 148-49. I add the terms "micro" and "macro" to Canale's terminology to provide further clarity regarding the complementary levels of exegetical operation.

These two reciprocally operative levels of exegesis function against the background of three levels of macro-, meso-, and microhermeneutical principles of theological conceptualization. Microhermeneutical principles refer to those at the level of examination of individual texts and pericopes, macrohermeneutical principles refer to the overarching conceptual framework, and mesohermeneutical principles refer to individual doctrines in between. In theological interpretation of the biblical text, each of these levels operates and impinges upon the others.

That is, one's conceptual framework (macro) sets the ontological and epistemological parameters within which doctrines (meso) are conceptualized, both of which impinge upon one's reading of the text itself (micro). Conversely, one's reading of the text itself (micro) *should* impinge upon one's meso- and macrohermeneutical presuppositions. In this regard, the canonical approach supposes that the divinely commissioned canon conveys (via individual texts and the text as canon) an overarching canonical conceptual framework within which doctrines are articulated (though with some indeterminacy at both levels).[54] However, the interpreter's conceptual framework and doctrinal understanding inevitably depart (to some extent) from that of the canonical text itself and, to the extent that such divergent macro- and mesohermeneutical presuppositions go unchallenged, this leads to a failure of canonical correspondence of the resultant system. With a canonical approach, therefore, one closely reads and exegetes the canonical text itself in order to inform and (where necessary) transform one's doctrines (meso) and the wider conceptual framework (macro) via an ongoing hermeneutical spiral that brings one's conceptual framework and dogmatic perspectives closer and closer to those discernible in the canonical text itself.[55] Here, one aims at moving from the particulars of the canonical text to the derivation of broader conclusions, rather than starting from universal ontological or epistemological presuppositions that methodologically determine the particulars.

This spiral takes place via the reciprocal operation of microhermeneutical

---

54. In my view, this idea of the "canonical horizon" is due to the divine authorship of the canon. But one might also operate minimally in this regard with a conception of canon consciousness where the conceptual framework and doctrines were transmitted intergenerationally to selected canonical writers via catechesis, or with a literary or canon-critical view of the final-form canon as unified literary document received/redacted by the community.

55. Anthony C. Thiselton, *New Horizons in Hermeneutics* (Grand Rapids: Zondervan, 1992), 31, notes, "Texts can actively shape and transform the perceptions, understandings, and actions of readers." Yielding to the canon thus yields a more canonical system.

and macrophenomenological exegesis.[56] Whereas microhermeneutical exegesis refers to the philological and historical dimensions of the grammatical-historical exegetical method, essential to the task of locating the range of the specific meaning in the text, macrophenomenological exegesis consists of looking for the conceptual framework implicit in the text as canon.[57] That is, macrophenomenological exegesis utilizes exegetically derived canonical data in order to uncover and abstract the (metaphysical, epistemological, and axiological) conceptual framework implicit in the canon, which itself undergirds the text's meaningfulness in communication.[58] This level of interpretation goes beyond the limited pericope to seek the horizon of the text as canon, which also impacts textual meaning itself.

One way of conceptualizing the difference between these complementary levels of exegesis is to recognize that they ask different questions of the text, the microlevel in reference to the intention discernible in the text in its immediate context and the macrolevel in reference to the conceptual framework conveyed in the text that both undergirds and circumscribes its meaning. Methodologically, the text at the microhermeneutical level holds priority and one thus intends to recognize, temporarily suspend, and put on the table for examination one's *pertinent* and *identifiable* operative macro and meso presuppositions, toward allowing the text as canon to inform all three levels in an ongoing hermeneutical spiral.[59]

56. Both the micro and macro levels of exegesis impinge also on the meso or doctrinal level and vice versa in a complex and dynamic fashion. Cf. Vanhoozer's view that "doctrine is largely a matter of exegesis, of providing 'analyses of the logic of the scriptural discourse'" (*Drama*, 20).

57. Note that phenomenological exegesis here differs considerably from the ontological and epistemological suppositions of Edmund Husserl (and those of other phenomenologists), particularly any suggestion that reality might be grounded in human perception as opposed to reality independent of human consciousness. Here, the term minimally refers to a close reading of the text that seeks to derive the conceptual framework assumed in and by the phenomena in the text as its context, toward informing and shaping the interpreter's framework via engagement with the phenomena of the canonical text.

58. For example, any communication between persons requires some minimal ontological, epistemological, and axiological underpinnings. For one, the intent to communicate presupposes (rightly or wrongly) that some other exists and might be able to receive and understand such communication and it is worth the attempt to communicate.

59. This approach thus employs a minimal, targeted *epoché* without expecting to arrive at presuppositionless interpretation, intentionally bracketing or tabling (as far as possible) known relevant presuppositions toward understanding the canon in terms of its internal logic/system of meaning. For Canale, in "this phase of data interpretation, exegetes and theologians cancel out all previously inherited theories that could prove to be hindrances to the understanding of

This latter interpretive task of asking questions regarding the operative conceptual framework of the text as canon is crucial given the recognition that each interpreter unavoidably brings their own conceptual framework (including sometimes mistaken presuppositions and misdirected idiosyncrasies) to the reading of the text. This has significant impact on the practice of exegesis, which is sometimes undertaken without consciously engaging (and thus uncritically presupposing and perhaps conflating) the metaphysical framework of both the text and the reader, in which case it offers little methodological advice directed toward such engagement.[60] The usual approach to exegesis begins with a limited pericope, seeks the historical and literary context, etc. However, the interpreter (wittingly or unwittingly) brings a horizon, including a conceptual framework that constitutes the environment of meaning. The exegetical product may be influenced significantly when the interpreter relies upon such preunderstandings rather than seeking to be informed by the conceptual framework assumed by the inner logic of the text. For instance, an interpretation predicated on methodological naturalism would be hard pressed to preserve even the spirit, much less the letter, of the miracle-filled account of the exodus (which assumes supernatural theism). A method that precludes a supernatural metaphysical framework for the meaning of the text — regardless of opinion regarding its correspondence to historical reality — has subverted its own attempt to understand the canonical intention.[61] Thus, macrophenomenological exegesis seeks to ascertain the canonical horizon to provide, among other things, the first principles thereof that themselves impact exegetical interpretation.[62]

Scripture" on its own terms (*Back to Revelation–Inspiration*, 149). Osborne adds, "The key is to 'bracket' out our own beliefs and to allow the other side to challenge our preferred positions. This will drive us to examine the biblical data anew and to allow all passages on the topic to have equal weight" (*Hermeneutical Spiral*, 373).

60. Such oversights might be (partially) due to the methodological vestiges of the modernistic ideal of neutrality, which purported to be able to interpret the text "objectively" independent of (and thus perhaps blind to) an operative conceptual framework. Insofar as we recognize the impossibility of such an approach (after modernism) it stands to reason that, while many exegetical procedures of analysis may yet be appropriate, one's overarching methodological framework may require modification of expectation about what is sought and what is achievable and in what way, giving particular attention to the unavoidable situatedness of the interpreter and of the text itself.

61. As Thiselton points out, "Non-theism or positivism is no more value-free than *theism*" ("Canon, Community, and Theological Construction," 4).

62. Consider Rob Lister's view, *God Is Impassible and Impassioned* (Wheaton, IL: Crossway, 2012), 174, that "metaphysical reflection on scriptural revelation is not, in principle, unac-

Alongside the crucial hermeneutical circle of text and reader/interpreter, canonical theological method also emphasizes the hermeneutical circle between the parts and the whole of the canon. Accordingly, macrophenomenological exegesis aims at the horizon of the canonical text while microhermeneutical exegesis focuses on the level of pericope, which itself contributes to and corrects the wider conceptual framework in an ongoing reciprocal relationship, never attempting to reduce the multivalency of the text, but seeking the wider canonical context that preserves the individual nuances of the texts.[63] Concomitantly, it brackets and tables, as much as possible, the recognizably pertinent elements of the interpreter's conceptual framework that impinge upon the interpretation of the text in favor of the conceptual framework required by the text in its pericope as well as the text as canon, thus attempting to allow the canon to provide its own conceptual framework. Thus, while looking at the text microhermeneutically to ascertain the textual intent it also looks for the biblical ontological suppositions that provide the framework for the text's communication. In this way, macrophenomenological exegesis and microhermeneutical exegesis function concurrently in an ongoing, reciprocally correcting manner.

Much more than providing merely a glorified exegetical outline or summary, the systematic theologian plays a vital role in asking questions of the text while deliberately requiring text-based and text-controlled answers, continually seeking the inner logic of the canon. This canonical systematic approach thus steers clear of a dichotomy between what the text *meant* and what it *means* in favor of a holistic canonical approach, seeking the meaning that is preserved *in* the text as received and situated within the wider narrative context that itself is crucial to the canonical conceptual framework.[64] This concep-

---

ceptable" but is actually "unavoidable. Indeed, Scripture does commend a metaphysic (e.g., the Creator/creature distinction)." It is crucial, however, to intentionally subject one's own preconception of the content of that metaphysic to the data of Scripture (see chapter 9). Cf. Canale, *Back to Revelation–Inspiration*, 149.

63. One must here distinguish between multivalency *in* the text and multivalency that various scholars might perceive *behind* the text. Since this approach is not concerned with the precanonical history of the text, issues regarding perceived multivalency *behind* the text (e.g., multiple cultural contexts and different historical situations) are left for further investigation as needed on a case-by-case basis. This basic delimitation is necessary for the manageability of a canonical approach, which itself then invites dialogue and further investigation of each individual pericope. The multivalency *in* the text, on the other hand, is preserved in this canonical approach by attempting to recognize the complexity of exegetical upshot(s) of the text(s) (via grammatical-historical procedures) and to do justice to all of it without injury to any of it.

64. What the text meant is not entirely recoverable but, as cause of the text, grounds the

tual framework arises in communication with and continual dependence on the text. It is by the words of the text itself that the macrophenomenological questions are addressed without the expectation that each question will receive a determinate answer. Thus, although macrophenomenological interpretations are logically prior to hermeneutical ones, they are methodologically posterior and should be recognized from within the ongoing, reciprocal, correcting task of interpretation.

CONCLUSION

Overall, canonical theological method uses the canon as source in the rigorous quest for a coherent system which corresponds to the text, as much as is achievable. It utilizes both microhermeneutical exegesis and macrophenomenological exegesis in order to provide canonical-textual answers to philosophical and theological questions. The systematic conclusions themselves remain tentative, continually subject to the recurring hermeneutical spiral where textual horizon judges interpreter's horizon as well as all current theological constructions. At each step this spiral is operative. The community that chooses to operate within such a framework may shed further light on where the interpreter's horizon or other human imperfection has led to error, but it is not itself authoritative over against the text. Moreover, the extracted canonical systematic theology is not the final word; the final-form canonical text is the final word, and the system is thus always secondary and must always appeal back to the text. The methodology arrives only at tentative conclusions such that the text is never replaced by any theological construction but, rather, remains the locus of continual correction and re-correction. Hence, the system will never exhaust the canonical text but endeavors to persistently move toward thorough correspondence and rigorous inner coherence. In this regard, we now turn to an exposition of canonical hermeneutics and the application thereof.

---

latter such that contemporary meaning in the text should not be separated from the original meaning *in* the text insofar as that can be discovered. See the compelling criticism of this distinction in favor of a canonical biblical theology in Gerhard F. Hasel, "The Relationship between Biblical Theology and Systematic Theology," *TJ* 5/2 (1984): 113-27. Cf. Osborne, *Hermeneutical Spiral*, 32. Further, this canonical approach does not wish to atomistically extract "theology" from the canonical context in all its rich narrative and other genres but sees the canonical theology itself as inextricably situated within the dynamic narrative of the God–world relationship (see chapter 10), the canon itself being the covenant document thereof.

CHAPTER 9

Canonical Hermeneutics and Theopathic Language

While the canonical theologian aims at a conceptual framework and resultant theology shaped, reformed, and brought into union with the canonical horizon, the interpreter's horizon always impinges on interpretation. The fact that methodological rigor is insufficient to yield *purely* canonical theology indicates that far more than methodological procedures and conceptual frameworks are at work in doing theology. Operating in conjunction with these are the interpreter's posture and orientation toward the text specifically and the task of theology broadly.

Crucial commitments in this regard undergird the implementation of canonical theological method. This chapter takes up issues regarding such implementation by addressing the interpretation of theological language, including a case study of how to interpret purportedly anthropopathic language canonically, thereby shedding light on canonical hermeneutical procedures and controls. We begin, however, with a discussion of the hermeneutical posture that motivates and guides canonical theology.

CANONICAL HERMENEUTICS

Humble Theological Construction

The psalmist proclaims, "My heart stands in awe of your words" (Ps 119:161). For the canonical interpreter, similarly, recognition of the nature of the canon as canon engenders the posture of humility and submission to Scripture, willingness to have one's theology ruled by the canon. This entails a self-critical posture that allows oneself and one's community to be judged by the canon and not vice versa.

Such humility engenders an approach that attempts to avoid reductionism on the one hand and overreaching dogmatism on the other.[1] Here, the interpreter is willing to allow questions and tensions to remain on the table whenever one's investigation of the textual data is underdeterminative, that is, where the canonical interpretation of the data does not offer a conclusion that rises to the level of confidence (e.g., lack of discernibility, demonstrability, or defensibility).

In this manner, canonical theological method attempts to restrict itself to theological derivation from the particulars of the canonical data, which indicate what can be stated with confidence theologically and within what parameters. In other words, abstraction is (partially) controlled by the particulars of the concrete textual data and continually tested against those particulars via the hermeneutical spiral (e.g., macrophenomenological and microhermeneutical exegesis).

This provides a methodologically delimited scope of *canonical* theology, which does not exclude further theologizing that takes the results of a canonical theology and employs them in dialogue with a broader scope of data.[2] Indeed, it seems to me that employment of canonical methodology on various theological matters might itself provide considerable fodder for fruitful engagement with wider dialogue partners.

This minimal but not minimalistic approach to canonical interpretation aims at deriving from the canon only what can be derived with confidence, keeping in mind that certainty (interpretive and otherwise) is beyond our ken.[3] Thus, canonical theology is restricted to the discernible, demonstrable, and defensible upshot of the canonical data (the parts and the whole) that can thereby be confidently held and is, as such, actionable and professable.

This requires willingness to recognize that there may be fewer conclusions held with confidence that one might have initially hoped, subject to further in-

---

1. Here "a healthy dose of fallibilism is needed, and rational certainty must be tempered by God's ability to judge all human certainties at the end of time"; C. C. Pecknold, *Transforming Postliberal Theology: George Lindbeck, Pragmatism and Scripture* (New York: T&T Clark International, 2005), 6.

2. I do not mean to suggest that theological scholarship as a whole should be delimited by this methodology but that this might provide a delimited theological method as the starting point from which other areas and issues might be more fruitfully engaged systematically.

3. Here "minimal" is a shorthand way of describing the restriction of the upshot to that which is confidently derivable from the canon (i.e., minimal canonical derivation).

vestigation. Working hypotheses that do not rise to the level of confidence are held loosely and even confident beliefs are always subject to defeat by further investigation of the canonical data. Whereas confidence is invested in theological matters in proportion to their perceived canonical grounding via rigorous canonical study and is subject to the ongoing hermeneutical spiral, this does not mean that one holds no beliefs beyond those canonically derived.[4] That would be impossible. However, such beliefs are to be progressively tabled (targeted *epoché*), measured against the canon as rule, and informed and transformed (insofar as is achievable) by the continual process of canonical reading.

This requires intentional movement away from any predisposition to theological pretense, which leads to overdeterminative readings of *what might be* underdeterminative texts, and movement toward recognizing how little one knows and understands with confidence, particularly in comparison to the divine author of the canon (cf. Job 38). Given my cognitive limitations and other inadequacies (canonically humbled cognition), I do not expect to be able to unravel the mysteries of God and construct an immovable, cathedral-like systematic theology. There remain many mysteries, "things into which [even the] angels long to look" (1 Pet 1:12). Rather, via an ongoing hermeneutical spiral, canonical theological method aims at constructing dynamic and ambulatory models analogous to Israel's traveling wilderness tabernacle.

As the wilderness tabernacle was constructed as a type of the heavenly temple not made with human hands (Heb 9:24), canonical theology is a theological approximation in human language of the revelation of the one true Theo-Logos. It is thus continuously disposed to improvement and correction as the interpreter moves along the ever-continuing journey of immersive reading and analysis of the inexhaustible riches of the canonical data, the interpreter's horizon (ideally) spiraling ever closer to the canonical horizon. Accordingly, a wilderness sanctuary model of theological construction takes the minimal data of the canon and uses it to construct theological models that are adaptable to further canonical investigation.[5]

In this vein, canonical theological method rejects the modernistic supposition that "foundational" philosophical questions must be conclusively answered *a priori* or via generalized abstraction from limited data. Departing from many classical systems in this regard, canonical theological method nei-

---

4. In my experience, subjecting beliefs to ongoing rigorous study provides more confidence regarding what is canonically derived.

5. Canonical theology need not lack robustness or conviction but, in my view, warrants a missional strategy of dissemination that might itself be furthered by a humble approach to canonical catechization.

ther starts from, nor expects to yield, conclusive positions regarding many of the intricacies of metaphysics and epistemology, focusing instead on careful examination of particulars within their canonical context without delimiting the options of what might be the case generally via the imposition of a universalized conceptual framework (see chapter 10). Thus, canonical theological method focuses on moving from the particulars of canonical data (insofar as they are confidently derivable) to what those particulars (minimally) yield regarding universal matters (conceptual framework).

This aims at minimally confidently derivable, but nonreductionist, canonical theology that is ever moving and ever reforming in (attempted) correspondence to the canonical text as God's rule and expression of his rulership. This humble, wilderness-sanctuary approach to theological construction itself rests on commitment to a posture of ethical reading.

Ethical and Charitable Reading

Ethical reading entails a charitable posture that intends to understand what someone has written for some purpose, interpreting and representing that communication in a way that its author(s) might be able to affirm. The practice of ethical reading involves the choice to listen to and try to understand what has been written by someone for some purpose, reserving judgment until after the attempt to understand.[6] Such reading includes seeking to allow one's words to guide the interpretation thereof, analogous to active listening and asking: Have I understood you correctly? and carefully listening for the answer.[7] In short, it hermeneutically applies the golden rule: read as you would want your words to be read.[8]

---

6. Cf. Daniel R. Schwarz's five stages of ethical reading of literature, "The Ethics of Reading Elie Wiesel's *Night*," in *Elie Wiesel's Night*, edited by Harold Bloom (New York: Bloom's Literary Criticism, 2010), 72-74: (1) "immersion in the process of reading and the discovery of imagined worlds"; (2) "quest for understanding," including seeking "to discover the principles and worldview by which the author expects us to understand characters' behavior"; (3) "self-conscious reflection"; (4) "critical analysis"; and (5) "cognition in terms of what we know," moving "back and forth from the whole to the part."

7. Put simply, ethical reading is analogous to the virtue of listening, without which there can be no communication. Choices in this regard are ethically impactful. For instance, suppose one interprets the command of another, "Stop touching me," to mean keep touching me. That one *can* choose to interpret another's words in a variety of ways does not mean that one should do so and, indeed, if everyone did so what would be left of meaningful communication?

8. This does not exclude criticism but is restricted to fair, potentially constructive, crit-

Canonical hermeneutics seek to read the canon ethically, actively listening to the text as canon and allowing the text itself to guide and correct one's reading of it (*analogia scriptura*). Recognizing that one's horizon inevitably imposes upon and limits understanding, it is essential, first, to carefully employ sound exegetical procedures to mitigate eisegesis and, second, to engage the readings of other careful readers to illuminate some of the limitations, blind spots, and impositions of one's own horizon. Here, if I am reading ethically, my priority is not what I want the text to mean or the use I can make of it to advance my own purposes. Rather, my priority is to receive and understand the intention inscripturated *in* the text, toward reforming my desires and purposes (among other things).

Precisely because humans tend to be skilled at deceiving both themselves and others (Jer 17:9), there is need of spiritual discernment and communion with God toward the cultivation of a sanctified mind (cf. 1 Cor 2). In no small fashion, the hermeneutical spiral that ideally moves the interpreter's horizon closer and closer to the canonical horizon at each pass also might, in so doing, reform and transform the interpreter's conceptual framework in a manner akin (and contributing) to the process of sanctification (cf. Pss. 19:7-14; 119:1-16; 2 Tim 3:16). That is, the "fusion" of my horizon with that of the canonical text will change me insofar as I am open to such change.[9]

However, this raises concerns regarding to what extent my own horizon generally, or my interpretations particularly, limited as they are by my finite cognition and linguistic capacity, might correspond to that intended by the divine author of the canon. That is, even given a humble posture, ethical reading, and openness to the Spirit's illumination of my mind and sanctification of my heart, to what extent might I come to know God, particularly via the human language used in the canon?

The Limits of Human Language

In keeping with my minimal canonical approach, I make no attempt to set forth anything like a thoroughgoing philosophy of language. Like any other question of import, I would like to see this engaged via a canonical meth-

---

icism. Further, in theological exposition, this entails representing the positions of others as you would have them represent your own.

9. This disposition might be aimed at and approximated but the requisite heart transformation is the Spirit's work.

odology.[10] Nevertheless, some working assumptions regarding language are necessary even to begin such a process. I adopt the minimal working approach that words mean what they are used to mean by their speakers/writers within their particular context(s).[11] Further, I believe that human language is at least minimally sufficient for communication.[12]

This minimal approach appears to be supportable by canonical data and derivable via minimal phenomenological analysis. For example, if you expect that you can or do (at least partially) understand what I mean by the words you are reading, then you appear to be operating on an approach like this.[13] Further, it appears that canonical writers likewise supposed this much about the efficacy of language, particularly regarding effective communication via their written words and of divine–human communication. Otherwise, it is difficult to make sense of the record of God commanding particular divine messages to be written down for dissemination (Deut 4:5-10; Ps 78:5).[14]

That God can effectively communicate with humans via language is unsur-

---

10. By this I do not mean that I expect the canon to deliver a full-fledged philosophy of language analogous to existing philosophical forms but a minimal working conception against which more detailed conceptions might be measured.

11. As A. B. Caneday, "Is Theological Truth Functional or Propositional? Postconservatism's Use of Language Games and Speech-Act Theory," in *Reclaiming the Center: Confronting Evangelical Accommodation in Postmodern Times*, ed. Millard J. Erickson, Paul Kjoss Helseth, and Justin Taylor (Wheaton, IL: Crossway, 2004), 146, notes, "to agree with Wittgenstein concerning how words and sentences denote meaning does not require agreement with" the view that "meaning and truth are not related — at least not directly or primarily — to an external world of 'facts' waiting to be apprehended." Further, this does not mean that authorial intention is recoverable as an object of study but undergirds the hermeneutical critical realism surveyed in chapter 8, wherein the author is the cause of the intention *in* the text.

12. This is a somewhat pragmatic approach to language but does not require adoption of a merely pragmatic theory of truth or the tenets of pragmatism or pragmaticism generally.

13. Further, if you are now pondering the question of whether or to what extent a philosophy of language might be employed for theological construction, you have at least minimally understood and been affected by my use of language. See Bruce Ellis Benson's excellent essay, "Now I Would Not Have You Ignorant: Derrida, Gadamer, Hirsch and Husserl on Authors' Intentions," in *Evangelicals & Scripture: Tradition, Authority, and Hermeneutics*, ed. Vincent Bacote, Laura C. Miguélez, and Dennis L. Okholm (Downers Grove, IL: InterVarsity, 2004), in which he argues that "readers and listeners are able to discern" the "intentions" of "authors," but "our understanding is, in some senses, the 'same' as that of the author and also, in some senses, 'different' from that of the author" (191).

14. Minimally, the canon itself appears to presuppose that communication takes place (Dan 10:11; Matt 15:10; Luke 24:45) and that words mean what agents use them to mean (cf. 1 Cor 2:11-16), while also recognizing hermeneutical diversity (e.g., how do you read this? Luke 10:26; John 20:29).

prising given the canonical depiction of God as omniscient, omnipotent, and willing to condescend to communicate with humans and illuminate human understanding (cf. 1 Cor 2). However, the canon presents human reception of God's linguistic communication as partial. Whereas numerous instances depict divine communication as understood to a degree that renders humans morally responsible, which is acted upon (or actionable) by humans (e.g., Deut 7:11-13; Neh 8:3; Luke 24:45; John 10:38), there is also considerable evidence of human misunderstanding of divine communication (e.g., Deut 8:3; Ps 14:2; Isa 1:3; Matt 13:19; 16:11; Mark 9:32; 12:24; John 8:43; 10:6; 12:16; 13:7).

The canon posits, then, both understanding and misunderstanding of divine communication, a partial overlap between that which God intends to convey via human language and that which a given human understands. To the extent that God elects to communicate to humans via language, our access to such communication is limited to that which is conveyed via human language such that there appears to be no getting behind language in this regard. Further, given human limitations, including that we are unavoidably impacted by our communities' language games, it seems that all we can do is seek to recognize and understand divine communication as best we can (via human language or otherwise), believing the canon's claims that humans can understand in part while recognizing that our understanding is always incomplete and susceptible to misunderstanding.[15] As Paul puts it, "now I know in part, but then I will know fully just as I have been fully known" (1 Cor 13:12).

Instead of dissuading from the attempt to understand, such recognition might remind of our limitations, engender humility and openness to the text, and motivate us to continually submit to the canon insofar as we take it to be the divinely commissioned rule of faith. From this standpoint, we can attempt to grasp and appropriate, by canonical immersion, the language games used within the canon itself.[16] As such, the canonical hermeneutical approach seeks to discern as far as possible the intentions inscripturated in the canonical text in keeping with the grammatical "rules" of human language as employed by

---

15. Fully effective communication appears to be beyond our abilities. As Wilhelm von Humboldt, *Humanist without Portfolio* (Detroit: Wayne State University Press, 1963), 235, states: "No one when he uses a word has in mind exactly the same thing that another has, and the difference, however tiny, sends its tremors throughout language."

16. Recall that, according to the intrinsic canon view, God utilized a particular community of prophets and apostles to convey his messages via their human language from within their cultural-linguistic context, which was itself shaped by God's covenantal leading, resulting in sufficiently effective, albeit partial, communication. Cf. Fernando Canale, *Back to Revelation–Inspiration* (Lanham, MD: University Press of America, 2001).

the canonical writers, which are believed to be sufficient for the communication for which they were employed (cf. 2 Tim 3:16).

Theological Language as Accommodative and Analogical

Long-standing debate continues, however, over the extent to which human language is descriptive of God, that is, whether theological language is univocal, analogical, or equivocal.[17] In this treatment, univocal predication is that which applies to God and creatures in exactly the same way,[18] equivocal predication is that which holds entirely different meaning when applied to God than when applied to creatures,[19] and analogical predication is that which holds some degree of similarity and dissimilarity when applied to God and creatures.[20] Accordingly, "analogical" encapsulates a vast spectrum between univocal and equivocal predication such that one might mean by analogical a great deal of dissimilarity and a minimum of similarity, or vice versa.[21]

17. The distinction between the univocal, analogical, and equivocal use of language has a long history. See Thomas Aquinas's influential treatment of language (which utilizes Aristotle's treatment) in reference to God as "analogical" in *Summa theologica* 1.1.13. Note, however, that my use of these categories and terminology should not be confused with an endorsement of the way Aquinas employs them relative to the *analogia entis* (the analogy of being) and divine simplicity.

18. Thomas Williams, "The Doctrine of Univocity Is True and Salutary," *Modern Theology* 21/4 (2005): 578, states, "Notwithstanding the irreducible ontological diversity between God and creatures, there are concepts under whose extension both God and creatures fall, so that the corresponding predicate expressions are used with exactly the same sense in predications about God as in predications about creatures." He believes the only two options are "either unintelligibility or univocity" ("Doctrine of Univocity," 578). William P. Alston, "Aquinas on Theological Predication: A Look Backward and a Look Forward," in *Reasoned Faith*, ed. Eleonore Stump (Ithaca: Cornell University Press, 1993), 178, believes that "we may be able in some cases to use terms univocally of God and creature so far as the *res significata* [a property signified by a predicate term] is concerned, even though the mode of signification will misrepresent the divine being." Yet, he also admits that "it may be that no creaturely terms, as they stand, can be so applied."

19. Jordan Wessling, "Colin Gunton, Divine Love, and Univocal Predication," *JRT* 7 (2013): 95-96, defines "theological equivocation" as "the view that there are no concepts under whose extension both God and creatures fall; the same term has an altogether different meaning when applied to either God or creature."

20. For Wessling, "Analogy is the doctrine that the relevant predicates have different but related senses" ("Colin Gunton, Divine Love," 95).

21. That is, "analogical" might refer to similarity within the greater context of dissimilarity on the one hand or it might refer to dissimilarity within the greater context of similarity on

In this treatment, I am most interested in the correspondence of canonical theological language to God as he is (see chapter 10). This relates to and overlaps with the issues regarding the similarity or dissimilarity of the same language relative to God and creatures but focuses particularly on the presence or absence of correspondence between one's conceptualization of the meaning of language and God as he actually is.

Canonical theology views biblical theological language as analogical without attempting to specify the degree of similarity or dissimilarity of theological language relative to God. Treatment of theological language as analogical might guard against the extremes of treating language as purely univocal in a way that might collapse the Creator–creature distinction on the one hand, such that language conveys exactly "the same meaning or sense when applied to God and creature," and purely equivocal on the other hand, where theological language bears no relation to God as he is, rendering humans unable to speak intelligibly of God.[22] As a faith claim grounded in my view of the revealed and inspired nature of the canon, I do believe that canonical language of God *suffi-*

the other, or anything in between. That language is "analogical," according to this view, does not indicate whether such language is closer to being univocal or equivocal.

22. Wessling, "Colin Gunton, Divine Love," 94. Wessling distinguishes between this "pure univocity," where "the concepts embedded in a predicate share [exactly] the same meaning or sense when applied to God and creature," and "partial univocity," where "a predicate shares the same sense when applied either to God or creature, only this predicate might have either additional or abridged meaning when applied to one of its referents." With my definitions of univocity, analogy, and equivocity, what Wessling calls "partial univocity" seems to fall within the broad spectrum of analogy (closer to univocity, but nevertheless within analogy). For a further discussion of these issues and my preference for treating canonical language as analogical but sufficiently descriptive of God (erring toward the univocal end of the spectrum), see John C. Peckham, *The Love of God: A Canonical Model* (Downers Grove, IL: IVP Academic, 2015), 171-87. There I explain further my view that whereas I share Wessling's belief that there might be a common conceptual core of some theological language, I am not confident that humans possess adequate knowledge to identify it. Cf. Wessling, "Colin Gunton, Divine Love," 95-96.

Compare William Alston's argument, "Divine and Human Action," in *Divine and Human Action: Essays in the Metaphysics of Theism*, ed. Thomas V. Morris (Ithaca: Cornell University Press, 1988), 258, 266, 273, for "partial univocity" of "divine and human action," by which he means there is "a partial overlap between concepts of divine and human action" such that there is "some commonality between our thought of human and divine action and motivation." In contrast, Philip A. Rolnick, "Realist Reference to God: Analogy or Univocity?" in *Realism & Antirealism*, ed. William P. Alston (Ithaca: Cornell University Press, 2002), 234, argues: "Unless Alston is prepared to specify what the meaning is to God, he can hardly claim to have depicted 'a core of common meaning.'" According to his view, "Alston has misunderstood analogy as keeping God and humankind too far separated" ("Realist Reference to God," 236).

ciently corresponds to God as he is but I do not believe that I possess adequate knowledge of God to precisely identify the extent of that correspondence.[23]

In my view, even the best available theological language is accommodative. Indeed, it seems that all communicably meaningful language is in some sense accommodative to the parameters within which another might understand it (e.g., my communication with my five-year-old son). Similarly, any language used by God to communicate with humans would be limited by (if nothing else) human finitude and cognitive-linguistic limitations such that any language understandable by humans would not fully correspond to God as he is.

Given that canonical language itself is accommodative, it follows that canonical language is analogical at least in the sense that, as accommodative, it partially corresponds to God as he is. Without utilizing the term "analogy" in this regard, Scripture depicts (at least some) theological language as analogical in this minimal sense of similarity and dissimilarity. For instance, anger (among other emotions) is ascribed to God alongside the proviso that God is "not a man" (Hos 11:9; cf. Isa 55:8). To speak of canonical theological language as accommodative and analogical simply entails that there are an "is" and an "is not," a likeness and unlikeness, between the canonical words and concepts used of God and God as he is.

In my view, such recognition should not dissuade from confidence in the canonical word of God and pursuit of the highest understanding of it but should engender theological humility.[24] If even the best available theological language is accommodative, it seems futile to try to get beyond accommodative (and analogical) language. Accordingly, insofar as canonical language is believed to be infallibly revealed and inspired or recognized to be the divinely commissioned rule, canonical theology employs the exegetical upshot of canonical language as the minimal basis of, and control for, theological construction, while recognizing the analogical character thereof in accommodation to our own cognitive-linguistic limitations.

---

23. Whereas Thomas Williams contends that "*either* the doctrine of univocity is true or . . . everything we say about God is in the most straightforward sense unintelligible — that is, that we literally do not know what we are saying when we say of God that he is good, just, wise, loving, or what have you" ("Doctrine of Univocity," 579-80), might it not be the case that we do know what *we mean to say* of God in such instances but we do not know the extent to which our conception(s) apply to God? It would seem the burden of proof lies with those who claim to know the extent of the correspondence between our language of God and God as he is.

24. Even as epistemological certainty is beyond my grasp but that does not dissuade me from theological convictions, recognizing theological language as analogous need not deter from theological convictions.

With a canonical approach, knowledge of God is limited to that which God reveals and even this we "see through a glass, darkly" (1 Cor 13:12, KJV).[25] As such, "'final' or absolute biblical interpretations are properly eschatological. For the moment, we must cast our doctrines not in the language of heaven" but in the "culture-bound languages of earth, governed, of course, by the dialogue we find in Scripture itself."[26] The recognition that our human conceptualizations and language about God cannot reach beyond accommodation and some (apparently unspecifiable) degree of analogical predication recommends the continual subjection of all theological claims to the canon itself. Canonical theological method thus recognizes the priority of canonical language as theological rule, affirming and using the exegetical upshot of such language as genuinely (albeit analogically) applicable to God and useful for (humble and tentative) theological construction.

Clarity and Precision in Theological Construction

Recognition of our cognitive and linguistic finitude, and the humility engendered thereby, might caution us against overinterpretation (treating a text as more determinative than it is) and motivate us to clarity of communication within our theological models. Accordingly, toward constructing ambulatory and humble theological models that offer minimal systematic descriptions of the canonical data, it is important to carefully define and consistently employ one's terms in order to leave less room for our words to imply more or less than we mean to convey. Further, it is important to restrict inferences to those that are confidently defensible given the data at hand.

Canonical theology, then, treasures clarity of definitions and soundly derived inferences that tie theological construction to progressive understanding of the canonical data.[27] Accordingly, it aims at clarity and precision except

25. If the canon contains successful communication from God to humans regarding Godself (as it claims), it follows that, whereas full correspondence of humanly understandable language to God is beyond our ken, there is some degree of correspondence (similarity and dissimilarity) between the meaning of words/concepts and God as he is (1 Cor 13:12).

26. Kevin J. Vanhoozer, "The Voice and the Actor: A Dramatic Proposal about the Ministry and Minstrelsy of Theology," in *Evangelical Futures: A Conversation on Theological Method*, ed. John G. Stackhouse, Jr. (Grand Rapids: Baker, 2000), 80.

27. This aim toward minimal canonical derivation with clarity of terminology dovetails with some values of analytic theology. In this and other respects, various analytic tools might be helpfully employed in a canonical approach, with the proviso that such tools are

where precision might injure any text or result in overinterpretation. The goal of the canonical interpreter, as such, is not to develop a theology to replace the canon but to analyze the canon itself as clearly and precisely as one can without doing injury to any of it, including the avoidance of sidelining, obscuring, or minimizing its narrativity, poetry, and other elements. Whereas canonical theology does not (and cannot) replicate the form(s) of Scripture, it aims at avoiding subsuming the canon itself within a "system," instead continually directing attention back to Scripture in its rich, diverse, and beautiful forms.

Among the beautiful forms of Scripture is language that ascribes profound emotions to God himself. There is considerable disagreement about how such language should be interpreted, a discussion of which will illuminate how the above-described approach to canonical hermeneutics may be applied.

ANTHROPOPATHIC IMAGERY OF DIVINE EMOTION?

Many theologians treat biblical language that ascribes emotion to God as anthropopathic, that is, as merely accommodative attributions of human pathos to God.[28] Whereas it is widely recognized that the canon repeatedly depicts divine emotions, how such language should be interpreted theologically is a matter of considerable disagreement.[29]

---

conscientiously utilized to clarify articulation of minimal systematic description such that the canon is ruler, not ruled, and with the recognition that there is no available human language that is theologically superior to the uniquely infallible canonical language, which is unavoidably analogical.

28. Examples of this interpretive maneuver abound and only a few will be mentioned here. Millard Erickson, *Christian Theology* (Grand Rapids: Baker, 1998), 304, notes some passages that "are to be understood as anthropomorphisms and anthropopathisms" being "simply descriptions of God's actions and feelings in human terms, and from a human perspective." So John W. Cooper, *Panentheism, the Other God of the Philosophers: From Plato to the Present* (Grand Rapids: Baker Academic, 2006), 332; Phillip R. Johnson, "God without Mood Swings," in *Bound Only Once: The Failure of Open Theism*, ed. D. Wilson (Moscow, ID: Canon, 2001), 116. Martin Luther, *Luther's Works*, ed. J. Pelikan et al.; 55 vols. (Philadelphia: Fortress, 1999), 17:358, took a similar position with regard to divine grief in Gen 6:7, stating: "Such an emotion is attributed to God, not as though He were thus moved, but the holy prophets, Moses, and Noah conceived of Him in this way."

29. As Rob Lister, *God Is Impassible and Impassioned: Toward a Theology of Divine Emotion* (Wheaton, IL: Crossway, 2013), 195, recognizes, "the biblical portrayal of divine emotion is both powerful and pervasive. One cannot read Scripture and come away with the conclusion that God is affectionless." Lister nevertheless adopts what he calls a qualified impassibilist perspective (see below).

Hosea 11:8-9 provides an apt instance in this regard, the consideration of which will model one way of implementing canonical hermeneutics. Therein God states, "How can I give you up, O Ephraim? How can I surrender you, O Israel? How can I make you like Admah? How can I treat you like Zeboiim? My heart is turned over within Me, all My compassions are kindled. I will not execute My fierce anger; I will not destroy Ephraim again. For I am God and not man, the Holy One in your midst, and I will not come in wrath." This passage depicts intense divine emotions, prompted by human unfaithfulness.

John Calvin, however, comments regarding this passage, "God, we know, is subject to no passions, and we know that no change takes place in him. What then do these expressions mean, by which he appears to be changeable? Doubtless he accommodates himself to our ignorances whenever he puts on a character foreign to himself." Further, "the same mode of speaking after the manner of men is adopted; for we know that these feelings belong not to God; he cannot be touched with repentance, and his heart cannot undergo changes."[30]

Calvin thus employs the first two of three prominent rationales for the exclusion of divine pathos in the interpretation of purportedly anthropopathic imagery relative to God, which are:

1. The language of Scripture is human language accommodative of human thought patterns.
2. God is impassible; thus biblical language suggesting passibility cannot correspond to God as he is.
3. Passages that appear to ascribe passible emotion to God often utilize anatomical imagery. Since God is incorporeal (i.e., lacks a physical body), such language cannot correspond to God as he is.

These rationales will be evaluated one by one.

The Accommodative Language Rationale

The dismissal of purportedly anthropopathic language relative to God *because* it is accommodative as "human" language faces numerous problems. First, it appears to overlook the fact that all language to which the interpreter is privy

30. John Calvin, *Commentaries on the Twelve Minor Prophets* (Grand Rapids: Eerdmans, 1950), 400-401.

is accommodative human language. Since theology unavoidably consists of accommodative language, identifying language as accommodative provides no basis for distinguishing between canonical (or any other) language that is intended to correspond to God and that which is not.[31]

Given that I lack direct access to God as an object of examination and do not possess the cognitive-linguistic capacity to know with specificity the extent to which canonical language corresponds to God, with Vanhoozer I aim to avoid overestimating "the adequacy of human language and thought" while also avoiding underestimating "the importance of responding to the provocations of God's self-revelation."[32] Accordingly, a canonical approach attempts to remain close to the canonical language itself, carefully interpreted in light of the details of individual texts and the wider canonical context.

This includes taking canonical language in its minimally demonstrable exegetical sense (in light of the entire canon) while recognizing that my resulting conception of God is unavoidably imperfect (as is all God-talk). As Wolterstorff puts it, "an implication of accepting Scripture as canonical is that one affirms, as literally true, Scripture's representation of God unless, on some point, one has good reason not to do so."[33] Here, even language that is properly taken as literal is nevertheless analogical and taking the exegetical upshot as true itself entails careful sensitivity to identifiable metaphors and idiomatic expressions.[34]

---

31. It seems inappropriate to sideline the apparent exegetical meaning of biblical language about God on the premise that it is accommodative language, since this is true of all available theological language. G. B. Caird, *The Language and Imagery of the Bible* (Philadelphia: Westminster, 1980), 174, states, "We have no other language besides metaphor with which to speak about God." So also John C. L. Gibson, *Language and Imagery in the Old Testament* (Peabody, MA: Hendrickson, 1998), 26.

32. Kevin J. Vanhoozer, *Remythologizing Theology* (Cambridge: Cambridge University Press, 2010), 16.

33. Nicholas Wolterstorff, "Could Not God Sorrow If We Do?" in *The Papers of the Henry Luce III Fellows in Theology*, ed. Christopher I. Wilkins (Atlanta: Scholars, 2002), 140.

34. Using Alston's distinction between literal and univocal, Vanhoozer states, "Two things are 'univocal' if they have the same meaning. To use a term 'literally,' by contrast, is to use it in its conventional rather than figurative sense. God literally speaks and acts, but because God does so in his own way, these terms are only partially univocal when applied to God and human beings" (*Remythologizing Theology*, 211 n. 118). Vanhoozer prefers "to say the two terms ["speaks" and "acts"] are 'literal and analogical' rather than [Alston's preference for] 'partially univocal.' The key is to remember that 'univocal' pertains to the mode of God's acting, 'literal' to the kind of action done" (*Remythologizing Theology*, 211 n. 118). Cf. William P. Alston, "How to Think about Divine Action," in *Divine Action*, ed. B. Hebblethwaite and E. Henderson (Edinburgh: T&T Clark, 1990), 52, 68-69. See also Merold Westphal's view, "On

According to canonical theological method, biblical language should be interpreted with careful attention to its genre, context, and other textual indicators, in order to avoid dismissing the exegetical content of the text (figurative or otherwise) based on extratextual presuppositions or dogmatic pressures.[35] This includes recognizing instances where biblical language is demonstrably figurative, by way of metaphor, idiom, hyperbole, etc. However, even where language is appropriately identified as metaphorical, there remains the danger of "either interpreting metaphors literally in every respect or (more commonly today) denying any essential relationship between the metaphor and God."[36]

Dismissal of the emotional aspects of canonical language as inappropriate to God because it is accommodative or figurative language seems to require that the interpreter already knows either what God is like or what the author of the text thought that God is like, and can thus differentiate between canonical language that is intended to correspond to God's being or actions and that which is not. This relates closely to the impassibility rationale.

Reading God the Author," *RelS* 37/3 (2001): 273, that "we need two distinctions, one between literal and metaphorical and the other between analogical and univocal." The theist can then say, "'God speaks' is a literal but analogical claim. It is analogical because divine discourse is both like and unlike human discourse; but this is not metaphor, because the performance of illocutionary acts belongs properly and primarily to God and only derivatively" to humans."

35. Nonliteral use of language may convey true content that exceeds what may have been conveyed by strictly literal speech. That language is literal or nonliteral does not mean it is thereby true or untrue.

36. Terence E. Fretheim, "The Repentance of God: A Key to Evaluating Old Testament God-Talk," *HBT* 10/1 (1988): 51. I prefer to use "literal" and "figurative" as shorthand ways to distinguish between that which is conventionally presumed to be the strict, primary sense of a term and the use of figures of speech (e.g., metaphors, metonyms, idioms, etc.) wherein the literal meaning (as defined above) of the word is untrue or nonsensical. Metaphor has often been defined as a kind of figurative language (though it may also be employed broadly as a near synonym of figurative) that compares two unlike things that have some point(s) of commonality. According to the cognitive-linguistic view, however, metaphor uses the terms of one conceptual domain to understand another (e.g., life as a journey), whether or not there is obvious similarity between them. The nature of metaphor (and figurative language broadly) and how it is to be understood and related to or distinguished from the literal sense of language has been (and continues to be) the subject of complex, protracted debate. For an introductory discussion of perspectives on metaphor in the philosophy of language see William G. Lycan, *Philosophy of Language: A Contemporary Introduction*, 2nd ed. (New York: Routledge, 2008), 175-90. Recognizing the difficulty in defining and understanding the nature, meaning, and operation of literal and figurative language only strengthens the approach advocated here that, since our language is insufficient, one should interpret canonical language in a way that errs on the side of remaining close to Scripture's language and thought patterns.

The Divine Impassibility Rationale

Some claim that God cannot be affected by anything external to himself, thus biblical language suggesting passibility must not be descriptive of God.[37] Paul Helm, for instance, reasons to (unqualified) divine impassibility as follows: "(1) God is timelessly eternal. (2) Whatever is timelessly eternal is unchangeable. (3) Whatever is unchangeable is impassible. (4) Therefore, God is impassible."[38] Given this conception of God, Helm employs the accommodative language rationale to interpret canonical texts suggestive of divine passibility, stating that it "is because God wishes people to respond to him that he *must* represent himself to them as one to whom response is possible," but God does not, properly speaking, respond to humans or experience emotions as "affect."[39]

Beyond Helm's rationale, divine impassibility has been promoted for a host of complex reasons, including the desires to promote the view that God transcends creaturely limitations as the self-sufficient Creator of all,[40] to starkly

37. Divine impassibility may be defined in a variety of ways. Unless otherwise specified, I use it to refer to the notion that God cannot be affected by anything outside of himself. Passibility, then, refers to being affected by and responsive to the external world. See Peckham, *Love of God*, 147-89.

38. Paul Helm, "The Impossibility of Divine Passibility," in *The Power and Weakness of God: Impassibility and Orthodoxy*, ed. Nigel M. de S. Cameron (Edinburgh: Rutherford, 1990), 119. Helm's premise of divine timelessness has been (and continues to be) a matter of considerable theological debate and there is considerable biblical material suggestive of (analogical) divine temporality. See the discussion of various views in Gregory E. Ganssle, ed., *God & Time: Four Views* (Downers Grove, IL: InterVarsity, 2001). Cf. Fernando Canale, *A Criticism of Theological Reason: Time and Timelessness as Primordial Presuppositions* (Berrien Springs, MI: Andrews University Press, 1987); John C. Peckham, "Divine Passibility, Analogical Temporality, and Theo-Ontology: Implications of a Canonical Approach," in *Scripture and Philosophy: Essays Honoring the Work and Vision of Fernando Luis Canale*, ed. Tiago Arrais, Kenneth Bergland, and Michael F. Younker (Berrien Springs, MI: Adventist Theological Society Publications, 2016), 32-53.

39. Helm, "Impossibility," 133-34. Helm does not intend to present a view at odds with Scripture but claims that "the metaphysical or ontological or strictly literal data must control the anthropomorphic and anthropopathic data, and not vice versa" ("Impossibility," 131). However, how does one know which language is metaphysical and which is "anthropopathic"?

40. Many theologians have argued that divine impassibility is a vestige of classical Greek ontology. See, for example, John Sanders, "Historical Considerations," in *The Openness of God: A Biblical Challenge to the Traditional Understanding of God* (Downers Grove, IL: InterVarsity, 1994), 59-91. However, some theologians maintain that the tradition has been misunderstood, positing that while some (Justin Martyr, Clement of Alexandria) presented impassibility as "hyper-transcendent," the traditional mainstream "understanding of a negative term like *impassible* did not prohibit the application of emotionally laden characteristics to God" (Lister,

distinguish the biblical God from the often immoral "anthropomorphic" gods of ancient religions,[41] and to avoid Feuerbachian criticisms of theology as merely human projection.[42] However, the impassibilist rationale risks imposing a preconception of God upon the canonical text, which repeatedly depicts God as passible (e.g., Gen 6:5-6; Hos 9:15; 11:8-9; Isa 49:15; 63:9, 15; 66:13; Jer 18:7-10; 31:20; Pss 78:40-41, 58-59; 103:13).

Adherence to sound principles of exegesis would require sufficient evidence that the canonical text supports the view that God is impassible. However, no canonical text or passage asserts divine impassibility. As Rob Lister comments,

---

God Is Impassible, 41-122, here 95, 103). Likewise, Paul Gavrilyuk, "God's Impassible Suffering in the Flesh: The Promise of Paradoxical Christology," in *Divine Impassibility and the Mystery of Human Suffering*, ed. James Keating and Thomas Joseph White (Grand Rapids: Eerdmans, 2009), 139, maintains that, for the patristics, "divine impassibility is primarily a metaphysical term, marking God's unlikeness to everything in the created order, not a psychological term denoting (as modern passibilists allege) God's emotional apathy." See the further discussion below.

Gavrilyuk thus contends that it was the heretical "Docetists, Arians, and Nestorians" who all "deployed divine impassibility in an unqualified sense, as a property that categorically excluded God's participation in any form of suffering," whereas "the Church Fathers defended the reality of Christ's suffering against the Docetists, the fullness of the incarnate Son's divinity against the Arians, and the unity of his person against the Nestorians" ("God's Impassible Suffering," 143). See Gavrilyuk's extended treatment in *The Suffering of the Impassible God: The Dialectics of Patristic Thought* (Oxford: Oxford University Press, 2004), 21-63. Consider also Thomas Weinandy, *Does God Suffer?* (Notre Dame: University of Notre Dame Press, 2000), 83-113. Regarding the historical theology, one should not confuse patripassianism or theopaschitism with passibility generally. Patripassianism assumes modalism because it claims that the Father suffers on the cross, which is rejected by most contemporary passibilists. Likewise, the early condemnation of theopaschitism related to its connotations (at the time) of monophysitism and should not be conflated with passibility generally. See the discussion of these distinctions in Lister, *God Is Impassible*, 33-35.

41. Thus "by calling the Christian God impassible the Fathers sought to distance God the creator from the gods of mythology" (Gavrilyuk, *Suffering of the Impassible God*, 48; see also his entire chapter, "The Christian God v. Passionate Pagan Deities: Impassibility as an Apophatic Qualifier of Divine Emotions," in *Suffering of the Impassible God*, 47-63; cf. Weinandy, *Does God Suffer?* 89). An antianthropomorphic tendency is apparent in the LXX, which often (though not always) downplays the portrayal of divine emotions. See especially the Septuagint rendering of Jer 31:20 [LXX Jer 38:20]. For a discussion of many examples, see Charles T. Fritsch, *The Anti-anthropomorphisms of the Greek Pentateuch* (Princeton: Princeton University Press, 1943), 17-18. Cf. Gavrilyuk, *Suffering of the Impassible God*, 39-46.

42. See Vanhoozer, *Remythologizing Theology*, 21-23. Charles Hartshorne, *Omnipotence and Other Theological Mistakes* (Albany: State University of New York Press, 1984), 29, believes, "A well-meaning attempt to purify theology of anthropomorphisms purified it of any genuine, consistent meaning at all."

"Scripture never makes a direct assertion of a metaphysical doctrine of divine impassibility"; the canon "does not supply" this "theological category."[43] On the contrary, though Lister himself advocates (qualified) impassibility, he recognizes the "powerful and pervasive" canonical "portrayal of divine emotions," which excludes "the conclusion that God is affectionless."[44]

Some impassibilists argue, conversely, that passages appearing to describe divine passibility should be interpreted in light of other texts that assert divine immutability. Trent Pomplun notes, "Satisfied that God was immutable (Mal 3:6) and invariable (James 1:17), theologians took it for granted that the Most High was impervious to any pathos external to his own nature."[45] However, the primary texts typically offered to prove divine immutability (e.g., Mal 3:6 and Num 23:19) themselves contextually suggest divine responsiveness, contra the kind of immutability needed to ground impassibility.[46] For example, the proclamation "I, the LORD, do not change; therefore you, O sons of Jacob, are not consumed" (Mal 3:6) appears within the context of responsive relationship, evident in the following verse where God states, "Return to Me, and I will return to you" (Mal 3:7).[47] The statement that God does "not change," then, does

---

43. Lister, *God Is Impassible*, 190, 173. He includes even his own view of qualified impassibility, for which there is no direct textual evidence. It is the product of "second-order theological reflection on Scripture's first-order statements" (*God Is Impassible*, 173). Thus "when biblical texts appear in the discussion [of the Fathers], it is because they seem to be evidence against God's impassibility, evidence which had then to be explained or accounted for by defenders of the doctrine"; Dennis Edward Johnson, "Immutability and Incarnation: An Historical and Theological Study of the Concepts of Christ's Divine Unchangeability and His Human Development" (PhD diss., Fuller Theological Seminary, 1984), 174, quoted in Lister, *God Is Impassible*, 103. Nevertheless, Johnson maintains that "the doctrine of impassibility was an attempt to express some broader biblical teachings about God" ("Immutability," 174).

44. Lister, *God Is Impassible*, 195. He thus adopts a temporally affected and responsively (though self-determinedly) emotional qualified impassibility over against the unqualified impassibility of Helm and others, claiming that God is "impassible and impassioned" (*God Is Impassible*, 171).

45. Trent Pomplun, "Impassibility in St. Hilary of Poitiers's *De Trinitate*," in *Divine Impassibility and the Mystery of Human Suffering*, 187. Calvin similarly held that Scripture depicts God as immutable in a way that requires the exclusion of divine pathos, a view still held by many. Lister notes, however, that Calvin was unfortunately "prone to shift 'negative' emotional terminology into categories of volition," thus "dissolving its affective content" *God Is Impassible*, 118, 121).

46. This has been recognized by many theologians, including those who advocate a qualified impassibility. See Bruce A. Ware, "An Evangelical Reexamination of the Doctrine of the Immutability of God" (PhD diss.; Fuller Theological Seminary, 1984), 433. Cf. Lister, *God Is Impassible*, 204-6.

47. Both Num 23:19 and 1 Sam 15:29 differentiate God's repenting (נחם) from that of hu-

not exclude relational responsiveness but appears to express the constancy of God's character, undergirding his appropriate wrath against evil.[48]

Whereas canonical evidence for divine impassibility is lacking, there is an abundance of canonical testimony that depicts God experiencing responsive emotions.[49] Thus, absent a compelling, canonical-exegetical argument asserting that emotive language in the Bible is not intended to apply to the conception of God proper, the impassibility rationale does not suffice to sideline the literary thrust of Hosea 11:8-9 and similar texts.

The Anatomical Imagery Rationale

Some, further, emphasize that Hosea 11:8-9 expresses emotional content by anatomical imagery, which cannot apply to God because God is incorporeal.[50] Consider the imagery in Hos 11:8-9 once again. God states, "How can I give you up, O Ephraim? How can I surrender you, O Israel? How can I make you like Admah? How can I treat you like Zeboiim? My heart [לֵב] is turned over [הָפַךְ] within Me, all My compassions [נִחֻם] are kindled [כָּמַר]. I will not execute My fierce anger [אַף]; I will not destroy Ephraim again. For I am God and not man, the Holy One in your midst, and I will not come in wrath."

Here, one need not rely on the presupposition that God is incorporeal in order to recognize that this imagery does not refer to divine anatomy. Such language is demonstrably idiomatic in that the same anatomical idioms of "heart" (לֵב) and "nose" (אַף) are also used of human agents with the widely recognized intent of conveying intense emotions without any intended ref-

mans, but neither rules out divine repenting altogether, lest they contradict the many other passages in which God is the subject of the verb נחם, including twice within 1 Sam 15 itself (e.g., Exod 32:14; 1 Sam 15:11, 35; Jer 18:7-10; Jon 3:9-10; 4:2). See Peckham, *Love of God*, 153-55, 185.

48. James 1:17 likewise refers to God's ethical immutability but makes no mention of ontological imperviousness to affect.

49. For the wider canonical evidence against the divine impassibility rationale see John C. Peckham, *The Concept of Divine Love in the Context of the God–World Relationship* (New York: Peter Lang, 2014), 256-99, 432-55, 510-20, 584-88; Peckham, *Love of God*, 147-89, 263-69.

50. How biblical language of divine embodiment should be taken is the subject of considerable debate. The primary upshot of this chapter, however, is not affected by whether one claims that Scripture views God as embodied, or that all divine "body language" consists of conceptual metaphor that does not convey that God possesses physical form, or something in between. Divine passibility does not require corporeality. Lister believes that God's "experience of emotion is certainly no less real than ours on account of the fact that he does not have a body" (*God Is Impassible*, 252).

erence to the anatomy of the human.[51] The expression "My heart is turned over within Me" should not be taken to refer to the physical turning of an anatomical heart but to profound emotions, and this would be so whether such language were used of God or humans (cf. Exod 14:5).[52]

Consider Jeremiah 31:20, wherein God declares: "Is Ephraim My dear son? Is he a delightful child? Indeed, as often as I have spoken against him, I certainly *still* remember him. Therefore My heart [מֵעִים] yearns [הָמָה] for him; I will surely have mercy [רחם] on him." The Hebrew term מֵעָה (here translated "heart") often refers to the intestines or abdomen but is commonly used idiomatically to refer to one's inner being, the seat of emotions.[53] מֵעִים is used alongside the verb רחם (here translated "have mercy" and typically rendered "have compassion"), which is itself probably denominative from the noun רַחֲמִים, which means abdomen or "womb" and thus evokes anatomical imagery in a similar fashion to that of מֵעִים.[54] Here again it is readily apparent that the imagery does not literally refer to internal organs roaring, moaning, or growling, but idiomatically refers to emotionally intense compassion.[55]

Elsewhere, the canon repeatedly depicts God by anatomical language in-

---

51. See the list below. The intensity of the emotionality conveyed here is evident by comparison to the similar imagery of human agents in Gen 43:30 and 1 Kgs 3:6, the only two other instances where the term כמר relates to emotions. In the one nonemotional instance it refers to skin becoming hot in the sun (Lam 5:10). Cf. Mike Butterworth, "רחם," *NIDOTTE* 3:1093; H. J. Stoebe, "רחם," *TLOT* 3:1226.

52. Consider John Sanders's cognitive-linguistic approach to metaphorical language of God, "Theological Muscle-Flexing: How Human Embodiment Shapes Discourse about God," in *Creation Made Free: Open Theology Engaging Science*, ed. Thomas Jay Oord (Eugene, OR: Pickwick, 2009), 236, wherein he posits that our reasoning depends heavily on conceptual metaphors derived from physical experience as embodied and it is thus "not surprising that we use the same processes to conceptualize God," that is, "by way of conceptual metaphors derived from our embodiment." Cf. Zoltán Kövecses, *Metaphor: A Practical Introduction*, 2nd ed. (New York: Oxford University Press, 2010).

53. מֵעִים is elsewhere used in instances of intense physical pain (Job 30:27; Ps 22:15) but more frequently denotes intense human emotions (Isa 16:11; Jer 4:19; Lam 1:20; 2:11). Stoebe thus correctly sees this as "expanded parallelism" that "approximate[s] *rahamim*" ("רחם," 1226). The collocation of מֵעִים and הָמָה ("murmur," "roar," sometimes "arouse") appears five times of strong emotions (Isa 16:11; 63:15; Jer 4:19; 31:20; Cant 5:4).

54. Phyllis Trible, *God and the Rhetoric of Sexuality* (Philadelphia: Fortress, 1978), 31-59, posits that it thus evokes the image of a womb-like mother love. Cf. Butterworth, "רחם," 1093; Stoebe, "רחם," 1226; H. Simian-Yofre, "רחם," *TDOT* 13:438.

55. I use the term "idiomatic" to refer simply to a common use of a phrase (or a single term in Hebrew) that has figurative meaning divergent from the literal meaning of its component term(s).

cluding that of ears,[56] eyes,[57] nose,[58] mouth,[59] face,[60] hands,[61] arms,[62] and heart.[63] Significantly, this same idiomatic phraseology that is used of God is also used of humans and, in each case, it is readily apparent that the intended meanings of the idiomatic expressions are independent of physical anatomy, whether referring to humans or God.[64] For instance, the idiom of finding favor in someone's sight (Gen 6:8; 1 Sam 25:8) corresponds to favor in one's estimation. The anatomical referent is beside the point because the idiom is not dependent upon the physiological phenomena that might have undergirded the origin of such metaphorical usage.

It will not do to assert that God has no body parts, therefore the language

56. For example, consider the idiom of inclining one's ear (נטה + אֹזֶן), which refers to attentively listening, used of both God (2 Kgs 19:16) and humans (Prov 5:1).

57. Consider the frequent idiom of finding favor (מצא + חן + עין) in one's sight, used of both God and humans (Gen 6:8; 32:5). Consider also the idiom that is often rendered by the English idiom "apple" of the "eye," which in Hebrew literally means "little man of the eye [עין]" and appears of both God and humans (Deut 32:10; Zech 2:8; Prov 7:2). For many other anatomical idioms in the OT see Jeffery D. Griffin, "An Investigation of Idiomatic Expressions in the Hebrew Bible with a Case Study of Anatomical Idioms" (PhD diss.; Mid-America Baptist Theological Seminary, 1999), 111.

58. For example, God is described as "long of nose" (אֶרֶךְ אַפַּיִם), which is translated "slow to anger" (Exod 34:6) and may be used of humans (Prov 14:29). Consider also the description of divine anger as the "heat of my nostrils" in Exod 32:10, 12. Here and elsewhere the term אַף, literally "nose," idiomatically refers to anger by metonymy, as it does also with human referents (Gen 30:2; Exod 32:10). On the other hand, a human may be "quick-tempered," that is, "short of nose" (Prov 14:17).

59. Frequently the "mouth" (פֶּה) of someone idiomatically refers to their speech in the sense of command or proclamation, of God and humans (Gen 45:21; Deut 8:3; 2 Sam 14:19).

60. The term that literally refers to one's face (פָּנִים) may be used idiomatically of one's presence (Exod 33:14), both divine and human (Exod 10:11). Consider also the concept of "hiding" one's "face," which is a sign of displeasure, used with divine (Deut 31:17-18) and human subjects (Isa 53:3). See Mayer I. Gruber, "The Many Faces of Hebrew nāśā' pānîm 'lift up the face,'" ZAW 95/2 (1983): 252-60.

61. One's "hand" (יד) may appear idiomatically in various ways, including in many verbal phrases, of God and humans (Gen 14:20; 49:24; cf. Deut 4:34).

62. Language of "arm" (זרוע) may refer to one's strength or power, of God and humans (Exod 6:6; 15:16; Job 35:9; 40:9).

63. In Hebrew, the word that literally refers to one's "heart" (לב) is a rich term of the totality of human disposition. It may idiomatically describe many different mental aspects including one's thoughts, will, and emotions and is used of both divine and human referents (Gen 6:5-6).

64. There is an evident "proclivity" in Semitic languages "to utilize anatomical terms in the creation of new idioms" (Griffin, "Investigation of Idiomatic Expressions," 39). Cf. E. Dhorme, L'emploi métaphorique des noms de parties du corps en hébreu et en akkadien (Paris: Geuthner, 1963). Caird suggests this is true of all languages (Language and Imagery of the Bible, 172-73).

is nonliteral, therefore it does not correspond to God.[65] If such idiomatic language used of God is to be dismissed *because* of its anatomical imagery, consistency would require that the identical idioms with reference to humans also be interpreted either as literal references to anatomy or as expressions that do not actually correspond to the human subjects. Yet neither of these options would be applied by competent interpreters. As Caird puts it, "Only captious pedantry or childish humour will find it necessary to remark that the eye of a needle cannot see or a tongue of land speak."[66] Why, then, should references to divine agency be divested of the intended meaning of well-understood idiomatic phraseology?[67]

If one insists on dismissing such language as anthropomorphic or anthropopathic, one should rule out divine speech and many other divine actions that are also often conveyed by anatomical idiom. At what point would one draw the line with regard to which language is intended to refer to God and which is not? With regard to divine action, Vanhoozer recognizes that "while it is a contingent fact about human beings that we can only act or bring about changes in the world through some bodily movement, the latter is not a necessary part of the meaning of the concept."[68] Applied broadly, such a principle entails that the anatomical imagery rationale fails to provide grounds for dismissing the apparent exegetical meaning of canonical imagery

---

65. See James Barr, "Literality," *Faith and Philosophy* 6/4 (1989); Eugene Albert Nida, *Componential Analysis of Meaning: An Introduction to Semantic Structures*, Approaches to Semiotics 57 (The Hague: Mouton, 1975). See also Paul Ricoeur's classic consideration, *The Rule of Metaphor: Multi-Disciplinary Studies of the Creation of Meaning in Language* (Toronto: University of Toronto Press, 1977), of the referential function of language by way of living metaphor that corresponds to reality, but neither univocally nor equivocally. Cf. the cognitive-linguistic approach in Kövecses, *Metaphor*.

66. Caird, *Language and Imagery of the Bible*, 173.

67. Graham Cole, "The Living God: Anthropomorphic or Anthropopathic?" *RTR* 59/1 (2000): 23, contends that "an anthropopathism such as God's grief is to be given its face value. God does not merely *seem* to have grief in Genesis 6:6; He is grieved, *contra* Calvin." In his view, "to argue otherwise is to beg the question of why we should not dismiss references to the divine love and compassion also as mere anthropopathisms" ("Living God," 23). Cf. Robert B. Chisholm, Jr.'s argument, "Anatomy of an Anthropomorphism: Does God Discover Facts?" *BSac* 164 (2007): 3-20, that while so-called anthropomorphic language is metaphorical, it conveys the reality that God enters into real relationship with his creatures. Cf. Terence E. Fretheim, *The Suffering of God: An Old Testament Perspective* (Philadelphia: Fortress, 1984), 99.

68. Vanhoozer, *Remythologizing Theology*, 58. John Gibson adds, the "issue in biblical anthropomorphisms is understanding them, not approving or disapproving them" (*Language and Imagery in the Old Testament*, 26).

of divine emotion. How, then, should such language be interpreted with a canonical approach?

DIVINE EMOTION AS "THEOPATHIC"

In contrast to the three prominent rationales for treating imagery of divine emotion as anthropopathic, I posit three counterprinciples for interpreting imagery of divine emotion:

1. Since all available language is human and thus accommodative, the dismissal of the exegetical force of figurative language for this reason is self-defeating.
2. The interpreter should not presume to know what God is like, or what the author of a given text thought that God is like, prior to or independent of the canonical data itself.
3. The frequent idiomatic usage of figurative anatomical expressions, with both divine and human referents, demonstrates that such idioms are not intended to refer to, or depend upon, anatomical referents. Therefore, interpretation should include the well-known exegetical meaning of a given idiom, even in reference to God (analogically), unless there is a compelling canonical rationale otherwise.

Beyond these principles, the wider data of the canon provides additional insights that assist in the interpretation of the imagery of divine emotion as analogical, without precisely specifying the extent of similarity and dissimilarity. For instance, Hos 11:8-9 includes an interpretive control in God's statement, "I am God and not man" (cf. Isa 55:8).[69] It is therefore apparent in the text itself that the imagery therein should not be applied to God univocally, that is, as identical to such language with reference to humans. The text indicates, rather, that the language should be interpreted as analogical.[70]

---

69. Similarly, God is depicted as being "wearied" (יגע) by his people (Mal 2:17) or "weary" (לאה) of bearing feasts and festivals that are merely for show (Isa 1:14) yet elsewhere Scripture states that God does "not become weary [יגע] or tired" (Isa 40:28). It seems the former instances express God's emotional displeasure and disappointment yet without the fatigue that is excluded by Isa 40.

70. Vanhoozer notes that such "metaphors assert both 'is' and 'is not,' and thus may be indicative not of sheer contradiction ... but partial description" (*Remythologizing Theology*, 62). However, it appears to me to be beyond the interpreter's abilities to specify

Likewise, the canon explicitly differentiates divine "repentance" from human "repentance," stating "the Glory of Israel will not lie or change His mind [נחם]; for He is not a man that He should change His mind [נחם]" (1 Sam 15:29; cf. Num 23:19; Mal 3:6). Scripture, however, repeatedly depicts divine נחם, including twice in 1 Sam 15 where God is grieved by the outcome of his election of Saul (1 Sam 15:11, 35). Similarly, prior to the flood, God is "sorry" (נחם) (Gen 6:6) and in many other instances God declares or exhibits willingness to relent (נחם) in response to humans (Exod 32:14; Jer 18:7-10; Jon 3:10; 4:2; etc.). Yet whereas humans repent of wrongdoing, "God is never said to have committed any sin of which God needs to repent."[71] In this and other ways, God does נחם but in a way appropriate to divinity that differs from human repentance.[72]

To take another example, some interpreters dismiss God's passion, or jealousy (קנא), as anthropopathic. But careful examination of divine jealousy in the canon demonstrates that it is both like and unlike human jealousy. God's passion for relationship with his people is always appropriate, analogous to the proper passion of a husband for his wife.[73] God's jealousy, however, portrays none of the flawed characteristics manifest in human jealousy, such as envy.[74] Likewise, whereas humans may hate arbitrarily or unjustly, divine displeasure is always accurately evaluative and appropriate.[75] Whereas humans may overreact in anger, God restrains his anger, despite provocation, always responding appropriately (Ps 78:38, 58).

Consistently, then, the canon depicts God as having emotions that are anal-

---

what corresponds to God (the "is") and what does not (the "is not") apart from canonical information.

71. See Fretheim, "Repentance of God," 50. Cf. Matthew R. Schlimm, "Different Perspectives on Divine Pathos: An Examination of Hermeneutics in Biblical Theology," *CBQ* 69/4 (2007): 673-94.

72. See page 235, note 47, and Peckham, *Love of God*, 153-55, 185.

73. E. Reuter, "קנא," *TDOT* 13:53, points out that the dismissal of divine jealousy as a so-called anthropopathism "only serves the Stoic notion of divine impassibility, which is inconsistent with the biblical understanding of God but is often espoused nevertheless by both Christian and Jewish theology, creating problems of exegesis."

74. The combination of ב + קנא suggests the negative emotion of envy (e.g., "envy" in Prov 3:31), never used of God, whereas the construction of ל + קנא suggests an appropriate passion or righteous ardor with action on behalf of its object, of both humans (e.g., "zealous" in 1 Kgs 19:10) and of God (e.g., Zech 8:2). See Peckham, *Love of God*, 156-59; Peckham, *Concept of Divine Love*, 261-64, 439-40.

75. See Peckham, *Concept of Divine Love*, 250-56, 428-32, 503-4; Peckham, *Love of God*, 125-28.

ogous to human emotions (or vice versa), but his are wholly good, appropriate, and without fault.[76] Whereas human judges may be corrupted (1 Sam 8:3), God always judges righteously (Gen 18:25). Whereas human love may fail, God's exceeds all expectations (Isa 49:15). Israel's lovingkindness is transient (Hos 6:4) but God's is everlasting (Ps 100:5). Thus, the biblical data provides *some* guidelines and controls with regard to the interpretation of the language used of God, figurative and otherwise, and it sheds light on some of the ways language about God differs from the same or similar language used of humans.

In some sense, then, theological predications should be qualified according to any canonically indicated qualifications alongside continual recognition of the partially corresponding and accommodatively analogical character of theological language. Accordingly, one should carefully and humbly attempt to avoid imposing any extracanonical conception about God, especially one that would exclude what would otherwise be the exegetical upshot of the canonical language. Given that I lack a perfect understanding of God such that I cannot with confidence specify all of the ways in which divine repentance (or any other attribution to God) differs from human repentance, canonical hermeneutics restricts such specification to that which is indicated by the canonical text itself, recognizing that there are surely other differences beyond those indicated in the canon but which are better left without speculation.

Accordingly, canonical hermeneutics do not employ the way of eminence or the way of negation. Whereas it is true that only good characteristics apply to God, and do so maximally (or eminently), the way of eminence is incapable of objective usefulness since different interpreters will find different characteristics "good" and derive widely differing "positive" aspects. The *via negativa* (way of negation, i.e., apophatic theology), which purports to negate those characteristics that do not apply to God, is similarly problematic since it requires decisions regarding which characteristics should be excluded and thus runs the risk of excluding characteristics that seem inappropriate to God from our limited perspective but that God may possess analogically, or characteristics that God may condescend to take on in relation to the world.

Canonical theology focuses on and attempts to restrict itself to textual indicators while remaining cognizant of the limitations of human understanding, with the goal of avoiding the temptation to overdetermine the conception of God. Conversely, no harbor is given to overly literalistic or naïve approaches

76. Here, divine omnibenevolence is not an extracanonical presupposition but is derived from the frequent, canon-wide data that describe God as always, and in all things, good (omnibenevolent).

to the text, which falsely suggest that an interpreter may achieve complete success in avoiding the influence of presuppositions, errors, and other qualifiers. Questions will remain and differing interpretations by competent biblical scholars and theologians regarding the extent of the "is" and "is not" of biblical language of God will persist. However, precisely because the interpretation of such language is not self-evident, in the absence of compelling exegetically and canonically sound argument that emotive language in Scripture is not intended to apply to the conception of God proper, I believe the literary thrust of the biblical text(s) should be taken seriously, in conjunction with all available intertextual canonical controls.

To his credit, Lister's model moves in this direction, attempting to provide a positive explication of how "emotional predications of God in Scripture refer literally and truthfully [but not univocally] to him" such that "God is truly impassioned," alongside a qualified notion of divine impassibility wherein God is "invulnerable to *involuntarily* precipitated emotional vicissitude."[77] He thus utilizes "analogical hermeneutics" in the attempt to identify "what the ascription of emotional terminology to God does not mean" while also suggesting "positively what affective content is true of God's experience according to Scripture."[78] Lister's interpretation of "the language of divine passion" is constrained by his commitment to qualified impassibility, which is grounded in the "Creator/creature distinction," the "transcendence/immanence balance, incorporeality, self-sufficiency, eternality, omniscience, exhaustive sovereignty, immutability, [and] intra-Trinitarian love and holiness," all of which he considers to be derived from Scripture.[79] Yet, Lister breaks from significant streams of Christian tradition in numerous ways, including his rejection of the dissolution of "all of the affective connotations into expressions of the divine will" and "adjustment of the Augustinian stance on divine eternity, such that the eternal God is capable of having actual in-time [and responsive] relations with his creatures."[80]

On the contrary, although I also maintain important distinctions between divine and human emotions, I do not think there is sufficient reason to label God as impassible. Impassibility is neither referred to in Scripture (semantically or conceptually) nor does its qualified sense provide explanatory value

---

77. Lister, *God Is Impassible*, 187, 175.

78. Lister, *God Is Impassible*, 106.

79. Lister, *God Is Impassible*, 184.

80. Lister, *God Is Impassible*, 184. At the same time, he considers his qualified passibility to be in agreement with the mainstream tradition. *God Is Impassible*, 95, 103, 106. Similarly, see Gavrilyuk, "God's Impassible Suffering," 131.

that is not already capably conveyed by other theological concepts that may be confidently derived from the canon (e.g., creation, transcendence, omnipotence, omniscience). What is the benefit, then, of continuing to use terminology that is often taken to mean that God has no emotions or, at least, cannot be affected by the world?

Why not, instead, speak of divine emotions as theopathic? According to the canon, humans were created in the image of God (Gen 1:26-27). It may therefore be more accurate to say that the canon considers humans to be theomorphic and theopathic than to say that language of God that Scripture also uses of humans is anthropopathic.[81] The term theopathic itself conveys positively that God does have emotions (the "is") while qualifying those emotions as distinctly divine (the "is not") without either committing the users of such terminology to a particular conception of God's nature or conveying a particular (and, perhaps, idiosyncratic) delimitation of the extent of similarity or dissimilarity between such language and the way the same language would apply to humans. This would avoid some of the negative and sometimes misleading connotations of the term anthropopathic while offering the benefit of a shorthand moniker for use by interpreters who may nevertheless come to various conclusions about the manner in which theopathisms should ultimately be understood.

Conclusion

This chapter has focused on how to interpret theological language relative to God canonically, with attention first to crucial underlying issues regarding the humble posture of canonical theology, commitment to ethical reading, and recognition of the limits of divinely commissioned theological language as unavoidably accommodative and analogical.

Toward understanding how canonical theology functions in practice, attention turned to the treatment of purportedly anthropopathic language used of God. In contrast to the view that figurative anatomical expressions of divine

81. See Vanhoozer's view that the "human capacities to know, will, and love are themselves theomorphic" (*Remythologizing Theology,* 64). Further, "perhaps the Bible's depiction of divine suffering is less a matter of anthropopathic projection than it is a case of human suffering being theopathic (God-like)" (*Remythologizing Theology,* 77-88). Moisés Silva, *God, Language, and Scripture: Reading the Bible in the Light of General Linguistics* (Grand Rapids: Zondervan, 1990), 22, adds, "our human qualities are themselves but a reflection of God's person and attributes."

emotion are nondescriptive of God, canonical theology posits an alternative approach that views such language as theopathic and intentionally avoids subverting the text to extracanonical imposition.

Although divine emotions surely differ considerably from those of humans, absent canonical evidence that suggests otherwise, they should be treated as sufficiently analogical without attempting to parse the specific manner in which they correspond to God (beyond the limits of what is offered by the canonical data). That is, in accordance with appropriate epistemic humility and caution against human presuppositions (as far as possible), where the Bible does not provide a discernible indication of the extent of similarity or dissimilarity of divine emotive language to that of humans, it seems most prudent to err toward the univocal end of the spectrum, in deference to the words of the canon as theological rule.

CHAPTER 10

What Might a Canonical Theology Look Like?
The Nature of Divine Love

What does canonical theology look like more broadly? This chapter examines how canonical theological method was applied to my own study of the nature of divine love, illustrating how this method applies and functions in systematic theology. This examination includes a step-by-step description of my implementation of this method toward addressing the conflict of interpretations over the nature of divine love and the broader issues of divine ontology that undergird and drive that conflict.[1] Such description provides an example of the postures, procedures, implementation, and implications of a canonical approach to systematic theology, which provides guidelines applicable to the study of other topics.

Toward a Canonical Model of Divine Love

Identifying the Issues/Questions

Over a number of years, I implemented this canonical theological method toward addressing the concept of divine love in relationship to the world, the first step of which was to identify the issues and engage the ongoing scholarly conversation by way of a careful literature review of theological perspectives

---

1. For an exposition of the results of my study of divine love see John C. Peckham, *The Love of God: A Canonical Model* (Downers Grove, IL: IVP Academic, 2015); also John C. Peckham, *The Concept of Divine Love in the Context of the God–World Relationship* (New York: Peter Lang, 2014).

on divine love.[2] This investigation identified an irreconcilable conflict of interpretations between two prominent models of divine love, the consideration of which, via major points of divergence, holds major implications across the broad spectrum of positions.

The transcendent-voluntarist model posits that divine love in relationship to the world is freely willed, unilateral, unmotivated, and unconditional beneficence. The immanent-experientialist model defines divine love in relationship to the world as essentially relational, universally sympathetic, and primarily passive. In the former, to love is primarily to freely will good to another; in the latter, to love is primarily to feel the feelings of others.

The underlying ontological systems of both of these models determine the nature of divine love.[3] The latter flows from process panentheism wherein reality *is* social relationship and, thus, the God–world relationship is itself love (i.e., sympathy). The former adopts a more traditional ontology of God as simple, timeless, self-sufficient, perfect, immutable, impassible, and sovereign will such that divine love must be unilaterally willed beneficence.

Examination of these two models, and of critics of both, highlighted crucial theological questions at the center of the conflict. Such questions were themselves shaped by investigation of the canonical data, resulting in five questions revolving around whether the God–world relationship is unilateral or bilateral.[4] First, does God choose to fully love only some, or all, or is he essentially related to all such that he necessarily loves all? Second, does God only bestow or create value, or might he also appraise, appreciate, and receive value? Third, does God's love include affection or emotionality such that God is concerned for the world, sympathetically or otherwise? Fourth, is divine love unconditional or conditional? Fifth, can God and humans be involved in a reciprocal (albeit asymmetrical) love relationship? Notably, each of these five questions themselves impinge upon weighty issues regarding the nature of God (divine ontology) and the God–world relationship.

Some might ask, at this juncture, about the validity of extracanonical ques-

---

2. This step of identifying and isolating the questions is crucial not only to know what questions to have in mind when consulting the canon but also to be engaged in the ongoing conversation among scholars toward avoiding isolationism and thus being ignorant of what has been said and what might be learned thereby. At this and other stages it is crucial first to read to understand and only thereafter to critically analyze the secondary material.

3. See Peckham, *Love of God*, 15-31.

4. These are later forms of the five questions that went through stages of revision and fine-tuning throughout the study, which began with the simple query: How does the canon depict divine love in relationship to the world?

tions that might themselves predetermine the results of canonical study. To be sure, questions might be framed and pursued in such a way that the results of a study are predetermined by them. To some degree, this seems unavoidable. With *any* methodology the interpreter brings a horizon and has questions in mind that do not derive purely from the canonical text itself. Toward mitigating undue imposition, however, the questions brought to the investigation are themselves to be revised by what is discovered in the canon and the canonical interpreter remains open to whatever might be found in the text and intentionally guards against presupposed conclusions and premature evaluation of existing positions.

Inductive Reading of the Canon

With major issues regarding the conception of divine love in mind, I conducted an inductive reading of the entire canon, isolating any texts that even slightly impinged on such issues — with care to avoid selecting passages based on my predispositions (insofar as is achievable). Among the most crucial elements of this approach is the application of *targeted* epoché, that is, the careful and intentional recognition and "tabling" of presuppositions that impinge upon the question(s) at hand.

Here, I attempted to table my presuppositions regarding divine ontology (particularly relative to divine love), not ignoring such presuppositions or those of others but attempting to subject them to the test of the canonical data, aiming first to ascertain the canonical description of divine love and only thereafter to ask what God must be like in order to cohere with such canonical description(s). That is, rather than filtering the canonical data by assuming that God is like x and therefore divine love is x, I attempted to invert the typical order and first ask what divine love is, starting from and prioritizing the particulars in the economy of God's revelation via the canonical data toward eventually informing the broader conception of God.[5]

---

5. Here, I attempted to allow the canonical data to offer answers to the questions without filtering the "answers" of the canon by presupposing what God *must* be or not be like a priori. Compare Kevin Vanhoozer's question, *Remythologizing Theology* (Cambridge: Cambridge University Press, 2010), 23: "What must God be like if he is actually the speaking and acting agent depicted in the Bible?" Elsewhere, "What must God be in order truthfully to be represented as repenting, grieving, compassionate?" (*Remythologizing Theology*, 50, cf. 3, 13). Vanhoozer attempts to avoid ontotheology in favor of theo-ontology, that is, to avoid "'bad' metaphysics" which impose "a system of categories on God without attending to God's own

This does not attempt to bracket, suspend, or table *all* of one's presuppositions. Were this even possible, the success of such radical epoché would remove the ability to conduct the investigation itself. Rather, epoché is targeted to suspend presuppositions in those areas that might be reasonably expected to impinge upon the study in the attempt to let the text speak for itself rather than being forced into an alien mold.[6] This is crucial to canonical theological method, which attempts to subject the interpreter's horizon to that of the canon via an ongoing hermeneutical spiral toward yielding a minimal confidently derived canonical theology that corresponds to the text as nearly as is achievable.[7]

This requires a commitment to self-examination, self-criticism, and willingness to follow the canonical data wherever it leads. In this case, I was conscientiously willing to embrace whatever model of divine love fit the canonical data, including any one of the existing models.[8] Notably, the answers I would have posited at the outset of the study markedly differ from the conclusions that I arrived at via the canonical theological method. This was unsettling, at times, during the investigation itself but, in retrospect, quite encouraging in that it appears that I was at least partially successful in allowing the canonical data to reform my own preconceptions in this regard.

My inductive reading of the entire canon cast a very wide net, isolating any texts that even slightly impinged on the previously identified issues. In doing so, I attempted to lay my predispositions on the table and to challenge and question them by close reading of the texts. I resolved not to artificially delimit my field of investigation or dodge the "hard" texts, but to allow any and all texts to inform my investigation and expand my conceptions as much as possible.

---

self-communication." (*Remythologizing Theology*, 8, cf. 36, 175). In his view, "the character, and fate, of theism depends on how one relates biblical representations (the dramatic mythos) to metaphysical conceptualizations (logos). Metaphysics plays a magisterial role (i.e., system-building) in ontotheology (i.e., perfect being analysis). By contrast, a theo-ontology that hearkens first of all to God's self-naming in the biblical record (i.e., *mythos*) accords metaphysics the more modest, ministerial role of conceptual elaboration" (*Remythologizing Theology*, 104).

6. Some minimal presuppositions are needed as requisite to the methodology of the investigation itself. Among them (for a canonical approach) is that there is an interpreter, there is a text, and that text is canon.

7. See the discussion of the minimal (but not minimalistic), humble approach of canonical hermeneutics in chapter 9.

8. Whereas only I can know the sincerity of this posture, others can check and see how my intention in this regard manifested itself in my study. Despite the best of intentions, one might deceive oneself and be bound more by one's presuppositions than one recognizes. Thus it is crucial to dialogue with and listen to others who might also review one's work and provide critical suggestions or corrections.

Analyzing the Canonical Data

The large amount of data extracted from this reading was then analyzed and grouped in an ongoing spiral, which included both narrowing and expansion of the data when themes became more or less significant than originally thought throughout the ongoing analysis (see below). Initially, I grouped the data diacanonically according to the sections of the OT and NT canon, with the aim of respecting the canonical groupings and context(s) of the text(s) without speculating regarding the dating of specific passages and texts. Then I looked for patterns within the data and found that in each canonical section crucial themes recur prominently relative to the issues at hand, evincing striking continuity throughout the canon regarding the complex concept of divine love. Via a lengthy process of reviewing, analyzing, and organizing the canonical data based on the patterns that emerged, the data was eventually organized under five aspects of divine love: the volitional, evaluative, emotional, foreconditional, and ideally reciprocal aspects.

In the course of this analysis, I undertook far more semantic analysis than I had originally planned because I discovered considerable discrepancies between the exegetically apparent usage of terms in canonical context and the depiction of the meaning and semantic range of those terms in *some* lexicons, theological dictionaries, and commentaries. For example, the common representation of *agape* as uniquely descriptive of and appropriate to divine love did not match up with canonical evidence.[9] The *agape* root is not only used of God's perfect love in ways that do not match the popular conception of *agape* but is also used of a wide spectrum of human love, including misdirected love and rapacious lust.[10] Further, many other terms depict the richness of divine love and the canon depicts divine love in ways that are markedly incongruous with the popular conception of *agape* (cf. the agapism of Anders Nygren), which itself appears to have significantly impacted a broad range of secondary sources.[11]

Recognizing that (at least some) exegetical dictionaries and commentar-

9. Similar issues arose regarding the semantics of lovingkindness (*ḥesed*), calling, election, and others. I also began to find significant links between different words, via their usage and collocations, that bolstered the patterns I was finding and alerted me to some new ones.

10. See the discussion in Peckham, *Love of God*, 69-88.

11. See his classic and seminal work: Anders Nygren, *Agape and Eros*, trans. Philip S. Watson (London: SPCK, 1953). See also the discussion in Peckham, *Love of God*, 69-88. Conversely, see D. A. Carson's brief exposition of the popular fallacy regarding the meaning of *agape* and *philos* respectively, *Exegetical Fallacies*, 2nd ed. (Grand Rapids: Baker, 1996), 32, 51-53.

ies were even more significantly affected by the theological presuppositions of their authors than I had expected, it became apparent that I needed to conduct my own semantic analysis more rigorously, to couple with my exegetical analysis of the canonical material. I thus investigated various terms via a synchronic-canonical approach that considered every usage of every word that was readily identifiable as descriptive of divine love and many others that impinged significantly on the concept or related concepts.[12]

Such investigation was conducted with cognizance of the inherent limitations of semantic studies, including the fact that meanings of words vary depending upon their context and usage. Accordingly, I had no intention of prioritizing semantic study, reducing the terms to simple definitions, or suggesting that a nuance of meaning in one instance can be extrapolated to all other occurrences of a given term (illegitimate totality transfer).[13] Rather, I sought to identify and summarize the range of meaning of selected word groups (indicating their polysemy and multivalence) by way of their usage in the canon in their contexts to provide crucial background for engaging the wider canonical themes regarding divine love.[14]

Whereas some portray biblically based systematic theology as simply taking the preexisting fruit of the labor of professional exegetes, organizing it thematically, and contextualizing it for a contemporary audience, canonical theological method encourages the systematician to devote careful attention to the primary source material of the canon itself in order to guide effective discernment of what might be usefully and appropriately gleaned from secondary sources. Thus, while treasuring and learning a great deal from the work of exegetical scholars, canonical theological method challenges any rigid separation between exegetical and theological disciplines and refuses to outsource exegesis of the canonical data.[15] Canonical theology thus includes microher-

---

12. The terms included in my study were not selected arbitrarily but in conjunction with the inductive reading of the canon and the subsequent shaping of the canonical analysis.

13. See James Barr, *The Semantics of Biblical Language* (London: Oxford University Press, 1961); Moisés Silva, *Biblical Words and Their Meaning: An Introduction to Lexical Semantics* (Grand Rapids: Zondervan, 1994), 139. Consider also the methodology followed by Gordon R. Clark, *The Word Hesed in the Hebrew Bible* (Sheffield: JSOT Press, 1993), 24–34. For an introduction to the potential pitfalls of word studies see Carson, *Exegetical Fallacies*, 27-64; cf. also Grant R. Osborne, *The Hermeneutical Spiral* (Downers Grove, IL: IVP Academic, 2006), 83-93.

14. As Silva, *Biblical Words*, 139, puts it, "The context does not merely help us understand meaning; it virtually *makes* meaning."

15. Recall, at this juncture, that canonical theological method departs from the disjunction some posit between biblical and systematic theology and, accordingly, challenges rigid separation between exegetical and theological disciplines. Those theologians who have not been

meneutical and macrophenomenological exegesis in an ongoing hermeneutical spiral, intentionally engaging the very best of exegetical scholarship and thus learning from the careful reading of the canon by others without taking such readings as themselves determinative.[16]

In this and other ways, canonical theological method attempts to afford methodological primacy to the analysis of the canonical data, corresponding to the unique infallibility and sufficiency of Scripture (canonical *sola Scriptura*). However, this first and primary step of continual study of the canon itself is supplemented by careful consideration of the secondary data, including engagement with the very best exegetical scholarship and community interpretations past and present. This step is crucial to canonical theological method in (among other things) alerting the interpreter to significant issues, including a range of plausible interpretations, and guarding against solipsistic private interpretation.

Here it is important to engage sources across a broad spectrum. In my investigation of divine love, I therefore engaged major commentary series and selected commentaries from across the spectrum of exegetical approaches.[17] This kind of cross-fertilization via consideration of a variety of secondary

---

trained in doing exegesis might consider teaming up with an exegete and vice versa in order to conduct this kind of work. For helpful introductory works regarding the exegetical task see Osborne, *Hermeneutical Spiral;* Douglas K. Stuart, *Old Testament Exegesis: A Handbook for Students and Pastors* (Louisville: Westminster John Knox, 2008); Gordon D. Fee, *New Testament Exegesis: A Handbook for Students and Pastors* (Louisville: Westminster John Knox, 2002). Regarding wider hermeneutical issues, see Anthony C. Thiselton, *Hermeneutics: An Introduction* (Grand Rapids: Eerdmans, 2009).

16. There is no intention here to replace professional exegetes, exclude or diminish their exceptionally important and fruitful labors within their discipline, or suggest their work requires engagement with canonical theological method. Rather, the approach I have in mind complements their work and the work of many other people within their respective disciplines and does so in a way that does not disparage the disciplines themselves but looks for greater collaboration and cross-fertilization. In this regard, canonical theology itself especially requires the ability to engage the canon at a high level exegetically, knowledge of historical theology and the history and impact of philosophical thought, and an understanding of principles and methods of systematic theology. Such cross-disciplinary work would be greatly enhanced by collaboration among specialists.

17. This included, but was not limited to, Anchor, ICC, Hermeneia, JPS, Word, Interpreter's, NICOT/NICNT, NAC as well as standalone volumes and exegetical works on concepts, words, topics, etc. How much one engages is a decision that must be made by the interpreter. I wanted to consult every book from these series on the selected passages to avoid (as much as possible) missing something significant from the various angles. During such a process one comes to grasp the range of material on a given topic or passage.

sources helps to guard against myopia and inbred interpretation of Scripture. By reading and dialoguing with others I might see new questions raised, new potential insights that need to be brought to the canon and tested by it, and indications of what might need to be avoided and of my own blind spots.[18]

Constructing a Minimal Model from the Data

Via the lengthy process outlined above, five primary aspects of divine love in relationship to the world emerged from the canonical data: the volitional, evaluative, emotional, foreconditional, and ideally reciprocal aspects.[19] First, divine love is volitional but not merely volitional. It includes a free, volitional aspect that is neither essential nor necessary to God's being, yet it also is not arbitrary. God freely decided to create the world and bestow his love on all creatures. However, the divine–human love relationship is neither unilaterally deterministic nor essential or ontologically necessary to God but bilaterally volitional and contingent.

Second, divine love is evaluative. This means that God is capable of being affected by, and even benefitting from, the disposition and actions of his creatures. God enjoys, delights in, takes pleasure in, and receives value from the disposition and actions of creatures while being displeased by evil. Whereas absent God's prior initiative sinful humans would be incapable of bringing anything valuable to God, through Christ's mediation humans may bring pleasure to God.

Third, God's love is profoundly emotional, including deep and responsive affection and concern for creatures, without amounting to undifferentiated sympathy. God is intimately concerned with humans, feeling sorrow, passion, and intense anger at evil, but also compassion and the desire to restore creatures to relationship.

Fourth, divine love is foreconditional. That is, divine love is undeservedly bestowed prior to, but not exclusive of, conditions. While divine love is surpassingly enduring, steadfast, and reliable, humans may reject God's loving

18. Indeed, often one learns the most by engaging scholarship that works from a different background than one's own. This is particularly helpful in the ongoing task of recognizing and subjecting one's relevant presuppositions to the text as such may be highlighted when engaging the work of scholars who might not be impacted by the same or similar theological presuppositions.

19. While these five aspects may be distinguished, they are not altogether distinct. They overlap considerably, as evidenced by both the semantic and thematic canonical data.

overtures and, eventually, forfeit the benefits of his love. God's love is thus unconditional and conditional in different respects. God's disposition of love is unconditional and constant but love relationship and the benefits thereof are finally contingent upon response.

Fifth, God's love is ideally reciprocal. God desires and works toward bilateral love relationship with each human but does not unilaterally determine that anyone love him in response. While God loves all with a universal and prevenient love aimed at drawing humans into relationship with him, God's particular, relational love is conditional upon appropriate response, which he himself enables. Those who reciprocate God's love enjoy particular love relationship with God for eternity.

I cannot do justice here to the nuances of the canonical conception of divine love, which I have attempted to explicate in other full-length works, though even those barely scratched the surface of God's infinite love.[20] Here, however, it is worth noting that this foreconditional-reciprocal model of divine love includes many facets that I would not have anticipated at the outset of my study, with striking implications when brought into conversation with existing models of divine love. For one thing, I had previously assumed the popular view regarding the unqualified unconditionality of God's love, and I was rather surprised to find the concept of foreconditional love throughout the canon. This has significant implications for prevalent views regarding the relationship of divine love, covenant, and election. I also did not envision the evaluative aspect of divine love, which plays such a crucial role and opens to view a nuanced conception of unselfish love that overturns the prevalent altruism-egoism dichotomy in favor of love as other-inclusive, unselfish self-interest. I likewise had little idea of the importance in the canon of nonexclusive "insider love" that differs from the way in which God loves all humans generally but which God invites all humans to enjoy.

Whereas many other delightful "surprises" might be noted in this regard, I mention these to highlight the importance of remaining open to the text so as to allow one's preconceptions to be challenged and (if necessary) transformed by what emerges from the canonical text itself.[21] Faced with the canonical data depicting divine love as conditional, I might have excluded what I discovered

20. See the canonical and theological exposition of the foreconditional-reciprocal model of divine love in Peckham, *Love of God,* 191-217; Peckham, *Concept of Divine Love,* 300-336, 456-76, 520-31.

21. In this regard, there were also questions and issues regarding which I did not find the evidence sufficient to offer a confident perspective (e.g., regarding the extent of divine freedom and some Christological implications) and left the matters open to further investigation.

regarding foreconditional love on the presupposition that God's love *could not be* conditional by definition. For some time during my investigation, I wondered how the apparent tension between texts that present God's love as everlasting and those that present it as subject to forfeiture could be coherently understood (without injury to the exegetical upshot of any of the texts).[22] Over time, however, employment of the canonical method uncovered what I take to be sufficient grounds for recognizing that divine love is unconditional and conditional in different respects, that is, foreconditional (cf. Ps 103:17).[23]

Whereas others can assess whether and to what extent they find my interpretations adequately correspond to the canonical text and internally cohere systematically, I made every attempt, via the method described above, to humbly construct a discernible, demonstrable, and defensible conception of divine love that might account for all of the salient data without injury to any of it (canonical correspondence and coherence).

Systematizing the Model: Minimal Theo-ontological Implications

Up to this point, I have explained my attempt to follow through on inverting the typical methodology, focusing first on understanding the canonical conception of divine love in relationship to the world while leaving the issues of divine ontology and the wider God–world relationship open to shaping by these findings. With the foreconditional-reciprocal model in place, I turned to the question: If God loves in this way, what must God be like?[24]

A number of significant, though tentative, implications for divine ontology and the God–world relationship appear to follow from the foreconditional-reciprocal model of divine love. The first of these is bilateral freedom, which refers to God's granting of freedom to creatures while also possessing the free-

22. Whereas many scholars suggest that such passages represent at least two contradictory streams within the canonical data, my canonical approach led me to read all of the passages as a unified but not monolithic corpus such that I looked for congruity while attempting to refrain from any artificial smoothing out of or injury to the texts.

23. Two notable indicators were the combination of the two "streams" in passages such as Ps 103:17 and in larger thematic renderings across the canon and the wider conceptuality of the unconditionality and conditionality of covenants, particularly the nuance of the grant-type covenant that appears to permeate the canonical narrative of the God–world relationship (see Peckham, *Love of God,* 191-217; Peckham, *Concept of Divine Love,* 300-336, 456-76, 520-31).

24. See the brief discussion in page 248, note 5. This stage, of course, requires consideration of the wider landscape of systematic theology and (in this case) the particular issues and ongoing discussions regarding the nature of the God–world relationship.

dom to do otherwise than he does such that, whereas God desires reciprocal relationship with all humans, God does not unilaterally effect his will and thus does not always get what he wants.[25] Accordingly, whereas God is omnipotent, God does not (omnicausally) exercise all his power but allows creatures to affect history and himself, voluntarily limiting the exercise of his power. In this and other ways, God is passible (but not passive) and is affected by the disposition and actions of his creatures. In this way, while God is self-sufficient as ontologically independent on any world, he has voluntarily bound his own interests (including his joy and sorrow) to the best interests of his creatures, enjoying and appreciating value in relationship to his creation.

These implications, however, do not involve positing a fully developed conceptual framework and are themselves tentatively posited for at least four reasons.[26] First, the foreconditional-reciprocal model of divine love is itself tentative and open to revision based on further canonical investigation and systematic inquiry. Second, it could be misleading to attempt to derive a divine ontology from one divine characteristic, even one as major as divine love. Third, addressing the full scope of divine ontology canonically is well beyond the scope of the study of divine love and warrants input of many such investigations of the particulars of canonical data. Fourth, other outlines of divine ontology may also be able to harmonize with this model of divine love and should continue to be sought and considered.

Such implications (as well as other possible implications) require ongoing canonical investigation and systematic analysis and remain open to correction. However, insofar as the foreconditional-reciprocal model of divine love accurately accords with the canonical data, a canonical conception of God and the God-world relationship should be able to account for the volitional, evaluative, emotional, foreconditional, and ideally reciprocal aspects of divine love.

25. See John C. Peckham, "Does God Always Get What He Wants? A Theocentric Approach to Divine Providence and Human Freedom," *AUSS* 52/2 (2014): 195-212; John C. Peckham, "Providence and God's Unfulfilled Desires," *Philosophia Christi* 15/2 (2013):453-62.

26. Here, I attempted to refrain from overreaching regarding the positing of a conceptual framework beyond the upshot of my investigation. Methodologically, I attempted to derive from the particular revelation regarding divine love in the God–world relationship what appeared to me to be the minimal confidently derivable implications regarding the metaphysics of the God–world relationship.

Remaining Open to Further Investigation (the Ongoing Spiral)

The results of canonical theological method are not offered as the final word but remain secondary to the canonical text, which further corrects the system by way of ongoing canonical investigation via the hermeneutical spiral. Accordingly, a canonical theological system will never exhaust the text but endeavors to persistently move toward ever-greater correspondence and inner coherence. My own study of divine love is thus open to challenge and revision based on the implications of continued canonical investigation.

Further methodological issues and questions remain, particularly regarding the abstraction of a canonical conceptual framework. *Some* helpful postures, practices, and procedures toward carefully extracting or abstracting a canonical conceptual framework have been outlined here in the context of canonical theological method. Among others, the canonical interpreter should attempt to: (1) approach the canon humbly; (2) read ethically; (3) derive from the canon minimally that which can be held with confidence as discernible, demonstrable, and defensible; (4) move in a disciplined, delimited fashion from the particulars of divine revelation to universal (metaphysical) conceptions; and (5) refrain from premature conclusions and overreaching extrapolations by restricting conclusions to minimal sound inferences that are also discernible, demonstrable, and defensible.

While such postures, practices, and procedures are indeed crucial, I do not currently see any way to abstract a canonical conceptual framework without careful and ongoing trial and error. As it stands now, I have not discerned explicit rules for *each turn* of the implementation of canonical theological method, and I wonder whether it would be possible or desirable to do so. With *any* method, decisions will have to be made during the course of the investigation and, it seems to me, the best one can do is attempt to make such decisions in accordance with the aforementioned hermeneutical commitments and virtues.

Whereas canonical theological method involves a commitment to the investigation of a large amount of data and requires at least a working proficiency across a number of disciplines, I am convinced that such a commitment is more than worth it, particularly insofar as one has confidence in the canon as the rule of faith. I have found this to be the case with regard to divine love and my hope is to implement this approach on a number of other topics in the future.

Conclusion

This work has addressed the crucial divide among Christians regarding the respective theological authority of the canon and community, with particular attention to the sharp divide regarding the nature and function of the biblical canon and the ongoing debate regarding whether (and to what extent) an extracanonical interpretive arbiter should be adopted as the "rule" of Christian theology. Toward addressing this divide, I have advocated an intrinsic canon model wherein books are canonical in virtue of being divinely commissioned such that the community does not determine canonicity and is, accordingly, not authoritative relative to the canon. In my view, this intrinsic canon model undergirds (without requiring) canonical theological method, which recognizes the canon itself as the rule of faith (apart from any extracanonical normative interpreter).

Whereas communitarian approaches posit some extracanonical normative interpretive arbiter in order to rule the reading of Scripture toward assuaging rampant hermeneutical diversity, canonical theology accepts hermeneutical diversity as an unavoidable result of the universal hermeneutical circle. Advocates of this approach maintain the canon itself as the formal and functional rule of theology against which all interpretations should be continually brought without neglecting engagement with the wider Christian community past and present. In this regard, canonical *sola Scriptura* posits the canon as the uniquely infallible, sufficient, and fully trustworthy basis and rule of theology and theological interpretation. Here, the entire canon is to rule (*tota* and *analogia* Scriptura via spiritual discernment) without overlooking the fact that there are other sources of revelation specifically and knowledge generally and that all interpreters (individually and collectively) are fallible and unavoidably bring their own horizons to interpretation.[27]

Further, communitarian approaches appear to be inadequate to address contemporary debates over the Trinity, function as the rule of faith, function as interpretive authority, and answer the questions "which tradition?" and "on whose interpretation?" Conversely, canonical theological method does not expect to be able to settle all theological debates or eliminate hermeneutical diversity. Canonical theology embraces the reality that all communication requires interpretation. Further, canonical theology recognizes the common

---

27. Accordingly, canonical *sola Scriptura* contends that the canon *qua* canon is the rule and standard of Christian theology while recognizing that the canon requires interpretation (cf. Luke 10:26), rejecting isolationism and the private interpretation of Scripture.

canonical core of sixty-six books as theological rule, noting that this canonical core enjoys the most widespread consensus among self-identifying Christians and thus appears to be preferable even on (minimal) communitarian grounds.

Canonical theological method itself operates via the ever-ongoing hermeneutical spiral of microhermeneutical and macrophenomenological exegesis, working from the particulars of the text as canon toward deriving a minimal canonical system that itself directs attention back to further investigation of the canon.[28] This method includes a self-critical, humble posture directed toward ethical reading with awareness of the limits of language and, particularly, the unavoidably accommodative and thus analogical character of theological language. Explanation of this approach culminated in the step-by-step explication of my implementation of this canonical theological method via the steps of (1) identifying the issues/questions, (2) reading the canon inductively, (3) analyzing the canonical data, (4) constructing a minimal model from the data, (5) systematizing the model, and (6) remaining open to further investigation via the ongoing hermeneutical spiral.

One of my goals in this work has been to lay out a plausible and workable canonical approach to systematic theology, which can be practiced by others across the vast range of Christian communities who recognize the common canonical core and might engender dialogue via a common starting point and preliminary approach. Thus, while I do not expect this canonical theological method to be endorsed by all readers, I do hope that this treatment might stimulate thought and advance the conversation regarding the role of canon and community in theological method. In this regard, I hope this work illuminates some avenues toward continual retrieval and implementation of the guiding canonical principles, "To the law and to the testimony! If they do not speak according to this word, it is because they have no dawn" (Isa 8:20), and "All Scripture is inspired by God and profitable for teaching, for reproof, for correction, for training in righteousness" (2 Tim 3:16). As such, we might together proclaim along with the psalmist: "Your word is a lamp to my feet and a light to my path" (Ps 119:105).

---

28. Notably, these two forms of exegesis impinge upon both of the crucial hermeneutical circles at work in canonical theology, that of (1) the parts and the whole of the text(s) as canon, and (2) the reader and the text.

Bibliography

Abraham, William. *Canon and Criterion in Christian Theology*. Oxford: Clarendon, 1998.

Abraham, William J. "Canonical Theism: Thirty Theses." Pages 1-7 in *Canonical Theism: A Proposal for Theology and the Church*. Edited by William J. Abraham, Jason E. Vickers, and Natalie B. Van Kirk. Grand Rapids: Eerdmans, 2008.

Abraham, William J. "The Emergence of Canonical Theism." Pages 141-55 in *Canonical Theism: A Proposal for Theology and the Church*. Edited by William J. Abraham, Jason E. Vickers, and Natalie B. Van Kirk. Grand Rapids: Eerdmans, 2008.

Abramowski, Luise. "Irenaeus, Adv Haer III 3,2: Ecclesia Romana and Omnis Ecclesia; and Ibid 3,3: Anacletus of Rome." *Journal of Theological Studies* 28 (1977): 101-4.

Adam, A. K. M., Stephen E. Fowl, Kevin J. Vanhoozer, and Francis Watson. *Reading Scripture with the Church: Toward a Hermeneutic for Theological Interpretation*. Grand Rapids: Baker Academic, 2006.

Allen, Michael, and Scott R. Swain, *Reformed Catholicity: The Promise of Retrieval for Theology and Biblical Interpretation*. Grand Rapids: Baker, 2015.

Allert, Craig D. *A High View of Scripture? The Authority of the Bible and the Formation of the New Testament Canon*. Grand Rapids: Baker Academic, 2007.

Allert, Craig D. "What Are We Trying to Conserve? Evangelicalism and *Sola Scriptura*." *Evangelical Quarterly* 76/4 (2004): 327-48.

Allison, Gregg R. "Theological Interpretation of Scripture: An Introduction and Preliminary Evaluation." *Southern Baptist Journal of Theology* 14/2 (2010): 28-36.

Alter, Robert. *The Art of Biblical Narrative*. New York: Basic, 1981.

Alston, William P. "Aquinas on Theological Predication: A Look Backward and a Look Forward." Pages 145-78 in *Reasoned Faith*. Edited by Eleonore Stump. Ithaca: Cornell University Press, 1993.

Alston, William P. "Divine and Human Action." Pages 257-80 in *Divine and Human Action: Essays in the Metaphysics of Theism*. Edited by Thomas V. Morris. Ithaca: Cornell University Press, 1988.

Alston, William P. "How to Think about Divine Action." Pages 51-70 in *Divine Action*.

Edited by Brian Hebblethwaite and Edward Henderson. Edinburgh: T&T Clark, 1990.

Ammundsen, Valdemar. "The Rule of Truth in Irenaeus," *Journal of Theological Studies* 13 (1911): 574-80.

Aquinas, Thomas. *Summa Theologica*. Translated by Fathers of the English Dominican Province. Albany, OR: Ages, 1997.

Archer, Gleason. *A Survey of Old Testament Introduction*. 3rd ed. Chicago: Moody, 1998.

Armstrong, Jonathan J. "From the κανὼν τῆς ἀληθείας to the κανὼν τῶν γραφῶν: The Role of the Rule of Faith in the Formation of the New Testament Canon." Pages 30-47 in *Tradition and the Rule of Faith in the Early Church*. Edited by Ronnie J. Rombs and Alexander Y. Hwang. Washington, DC: Catholic University of America Press, 2010.

Awad, Najeeb George. "Should We Dispense with *Sola Scriptura*? Scripture, Tradition and Postmodern Theology." *Dialog: A Journal of Theology* 47/1 (2008): 64-79.

Bacote, Vincent, Laura C. Miguélez, and Dennis L. Okholm, eds. *Evangelicals & Scripture: Tradition, Authority, and Hermeneutics*. Downers Grove, IL: InterVarsity Press, 2004.

Balla, Peter. "Evidence for an Early Christian Canon (Second and Third Century)." Pages 372-85 in *The Canon Debate*. Edited by Lee Martin McDonald and James A. Sanders. Peabody, MA: Hendrickson, 2002.

Balmer, Randall Herbert. "*Sola Scriptura*: The Protestant Reformation and the Eastern Orthodox Church." *Trinity Journal* 3/1 (1982): 51-56.

Barnes, Michael René. "De Régnon Reconsidered." *Augustine Studies* 26 (1995): 51-79.

Barr, James. *Holy Scripture: Canon, Authority and Criticism*. Philadelphia: Westminster, 1983.

Barr, James. "Literality." *Faith and Philosophy* 6/4 (1989): 412-28.

Barr, James. *The Semantics of Biblical Language*. London: Oxford University Press, 1961.

Bartholomew, Craig G., Scott Hahn, Robin Parry, Christopher Seitz, and Al Wolters, eds. *Canon and Biblical Interpretation*. Grand Rapids: Zondervan, 2006.

Barton, John. *Holy Writings, Sacred Text: The Canon in Early Christianity*. Louisville: Westminster John Knox, 1997.

Barton, John. "Marcion Revisited." Pages 341-54 in *The Canon Debate*. Edited by Lee Martin McDonald and James A. Sanders. Peabody, MA: Hendrickson, 2002.

Bauckham, Richard. "Tradition in Relation to Scripture and Reason." Pages 117-45 in *Scripture, Tradition, and Reason: A Study in the Criteria of Christian Doctrine*. Edited by Richard Bauckham and Benjamin Drewery. New York: T.&T. Clark, 2004.

Bauer, Walter, *Orthodoxy and Heresy in Earliest Christianity*, trans. Paul J. Achtemeier. Philadelphia: Fortress, 1971.

Beckwith, Roger T. *The Old Testament Canon of the New Testament Church*. Grand Rapids: Eerdmans, 1986.

Behr, John. "The Word of God in the Second Century." *Pro Ecclesia* 9/1 (2000): 85-107.

Benoit, André. "Ecriture et tradition chez Saint Irénée." *Revue d'histoire et de philosophie religieuses* 40/1 (1960): 32-43.

Benson, Bruce Ellis. "'Now I Would Not Have You Ignorant': Derrida, Gadamer, Hirsch and Husserl on Authors' Intentions." Pages 173-91 in *Evangelicals & Scripture: Tradition, Authority, and Hermeneutics*. Edited by Vincent Bacote, Laura C. Miguélez, and Dennis L. Okholm. Downers Grove, IL: InterVarsity Press, 2004.

Bilezikian, Gilbert. "Hermeneutical Bungee-Jumping: Subordination in the Godhead." *Journal of the Evangelical Theological Society* 40/1 (1997): 57-68.

Billings, J. Todd. *The Word of God for the People of God: An Entryway to the Theological Interpretation of Scripture*. Grand Rapids: Eerdmans, 2010.

Blomberg, Craig. *Can We Still Believe the Bible?* Grand Rapids: Brazos, 2014.

Blosser, Philip. "What Are the Philosophical and Practical Problems with *Sola Scriptura*?" Pages 31-108 in *Not by Scripture Alone: A Catholic Critique of the Protestant Doctrine of* Sola Scriptura. Edited by Robert A. Sungenis. Santa Barbara, CA: Queenship Pub. Co., 1997.

Boersma, Hans. Nouvelle Théologie *and Sacramental Ontology: A Return to Mystery*. Oxford: Oxford University Press, 2009.

Boettner, Loraine. *Studies in Theology*. Philadelphia: P & R, 1964.

Brash, Donald James. "Pastoral Authority in the Churches of the First and Second Centuries." PhD dissertation. Drew University, 1987.

Bromiley, Geoffrey. "The Church Fathers and Holy Scripture." Pages 199-224 in *Scripture and Truth*. Edited by D. A. Carson and John D. Woodbridge. Grand Rapids: Zondervan, 1983.

Brower, Jeffrey E., and Michael C. Rea. "Material Constitution and the Trinity." Pages 263-82 in *Philosophical and Theological Essays on the Trinity*. Edited by Thomas H. McCall and Michael C. Rea. New York: Oxford University Press, 2009.

Brown, Colin. "Evangelical Tradition." *Evangel* (2007): 1-2.

Bruce, F. F. "The Bible." Pages 3-12 in *The Origin of the Bible*. Edited by Philip Wesley Comfort. Wheaton, IL: Tyndale, 1992.

Bruce, F. F. *The Books and the Parchments*. Glasgow: HarperCollins, 1991.

Bruce, F. F. *The Canon of Scripture*. Downers Grove, IL: InterVarsity, 1988.

Buschart, David, and Kent D. Eilers, *Theology as Retrieval: Receiving the Past, Renewing the Church*. Downers Grove, IL: IVP Academic, 2015.

Caird, G. B. *The Language and Imagery of the Bible*. Philadelphia: Westminster, 1980.

Calvin, John. *Commentaries on the Twelve Minor Prophets*. Grand Rapids: Eerdmans, 1950.

Campenhausen, Hans von. *Ecclesiastical Authority and Spiritual Power in the Church of the First Three Centuries*. Peabody, MA: Hendrickson, 1997.

Campenhausen, Hans von. *The Formation of the Christian Bible*. Philadelphia: Augsburg Fortress, 1972.

Canale, Fernando. *A Criticism of Theological Reason: Time and Timelessness as Primordial Presuppositions*. Berrien Springs, MI: Andrews University Press, 1987.

Canale, Fernando. *Back to Revelation–Inspiration: Searching for the Cognitive Foundation of Christian Theology in a Postmodern World*. Lanham, MD: University Press of America, 2001.

Caneday, A. B. "Is Theological Truth Functional or Propositional? Postconservatism's Use of Language Games and Speech-Act Theory." Pages 137-60 in *Reclaiming* the Center: Confronting Evangelical Accommodation in Postmodern Times. Edited by Millard J. Erickson, Paul Kjoss Helseth, and Justin Taylor. Wheaton, IL: Crossway, 2004.

Carlton, Clark. *The Way: What Every Protestant Should Know about the Orthodox Church.* Salisbury, MA: Regina Orthodox Press, 1997.

Carson, D. A. *Exegetical Fallacies.* 2nd ed. Grand Rapids: Baker, 1996.

Carson, D. A. "The Role of Exegesis in Systematic Theology." Pages 39-76 in *Doing Theology in Today's World: Essays in Honor of Kenneth S. Kantzer.* Edited by J. D. Woodbridge and T. E. McComiskey. Grand Rapids: Zondervan, 1991.

Carson, D. A., and Douglas J. Moo. *An Introduction to the New Testament.* 2nd ed. Grand Rapids: Zondervan, 2005.

Carson, D. A., and John D. Woodbridge. *Scripture and Truth.* Grand Rapids: Zondervan, 1983.

Cary, Phillip. "The New Evangelical Subordinationism: Reading Inequality into the Trinity." Pages 1-12 in *The New Evangelical Subordinationism? Perspectives on the Equality of God the Father and God the Son.* Edited by Dennis W. Jowers and H. Wayne House. Eugene, OR: Pickwick Publications, 2012.

Catechism of the Catholic Church. 2nd ed. Washington, DC: United States Catholic Conference, 2000.

Chadwick, Henry. *The Early Church.* London: Penguin, 1993.

Chapman, Stephen B. "The Canon Debate: What It Is and Why It Matters." *Journal of Theological Interpretation* 4.2 (2010): 273-94.

Chapman, Stephen B. "How the Biblical Canon Began: Working Models and Open Questions." Pages 29-51 in *Homer, the Bible and Beyond: Literary and Religious Canons in the Ancient World.* Edited by Margalit Finkelberg and Guy Stroumsa. Leiden: Brill, 2003.

Chapman, Stephen B. *The Law and the Prophets: A Study in Old Testament Canon Formation.* Tübingen: Mohr Siebeck, 2009.

Chapman, Stephen B. "The Old Testament Canon and Its Authority for the Christian Church." *Ex Auditu* 19 (2003): 125-48.

Childs, Brevard S. *Biblical Theology in Crisis.* Philadelphia: Westminster, 1970.

Childs, Brevard S. "The Canon in Recent Biblical Studies: Reflections on an Era." Pages 33-57 in *Canon and Biblical Interpretation.* Edited by Craig G. Bartholomew, Scott Hahn, Robin Parry, Christopher Seitz, and Al Wolters. Grand Rapids: Zondervan, 2006.

Childs, Brevard S. *Introduction to the Old Testament as Scripture.* Philadelphia: Fortress, 1980.

Childs, Brevard S. *The New Testament as Canon: An Introduction.* London: SCM, 1984.

Childs, Brevard S. "*Sensus Literalis* of Scripture: An Ancient and Modern Problem." Pages 80-93 in *Beiträge zur Alttestamentlichen Theologie: Festschrift für Walther Zimmerli.* Göttingen: Vandenhoeck & Ruprecht, 1977.

Chisholm, Robert B., Jr. "Anatomy of an Anthropomorphism: Does God Discover Facts?" *Bibliotheca Sacra* 164 (2007): 3-20.

Clark, David K. "Relativism, Fideism & the Promise of Postliberalism." Pages 107-20 in

The Nature of Confession: Evangelicals & Postliberals in Conversation. Edited by Timothy R. Phillips and Dennis L. Okholm. Downers Grove, IL: InterVarsity, 1996.

Clark, David K. *To Know and Love God.* Wheaton, IL: Crossway, 2003.

Clark, Gordon R. *The Word Hesed in the Hebrew Bible.* Sheffield: JSOT Press, 1993.

Cole, Graham. "The Living God: Anthropomorphic or Anthropopathic?" *The Reformed Theological Review* 59/1 (2000): 16-27.

Congar, Yves. *Tradition and Traditions.* New York: Macmillan, 1966.

Cook, L. Stephen. *On the Question of the "Cessation of Prophecy" in Ancient Judaism.* Tübingen: Mohr Siebeck, 2011.

Cooper, John W. *Panentheism, the Other God of the Philosophers: From Plato to the Present.* Grand Rapids: Baker Academic, 2006.

Craig, William Lane. "Toward a Tenable Social Trinitarianism." Pages 89-99 in *Philosophical and Theological Essays on the Trinity.* Edited by Thomas H. McCall and Michael C. Rea. New York: Oxford University Press, 2009.

Croy, N. Clayton. *Prima Scriptura: An Introduction to New Testament Interpretation.* Grand Rapids: Baker Academic, 2011.

Daniélou, Jean. "Les orientations presents de la Pensée religieuse." *Études* 249 (1946): 1-21.

Davidson, Richard M. "The Divine Covenant Lawsuit Motif in Biblical Perspective." *Journal of the Adventist Theological Society* 21/1-2 (2010): 45-84.

Davidson, Richard M. *Flame of Yahweh: Sexuality in the Old Testament.* Grand Rapids: Baker, 2007.

Davidson, Richard M. "Interpreting Scripture: An Hermeneutical 'Decalogue.'" *Journal of the Adventist Theological Society* 4/2 (1993): 95-114.

D'Costa, Gavin. "Revelation, Scripture and Tradition: Some Comments on John Webster's Conception of 'Holy Scripture.'" *International Journal of Systematic Theology* 6/4 (2004): 337-50.

Dei Verbum. Dogmatic Constitution on the Church. (1965): http://www.vatican.va/archive/hist_councils/ii_vatican_council/documents/vat-ii_const_19651118_dei -verbum_en.html. Accessed May 23, 2016.

Dempster, Stephen G. "Canons on the Right and Canons on the Left: Finding a Resolution in the Canon Debate." *Journal of the Evangelical Theological Society* 52 (2009): 47-77.

Dempster, Stephen G. *Dominion and Dynasty: A Biblical Theology of the Hebrew Bible.* Downers Grove, IL: InterVarsity, 2003.

Dempster, Stephen G. "Torah, Torah, Torah: The Emergence of the Tripartite Canon." Pages 87-127 in *Exploring the Origins of the Bible: Canon Formation in Historical, Literary, and Theological Perspective.* Edited by Craig A. Evans and Emanuel Tov. Grand Rapids: Baker, 2008.

Dhorme, E. *L'emploi métaphorique des noms de parties du corps en hébreu et en akkadien.* Paris: Geuthner, 1963.

Dolezal, James E. *God without Parts: Divine Simplicity and the Metaphysics of God's Absoluteness.* Eugene, OR: Pickwick, 2011.

Donkor, Kwabena. "Postconservatism: A Third World Perspective." Pages 199-221 in *Reclaiming the Center: Confronting Evangelical Accommodation in Postmodern*

Times. Edited by Millard J. Erickson, Paul Kjoss Helseth, and Justin Taylor. Wheaton, IL: Crossway Books, 2004.

Dorrien, Gary. *The Remaking of Evangelical Theology*. Louisville: Westminster John Knox, 1998.

Dungan, David L. *Constantine's Bible: Politics and the Making of the New Testament*. Minneapolis: Fortress, 2007.

Dunn, James D. G. "Has the Canon a Continuing Function?" Pages 558-79 in *The Canon Debate*. Edited by Lee Martin McDonald and James A. Sanders. Peabody, MA: Hendrickson, 2002.

Dunn, James D. G. *Unity and Diversity in the New Testament: An Inquiry into the Character of Earliest Christianity*. London: SCM, 1990.

Erickson, Millard J., *Christian Theology*. 2nd ed. Grand Rapids: Baker, 1998.

Erickson, Millard J. *God in Three Persons: A Contemporary Interpretation of the Trinity*. Grand Rapids: Baker, 1995.

Erickson, Millard J. *God the Father Almighty: A Contemporary Exploration of the Divine Attributes*. Grand Rapids: Baker, 1998.

Erickson, Millard J. *Who's Tampering with the Trinity? An Assessment of the Subordination Debate*. Grand Rapids: Kregel Academic, 2009.

Erickson, Millard J., Paul Kjoss Helseth, and Justin Taylor, eds. *Reclaiming the Center: Confronting Evangelical Accommodation in Postmodern Times*. Wheaton, IL: Crossway, 2004.

Evans, Craig A. "The Scriptures of Jesus and His Earliest Followers." Pages 185-95 in *The Canon Debate*. Edited by Lee Martin McDonald and James A. Sanders. Peabody, MA: Hendrickson, 2002.

Evans, C. Stephen, "Canonicity, Apostolicity, and Biblical Authority: Some Kierkegaardian Reflections." Pages 146-66 in *Canon and Biblical Interpretation*. Edited by Craig G. Bartholomew, Scott Hahn, Robin Parry, Christopher Seitz, and Al Wolters. Grand Rapids: Zondervan, 2006.

Farkasfalvy, Denis. "'Prophets and Apostles': The Conjunction of the Two Terms before Irenaeus." Pages 109-34 in *Texts and Testaments*. Edited by Eugene March. San Antonio: Trinity University Press, 1980.

Fee, Gordon D. *New Testament Exegesis: A Handbook for Students and Pastors*. Louisville: Westminster John Knox, 2002.

Feinberg, John S. *No One like Him: The Doctrine of God*. The Foundations of Evangelical Theology. Wheaton, IL: Crossway, 2001.

Ferguson, Everett. "Canon Muratori: Date and Provenance." *Studia Patristica* 17/2 (1982): 677-83.

Ferguson, Everett. "*Paradosis* and *Traditio*: A Word Study." Pages 3-29 in *Tradition and the Rule of Faith in the Early Church*. Edited by Ronnie J. Rombs and Alexander Y. Hwang. Washington, DC: Catholic University of America Press, 2010.

Ferguson, Everett, ed. *Orthodoxy, Heresy, and Schism in Early Christianity*. New York: Garland Publishing, 1993.

Fish, Stanley. *Is There a Text in This Class? The Authority of Interpretive Communities*. Cambridge, MA: Harvard University Press, 1980.

Fisher, Milton. "The Canon of the New Testament." Pages 65-78 in *The Origin of the Bible*. Edited by Philip Wesley Comfort. Wheaton, IL: Tyndale, 1992.

Flynn, Gabriel, and Paul D. Murray, eds. *Ressourcement: A Movement for Renewal in Twentieth-Century Catholic Theology*. Oxford: Oxford University Press, 2012.

Ford, David F. "Radical Orthodoxy and the Future of British Theology." *Scottish Journal of Theology* 54 (2001): 385-404.

The Formula of Concord. In *The Creeds of Christendom*. Edited by Philip Schaff. New York: Harper & Brothers, 1882.

Fowl, Stephen E. *Engaging Scripture: A Model for Theological Interpretation*. Challenges in Contemporary Theology. Malden, MA: Blackwell, 1998.

Fowl, Stephen E. "The Importance of a Multivoiced Literal Sense of Scripture: The Example of Thomas Aquinas." Pages 35-50 in *Reading Scripture with the Church: Toward a Hermeneutic for Theological Interpretation*. Grand Rapids: Baker Academic, 2006.

Fowl, Stephen E. "Introduction." Pages xii-xxx in *The Theological Interpretation of Scripture*. Edited by Stephen E. Fowl. Cambridge, MA: Blackwell, 1997.

Fowl, Stephen E. *Theological Interpretation of Scripture*. Eugene, OR: Cascade, 2009.

Fowl, Stephen E., ed. *The Theological Interpretation of Scripture: Classic and Contemporary Readings*. Malden, MA: Blackwell, 1997.

Frame, John M. "In Defense of Something Close to Biblicism: Reflections on Sola Scriptura and History in Theological Method." *Westminster Theological Journal* 59 (1997): 269-91.

France, R. T. *Jesus and the Old Testament*. Grand Rapids: Baker, 1982.

Franke, John R. "Scripture, Tradition, and Authority: Reconstructing the Evangelical Conception of Sola Scriptura." Pages 192-210 in *Evangelicals & Scripture: Tradition, Authority, and Hermeneutics*. Edited by Vincent Bacote, Laura C. Miguélez, and Dennis L. Okholm. Downers Grove, IL: InterVarsity Press, 2004.

Freedman, David Noel. "Canon of the Old Testament." Pages 130-36 in *Interpreter's Dictionary of the Bible Supplemental Volume*. Nashville: Abingdon, 1976.

Freedman, David Noel. *The Unity of the Hebrew Bible*. Ann Arbor: University of Michigan Press, 1991.

Frei, Hans W. *The Eclipse of Biblical Narrative*. New Haven: Yale University Press, 1974.

Fretheim, Terence E. "The Repentance of God: A Key to Evaluating Old Testament God-Talk." *Horizons in Biblical Theology* 10/1 (1988): 47-70.

Fretheim, Terence E. *The Suffering of God: An Old Testament Perspective*. Philadelphia: Fortress, 1984.

Fritsch, Charles T. *The Anti-anthropomorphisms of the Greek Pentateuch*. Princeton: Princeton University Press, 1943.

Funk, Robert W. "The Once and Future New Testament." Pages 541-57 in *The Canon Debate*. Edited by Lee Martin McDonald and James A. Sanders. Peabody, MA: Hendrickson, 2002.

Gadamer, Hans-Georg. *Truth and Method*. Translated by Joel Weinsheimer and Donald G. Marshall. New York: Continuum, 2004.

Gamble, Harry Y., Jr. "Christianity: Scripture and Canon." Pages 36-62 in *The Holy Book in Comparative Perspective*. Edited by Frederick M. Denny and Rodney L. Taylor. Columbia: University of South Carolina Press, 1985.

Gamble, Harry Y., Jr. *The New Testament Canon: Its Making and Meaning*. Philadelphia: Fortress, 1985.

Ganssle, Gregory E., ed. *God & Time: Four Views*. Downers Grove, IL: InterVarsity, 2001.

Gavrilyuk, Paul L. "God's Impassible Suffering in the Flesh: The Promise of Paradoxical Christology." Pages 127-49 in *Divine Impassibility and the Mystery of Human Suffering*. Edited by James Keating and Thomas Joseph White. Grand Rapids: Eerdmans, 2009.

Gavrilyuk, Paul L. "Scripture and the *Regula Fidei*: Two Interlocking Components of the Canonical Heritage." Pages 27-42 in *Canonical Theism: A Proposal for Theology and the Church*. Edited by William J. Abraham, Jason E. Vickers, and Natalie B. Van Kirk. Grand Rapids: Eerdmans, 2008.

Gavrilyuk, Paul L. *The Suffering of the Impassible God: The Dialectics of Patristic Thought*. New York: Oxford University Press, 2004.

Geisler, Norman L., and William E. Nix. *A General Introduction to the Bible: Revised and Expanded*. Chicago: Moody, 1986.

Gibson, John C. L. *Language and Imagery in the Old Testament*. Peabody, MA: Hendrickson, 1998.

Giles, Kevin. "The Authority of the Bible and the Authority of the Theological Tradition." *The Priscilla Papers* 27/4 (2013): 17-18.

Giles, Kevin. *The Eternal Generation of the Son: Maintaining Orthodoxy in Trinitarian Theology*. Downers Grove, IL: IVP Academic, 2012.

Giles, Kevin. "The Evangelical Theological Society and the Doctrine of the Trinity." *Evangelical Quarterly* 80/4 (2008): 323-38.

Giles, Kevin. *Jesus and the Father: Modern Evangelicals Reinvent the Doctrine of the Trinity*. Grand Rapids: Zondervan, 2006.

Giles, Kevin. *The Trinity and Subordinationism: The Doctrine of God and the Contemporary Gender Debate*. Downers Grove, IL: InterVarsity Press, 2002.

Giles, Kevin. "The Trinity without Tiers." Pages 262-87 in *The New Evangelical Subordinationism? Perspectives on the Equality of God the Father and God the Son*. Edited by Dennis W. Jowers and H. Wayne House. Eugene, OR: Pickwick, 2012.

Grant, Robert F. *Irenaeus of Lyons*. New York: Routledge, 1996.

Green, Joel B. *Practicing Theological Interpretation: Engaging Biblical Texts for Faith and Formation*. Grand Rapids: Baker Academic, 2011.

Green, Joel B. *Seized by Truth: Reading the Bible as Scripture*. Nashville: Abingdon, 2007.

Greene-McCreight, Kathryn. "Rule of Faith." Pages 703-4 in *Dictionary for Theological Interpretation of the Bible*. Edited by Kevin J. Vanhoozer. Grand Rapids: Baker Academic, 2005.

Gregory, Brad S. *The Unintended Reformation: How a Religious Revolution Secularized Society*. Cambridge, MA: Belknap, 2012.

Grenz, Stanley J. "Articulating the Christian Belief-Mosaic: Theological Method after the Demise of Foundationalism." Pages 107-36 in *Evangelical Futures: A Conversation on Theological Method*. Edited by John G. Stackhouse, Jr. Grand Rapids: Baker, 2000.

Grenz, Stanley J. "Nurturing the Soul, Informing the Mind: The Genesis of the Evangelical Scripture Principle." Pages 21-41 in *Evangelicals & Scripture: Tradition, Authority, and Hermeneutics.* Edited by Vincent Bacote, Laura C. Miguélez, and Dennis L. Okholm. Downers Grove, IL: InterVarsity Press, 2004.

Grenz, Stanley J. *Renewing the Center: Evangelical Theology in a Post-theological Era.* 2nd ed. Grand Rapids: Baker, 2006.

Grenz, Stanley J. *Revisioning Evangelical Theology.* Downers Grove, IL: InterVarsity, 1993.

Grenz, Stanley J., and John R. Franke. *Beyond Foundationalism: Shaping Theology in a Postmodern Context.* Louisville: Westminster John Knox, 2001.

Grondin, Jean. *Introduction to Philosophical Hermeneutics.* New Haven: Yale University Press, 1994.

Gruber, Mayer I. "The Many Faces of Hebrew *nāśā' pānîm* 'lift up the face,'" *Zeitschrift für die alttestamentliche Wissenschaft* 95/2 (1983): 252-60.

Grudem, Wayne A. "Biblical Evidence for the Eternal Submission of the Son to the Father." Pages 223-61 in *The New Evangelical Subordinationism? Perspectives on the Equality of God the Father and God the Son.* Edited by Dennis W. Jowers and H. Wayne House. Eugene, OR: Pickwick, 2012.

Grudem, Wayne. "Do We Act As If We Really Believe That 'the Bible Alone, and the Bible in Its Entirety Is the Word of God Written?'" *Journal of the Evangelical Theological Society* 43/1 (2000): 5-26.

Grudem, Wayne A. *Evangelical Feminism and Biblical Truth: An Analysis of More than One Hundred Disputed Questions.* Sisters, OR: Multnomah, 2004.

Grudem, Wayne A. *Systematic Theology.* Grand Rapids: Zondervan, 1994.

Grudem, Wayne A., C. John Collins, and Thomas R. Schreiner, eds. *Understanding Scripture: An Overview of the Bible's Origin, Reliability, and Meaning.* Wheaton, IL: Crossway, 2012.

Hahneman, Geoffrey M. *The Muratorian Fragment and the Development of the Canon.* Oxford: Clarendon, 1992.

Hahneman, Geoffrey M. "The Muratorian Fragment and the Origins of the New Testament Canon." Pages 405-15 in *The Canon Debate.* Edited by Lee Martin McDonald and James A. Sanders. Peabody, MA: Hendrickson, 2002.

Hall, Christopher A. *Reading Scripture with the Church Fathers.* Downers Grove, IL: InterVarsity, 1998.

Hall, Christopher A. "What Evangelicals and Liberals Can Learn from the Church Fathers." *Journal of the Evangelical Theological Society* 49/1 (2006): 81-96.

Hankey, W. J., and Douglas Hedley, eds. *Deconstructing Radical Orthodoxy: Postmodern Theology, Rhetoric, and Truth.* Burlington, VT: Ashgate, 2005.

Hanson, R. P. C. "The Church and Tradition in the Pre-Nicene Fathers." *Scottish Journal of Theology* 12 (1959): 21-31.

Hanson, R. P. C. *Tradition in the Early Church.* London: SCM, 1962.

Harnack, Adolf von. *History of Dogma.* 7 vols. New York: Dover, 1961.

Harnack, Adolf von. *The Origin of the New Testament and the Most Important Consequences of the New Creation.* New York: Macmillan, 1925.

Harris, R. L., and Gleason L. Archer Jr. *Theological Wordbook of the Old Testament*. 2 vols. Chicago: Moody, 1980.

Hartshorne, Charles. *Omnipotence and Other Theological Mistakes*. Albany: State University of New York Press, 1984.

Harvey, W. Wigan, ed. *Libros Quinque Adversus Haereses*. Cambridge: Typis Academicis, 1857.

Hasel, Gerhard F. "Divine Inspiration and the Canon of the Bible." *Journal of the Adventist Theological Society* 5/1 (1994): 68-105.

Hasel, Gerhard F. "The Relationship between Biblical Theology and Systematic Theology." *Trinity Journal* 5/2 (1984): 113-27.

Hauerwas, Stanley. "The Church's One Foundation Is Jesus Christ Her Lord; or, in a World without Foundations: All We Have Is the Church." Pages 143-62 in *Theology Without Foundations*. Edited by Stanley Hauerwas, Nancey Murphy, and Mark Nation. Nashville: Abingdon, 1994.

Hauerwas, Stanley. *A Community of Character: Toward a Constructive Christian Social Ethic*. Notre Dame: University of Notre Dame Press, 1981.

Hauerwas, Stanley. *Unleashing the Scripture: Freeing the Bible from Captivity to America*. Nashville: Abingdon, 1993.

Hauerwas, Stanley, Nancey Murphy, and Mark Nation, eds. *Theology without Foundations*. Nashville: Abingdon, 1994.

Hefner, Philip J. "Saint Irenaeus and the Hypothesis of Faith." *Dialog* 2 (1963): 300-306.

Helm, Paul. "The Impossibility of Divine Passibility." Pages 119-40 in *The Power and Weakness of God: Impassibility and Orthodoxy*. Edited by Nigel M. de S. Cameron. Edinburgh: Rutherford, 1990.

Helm, Paul. "Of God, and of the Holy Trinity: A Response to Dr. Beckwith." *Churchman* 115/4 (2001): 350-57.

Hemming, Laurence Paul, ed. *Radical Orthodoxy? A Catholic Enquiry*. Burlington, VT: Ashgate, 2000.

Hennessy, Kristin. "An Answer to de Régnon's Accusers: Why We Should Not Speak of 'His' Paradigm." *Harvard Theological Review* 100/2 (2007): 179-97.

Hernando, James Daniel. "Irenaeus and the Apostolic Fathers: An Inquiry into the Development of the New Testament Canon." PhD dissertation. Drew University, 1990.

Hill, Andrew E., and John H. Walton. *A Survey of the Old Testament*. 3rd ed. Grand Rapids: Zondervan, 2009.

Hill, Charles E. "The Debate over the Muratorian Fragment and the Development of the Canon." *Westminster Theological Journal* 57 (1995): 437-52.

Hill, Charles E. "The New Testament Canon: Deconstructio ad absurdum?" *Journal of the Evangelical Theological Society* 52/1 (2009): 101-19.

Hirsch, E. D. *Validity in Interpretation*. New Haven: Yale University Press, 1967.

Holmer, Paul. *The Grammar of Faith*. San Francisco: Harper & Row, 1978.

Holmes, Stephen R. *Listening to the Past: The Place of Tradition in Theology*. Grand Rapids: Baker Academic, 2002.

Holmes, Stephen R. *The Quest for the Trinity: The Doctrine of God in Scripture, History, and Modernity*. Downers Grove, IL: IVP Academic, 2012.

Humboldt, Wilhelm von. *Humanist without Portfolio*. Detroit: Wayne State University Press, 1963.

Humphrey, Edith. *Scripture and Tradition: What the Bible Really Says*. Grand Rapids: Baker, 2013.

Hwang, Alexander Y. "Prosper, Cassian, and Vincent: The Rule of Faith in the Augustinian Controversy." Pages 68-87 in *Tradition and the Rule of Faith in the Early Church*. Edited by Ronnie J. Rombs and Alexander Y. Hwang. Washington, DC: Catholic University of America Press, 2010.

Irenaeus. *Contre Les Hérésies*. Sources Chrétiennes. Paris: Cerf, 1969.

Irenaeus. *Proof of the Apostolic Preaching*. Translated by Joseph P. Smith. Ancient Christian Writers 16. New York: Newman, 1952.

Jenni, Ernst, and Claus Westermann. *Theological Lexicon of the Old Testament*. Translated by Mark E. Biddle. 3 vols. Peabody, MA: Hendrickson, 1997.

Jenson, Robert W. *Systematic Theology*. 2 vols. New York: Oxford University Press, 1997.

Johnson, Dennis Edward. "Immutability and Incarnation: An Historical and Theological Study of the Concepts of Christ's Divine Unchangeability and His Human Development." PhD dissertation. Fuller Theological Seminary, 1984.

Johnson, Phillip R. "God without Mood Swings." Pages 109-21 in *Bound Only Once: The Failure of Open Theism*. Edited by D. Wilson. Moscow, ID: Canon, 2001.

Josephus. *The Life; Against Apion*. Translated by H. St. J. Thackeray. Loeb Classical Library 186. Cambridge, MA: Harvard University Press, 1926.

Jowers, Dennis W. "The Inconceivability of Subordination within a Simple God." Pages 375-410 in *The New Evangelical Subordinationism? Perspectives on the Equality of God the Father and God the Son*. Edited by Dennis W. Jowers and H. Wayne House. Eugene, OR: Pickwick, 2012.

Jowers, Dennis W., and H. Wayne House, eds. *The New Evangelical Subordinationism? Perspectives on the Equality of God the Father and God the Son*. Eugene, OR: Pickwick, 2012.

Kaiser, Walter C., Jr. "Prophet, Prophetess, Prophecy." Pages 641-47 in *Evangelical Dictionary of Biblical Theology*. Edited by Walter A. Elwell. Grand Rapids: Baker, 1996.

Kaiser, Walter C., Jr. *Recovering the Unity of the Bible: One Continuous Story, Plan, and Purpose*. Grand Rapids: Zondervan, 2009.

Kaiser, Walter C., Jr. *Toward an Exegetical Theology: Biblical Exegesis for Preaching and Teaching*. Grand Rapids: Baker Academic, 1998.

Kaiser, Walter C., Jr. *Toward an Old Testament Theology*. Grand Rapids, Zondervan, 2001.

Keating, James, and Thomas Joseph White, eds. *Divine Impassibility and the Mystery of Human Suffering*. Grand Rapids: Eerdmans, 2009.

Keener, Craig. "Subordination within the Trinity: John 5:18 and 1 Cor 15:28." Pages 39-58 in *The New Evangelical Subordinationism? Perspectives on the Equality of God the Father and God the Son*. Edited by Dennis W. Jowers and H. Wayne House. Eugene, OR: Pickwick, 2012.

Kelsey, David H. *The Uses of Scripture in Recent Theology*. Philadelphia: Fortress, 1975.

Kittel, Gerhard, and Gerhard Friedrich, eds. *Theological Dictionary of the New Testament*. Translated by Geoffrey W. Bromiley. 10 vols. Grand Rapids: Eerdmans, 1964–1976.

Kline, Meredith G. *The Structure of Biblical Authority*. Grand Rapids: Eerdmans, 1972.

Koester, Helmut. *Introduction to the New Testament*, vol. 2: *History and Literature of Early Christianity*. Philadelphia: Fortress, 2000.

Köstenberger, Andreas J., and Michael J. Kruger. *The Heresy of Orthodoxy*. Wheaton, IL: Crossway, 2010.

Kövecses, Zoltán. *Metaphor: A Practical Introduction*. 2nd ed. New York: Oxford University Press, 2010.

Kreeft, Peter. *Fundamentals of the Faith: Essays in Christian Apologetics*. San Francisco: Ignatius, 1988.

Kruger, Michael J. *Canon Revisited: Establishing the Origins and Authority of the New Testament Books*. Wheaton, IL: Crossway, 2012.

Kruger, Michael J. *The Question of Canon: Challenging the Status Quo in the New Testament Debate*. Downers Grove, IL: IVP Academic, 2013.

Lane, Anthony N. S. "Scripture, Tradition and Church: An Historical Survey." *Vox Evangelica* 9 (1975): 37-55.

Lane, Anthony N. S. "*Sola Scriptura*? Making Sense of a Post-Reformation Slogan." Pages 297-328 in *A Pathway into the Holy Scripture*. Edited by P. E. Satterthwaite and David F. Wright. Grand Rapids: Eerdmans, 1994.

Lawson, John. *The Biblical Theology of Saint Irenaeus*. London: Epworth, 1948.

Leiman, Sid Z. *The Canonization of Hebrew Scripture: The Talmudic and Midrashic Evidence*. Hamden, CT: Archon Books, 1976.

Leithart, Peter J. "The Word and the Rule of Faith." *First Things* (2015). http://www.firstthings .com/web-exclusives/2015/01/the-word-and-the-rule-of-faith. Accessed 1/30/15.

Letham, Robert, *The Holy Trinity: In Scripture, History, Theology, and Worship*. Phillipsburg, NJ: Presbyterian & Reformed, 2004.

Letham, Robert. "Reply to Kevin Giles." *Evangelical Quarterly* 80/4 (2008): 339-45.

Lewis, Jack P. "Jamnia Revisited." Pages 146-62 in *The Canon Debate*. Edited by Lee Martin McDonald and James A. Sanders. Peabody, MA: Hendrickson, 2002.

Lienhard, Joseph T. *The Bible, the Church, and Authority: The Canon of the Christian Bible in History and Theology*. Collegeville, MN: Liturgical, 1995.

Lindbeck, George. *The Nature of Doctrine: Religion and Theology in a Postliberal Age*. 1st ed. Philadelphia: Westminster, 1984.

Lister, Rob. *God Is Impassible and Impassioned*. Wheaton, IL: Crossway, 2012.

Löfstedt, Torsten. "In Defence of the Scripture Principle: An Evangelical Reply to A. S. Khomiakov." *Evangelical Quarterly* 83/1 (2011): 49-72.

Lubac, Henri de. *History and Spirit: The Understanding of Scripture according to Origen*. San Francisco: Ignatius, 2007.

Lumen Gentium. Dogmatic Constitution on the Church. 1964. http://www.vatican.va/ archive/hist_councils/ii_vatican_council/documents/vat-ii_const_19641121 _lumen-gentium_en.html. Accessed May 23, 2016.

Luther, Martin. *Luther's Works*. Edited by Jaroslav Pelikan, Hilton C. Oswald, and Helmut T. Lehmann. 55 vols. Philadelphia: Fortress, 1999.

Lycan, William G. *Philosophy of Language: A Contemporary Introduction*. 2nd ed. New York: Routledge, 2008.

Lyon, J. A. *The Cosmic Christ in Origen and Teilhard de Chardin: A Comparative Study*. New York: Oxford University Press, 1982.

MacIntyre, Alasdair. *After Virtue*. London: Duckworth, 1984.

MacIntyre, Alasdair. *Whose Justice? Which Rationality?* London: Duckworth, 1988.

Mackenzie, Jon. "A Double-Headed Luther? A Lutheran Response to *The Holy Trinity* by Stephen R. Holmes." *Evangelical Quarterly* 86/1 (2014): 39-54.

Madrid, Patrick. "*Sola Scriptura*: A Blueprint for Anarchy." Pages 1-30 in *Not by Scripture Alone: A Catholic Critique of the Protestant Doctrine of* Sola Scriptura. Edited by Robert A. Sungenis. Santa Barbara, CA: Queenship Pub. Co., 1997.

Maier, Gerhard. *Biblical Hermeneutics*. Wheaton, IL: Crossway, 1994.

Markschies, Christoph. *Gnosis: An Introduction*. London: T&T Clark, 2003.

Markschies, Christoph. *Kaiserzeitliche christliche Theologie und ihre Institutionen: Prolegomena zu einer Geschichte der antiken christlichen Theologie*. Tübingen: Mohr Siebeck, 2009.

Marshall, I. Howard, *Beyond the Bible: Moving from Scripture to Theology*. Acadia Studies in Bible and Theology. Grand Rapids: Baker Academic, 2004.

Mathison, Keith A. *The Shape of Sola Scriptura*. Moscow, ID: Canon, 2001.

McCall, Thomas H. *Which Trinity? Whose Monotheism? Philosophical and Systematic Theologians on the Metaphysics of Trinitarian Theology*. Grand Rapids: Eerdmans, 2010.

McCall, Thomas H., and Michael C. Rea. "Theologians, Philosophers, and the Doctrine of the Trinity." Pages 336-49 in *Philosophical and Theological Essays on the Trinity*. Edited by Thomas H. McCall and Michael C. Rea. New York: Oxford University Press, 2009.

McDermott, Gerald. "Evangelicals Divided: The Battle between Meliorists and Traditionalists to Define Evangelicalism." *First Things* (April 2011). http://www.firstthings.com/article/2011/04/evangelicals-divided. Accessed 7/19/15.

McDonald, Lee Martin. *The Biblical Canon: Its Origin, Transmission, and Authority*. Peabody, MA: Hendrickson, 2007.

McDonald, Lee Martin. *The Formation of the Christian Biblical Canon*. Peabody, MA: Hendrickson, 1995.

McDonald, Lee Martin. "Identifying Scripture and Canon in the Early Church: The Criteria Question." Pages 416-39 in *The Canon Debate*. Edited by Lee Martin McDonald and James A. Sanders. Peabody, MA: Hendrickson, 2002.

McDonald, Lee Martin, and James A. Sanders, eds. *The Canon Debate*. Peabody, MA: Hendrickson, 2002.

McDonald, Lee Martin, and Stanley E. Porter, *Early Christianity and Its Sacred Literature*. Peabody, MA: Hendrickson, 2000.

McGlasson, Paul. *Invitation to Dogmatic Theology: A Canonical Approach*. Grand Rapids: Brazos, 2006.

McGrath, Alister E. "An Evangelical Evaluation of Postliberalism." Pages 23-44 in *The Nature of Confession: Evangelicals & Postliberals in Conversation*. Edited by Timothy R. Phillips and Dennis L. Okholm. Downers Grove, IL: InterVarsity, 1996.

McGrath, Alister E. *Christian Theology: An Introduction.* 5th ed. Malden, MA: Wiley-Blackwell, 2011.

McGrath, Alister E. "Engaging the Great Tradition: Evangelical Theology and the Role of Tradition." Pages 139-58 in *Evangelical Futures: A Conversation on Theological Method.* Edited by John G. Stackhouse, Jr. Grand Rapids: Baker, 2000.

McGrath, Alister E. "Evangelical Theological Method: The State of the Art." Pages 15-38 in *Evangelical Futures: A Conversation on Theological Method.* Edited by John G. Stackhouse, Jr. Grand Rapids: Baker, 2000.

McGrath, Alister E. *The Intellectual Origins of the European Reformation.* 2nd ed. Malden, MA: Blackwell, 2004.

McGrath, Alister E. *Reformation Thought: An Introduction.* 3rd ed. Malden, MA: Blackwell Publishers, 2001.

McGrath, Alister E. *Reformation Thought: An Introduction.* 4th ed. Malden, MA: Wiley-Blackwell, 2012.

McLaren, Brian D. *A Generous Orthodoxy.* Grand Rapids: Zondervan, 2006.

Metzger, Bruce M. *The Canon of the New Testament: Its Origin, Development, and Significance.* Oxford: Clarendon, 1987.

Metzger, Bruce M. *The Text of the New Testament: Its Transmission, Corruption, and Restoration.* 3rd ed. New York: Oxford University Press, 1992.

Milbank, John. "'Postmodern Critical Augustinianism': A Short Summa in Forty-two Responses to Unasked Questions." Pages 49-62 in *The Radical Orthodoxy Reader.* Edited by Simon Oliver and John Milbank. New York: Routledge, 2009.

Milbank, John. "The Programme of Radical Orthodoxy." Pages 33-45 in *Radical Orthodoxy? A Catholic Enquiry.* Edited by Laurence Paul Hemming. Burlington, VT: Ashgate, 2000.

Milbank, John. *Theology and Social Theory: Beyond Secular Reason.* Cambridge, MA: Blackwell, 1990.

Milbank, John, Catherine Pickstock, and Graham Ward. "Introduction: Suspending the Material: The Turn of Radical Orthodoxy." Pages 1-20 in *Radical Orthodoxy: A New Theology.* Edited by John Milbank, Catherine Pickstock, and Graham Ward. New York: Routledge, 1999.

Milbank, John, Catherine Pickstock, and Graham Ward, eds. *Radical Orthodoxy: A New Theology.* New York: Routledge, 1999.

Minns, Denis. *Irenaeus.* Washington, DC: Georgetown University Press, 1994.

Mitros, Joseph F. "The Norm of Faith in the Patristic Age." Pages 78-105 in *Orthodoxy, Heresy, and Schism in Early Christianity.* Edited by Everett Ferguson. New York: Garland, 1993.

Molland, Einar. "Irenaeus of Lugdunum and the Apostolic Succession." *Journal of Ecclesiastical History* 1/1 (1950): 12-28.

Moreland, James Porter, and William Lane Craig. *Philosophical Foundations for a Christian Worldview.* Downers Grove, IL: InterVarsity, 2003.

Moreland, James Porter, and Garrett DeWeese. "The Premature Report of Foundationalism's Demise." Pages 81-108 in *Reclaiming the Center: Confronting Evangelical*

Accommodation in Postmodern Times. Edited by Millard J. Erickson, Paul Kjoss Helseth, and Justin Taylor. Wheaton, IL: Crossway, 2004.

Mullins, R. T. "Simply Impossible: A Case against Divine Simplicity." *Journal of Reformed Theology* 7/2 (2013): 181-203.

Murphy, Nancey. *Beyond Liberalism and Fundamentalism: How Modern and Postmodern Philosophy Set the Theological Agenda.* Valley Forge, PA: Trinity Press International, 1996.

Nautin, Pierre. "Irénée, Adv haer, III 3,2 : Eglise de Rome ou église universelle?" *Revue de l'histoire des religions* 151 (1957): 37-78.

Nicole, Roger. "New Testament Use of the Old Testament." Pages 135-51 in *Revelation and the Bible.* Edited by Carl F. H. Henry. Grand Rapids: Baker, 1958.

Nida, Eugene Albert. *Componential Analysis of Meaning: An Introduction to Semantic Structures.* Approaches to Semiotics 57. The Hague: Mouton, 1975.

Noble, Paul R. *The Canonical Approach: A Critical Reconstruction of the Hermeneutics of Brevard S. Childs.* Leiden: Brill, 1995.

Norris, Richard A. "Theology and Language in Irenaeus of Lyon." *Anglican Theological Review* 73/3 (1994): 285-95.

Nygren, Anders. *Agape and Eros.* Translated by Philip S. Watson. London: SPCK, 1953.

Oberman, Heiko A. *The Dawn of the Reformation: Essays in Late Medieval and Early Reformation Thought.* Edinburgh: T&T Clark, 1986.

Oberman, Heiko A. *The Harvest of Medieval Theology.* Grand Rapids: Eerdmans, 1967.

Oden, Thomas C. *After Modernity . . . What? Agenda for Theology.* Grand Rapids: Zondervan, 1990.

Oden, Thomas C. *Classic Christianity.* San Francisco: HarperOne, 2009.

Oden, Thomas C. *The Rebirth of Orthodoxy: Signs of New Life in Christianity.* 1st ed. San Francisco: HarperSanFrancisco, 2003.

Oden, Thomas C. *Turning Around the Mainline: How Renewal Movements Are Changing the Church.* Grand Rapids: Baker, 2006.

Ohme, Heinz. *Kanon ekklesiastikos: Die Bedeutung des altkirchlichen Kanonbegriffs.* Berlin: de Gruyter, 1998.

Oliver, Simon. "Introducing Radical Orthodoxy: From Participation to Late Modernity." Pages 3-27 in *The Radical Orthodoxy Reader.* Edited by Simon Oliver and John Milbank. New York: Routledge, 2009.

Oliver, Simon, and John Milbank, eds. *The Radical Orthodoxy Reader.* New York: Routledge, 2009.

Olson, Roger E. *Reformed and Always Reforming: The Postconservative Approach to Evangelical Theology.* Grand Rapids: Baker Academic, 2007.

Olson, Roger E. "Reforming Evangelical Theology." Pages 201-7 in *Evangelical Futures: A Conversation on Theological Method.* Edited by John G. Stackhouse, Jr. Grand Rapids: Baker, 2000.

Osborne, Grant R. *The Hermeneutical Spiral: A Comprehensive Introduction to Biblical Interpretation.* 2nd ed. Downers Grove, IL: InterVarsity, 2006.

"A Panel Discussion: Lindbeck, Hunsinger, McGrath & Fackre." Pages 246-53 in *The Na-*

ture of Confession: Evangelicals & Postliberals in Conversation. Edited by Timothy R. Phillips and Dennis L. Okholm. Downers Grove, IL: InterVarsity, 1996.

Pannenberg, Wolfhart. *Systematic Theology*. 3 vols. Grand Rapids: Eerdmans, 1991.

Peckham, John C. "The Analogy of Scripture Revisited: A Final Form Canonical Approach to Systematic Theology." *Mid-America Journal of Theology* 22 (2011): 41-53.

Peckham, John C. "The Canon and Biblical Authority: A Critical Comparison of Two Models of Canonicity." *Trinity Journal* 28/2 (2007): 229-49.

Peckham, John C. *The Concept of Divine Love in the Context of the God–World Relationship*. New York: Peter Lang, 2014.

Peckham, John C. "Divine Passibility, Analogical Temporality, and Theo-Ontology: Implications of a Canonical Approach." Pages 32-53 in *Scripture and Philosophy: Essays Honoring the Work and Vision of Fernando Luis Canale*. Edited by Tiago Arrais, Kenneth Bergland, and Michael F. Younker. Berrien Springs, MI: Adventist Theological Society Publications, 2016.

Peckham, John C. "Does God Always Get What He Wants? A Theocentric Approach to Divine Providence and Human Freedom." *Andrews University Seminary Studies* 52/2 (2014): 195-212.

Peckham, John C. "Epistemological Authority in the Polemic of Irenaeus." *Didaskalia* 19 (2008): 51-70.

Peckham, John C. "Intrinsic Canonicity and the Inadequacy of the Community Approach to Canon Determination." *Themelios* 36/2 (2011): 203-15.

Peckham, John C. *The Love of God: A Canonical Model*. Downers Grove, IL: IVP Academic, 2015.

Peckham, John C. "Providence and God's Unfulfilled Desires." *Philosophia Christi* 15/2 (2013): 453-62.

Pecknold, C. C. *Transforming Postliberal Theology: George Lindbeck, Pragmatism and Scripture*. New York: T&T Clark International, 2005.

Perrin, Nicholas. "Thomas: The Fifth Gospel?" *Journal of the Evangelical Theological Society* 49/1 (2006): 67-80.

Phillips, Timothy R., and Dennis L. Okholm. "The Nature of Confession: Evangelicals & Postliberals." Pages 7-20 in *The Nature of Confession: Evangelicals & Postliberals in Conversation*. Edited by Timothy R. Phillips and Dennis L. Okholm. Downers Grove, IL: InterVarsity, 1996.

Phillips, Timothy R., and Dennis L. Okholm, eds. *The Nature of Confession: Evangelicals & Postliberals in Conversation*. Downers Grove, IL: InterVarsity, 1996.

Pickstock, Catherine. *After Writing: On the Liturgical Consummation of Philosophy*. Oxford: Blackwell, 1998.

Pickstock, Catherine. "Radical Orthodoxy and the Meditations of Time." Pages 63-75 in *Radical Orthodoxy? A Catholic Enquiry*. Edited by Laurence Paul Hemming. Burlington, VT: Ashgate, 2000.

Pickstock, Catherine. "Reply to David Ford and Guy Collins." *Scottish Journal of Theology* 54 (2001): 405-22.

Plantinga, Alvin. *Does God Have a Nature?* Milwaukee: Marquette University Press, 1980.

Plantinga, Alvin. *Warranted Christian Belief*. New York: Oxford University Press, 2000.

Plantinga, Cornelius, Jr. "Social Trinity and Tritheism." Pages 21-37 in *Trinity, Incarnation, and Atonement: Philosophical and Theological Essays*. Edited by Cornelius Plantinga, Jr. and Ronald J. Feenstra. Notre Dame: University of Notre Dame Press, 1989.

Pomplun, Trent. "Impassibility in St. Hilary of Poitiers's *De Trinitate*." Pages 187-213 in *Divine Impassibility and the Mystery of Human Suffering*. Edited by James Keating and Thomas Joseph White. Grand Rapids: Eerdmans, 2009.

Porter, Stanley E. "When and How Was the Pauline Canon Compiled? An Assessment of Theories." Pages 95-127 in *The Pauline Canon*. Edited by Stanley E. Porter. Leiden: Brill, 2004.

Provan, Iain. "Canons to the Left of Him: Brevard Childs, His Critics, and the Future of Old Testament Theology." *Scottish Journal of Theology* 50/1 (1997): 1-38.

Quine, W. V., and J. S. Ullian. *The Web of Belief*. New York: Random House, 1970.

Reno, R. R. "Series Preface." In Jaroslav Pelikan, *Acts*, Brazos Theological Commentary on the Bible. Grand Rapids: Brazos, 2005.

Ricœur, Paul. *Interpretation Theory: Discourse and the Surplus of Meaning*. Fort Worth: Texas Christian University Press, 1976.

Ricœur, Paul. *The Rule of Metaphor: Multi-Disciplinary Studies of the Creation of Meaning in Language*. Toronto: University of Toronto Press, 1977.

Ridderbos, Herman N. *Redemptive History and the New Testament Scriptures*. 2nd rev. ed. Phillipsburg, NJ: Presbyterian and Reformed, 1988.

Rittgers, Ronald K. "Blame It on Luther." *Christian Century* 130/2 (2013): 26-29.

Rolnick, Philip A. "Realist Reference to God: Analogy or Univocity?" Pages 211-37 in *Realism & Antirealism*. Edited by William P. Alston. Ithaca: Cornell University Press, 2002.

Rombs, Ronnie J., and Alexander Y. Hwang. *Tradition and the Rule of Faith in the Early Church*. Washington, DC: Catholic University of America Press, 2010.

Sanders, Fred. "Redefining Progress in Trinitarian Theology: Stephen R. Holmes on the Trinity." *Evangelical Quarterly* 86/1 (2014): 6-20.

Sanders, James A. *Canon and Community: A Guide to Canonical Criticism*. Philadelphia: Fortress, 1984.

Sanders, James A. "Canon: Hebrew Bible." Pages 837-52 in *The Anchor Bible Dictionary*. Edited by David Noel Freedman. 6 vols. New York: Doubleday, 1992.

Sanders, James A. "The Issue of Closure in the Canonical Process." Pages 252-66 in *The Canon Debate*. Edited by Lee Martin McDonald and James A. Sanders. Peabody, MA: Hendrickson, 2002.

Sanders, James A. *Torah and Canon*. Philadelphia: Fortress, 1972.

Sanders, John. "Historical Considerations." Pages 59-91 in *The Openness of God: A Biblical Challenge to the Traditional Understanding of God*. Downers Grove, IL: InterVarsity, 1994.

Sanders, John. "Theological Muscle-Flexing: How Human Embodiment Shapes Discourse about God." Pages 219-36 in *Creation Made Free: Open Theology Engaging Science*. Edited by Thomas Jay Oord. Eugene, OR: Pickwick, 2009.

Saucy, Mark R. "Canon as Tradition: The New Covenant and the Hermeneutical Question." *Themelios* 36/2 (2011): 216-37.

Scalise, Charles J. *From Scripture to Theology: A Canonical Journey into Hermeneutics.* Downers Grove, IL: InterVarsity, 1996.

Schaff, Philip, ed. *The Creeds of Christendom.* New York: Harper & Brothers, 1882.

Schlimm, Matthew R. "Different Perspectives on Divine Pathos: An Examination of Hermeneutics in Biblical Theology." *Catholic Biblical Quarterly* 69/4 (2007): 673-94.

Schwarz, Daniel R. "The Ethics of Reading Elie Wiesel's *Night.*" Pages 71-98 in *Elie Wiesel's Night.* Edited by Harold Bloom. New York: Bloom's Literary Criticism, 2010.

Seitz, Christopher. "Canonical Approach." Pages 100-102 in *Dictionary for Theological Interpretation of the Bible.* Edited by Kevin J. Vanhoozer. Grand Rapids: Baker Academic, 2005.

Seitz, Christopher. "The Canonical Approach and Theological Intepretation." Pages 58-110 in *Canon and Biblical Interpretation.* Edited by Craig G. Bartholomew, Scott Hahn, Robin Parry, Christopher Seitz, and Al Wolters. Grand Rapids: Zondervan, 2006.

Seitz, Christopher. *The Goodly Fellowship of the Prophets: The Achievement of Association in Canon Formation.* Grand Rapids: Baker Academic, 2009.

Sheppard, Gerald T. "Canon." Pages 62-69 in *The Encyclopedia of Religion.* Edited by Mircea Eliade. New York: Macmillan, 1987.

Silva, Moisés. *Biblical Words and Their Meaning: An Introduction to Lexical Semantics.* Grand Rapids: Zondervan, 1994.

Silva, Moisés. *God, Language, and Scripture: Reading the Bible in the Light of General Linguistics.* Grand Rapids: Zondervan, 1990.

Smith, Christian. *The Bible Made Impossible: Why Biblicism Is Not a Truly Evangelical Reading of Scripture.* Grand Rapids: Brazos, 2011.

Smith, James K. A. *Introducing Radical Orthodoxy: Mapping a Post-Secular Theology.* Grand Rapids: Baker Academic, 2004.

Stackhouse, John G., Jr., ed. *Evangelical Futures: A Conversation on Theological Method.* Grand Rapids: Baker, 2000.

Stackhouse, John G., Jr. "Evangelical Theology Should Be Evangelical." Pages 39-58 in *Evangelical Futures: A Conversation on Theological Method.* Edited by John G. Stackhouse, Jr. Grand Rapids: Baker, 2000.

Steinmann, Andrew E. *The Oracles of God.* Saint Louis: Concordia, 1999.

Steinmetz, David C. "The Superiority of Pre-Critical Exegesis." Pages 26-38 in *The Theological Interpretation of Scripture: Classic and Contemporary Readings.* Edited by Stephen E. Fowl. Malden, MA: Blackwell, 1997.

Sternberg, Meir. *The Poetics of Biblical Narrative.* Bloomington: Indiana University Press, 1985.

Stuart, Douglas K. *Old Testament Exegesis: A Handbook for Students and Pastors.* Louisville: Westminster John Knox, 2008.

Stylianopoulos, Theodore G. "Scripture and Tradition in the Church," Pages 21-34 in *The Cambridge Companion to Orthodox Christian Theology.* Edited by Mary Cunningham and Elizabeth Theokritoff. Cambridge: Cambridge University Press, 2008.

Sullivan, Francis A. *From Apostles to Bishops: The Development of the Episcopacy in the Early Church.* New York: Newman, 2001.

Sundberg, Albert C. "Canon Muratori: A Fourth-Century List." *Harvard Theological Review* 66 (1973): 1-41.

Sundberg, Albert C. *The Old Testament of the Early Church*. New York: Kraus, 1969.

Sundberg, Albert C. "Towards a Revised History of the New Testament Canon." *Studia Evangelica* 4 (1968): 452-61.

Sungenis, Robert A. "Point/Counterpoint: Protestant Objections and Catholic Answers." Pages 211-324 in *Not by Scripture Alone: A Catholic Critique of the Protestant Doctrine of Sola Scriptura*. Edited by Robert A. Sungenis. Santa Barbara, CA: Queenship Pub. Co., 1997.

Sungenis, Robert A., ed. *Not by Scripture Alone: A Catholic Critique of the Protestant Doctrine of Sola Scriptura*. Santa Barbara, CA: Queenship Pub. Co., 1997.

Thiselton, Anthony C. "Canon, Community, and Theological Construction." Pages 1-30 in *Canon and Biblical Interpretation*. Edited by Craig G. Bartholomew, Scott Hahn, Robin Parry, Christopher Seitz, and Al Wolters. Grand Rapids: Zondervan, 2006.

Thiselton, Anthony C. *Hermeneutics: An Introduction*. Grand Rapids: Eerdmans, 2009.

Thiselton, Anthony C. *New Horizons in Hermeneutics*. Grand Rapids: Zondervan, 1992.

Timothy, Hamilton. *The Early Christian Apologists and Greek Philosophy*. Assen: Van Gorcum, 1973.

Treier, Daniel J. "Canonical Unity and Commensurable Language: On Divine Action and Doctrine." Pages 211-28 in *Evangelicals & Scripture: Tradition, Authority, and Hermeneutics*. Edited by Vincent Bacote, Laura C. Miguélez, and Dennis L. Okholm. Downers Grove, IL: InterVarsity, 2004.

Treier, Daniel J. *Introducing Theological Interpretation of Scripture: Recovering a Christian Practice*. Grand Rapids: Baker Academic, 2008.

Treier, Daniel J. "Scripture, Unity of." Pages 731-34 in *Dictionary for Theological Interpretation of the Bible*. Edited by Kevin J. Vanhoozer. Grand Rapids: Baker Academic, 2005.

Treier, Daniel J. "What Is Theological Interpretation? An Ecclesiological Reduction." *International Journal of Systematic Theology* 12/2 (2010): 144-161.

Trible, Phyllis. *God and the Rhetoric of Sexuality*. Philadelphia: Fortress, 1978.

Tuckett, Christopher M. *Reading the New Testament: Methods of Interpretation*. Philadelphia: Fortress, 1987.

Ulrich, Eugene. "The Notion and Definition of Canon." Pages 21-35 in *The Canon Debate*. Edited by Lee McDonald and James A. Sanders. Peabody, MA: Hendrickson, 2002.

Vallée, Gérard. *A Study in Anti-Gnostic Polemics: Irenaeus, Hippolytus, and Epiphanius* Waterloo, Ontario: Wilfrid Laurier University Press, 1981.

VanGemeren, Willem A., ed. *New International Dictionary of Old Testament Theology & Exegesis*. 4 vols. Grand Rapids: Zondervan, 1997.

Vanhoozer, Kevin J., ed. *Dictionary for Theological Interpretation of the Bible*. Grand Rapids: Baker Academic, 2005.

Vanhoozer, Kevin J. *The Drama of Doctrine: A Canonical-Linguistic Approach to Christian Theology*. Louisville: Westminster John Knox, 2005.

Vanhoozer, Kevin J. *First Theology: God, Scripture & Hermeneutics.* Downers Grove, IL: InterVarsity, 2002.

Vanhoozer, Kevin J. "Introduction: What Is Theological Interpretation of the Bible?" Pages 19-25 in *Dictionary for Theological Interpretation of the Bible.* Edited by Kevin J. Vanhoozer. Grand Rapids: Baker Academic, 2005.

Vanhoozer, Kevin J. *Is There a Meaning in This Text?* Grand Rapids: Zondervan, 1998.

Vanhoozer, Kevin J. *Remythologizing Theology.* Cambridge: Cambridge University Press, 2010.

Vanhoozer, Kevin J. "The Voice and the Actor: A Dramatic Proposal about the Ministry and Minstrelsy of Theology." Pages 61-106 in *Evangelical Futures: A Conversation on Theological Method.* Edited by John G. Stackhouse, Jr. Grand Rapids: Baker, 2000.

Van Inwagen, Peter. *God, Knowledge & Mystery.* Ithaca: Cornell University Press, 1995.

Vorster, Nico. "*Sola Scriptura* and Western Hyperpluralism: A Critical Response to Brad Gregory's Unintended Reformation." *Review of European Studies* 5/1 (2013): 52-64.

Ward, Graham. "Radical Orthodoxy and/as Cultural Politics." Pages 97-111 in *Radical Orthodoxy? A Catholic Enquiry.* Edited by Laurence Paul Hemming. Burlington, VT: Ashgate, 2000.

Ware, Bruce A. "An Evangelical Reexamination of the Doctrine of the Immutability of God." PhD dissertation. Fuller Theological Seminary, 1984.

Ware, Bruce A. "Equal in Essence, Distinct in Roles: Eternal Functional Authority and Submission among the Essentially Equal Divine Persons of the Godhead." Pages 13-38 in *The New Evangelical Subordinationism? Perspectives on the Equality of God the Father and God the Son.* Edited by Dennis W. Jowers and H. Wayne House. Eugene, OR: Pickwick, 2012.

Ware, Bruce A. *Father, Son, and Holy Spirit: Relationships, Roles, and Relevance.* Wheaton, IL: Crossway, 2005.

Ware, Bruce. "Tampering with the Trinity: Does the Son Submit to His Father?" *Journal for Biblical Manhood and Womanhood* 6/1 (2001): 4-12.

Watson, Francis. "Authors, Readers, Hermeneutics." Pages 119-23 in *Reading Scripture with the Church: Toward a Hermeneutic for Theological Interpretation.* Grand Rapids: Baker Academic, 2006.

Webber, Robert. *Ancient-Future Faith: Rethinking Evangelicalism for a Postmodern World.* Grand Rapids: Baker, 1999.

Webster, John. "Principles of Systematic Theology." *International Journal of Systematic Theology* 11/1 (2009): 56-71.

Weinandy, Thomas. *Does God Suffer?* Notre Dame: University of Notre Dame Press, 2000.

Weiss, Meir. *The Bible from Within: The Method of Total Interpretation.* Jerusalem: Magnes, 1984.

Wellum, Stephen J. "Postconservatism, Biblical Authority, and Recent Proposals for Re-Doing Evangelical Theology: A Critical Analysis." Pages 161-98 in *Reclaiming the Center: Confronting Evangelical Accommodation in Postmodern Times.* Edited by Millard J. Erickson, Paul Kjoss Helseth, and Justin Taylor. Wheaton, IL: Crossway, 2004.

Wessling, Jordan. "Colin Gunton, Divine Love, and Univocal Predication." *Journal of Reformed Theology* 7 (2013): 91-107.

Westminster Confession of Faith. In *The Creeds of Christendom*. Edited by Philip Schaff. New York: Harper & Brothers, 1882.

Westphal, Merold. "A Reader's Guide to 'Reformed Epistemology.'" *Perspectives* 7/9 (1992): 10-13.

Westphal, Merold. "On Reading God the Author." *Religious Studies* 37/3 (2001): 271-91.

Westphal, Merold. *Whose Community? Which Interpretation? Philosophical Hermeneutics for the Church*. The Church and Postmodern Culture. Grand Rapids: Baker Academic, 2009.

Whidden, Woodrow W. "*Sola Scriptura*, Inerrantist Fundamentalism, and the Wesleyan Quadrilateral: Is 'No Creed but the Bible' a Workable Solution?" *Andrews University Seminary Studies* 35/2 (1997): 211-26.

Williams, D. H. *Evangelicals and Tradition: The Formative Influence of the Early Church*. Grand Rapids: Baker Academic, 2005.

Williams, D. H. *Retrieving the Tradition and Renewing Evangelicalism: A Primer for Suspicious Protestants*. Grand Rapids: Eerdmans, 1999.

Williams, D. H. "The Search for *Sola Scriptura* in the Early Church." *Interpretation: A Journal of Bible & Theology* 52/4 (1998): 354-66.

Williams, D. H. *Tradition, Scripture, and Interpretation*. Grand Rapids: Baker Academic, 2006.

Williams, Thomas. "The Doctrine of Univocity Is True and Salutary." *Modern Theology* 21/4 (2005): 575-85.

Wolterstorff, Nicholas. "Could Not God Sorrow If We Do?" Pages 139-63 in *The Papers of the Henry Luce III Fellows in Theology*. Edited by Christopher I. Wilkins. Atlanta: Scholars, 2002.

Wolterstorff, Nicholas. *Divine Discourse: Philosophical Reflections on the Claim That God Speaks*. Cambridge: Cambridge University Press, 1995.

Wright, N. T. "How Can the Bible Be Authoritative?" *Vox Evangelica* 21 (1991): 7-32.

Wright, N. T. *Scripture and the Authority of God*. San Francisco: HarperCollins, 2011.

Yandell, Keith. "How Many Times Does Three Go into One?" Pages 151-69 in *Philosophical and Theological Essays on the Trinity*. Edited by Thomas H. McCall and Michael C. Rea. New York: Oxford University Press, 2009.

Yeago, David. "The Bible: The Spirit, the Church, and the Scriptures." Page 49-93 in *Knowing the Triune God*. Edited by David Yeago and James Buckley. Grand Rapids: Eerdmans, 2001.

Yeago, David, and James Buckley, eds. *Knowing the Triune God*. Grand Rapids: Eerdmans, 2001.

Modern Author Index

Subject Index

accommodation. *See* language: accommodative

Acts of Paul, 66n57

agape. *See* love

allegorical interpretation, 75-76, 122, 203

Ambrose, 98n149

analogy. *See* language: analogical

analogy of being, 101, 225n17

analogy of Scripture. *See* Scripture: analogy of

analytic theology, 206, 228-29

anatomical imagery, 236-40, 244-45

anthropomorphisms. *See* language: anthropomorphic

antifoundationalism. *See* foundationalism: anti

antisupernaturalism. *See* hermeneutical presuppositions: naturalistic

Apocalypse of John, 66n57

Apocalypse of Peter, 66nn56-57

Apocrypha, OT, 25n29, 34n53, 44, 52n15, 58n30, 63n41

apostle, definition of, 27-28

Apostles' Creed, 96, 133n98

apostolicity, 21-22, 24, 26-39, 42-43, 45-47, 66, 110-17, 131-33, 147-48, 151, 158

apostolic succession, 113-19, 133, 158n59

Aquinas, Thomas, 101, 225n17

Arianism, 164n78, 168, 174n28, 178, 174n28, 191n91, 234n40

Aristotle, 225n17

Athanasian Creed, 97, 127, 133n98, 180n52, 181n57

Athanasius, 66, 98n149

Augustine, 75, 98n149, 130n87, 133-34, 172-73

authorial intention, 201n17, 209-11, 223n11

authorship of biblical books, questions regarding, 35-36n57, 42-43

B. Baba Bathra, 24n27, 62

Baruch, 66n58

Basil, 75, 98n149, 134n102

begottenness of the son. *See* eternal generation

Ben Sira, 62

biblical criticism: modern historical-critical, 85, 86n68, 92, 104, 199n11, 204n25, 204n26; canonical, 198 213n54

biblical theology: relationship to systematic theology, 196-217

biblicism, 9n31, 87n78, 99, 144n13, 155n46, 162n70

Calixtus, Georg, 98n146

historical-critical, *see* biblical criticism: modern historical-critical; macro-phenomenological, 212-17, 252, 259; microhermeneutical, 212-17, 251-52; precritical, 85, 92; postcritical, 85, 92

eyewitness testimony, 27-29, 35, 42, 117, 132

filioque. See Trinity: *filioque*

foundationalism: anti, 83-84, 137n112; classical, 84, 88, 103-5, 130, 136-38; definition of, 136-37; demise of (strong); modernistic, *see* strong; modest, 137-38; non, 87-89, 137n112; post, 88n81, 137n112; strong, *see* classical; weak, *see* modest

Formula of Concord, 133

gnosticism, 58, 110-15, 118-123

Gospel of Peter, 38n63

Gospel of Thomas, 38, 43n83, 59n31

Gregory of Nazianzus, 98n149, 176n34

Gregory the Great, 98n149

Hellenization hypothesis, 176, 233n40

hermeneutical authority: extracanonical arbiter of, 10-15, 73-74, 103, 105, 109-10, 123-24, 128-30, 132, 135, 169-70, 186-90; question of, 105-7, 115-18, 127, 152, 186-90

hermeneutical circle: parts–whole, 196, 216; reader–text, 145, 160, 169, 196, 210, 216, 258

hermeneutical diversity, 13, 126-30, 134, 140, 161-64, 186-88, 193-94, 258

hermeneutical presuppositions: macro, 213-15; micro, 213-14; meso, 213-14; naturalistic, 199, 204, 215

hermeneutical spiral, 12, 145, 164, 194, 212-17, 219-22, 249-50, 252, 257, 259

Hilary of Poitiers, 187n80

historical-critical method. *See* biblical criticism: modern historical-critical

historical-grammatical method. *See* exegesis: grammatical-historical

Holy Spirit, role of, 26-27, 33, 39, 46, 89-90, 95, 105-7, 135, 142, 154n45, 193, 202

humble approach to theology, 218-21

Ignatius of Antioch, 36n59, 64, 65

impassibility, 176n36, 229-36, 240-44, 247, 256

interpretive diversity. *See* hermeneutical diversity

intrinsic canon model. *See* canon: intrinsic

Irenaeus, 20n16, 33n49, 58, 63-65, 110-25, 131-32

isolationism, 12-13, 104, 138, 140-42, 150-51, 154, 157, 161, 164-65, 252

Jerome, 98n149

Josephus, 24n27, 34, 44, 62

Judas Maccabeus, 24n27, 51n12, 62

Justin Martyr, 36n59, 63, 187n80, 233n40

language: accommodative, 225-28, 230-33, 240, 242, 259; analogical, 225-28, 231-32, 240-43; anthropomorphic, 173n25, 229n28, 233n39, 234n41, 239; anthro-popathic, 229-41; equivocal, 225-26; figurative, 231-32, 237n55, 240, 242, 244; idiomatic, 244n81; literal, 155n48, 207n35, 231-32, 233n39, 237, 242-43; metaphorical, 231-32, 236n50, 237n52, 239nn65-66; philosophy of, 83, 93, 222-25; univocal, 101, 225-27, 231n34, 240, 245; theopathic, 240-45

literary criticism, 202n20, 204n26, 213n54

love, divine, 246-48, 250, 253-56

Lucaris, 78n26

Luther, Martin, 9-10, 155-57

magisterial reformers. *See* reformers: magisterial

Magisterium, 75-77, 86

Marcion, 33n49, 58, 118n39

Mishnah Yadaim, 51n10

modalism, 174n28, 234n40

Scripture Index